FREE MOVEMENT OF GOODS AND SERVICES WITHIN THE EUROPEAN COMMUNITY

Free Movement of Goods and Services within the European Community

LORNA WOODS
University of Essex

ASHGATE

Published by
Ashgate Publishing Limited
Gower House
Croft Road
Aldershot
Hants GU11 3HR
England

Ashgate Publishing Company
Suite 420
101 Cherry Street
Burlington, VT 05401-4405
USA

Ashgate website: http://www.ashgate.com

British Library Cataloguing in Publication Data
Woods, Lorna
Free movement of goods and services within the European community. - (European business law library)
1. Free trade - European Union countries 2. Service industries - Law and legislation - European Union countries
3. Freedom of movement - European Union countries
4. International and municipal law - European Union countries
I. Title
341.7'543'094

Library of Congress Cataloging-in-Publication Data
Woods, Lorna.
Free movement of goods and services within the European community / Lorna Woods.
p. cm. -- (European business law library)
Includes bibliographical references and index.
ISBN 1-85521-568-3
1. Free trade--European Union countries. I. Title. II. Series.

KJE5177.W66 2003
343.4'087--dc22

2003060499

ISBN 1 85521 568 3

Printed and bound by Athenaeum Press, Ltd.,
Gateshead, Tyne & Wear.

Contents

Table of Cases

Before the European Court of Justice

Alphabetical

Before the European Court of Justice

Numerical

Before the EFTA Court

Before the National Courts

England and Wales

Germany

Preface

It might seem that all that could possibly be said about the development of the free movement of goods has already been said, and repeatedly. Why then another book in this area? Simply, the freedoms are usually grouped in a way that the goods provisions are seen as isolated, whilst the provisions relating to services are usually grouped with the freedom of establishment and the free movement of workers. Services are a growing and important economic area and one to which insufficient attention has been paid in academic and even practitioner literature. Certainly they constitute an area in which significant difficulties remain, as the Commission's report of July 2002 illustrates. On this basis, services deserve attention in their own right separated from the other provisions providing for the free movement of people. Against a background of the 'Information Society', the question of the relationship between goods and services also deserves attention, as the boundaries between goods and services – at least in some areas – fade away. As society and technology have developed, so has the Community (and now the Union). Thus, the book takes into account changes in the drafting of the Treaty and their impact on the Court's interpretation of the freedom. This book then aims to provide an examination of the provisions relating the free movement of goods and services, tracing the development of the ECJ's jurisprudence. In doing so, the book has two main aims: to be informative as to the actual state of the law; and to provide a more detailed analysis of the Court's reasoning to identify areas of particular difficulty. Such difficulties may arise in relation to the individual freedoms, their relationship, or their relationship to the Treaty structure as a whole.

Despite the intention to treat both freedoms in equal depth, the book does not adopt a structure whereby the sections dealing with goods and services mirror each other exactly. Tellingly, there are differences in structure reflecting the different approach to the freedoms both in the Treaty provisions and the jurisprudence of the ECJ. Where there are similarities between the two freedoms, to avoid duplication the relevant issues have been dealt with once only, but with cross referencing where appropriate. Certain issues are common to both freedoms: the introductory section, the chapter on harmonization and the conclusion. The book includes developments up to and including January 2003. Although more cases have been handed down since then, at the time of going to press there seem to have been no major developments in this area of the law.

As ever, this book could not have been produced without the help of others. Whilst acknowledging the support of the departments of law in the universities of Sheffield and Essex, particular thanks must go to certain colleagues. Fiona Smith and Sabine Michalowski have each read sections of this book and pointed out to me when I was not making sense. If my arguments remain at any point incomprehensible, the fault is mine and not theirs. Invaluable assistance was also given to me in the typing of this book and preparing it for print by Kay Windust and Julie Prescott respectively. Finally, I should mention the contribution of my husband and the cats, all of whom gave support in various ways.

Lorna Woods
Essex, January 2004

Chapter 1

Introduction

The EU was originally formed in 1957 by the Treaty of Rome (EC Treaty), as the European Economic Community (now re-named the European Community and referred to as 'the Community' or 'the EC'). It may be presumed from the absence of any specific provision in that treaty dealing with the division of competence and the relative strength of the Member States and the Community that these issues were thought to be clear, at least by the Member States. In short, the Member States were 'masters of the Treaty'[1] and the Community was just another international law organisation, albeit one with – even then – a relatively wide remit and unusually independent institutions. Nonetheless, it was anticipated – or hoped – by at least some of those behind the Community project, that the Community's competence would expand, spilling over into increasing numbers of policy fields. Insofar as the Community was, at that stage, perceived to be any type of nascent federation, however, the power lay with the Member States through the limited competence conferred upon the Community.

The Preamble to the EC Treaty indicates the concerns of the founder Member States with rebuilding, after the ravages of World War II, a peaceful and prosperous Europe. Despite the lofty tones of the preamble to the Treaty, the tasks ascribed to the Community in the original EC Treaty had a strong economic focus, being the promotion of,

> 'a harmonious development of economic activities, a continuous and balanced expansion, an increase in stability, an accelerated raising of the standard of living and closer relations between the States belonging to [the Community].'[2]

The primary mechanism for achieving these aims was the common market, which was to be phased in gradually over a twelve-year period. The general powers to regulate, including the regulation of trade generally, remained with the Member States; further, those Member

---

1 This phrase is borrowed from the Bundesverfassunggericht's judgment in *Brunner* v. *TEU* [1994] 1 CMLR 57.

2 Article 2 EEC. See further below for current form.

States retained the loyalty and affection of their populations,[3] a state of affairs which, with rare individual exceptions, remains the case today.[4]

Although the balance of power in this relationship originally lay with the Member States, the picture has changed over the last five decades. Crucially, the European Court of Justice (ECJ) developed the doctrines of supremacy and direct effect, aimed at ensuring the effectiveness of Community law.[5] Further, the Court interpreted the scope of the EC Treaty broadly bringing Community law into fields that might not have been thought to be included in the original scope of the Treaty.[6] Culture is an example of an area of policy not expressly included in the original version of the EC Treaty, but in which the ECJ implicitly held the Community had competence.[7] It may be that certain of the political institutions colluded in this process through the enactment of secondary legislation based on the 'fall-back' provision, Article 308.[8] Many of these rulings have subsequently been confirmed by Treaty amendment and, indeed, Treaty amendments have broadened Community competence still further. Nonetheless Community competence is still limited to its attributed powers, however widely they are seen, a point re-emphasised by Article 5 EC.[9]

Given the priority of Community law in its relations with national law, the boundary between the competence of the Member States and that

---

3 This was the starting point for the American federal system in the Federalist Papers, Hamilton, Madison and Jay, *The Federalist* (William Benton, Chicago, London, Toronto, 1952).

4 Commission *Standard Barometer* (45) at point 7.1 shows that 40% of respondents perceived themselves to be nationals of their own country alone; and 61% felt first their own nationality and then European. Only 6% felt European and then their nationality. Only 5% felt themselves to be only European.

5 Case 26/62 *NV Algemene Transport- en Expedetie Onderneming Van Gend en Loos* v. *Nederlandse Administratie der Belastingen* [1963] ECR 1; Case 6/64 *Costa* v. *ENEL* [1964] ECR 425.

6 The ECJ determined that the EC had implied powers to carry out tasks where competence had not been expressly allocated under the Treaty: Cases 281, 283-5 and 287/85 *Commission* v. *Germany* [1987] ECR 3203; in *ERTA*, Case 22/70 *Commission* v. *Council* [1971] ECR 263, the EC was held to have power to act in the international sphere where it had competence to do so within the EC. Although the *ERTA* case gave the EC competence, in more recent cases there has been a tendency for the Court to find concurrent competence.

7 Case 7/68 *Commission* v. *Italy* (Tax on Art Treasures), [1968] ECR 428; Case 155/78 *Sacchi* [1974] ECR 409.

8 See further Chapter 13.

9 Subsidiarity together with the doctrines of pre-emption and implied powers are discussed further in Chapter 13.

of the Community is significant. There are, for example, possible conflicts in the policy-making and legislative fields and in any such conflict it seems that Community law, from the viewpoint of the Community, should triumph. This is important because such a result may lead to the disturbance of the political compromises constituting the lawmaking process within each Member State and the undermining of what each polity views as 'justice'. Furthermore, even within the scope of Community competence, the issue of the inter-relationships between Community and Member States' powers and between the Member States themselves arises. It is not possible to characterise the Community and the Member States as operating in some sort of dual federalist system, in which the powers are divided between levels of government and between which there are no areas of overlap. Instead, we see a more co-operative form of federalism, what seems to be called 'multi-level governance' within the sphere of European Community studies. In such a system, it is accepted that various actors have different roles to play. Certainly, the EC relies on Member States to implement its policies[10] and even within EC legislation – notably the directive – there is scope for Member State to make policy choices within the overarching Community framework. Nonetheless, given the potential consequences of supremacy, we need to identify the scope of Community competence. This issue is not just quantitative (which areas of law fall within Community competence) but also qualitative. What sort of competence does the Community have in specific policy fields and what the relative weight ascribed to different types of value?

Undeniably the Community in its original form had a free market emphasis: its primary goal was the creation of the common market via the introduction of the four freedoms, competition policy and certain sector specific policies, such as agriculture. The four freedoms are the free movement of goods, the free movement of people, the freedom to provide services and the free movement of capital.[11] With the various Treaty amendments, however, the Community can be seen as no longer principally focussed on trade and economic issues, but also as including more social questions and even such overtly political concepts as citizenship although the exact content of this concept may not have been

10 It should not be overlooked that the Member States' governments have a role to play in the formation of Community policies, via the Council, which is composed of representatives of each Member State.

11 Referred to in Article 3 as 'the abolition as between Member States, of obstacles to the free movement of persons services and capital'. The TEU amended this provision to refer to 'an internal market characterized by the abolition as between Member States of obstacles to the free movement of persons, services and capital' in Article 3(c) EC.

clear.[12] Notably, the Maastricht Treaty (TEU), which created the European Union, amended Articles 2 and 3 EC, the provisions setting out the tasks of the Community. After Maastricht, although the creation of the common market remained a primary vehicle for the attainment of Community objectives, it no longer was the only vehicle. In addition, and significantly, the objectives of the Community clearly reflected broader concerns, notably those relating to the environment and to social protection. Article 3 reflected these changes, containing amongst other activities, specific reference to the environment, to culture and to a high level of health protection. The Treaty of Amsterdam (ToA) further amended Article 2: economic activities are not only to be balanced and harmonious, but sustainable. A specific reference to 'a high level of protection and improvement of the quality of the environment' was included in that Article, whilst the reference to social protection features much higher up in the list of Community tasks. Despite these changes the common market, as primary mechanism for attaining these goals, remains fundamental to the Community project.

In this context, the four freedoms have particular significance. It is these provisions that give effect to the Community's objectives: Articles 2 and 3 EC, which set down the main tasks and aims, are not directly effective though they have interpretative value.[13] Not only are the four freedoms the framework of the common market (and constitute the internal market),[14] but they are capable of being relied on by private persons in national courts. The extent of each of the freedoms is therefore of great significance. This point, re-phrased, concerns the meaning of the term 'discrimination' and might seem non-contentious given that some of the Treaty provisions are phrased in terms of the elimination of discrimination, and one of the fundamental principles underlying the Community legal order is a prohibition on discrimination on the grounds of nationality.[15] Nonetheless there are difficulties in this area, relating to two linked points. First, what do we mean by discrimination? Secondly is discrimination an appropriate test for determining the boundaries of the internal market? The second point depends to a certain extent on the answer to the first question: it is difficult to assess the appropriateness of

12 Introduced by TEU, renumbered and amended by the Treaty of Amsterdam: now Article 18 EC *et seq*. On scope of citizenship see e.g. Reich, N., 'Union Citizenship – Metaphor or Source of Rights?' (2001) 7 *ELJ* 4.

13 See e.g. Case C-379/92 *Peralta* [1994] ECR I-3453.

14 This definition also does not consider expressly the issue of distortion of competition in the internal market, although this would seem also to be included: see Case C-300/89 *Commission* v. *Council* (Titanium Dioxide), [1991] ECR I-2866, at pp. 2899-2901.

15 Article 12 EC.

a particular conceptual tool for a task when that tool's nature or scope is unknown.

Clearly, different conceptions of discrimination may be identified. The most obvious is overt, direct discrimination. An example of this type of discrimination would be where national legislation expressly subjects foreign products to additional safety checks or licensing procedures. 'Local grab' measures, such as rules requiring the use of local facilities for waste, would also seem to fall into this category,[16] although some such measures may also affect non-local domestic production or service providers.[17] Direct discrimination can arise covertly: for example national measures may be phrased in an origin neutral way but in reality only affect imports. A number of cases of this sort of discrimination arose in relation to internal taxation, where particularly high rates of taxation fell on products with a specified alcohol content or on cars with certain engine sizes. In practice goods falling into the described categories were imported products.[18]

Indirect discrimination occurs where apparently neutral rules adversely affect imports more than domestic products or services. A common example is a dual burden rule, where imported products, having complied with safety or consumer protection requirements in the state or origin, then have to comply with additional, usually different, requirements aimed at protecting the same public interest in the importing or host Member State. Labelling requirements and 'recipe rules' are common examples of this sort of discrimination.[19] Similar problems may arise with services, for example if a service provider is required to comply with the broadcasting standards in all Member States in which the broadcast programming is received. Finally, there are rules that are applicable to domestic and foreign producers or service providers alike but which still affect access to the market, potentially, but not necessarily partitioning that market. This latter type of rule tends to be exemplified by rules regulating the market rather than the product or the service and have also been called 'single burden' rules. Examples include Sunday trading rules and rules limiting the establishments where certain types of

---

16 See e.g. Case 18/84 *Commission* v. *France* (Tax Breaks for Newspapers) [1985] ECR 1339 which concerned preferential tax treatment encouraging industry to locate in France.

17 See the discussion relating to export restrictions, discussed further in Chapter 6.

18 For example, in Case C-47/88 *Commission* v. *Denmark* (Car Tax) [1990] ECR I-4509, which was held to fall under Article 28 rather than 95, a tax affected only imports because there was no domestic product.

19 Case 120/78 *Rewe* v. *Bundesmonopolverwaltung für Branntwein* (Cassis de Dijon) [1979] ECR 649.

product may be sold.[20] It should be noted that the types of discrimination are not always clear-cut and there is a certain lack of clarity as to where the boundaries lie.[21]

One of the recurring questions in the internal market case law is which test of discrimination to use; further, what are the consequences of that choice. Where a narrower conception of discrimination is used, there is a lesser degree of impact on the Member States' rules. Discrimination in this case arises where there are overtly discriminatory rules. More broadly, it can arise from discrepancies between the various Member States' policy choices and levels of regulation. Even viewing discrimination quite narrowly, the four freedoms and discrimination have a harmonizing tendency, though there are concerns that such negative harmonization operates so as to lower protection and to deregulate. Of course, where the concern is discrepancies between different regulatory systems rather than the level of regulation per se, one solution would be to harmonize the sector at Community level. Although Community harmonization may protect public interests and thereby assuage concerns about lowering of standards, it has its own impact on the balance of power within the EC and Member States' regulatory choices. Tensions would therefore remain.

Alternatively, a broader notion of discrimination could be adopted, constituting a wide conception of each of the freedoms. The operation of such a broadly drawn rule would not be limited to circumstances where there are necessarily discrepancies between the regulatory systems of the Member. Instead, this view of discrimination covers rules that regulate access to the market. There is an obvious concern for the Community where such rules operate to partition off national markets; such rules would undermine the creation of a single market. Other rules relating to access, such as the Sunday trading rules, do not seem to have any such effect. Should these rules fall within the scope of Community law? The concern about deregulation present even in a relatively narrow conception of the freedoms is re-emphasised here, as a greater volume of national rules would be affected, including those not intended to discriminate or even to regulate trade. A broad view of discrimination may thus prove to be a political choice, limiting Member States' freedom to regulate at a general level. Arguably, and by contrast to the narrower view of discrimination, such an approach could also preclude Community regulatory action.[22] Regarding the free movement of goods, Advocate-General Tesauro commented:

---

20 Case C-23/89 *Quietlynn* [1990] ECR I-3059.

21 Discussed further in Chapters 5 and 11.

22 See discussion of Community law-making powers in Chapter 13.

> 'Is Article 30 [now 28] of the Treaty a provision intended to liberalise intra-Community trade or is it intended more generally to encourage the unhindered pursuit of commerce in individual Member States?'[23]

This comment could probably be generalised to refer to Article 49 as well, if not all the four freedoms.

To determine the appropriate test for the scope of the four freedoms, we might then question what functions we expect the Community in general and the freedoms in particular to fulfil. Are the freedoms aimed at eradicating the 'selfish' behaviour of Member States whereby each Member State seeks to further its own interests at the expense of those of its fellow Member States? A relatively narrow conception of discrimination would satisfy this goal. Discrimination in this sense seeks to ensure that market participants are not subject to added disadvantage depending on their origin. An alternative conception of the freedoms suggests that the emphasis on free competition between traders in the different Member States is essentially deregulatory. On this view, there has been a decision, made presumably in 1957, to roll back the state and to adopt a more laissez faire approach to the market. Such a decision may have had its basis in a desire on the part of the founder Member States to emulate the economic success of the United States of America, which itself favoured a free market approach. Similar concerns underpin the General Agreement on Tariffs and Trade (GATT), which was also established in the post war period.[24] Equally, such an approach would minimise the risk of a return to protectionism which could trigger disputes between the European states. Although such a decision may make sense half a century ago, a different emphasis may be appropriate now, given the change in political environment generally and the developments in the European Union. The question would then be not whether we would want to make such a change but, if we did, whether such a change would be possible. There is a possibility that the jurisprudence of the ECJ has entrenched certain values in the Community legal order, irrespective of the attempts of the Member States to change it. Thus, as well as discussing the nature of the test to determine the boundary between Member State and Community competence, the question of the values protected by the Community legal order needs to

---

23 Case C-292/92 *Hünermund* v. *Landesapothekerkammer Baden-Württemberg* [1993] ECR I-6787.

24 GATT was aimed at removing barriers to trade in the international community generally. It has now been succeeded by the WTO system, introduced in 1995 and which revised the GATT substantially. On foundation of GATT see generally Jackson, J. M., *World Trade and the Law of Gatt* (Bobbs-Merrill, 1969).

be addressed and the weight given to those respective values should be assessed.

As noted above, the Community legal order was originally given a clear purpose: the creation of the common market. That purpose was essentially trade-based and the values protected were economic values. The Member States, as political entities not subject to a limited purpose, had a wider range of values and concerns to deal with. The problem for the Community legal order was that, by virtue of the supremacy of Community law, trade concerns were given priority over other values, including fundamental political concerns, such as human rights. The response of the ECJ to the threatened rebellion of the constitutional courts is well known.[25] The recognition of fundamental values and human rights as forming part of the Community legal order illustrates one aspect of the broadening of the Community's values, although there have been some criticisms of the ECJ's interpretation of those values. The Treaty amendments identified earlier have successively introduced into the Community legal order wider values, including those that are clearly non-economic, such as sustainability and citizenship. As a result, there is now another possible area of tension in addition to those between the Member States and the Community: within the EU conflicts could arise between the different objectives of the EU. One question is the extent to which these changes have affected our understanding of the common market, if at all.

The relationship between the freedoms[26] and the provisions containing the principles on which the Community is based[27] will be crucial in this context. As noted, Articles 2 and 3 have interpretive value[28] but do not impose legal obligations on Member States or confer rights on individuals.[29] The value of the principles in concrete terms is, however, unclear. We might expect that a change in Articles 2 and 3 would have an impact on the provisions of the Treaty intended to implement them, such as the four freedoms. The ECJ has, however, suggested the opposite, at least as far as Article 2 and 3 and the free movement of goods are concerned. The Court has held that where the provisions designed to implement the Community's general policies have not themselves been amended, the ECJ's previous case law on those

25 Case 11/70 *Internationale Handelsgesellschaft mbH* v. *Einfuhr-und Vorratsstelle für Getriede and Futtermittel* [1970] ECR 1125. The Court's ruling was incorporated into the text of the Treaty on European Union itself: Article 6 TEU.

26 Contained in Part III of the Treaty: Community Policies.

27 Part I; Principles, Articles 1-16.

28 Case 270/80 *Polydor* v. *Harlequin Record Shops* [1982] ECR 329, paragraph 16.

29 Case C-379/92 *Peralta, supra* n. 12; Case C-339/89 *Alsthom Atlantique* [1991] ECR I-107, paragraph 9.

provisions may not be called into question, despite subsequent changes to the general objectives of the Community.[30] Whether this interpretation applies to all the principles contained in Part I of the Treaty is a different matter. Some provisions, such as Article 12, do have legal effect and may therefore be distinguished from Articles 2 and 3. Further, other articles specifically state that non-trade matters should be taken into account in other policy areas. Article 6, for example, provides that:

> 'Environmental protection requirements must be integrated into the definition and implementation of the Community policies and activities referred to in Article 3, in particular with a view to promoting sustainable development.'

It is debatable whether the general provisions have the same relationship with each of the implementing provisions. Some provisions seem designed to deal with specific areas: Article 16, for example, was introduced to protect the provision of services of general economic interest. The provisions relating to goods are unlikely to be affected by this article. Citizenship, contained in a separate section of the Treaty, also has the potential to affect the definition of other Treaty policies, notably those relating to the free movement of persons, suggesting that a wider, more social and political context should be given to those rights.[31] Indeed, citizenship signals a change in the conceptual status of the Community (and the Union). No longer are we talking about a trading agreement, but a political organisation including private parties as well as governments. This line of reasoning suggests that the Union should take into account a broad range of issues, reflecting social, cultural and political concerns, rather than focussing on the economic. Individuals should not be regarded as mere consumers in the Community legal order, but as citizens.

In one sense, there seems to have been a clear hierarchy governing the relationship between these general principles and the implementing provisions: the general provisions provide the framework within which the freedoms are interpreted. The relationship between the freedoms themselves and more particularly between the freedoms and sector specific provisions is less clear-cut. Particular problems arise when we consider the arguably deregulatory effect of the four freedoms and the obligation on the Community to take a high level of protection as its basis in some sectors, such as consumer protection, environment and public health. These provisions re-emphasise the point that the Community has a broader focus than hitherto and that the ECJ might consequently be able to take a wider range of issues into account when interpreting not only these provisions but also the

30 Case C-9/99 *Échirolles Distribution SA* v. *Association du Dauphiné and Others* [2000] ECR I-8207, paragraphs 22-24.

31 E.g. Case C-348/96 *Donatella Calfa* [1999] ECR I-11.

four freedoms. Nonetheless, it can be suggested that the four freedoms (and competition policy) have a very high value within the Community legal order, notwithstanding the original derogation provisions and the later Treaty amendments.[32] Again, the question is whether such an approach is appropriate in an organisation with the broad scope (in policy terms and geographically) of the Community (and Union).

Quite apart from the general discussion about the scope of the freedoms and the nature of discrimination, some might also question whether the ECJ has been consistent in its approach to discrimination, not only within its jurisprudence relating to one of the freedoms but as between those freedoms. Clearly, in a system that seeks to eliminate distortions in the trading environment, there should be coherence between the freedoms. It has been suggested that it would be inequitable for an individual's rights to vary depending on how the situation was categorised: whether as goods, people, services or capital.[33] Nonetheless, although some commentators have identified signs of unity in the ECJ's approach,[34] equally there are differences.[35] The question is to what extent are these differences the result of the different pressures on the four freedoms and the differences in drafting in the text of the EC Treaty. Implicit in the concern about deregulatory impact is the fact that the four freedoms – and harmonizing secondary Community legislation – identify the limits of acceptable state action. It is therefore important that those involved should have a clear and consistent understanding of where that boundary lies – or understand the criteria for identifying it.

This book will focus on two of the four freedoms: the free movement of goods and services. Rather than discuss fiscal barriers to trade, this book will focus on non-tariff barriers, as these are the areas in which the tension between the EC freedoms and the Member States' general regulatory competence can most clearly be seen. In considering these issues, the book will also consider the scope of the Community's power to legislate in this area.[36] Free movement of goods is clearly a central

32 The importance of free movement can be seen in other areas too, for example, in the relationship between the free movement of goods and the state aid rules: Case 18/84 *Commission* v. *France* (Tax Breaks for Newspapers), *supra* n. 16; Case C-21/88 *Du Pont de Nemours* v. *Unita Sanitaria Locale* [1990] ECR I-889.

33 See comments of Advocate-General Lenz in Case C-415/93 *Union Royale Belge des Sociétés de Football Association ASBL* v. *Jean-Marc Bosman* [1995] ECR I-4921.

34 Behrens (1992) EuR 145.

35 Contrast Joined Cases C-267 and 268/91 *Keck and Mithouard* [1993] ECR I-6097 and Case C-384/93 *Alpine Investments BV* v. *Minister van Financiën* [1995] ECR I-1141.

36 Article 3 EC provided for harmonization of laws to ensure the functioning of the common market. The original version of the Treaty referred to the 'proper'

freedom for any form of economic integration. The freedom to provide services, by contrast, although seen as analogous to goods and therefore the less sensitive aspect of the internal market, also has implications for the free movement of people. The discussion will attempt to determine the scope and content of the relevant Community law and consequently the freedom allowed to Member States to regulate in their respective territories. This book will not give an exhaustive analysis of the values inherent in the Community legal system, nor its flanking policies, but instead will seek to identify if the extensive changes to the Treaty, which emphasise different, non-economic values, have had any noticeable effect on the approach of the ECJ.

This book will be divided into two sections, one dealing with Articles 28-30, the other with Articles 49, 50 and 55. Broadly the issues relating to each freedom will be dealt with in the same order. Some points will be given greater emphasis in one freedom than the other, however, depending on the relevant case law. In each section, the terms will be defined before considering the beneficiaries of the rights and the persons against whom the rights may be enforced. A general overview of the scope of the right will be given before a separate chapter providing a detailed criticism of the ECJ's jurisprudence. Then, the scope of derogation from the relevant freedom will be discussed. In order to avoid duplication, some issues, where common principles appear, will be dealt with in relation to one of the freedoms only. The issues arising in the chapter on harmonization are, on the whole, common to both the free movement of goods and the freedom to provide services. Finally, the concluding chapter will seek to identify whether there are any common themes arising from the jurisprudence, as will divergences between the case law on the two articles in relation to the issues relating to the development of the Community legal order.

---

functioning of the common market, but this adjective was removed by TEU, presumably to avoid attempts to interpret 'proper' narrowly – though this does raise the question of what the 'improper functioning' of the common market might entail. See now Article 3(h). Harmonization is discussed further in Chapter 13.

Chapter 2

Meaning of 'Goods'

I Meaning of Goods

This section of the book deals with the free movement of goods, in particular the provisions dealing with quantitative restrictions on imports and exports and measures having equivalent effect (Articles 28 and 29 EC). A preliminary issue therefore must be to define what is meant by the term 'goods'. Any such definition should be determined by reference to Community law, rather than the law of the individual Member States, so as to ensure uniformity of approach across the Community. Although there are a number of provisions in the Treaty dealing with the free movement of goods, none define this term. Indeed, some provisions, such as Articles 28 and 29, do not even use the term, 'goods', but refer instead to 'products' or to 'imports' and 'exports'. Only the article containing the derogation from the free movement principle, Article 30, expressly refers to goods. The need to ensure that there are no gaps between the provisions ensuring free movement of goods would suggest that a consistent interpretation between all these provisions be adopted. In practice, it seems as though the different terms do have the same meaning. This is a view that is further supported by certain other language versions of the Treaty, which make no distinction between 'goods' and 'products'. The German version, for example, uses in both instances the same word, 'Waren'.

The starting point for any definition of goods, no matter which provision is in question, thus tends to be the same. The leading case is the decision of the ECJ in the *Export Tax on Art Treasures* case brought by the Commission against Italy.[1] Italian legislation aimed at making the export of art treasures from Italy less attractive by a number of measures, including the imposition of taxes on objects of historical, ethnographic or artistic importance. When the Commission claimed that this was contrary to the then Article 16 EEC, which abolished customs duties (now incorporated into Article 12 EC), the Italians argued that art treasures were not goods for the purposes of the EC Treaty because of their cultural nature. The ECJ found for the Commission, providing a definition of 'goods' as it did so as:

---

1 Case 7/68 *Commission* v. *Italy* (Tax on Art Treasures) [1968] ECR 428.

'... products which can be valued in money and which are capable, as such, of forming the subject matter of commercial transactions'.

Consequently, even if items might be valued for reasons other than economic (such as cultural, historical or artistic reasons), this does not mean that they are not goods for the purposes of the EC Treaty. Indeed, to have found otherwise would have created a significant weakness in the free movement provisions, particularly as notions such as 'culture' are difficult to define and may be broadly drawn.[2] A similar approach seems to be taken in relation to morality; the fact that certain goods are considered immoral in at least some Member States does not mean that they are not goods.[3] Furthermore, this approach to goods is implicit in the terms of new Article 30 EC (formerly Article 36). Were cultural items and objects viewed as immoral not to be considered as goods, they would not fall within Article 28 in the first place. There would therefore have been no need to provide exceptions for them in Article 30.[4]

Although this position may seem reasonable enough, there are a number of questions that arise from it. Any action by a Member State to ban a product will have to be justified by reference to Community objectives.[5] Obviously, an approach that takes a product outside the Treaty altogether by reference to an individual Member State's views of what was moral, or even what was legal, would have been open to abuse. If a product were to have fallen outside the scope of the Treaty because it did not fall within the definition of goods, this would have allowed Member States to enact discriminatory rules in relation to that product, arguably giving Member States an incentive to view a comparatively wide range of

---

2 On culture, see Chapters 7 and 13.

3 The comment of Advocate-General La Pegola in Case C-124/97 *Markku Juhani Läärä, Cotswold Microsystems Ltd, Oy Transatlantic Software Ltd v. Kihlakunnansyyttäjä (Jyväskylä), Suomen Valtio (Finnish State)* [1999] ECR I-6067 at paragraph 18, that the goods in question were capable of being the subject of '*lawful* commercial transactions' (emphasis added) would seem to suggest otherwise. The case law regarding Article 30, see Chapter 7, supports the view proposed in the text.

4 Some goods have generated special regimes, for example, guns. Note that this is not a matter of Community law alone; there has, for example, been action under the CFSP resulting in a joint action on the EU's contribution to combating the destabilising accumulation and uncontrolled spread of small arms and light weapons, 1999/34/CFSP. Similarly, the need to control certain drugs has led to action: Council Decision of 13 September 1999, relating to certain drugs to be subject to control measures and criminal penalties: OJ [1999] L 244/1.

5 It is not clear whether this means by reference to Article 30 as a quantitative restriction or whether bans that are imposed equally on domestic products and imports could be justified by mandatory requirements. See further Chapters 4 and 6.

products as illegal or immoral. Does this mean, however, that to ensure internal market objectives all things capable of satisfying the test in the *Italian Art* case[6] should be viewed as goods and subject to the rules in Articles 28-30, so that any concerns relating to morality or public policy are dealt with within the Treaty framework? Or, do we as a society object to the very act of viewing some things as commodities? What about the trafficking of children as slaves? The Union has felt the need to bring proposals to take action against this trade, so there is clearly a market attributing a price to children.[7] One might argue that people cannot be 'products', the term used by the Court in its judgment in the *Italian Art* case. Such an argument constitutes an *a priori* judgment about the nature of goods, which the ECJ has not yet considered. Although no-one would be likely to contend that individuals should be capable of being considered as goods, there are perhaps more difficult examples of what constitutes commodities, such as body parts. Medical services can, in principle, fall within the scope of Article 49 EC; presumably an organ transplant could be characterised as a commercial transaction, but would the European Union really want to regard the transplanted kidneys or heart in such an operation as goods?[8] In either case, should we decide that neither of the examples are goods, we need to be clear whether we are arguing that they are not goods because they are covered by another Treaty freedom (Article 49, for example) or that they are not goods because it is wrong to see certain things as the subject of trade in the first place. As a final point, the issue of whether the Community has power to ban certain items or services at the Community level is discussed further in Chapter 13. It does not seem, however, that such a Community prohibition would imply that the items are no longer capable of constituting goods.

Following the *Italian Art* judgment,[9] goods seemed to have two characteristics: being capable of having a value in money; and being capable of being the subject of a commercial transaction, although the possibility of there being a commercial transaction does seem to be linked to the object having a monetary value. In any event, the definition of

---

6 *Italian Art* case, *supra* n. 1.

7 The Union has sought to control trafficking in people generally: see e.g. Council Framework Decision of 19 July 2002 on Combating Trafficking in Human Beings, Doc No. ST9576/020RI and Article III-49 draft Constitutional Treaty.

8 Blood has been regarded as falling within the scope of the EC Treaty: see e.g. Directive 2001/104/EC of the European Parliament and of the Council of 7 December 2001 OJ [2002] L6/50 including within the scope of Council Directive 93/42/EEC medical devices which regulate medical devices derived from human blood, but note Article 3(2) of the EU Charter on Fundamental Rights, which would seem to preclude payment for body parts.

9 *Italian Art* case, *supra* n. 1.

'goods' was wide, ranging from cars[10] and fuel[11] to books[12] and videos[13] to food[14] and drink[15] and even agricultural[16] or fisheries products,[17] although the question of whether all animals constitute goods is a more difficult question. Not all animals have a value in money.[18]

The definition of goods has, however, been further refined in the *Belgian Waste* case,[19] which concerned waste that was neither reusable nor recyclable. Such waste was held to fall within the definition of goods, despite the fact that the subject matter of the contract, if it had a value at all, had a negative value. On the face of it, this fact would have seemed to exclude waste from the definition of goods.[20] In determining the question of whether such waste constituted goods, however, the ECJ focussed on the existence of the commercial transaction, rather than trying to identify a monetary value for the waste. The ECJ held that;

> 'objects which are shipped across borders for the purposes of commercial transactions are subject to Article 30 [now Article 28] et seq. of the Treaty, including non-recyclable waste.' [21]

---

10 See e.g. Case C-239/90 *SCP Boscher, Studer et Frometin* v. *SA British Motors Wright and Others* [1991] ECR I-2023; Case 50/85 *Schloh* v. *Auto Controle Technique* [1986] ECR 1855.

11 Case 231/83 *Cullet* v. *Centre Leclerc* [1985] ECR 305.

12 Case 286/81 *Oosthoek's Uitgeversmaatschappij BV* [1982] ECR 4575.

13 Joined Cases 60 and 61/84 *Cinéthèque SA* v. *Fédération Nationale des Cinémas Français* [1985] ECR 2605.

14 See e.g. Case 261/81 *Walter Rau Lebensmittlwerke* v. *de Smedt Pvba* [1982] ECR 3961; Case C-470/93 *Verein gegen Unwesen in Handel und Gewerbe Koln eV* v. *Mars GmbH* [1995] ECR I-1923.

15 Case 8/74 *Procureur du Roi* v. *Dassonville et al.* [1974] ECR 837.

16 See e.g. Cases 194 and 241/85 *Commission* v. *Greece* (Banana Licensing) [1988] ECR 1037; Case C-265/95 *Commission* v. *France* (Angry Farmers) [1997] ECR I-6959.

17 Case C-131/93 *Commission* v. *Germany* (Crayfish) [1994] ECR I-3303.

18 In the *Danish Bee* case, Case C-67/97 *Ditlev Bluhme* [1998] ECR I-8033, the question of the value of the imported bees was not discussed; they were however linked to the commercial production of honey and presumably therefore had some economic value. The position of pets, especially non-pedigree animals, would seem to be less clear-cut. The Commission, in answer to question E-3551/00 concerning the regulation of dangerous dogs, suggested that Articles 28-30 were relevant, implying that dogs are goods.

19 Case C-2/90 *Commission* v. *Belgium* (Walloon Waste) [1992] ECR I-4431.

20 Perhaps part of the difficulty in this area is that disposal of waste might well be considered as a contract for disposal; that is a contract for services. On the distinction between goods and services, see further below.

21 Case C-2/90 *Commission* v. *Belgium, supra* n. 19 at paragraph 26.

The argument seems to be that if a body wishes to make a business out of an object, then that business element should operate within the internal market; that is, within the scope of the EC Treaty. This element of being the subject of commercial transactions, rather than there being a given monetary value ascribed to the goods, now seems to be the crucial element in determining whether something can fall within the definition of goods. Arguably, there is a similar approach in relation to services.[22]

Clearly this definition is broad but, as it is based on the existence of a commercial transaction, it raises the question of which such transactions are included within the ECJ's ruling. The transactions covered are not limited to those involving the immediate disposal of the goods, but can include contracts following which the goods are stored, destroyed or tipped – as was the situation in the *Belgian Waste* case.[23] Similarly, the protection of free movement is not limited to transactions that are entered into by businesses but can include transactions involving consumers. Thus, an individual travelling to another Member State and buying goods there can rely on the treaty freedoms to bring them back to the Member State of origin.[24]

On one level the definition in *Belgian Waste*[25] is broader than that in *Italian Art Treasures*,[26] as it removes the necessity for a value to be ascribed to the goods. In another sense, however, it is narrower. In *Belgian Waste*, the ECJ stated that, to fall within the concept of goods for the EC Treaty, the items in question had to be shipped for the purposes of a commercial transaction. In the *Italian Art* case, the items needed only to be of the type of goods that are the subject of commercial transactions. This narrowing down could lead to some strange consequences, as can be illustrated by the following example. Were a famous artist to paint a picture and then sell that picture, the painting would clearly satisfy the ECJ's test for goods. The painting would be the subject matter of a commercial transaction (a contract of sale). Should the same artist produce another work but give that second picture away, would the second picture fall within the definition of goods? If we require the picture to be the subject of a commercial transaction, arguably the answer to this question would be 'no'. Making such a distinction between two such similar works seems to

22 On the definition of services, see further Chapter 9.

23 Case C-2/90 *Commission* v. *Belgium*, *supra* n. 19.

24 Case C- 362/88 *GB-Inno-BM* v. *Confederation du Commerce Luxembourgois* [1990] ECR I-667, Case 215/87 *Schumacher* v. *Hauptzollamt am Main-Ost* [1989] ECR 617, Case 34/79 *R.* v. *Henn and Darby* [1979] ECR 3795, especially p. 3827. Contrast the position for individuals, who, subject to Article 18 EC, to benefit from Community law rights, must be economically active.

25 *Belgian Waste* case, *supra* n. 19.

26 *Italian Art* case, *supra* n. 1.

have little to recommend it, especially as the recipient of the work could then sell the picture (or otherwise make it the subject of a commercial transaction), thus putting the work into the economic sphere.

One way of reconciling the two cases would be to argue that the *Belgian Waste* case[27] does not preclude the ECJ from looking at the test laid down in the *Italian Art Treasures* case;[28] the two cases simply apply to different situations. For most goods that have an intrinsic monetary value, as the paintings in the example clearly would, the appropriate test is that in the *Italian Art Treasures* case. The fact that they have value puts them *prima facie* within the economic sphere and renders the question of whether they are the subject of a commercial transaction less significant for determining whether they fall within the scope of the EC Treaty. For items with no intrinsic value, the contract is crucial for determining whether the objects fall within the economic sphere and thus whether they constitute goods for the purposes of the EC Treaty. The suggestion that the test for goods in the *Belgian Waste* case has not completely replaced that in the *Italian Art Treasures* case is reinforced by the approach in *Läärä*.[29] There, the Advocate-General in distinguishing slot machines from lottery tickets commented that;

> 'The products at issue here, by contrast, are "products which can be valued in money" and thus in abstract terms are capable of forming the subject of sales or other lawful commercial transactions.'[30]

The ECJ remarked in passing that slot machines 'constitute goods capable of being imported or exported'[31] showing again that the contractual status of the goods is both an abstract test and a secondary issue.

In some respects the definitions in the *Art Treasures* case[32] and that of the *Belgian Waste*[33] are in any event of limited utility. In both cases the status of the items in question as products or goods was not in question; the issue was whether they were goods for the purposes of the EC Treaty. The rulings thus do not help identify whether an item constitutes goods rather than something else, such as services. Some commentators have identified three differences between goods and services: 1) services cannot be stored whilst goods can be; 2) production and consumption of services must take

---

27 *Belgian Waste* case, *supra* n. 19.

28 *Italian Art* case, *supra* n. 1.

29 Case C-124/97 *Markku Juhani Läärä, supra* n. 3.

30 Case C-124/97 *Markku Juhani Läärä, supra* n. 3, Advocate-General's Opinion at paragraph 18.

31 Case C-124/97 *Markku Juhani Läärä, supra* n. 3, judgment at paragraph 24.

32 Case 7/68 *Commission* v. *Italy, supra* n. 1.

33 Case C-2/90 *Commission* v. *Belgium, supra* n. 19.

place simultaneously, whereas goods may be stored; and 3) services are intangible (although they may result in a tangible product).[34] As far as the ECJ is concerned, the term 'goods' is not synonymous with assets, so that fishing rights or intellectual property rights, for example, do not fall within the definition of goods.[35] The critical factor as regards goods appears to be their tangible nature. Although the ECJ has not expressly discussed the point, the Court has alluded to this element in passing. In *Sacchi*, when discussing the distinction between goods and services in the context of television broadcasting, the ECJ commented that;

> 'trade in material sound recordings and other products used for the diffusion of television signals are subject to the rules relating to the freedom of movement for goods.' [36]

In the context of this discussion, the key word in the quotation is 'material'.[37] As we shall see when discussing the boundary between goods and services, however, this approach is not unproblematic.

There are other criteria which affect the free movement of goods. Article 28 focuses on imports; there is no requirement that the person (legal or natural) seeking to rely on the free movement of goods be European (i.e. have the nationality of or be established in one of the Member States). Equally, 'imports' within the context of Article 28 are not limited to goods of European origin. Similar comments may be made in relation to Article 29 and exports. All goods in free circulation within the European Community may benefit from this right.[38] According to Article 24 EC, all products originating in a third country are considered to be in free circulation if the import formalities have been complied with and all customs duties or similar charges have been paid. Article 28 covers imports between Member States. This has two consequences: Articles 28 and 29 do not cover relations with third countries; further, Articles 28 and 29 do not

---

34 See for example Stern and Hoekman 'Negotiations in Services' (1987) 10 *The World Economy* 1 and Weatherill, S., *EC Consumer Law and Policy* (1997), Longmans: London, especially p. 46.

35 Case C-97/98 *Jägerskiöld* v. *Gustafsson*, judgment of 21 October 1999, especially paragraphs 32 and 38. As regards the relationship between intellectual property rights and services, see Cases 92 and 326/92 *Phil Collins* v. *Imtrat Handelsgesellschaft mbH* [1997] ECR I-5145 at paragraph 27.

36 Case 155/78 *Sacchi* [1974] ECR 409 at paragraph 7.

37 See also more recently Case C-2/90 *Commission* v. *Belgium, supra* n. 19, Opinion of Advocate-General Jacobs, Case C-97/98 *Jägerskiöld* v. *Gustafsson, supra* n. 35, Opinion of Advocate-General Jacobs, paragraph 20.

38 Article 23(2) EC.

relate to situations which are purely internal to one Member State. The ramifications of this latter requirement are discussed further in Chapter 5.

II Relationships with Other Freedoms

Given that there is no overlap between the free movement provisions, it is important to distinguish goods from the subject matter of the other freedoms. Difficulties may arise regarding the distinction between goods and services, and also goods and capital. Less obvious is the potential overlap between goods and people (through free movement of workers, freedom of establishment and also some aspects of freedom to provide services).

a) Relationship Between Goods and People

When individuals move from one Member State to another taking with them their belongings, are they relying on their own right to freedom of movement or on the free movement of goods? This issue has not been addressed directly and there are arguments for the use of either article. The argument for relying on Article 28 is clear; household possessions are clearly goods that are being moved from one Member State to another. As noted earlier, it does not matter that they are not directly linked to a commercial transaction,[39] provided they have a value and are capable of forming the subject matter of such an arrangement. Arguably, however, given the wide interpretation given to the rights of those who move, then the right to bring possessions with them is ancillary to migrants being able to exercise their own free movement rights. On a more macabre note, a written question from the European Parliament raised the question of the legal status of dead bodies.[40]

b) Relationship Between Goods and Capital

The distinction to be made here is between goods and currency payments. The problem is that, although money has a function in being used to pay for things, the physical manifestation of money may also have a value separate to that ascribed to it in its capacity as currency, for example, a collection of old coins. It would seem that legal tender should not be considered as goods, although other forms of currency might be. In

---

39 Presumably cross-border removal services could fall within Article 49.

40 Written Question E-3966/93 OJ [1994] C 340/60. It is to be hoped that the question of whether children constitute goods or people does not need to be addressed.

Thompson, Johnson and Woodwiss,[41] for example, the subject matter of the case was Krugerrands and other silver alloy coins, some but not all of which were legal tender. Each of the coins, however, had a value greater than its face value. The question before the ECJ was whether the coins should be considered as goods or as capital. Despite some suggestions that the ECJ should consider the purpose for which the items were imported, the ECJ focussed on the nature of the items, holding that 'monetary transfers' and 'means of payment' do not fall within the scope of 'goods'. Although, as noted, legal tender would seem to fall within these categories, the categories themselves have not been defined, leading to a certain lack of clarity in this area. The judgment in *Thompson* was confirmed in *Bordessa,*[42] which extended the same approach to banknotes and bearer cheques, although the ECJ left the definitional issues arising from *Thompson* unresolved.

Equally, the position of products which are closely associated with having an investment quality is not clear – what, for example, is the position of gold ingots or jewellery? They are tangible and capable of being the subject matter of a transaction. Presumably such items would be seen as capital only where they had a financial nature but would otherwise constitute goods. This suggests that context may be important in determining the question of whether items such as jewellery constitute goods or capital, despite the ECJ's failure to consider the point in *Thompson.*[43] It also means that such items may change from being, for example, goods to capital, depending on the operation of circumstances, with the result that different treaty provisions would apply to their movement between Member States. The potentially mutating nature of such items could prove particularly problematic were the change to occur in transit. Although the changes to the section on free movement of capital[44] have brought that section more closely into line with the provisions and jurisprudence on free movement of goods,[45] differences between the rights remain, particularly as the case law as regards capital is much less well developed than that in relation to goods. These differences mean that the categorisation of an item as goods or capital might be crucial in determining whether the national laws in issue are compatible with EC law or not.

---

41 Case 7/78 *R.* v. *Thompson, Johnson & Woodwiss* [1978] ECR 2247.

42 Case C-358/93 *Bordessa et al* [1993] ECR [1995] ECR I-361.

43 Case 7/78 *R.* v. *Thompson, Johnson & Woodwiss, supra* n. 41.

44 The original articles 67-73 have been replaced by Articles 56–60 (ex 73b–73g).

45 Contrast the earlier position where the ECJ emphasised that, by contrast to the other freedoms, the free movement of capital was binding only insofar as it was necessary to ensure the proper functioning of the common market: Case 203/80 *Casati* [1981] ECR 2595 at 2614.

Despite the changes to the Treaty provisions on capital, given the strong similarity between the new provisions and the terms of Directive 88/361,[46] the most recent directive to implement the original capital provisions, it would seem that the existing definition of capital (as regards means of payment) set down in *Thompson* and confirmed in *Bordessa* is still good law.[47]

c) Relationship Between Goods and Services

The relationship between goods and services creates its own special problems arising out of the fact that goods are often used within the provision of services, and vice versa. Thus, when one orders a new central heating system is this a question of goods or services or both? Additionally, questions arise regarding sales and advertising; should these be considered as part of the sale of the goods, or do they constitute a separate service? Finally, the development of e-commerce may cause further difficulties in the identification of a clear boundary between some goods and services. The problems relating to the determination of the boundary between the two categories are clearly not unique to the EC. Similar issues arise, for example, in the context of English commercial law, but it should be remembered that the dividing line will not necessarily be in the same place for EC law as for other legal systems, since they may have different conceptions of what constitutes goods and services respectively.[48]

The ECJ has generally taken the view that where the service is the main object of the transaction, then the issue falls to be considered under Article 49. For example, in *Schindler*,[49] which concerned the import of lottery tickets into the UK, the tickets were found to be merely instrumental to the provision of the game of chance, a service. Significantly, the tickets had no value in themselves but only as evidence of participation in the game of chance. Similarly, in *van Schaik*,[50] the ECJ found the supply of car parts was incidental to the contract for services to repair the car. By contrast, in the case of the manufacture of goods, because the process 'leads directly to the manufacture of a physical article', manufacture is viewed as the supply of goods rather than the provision of manufacturing services.[51]

---

46 Directive 88/361 OJ [1988] L 178/5.

47 Case C-358/93 *Bordessa*, *supra* n. 42, at paragraph 22.

48 For an example of this sort of dispute outside the confines of the EU, see the difference of opinion between the EC itself and the Americans as to whether television programmes constitute goods or services.

49 Case C-275/92 *Schindler* [1994] ECR I-1039.

50 Case C-55/93 *van Schaik* [1994] ECR I-4837.

51 Case 18/84 *Commission* v. *France* (Tax Breaks) [1985] ECR 1339.

There are a couple of problems with this distinction. One lies with how we define what the main object of the transaction is. The second is whether the use of one of the freedoms precludes the other. As regards the first point, the position in *Schindler*,[52] dealt with under the services provisions, seems unproblematic. *Läärä*[53] also concerned gambling, but with slot machines. The Court accepted that the national rules could affect the import of goods as well as fall within Article 49. In contrast to *Schindler*, slot machines were not merely ancillary to and necessary for the provisions of services; they also constituted capital goods.[54] Does this mean that any goods with an economic value justify the use of the provisions on goods? The spare parts in *van Schaik* equally had an economic value. They ceased, however, to have a separate independent existence following the carrying out of the service. This situation can therefore be distinguished from cases such as *Läärä* and those where tools of a trade, such as spanners, machines for carrying out eye examinations or scalpels, are involved. In each of the latter cases, the goods continue to have an existence independent of the service; in fact they can be re-used in the context of different contracts.

One case that might prove difficult to fit in with this analysis is that of *de Coster*.[55] The case concerning rules relating to the installation of satellite dishes. Despite the fact that satellite dishes surely constitute 'products used for the diffusion of television signals', a phrase from the earlier case of *Sacchi*[56] and used there to delineate the scope of goods, the Court held in *de Coster* that the issue should be dealt with as a matter of services. Clearly, the satellite dish was necessary for the receipt of the services, but so were the fruit machines in *Läärä*, so why were they treated differently? Any argument for determining that the rules related to services would have been stronger had the satellite dish been provided by the broadcaster, especially if ownership had not passed (see further below), as this would have formed part of the overall package supplied by the broadcaster. In circumstances where an individual has bought the satellite dish, the point is less convincing. It is unlikely that one would argue that the purchase of a television set, equally necessary for the receipt of television signals, constituted a situation falling within Article 49. One argument that might be put forward to justify this holding is that, in contrast to the position of tools of the trade that are re-used, the satellite dish can only be used in the context of one service relationship, whether or not contractual. It seems, therefore, that a broader picture relating to the

---

52 Case C-275/92 *Schindler*, *supra* n.49.

53 Case C-124/97 *Läärä*, *supra* n.3.

54 *Ibid.*, Opinion, paragraph 18.

55 Case C-17/00 *Françoise de Coster* v. *Collège des Bourgmestres et Echevins de Watermael-Boitsfort*, judgment 29 November 2001.

56 Case 155/78 *Sacchi*, *supra* n. 36, paragraph 7.

provision of services and goods will need to be taken into account to determine the boundary between the relevant provisions.

Middle ground between the circumstances in which goods have an independent existence and those in which they do not might be exemplified in the case of leasing of objects. One might argue that the fact that the object exists separately suggests that the independent value aspect noted in *Schindler* would be satisfied in such a case. Nonetheless, leasing an object, for example an aircraft or cars, has been considered to constitute a service, as what is being supplied is not the object itself but the use of the object.[57] It is tempting to assume that what is crucial in these leasing cases and what excluded the cases being considered as concerning the free movement of goods is the fact that there has been no transfer of ownership. The Advocate-General in *Läärä* discussed this point, however, rejecting the idea that the transfer of ownership is a necessary pre-requisite to the application of Article 28.[58] The fact that ownership is not transferred may point towards the provision of a service, but it does not mean that the operation of the goods provisions is excluded. Certainly, the relevance of the services provisions can clearly be seen when what is in issue is not just the use of the goods, but when servicing and other services are also included as a package. When might goods provisions be relevant, then? The distinction between the re-use of items in many contracts for service and the use of an item in respect of just one contract, implied in relation to tools, could be applied by analogy in the context of leasing. That is, there is a difference between an item supplied long-term to one customer, in the case of aircraft leasing, and goods supplied to a number of different customers, for shorter periods, as occurs in some aspects of the car hire business. The links with the provision of services rather than the provision of goods in the latter case seems much clearer. This is not a distinction the Court has developed, however, and has arguably been excluded by the Court's emphasis on the contract for use of the goods.

These cases, particularly those relating to tools and equipment, raise another question; that is, whether the services and goods provisions may be applied only in the alternative rather than in tandem. Certainly, the wording of Article 50 might suggest this, as services are described as falling within the Treaty 'when provided for remuneration, insofar as they are not governed by the provisions relating to freedom of movement for goods, capital and persons'. This point might also be inferred from *van Schaik*,[59] as although goods were clearly part of the transaction, the whole matter

---

57 Case C-294/97 *Eurowings Luftverkehr* [1999] ECR I-7447, at paragraph 33, confirmed in Case C-451/99 *Cura Anlagen GmbH* v. *ASL* [2002] ECR I-3193.

58 Case C-124/94 *Läärä, supra* n. 3.

59 Case C-55/93 *van Schaik, supra* n. 50.

(despite the wording of Article 50) was viewed as a question of services. In other words,

> 'does the import or export of goods for the sole purpose of providing services mean that such an operation forms part of the services themselves and accordingly escapes the rules governing the free movement of goods?[60]

Despite the approach in cases such as *van Schaik*, it would seem as though the ECJ has in some instances taken a different view. In the *Dundalk Water* case, the ECJ held that,

> 'the fact that a public works contract relates to the provision of services cannot remove a clause in an invitation to tender restricting the materials that may be used from the scope of the prohibitions set out in Article [28].'[61]

This reasoning undermines the independent economic existence argument put forward earlier, as the materials used would be incorporated into the final building project. *Dundalk Water* is hard to reconcile with *van Schaik*.

Much more recently, in a case which concerned surgeons purchasing scalpels, it was suggested that, as the sole purpose for the scalpels' acquisition was for the provision of services, the relevant national rules should be assessed by reference to Article 49. Despite this and the approach in *van Schaik*, the ECJ held that the fact that goods are to be used for the provision of specific services should not take them outside the scope of the provisions on goods.[62]

Thus both the goods and services provisions seem applicable. Perhaps the significance of these cases on tools, and by contrast to the situation where materials are incorporated during the provision of a service, is to identify when potentially two freedoms come into play rather than just one. Even accepting this point, the jurisprudence is not clear-cut as, in some cases where both goods and services have been involved, the ECJ has dealt with the case by reference to only one freedom. In *MacQuen*,[63] Belgian rules prohibited opticians from carrying out certain optical examinations and restricted the marketing of equipment used in such examinations. This case would seem to involve both goods and services. The ECJ, however, dealt with the issue as a matter of services (and establishment). The Court seemed to discount the argument relating to goods on the basis that a

---

60 Case C-124/94 *Läärä*, supra n. 3, Opinion of the Advocate-General, paragraph 19.

61 Case 45/87 *Commission* v. *Ireland* (Dundalk Water) [1988] ECR 4929, paragraph 17.

62 Cases C-157-160/94 *Commission* v. *Netherlands* [1997] ECR I-5699, at paragraphs 15–20 and the Opinion of the Advocate-General, paragraph 15.

63 Case C-108/96 *MacQuen et al* v. *Union Professionelle Belge des Médecins Spécialistes en Opthalmologie et Chirurgie Oculaire* [2001] ECR-I837.

violation of Article 28 was unlikely to be found.[64] This is open to criticism as surely it is proper to identify the provisions that deal with the relevant subject matter, before assessing the likelihood of a claim being made out. Nonetheless, this argument might well explain the approach in *de Coster*; there the rules could have been considered 'selling arrangements' and therefore outside the scope of Article 28 (see further Chapter 5).

What might be termed retail support services[65] also raised questions in this context. Rules relating to the conditions of retail of goods, such as opening hours, have been considered to be questions affecting goods. Similarly, auctioneers' services have been deemed to fall within the scope of Article 28 rather than 49.[66] Although advertising is clearly a service when provided by an advertising agency to a manufacturer,[67] the advertising itself is considered to form part of the goods or, where a service is being advertised, those services. Thus, advertising itself might become subject to different rules, depending on what is being advertised. Since *Keck*,[68] rules relating to selling arrangements which apply equally in law and in fact, including shop opening hours and some advertising, will fall outside Article 28, although a similar approach has not been taken with regard services.[69] Until recently, the impact on the service provider did not seem to be have been considered separately. Thus, in *Leclerc-Siplec*,[70] which concerned broadcast advertising, rules relating to certain restrictions on advertising were considered as a matter of the free movement of goods, and the impact on the advertising agency or the broadcaster, both service providers, was not considered. More recently in *GIP*,[71] which concerned restrictions on the advertisement of alcoholic beverages in magazines available at the point of sale, the ECJ considered both the impact on the

64 *Ibid.* paragraph 21.

65 See March Hunnings below on 'retail services'. See Case C-17/00 *de Coster supra* n. 63. The Commission Communication on the right to install a satellite dish considered the matter from the perspective of both goods and services.

66 Case C-239/90 *SCP Boscher, Studer et Frometin* v. *SA British Motors Wright and Others, supra* n. 10.

67 See e.g. Case C-405/98 *Konsumentombudsmannen* v. *Gourmet International Products AB* [2001] ECR 1-1795.

68 Joined Cases C-267 and 268/91 *Keck and Mithouard* [1993] ECR I-6097.

69 This issue is discussed further in Chapter 11.

70 Case C-412/93 *Société d'Importation Edouard Leclerc-Siplec v. TF 1 Publicité SA and M6 Publicité SA* [1995] ECR I-179, but contrast the approach of the Advocate-General and see also Joined Cases C-34-36/95 *Konsumentombudsmannen* v. *de Agostini* and *TV Shop* [1997] ECR I-3843.

71 Case C-405/98 *Konsumentombudsmannen* v. *Gourmet International Products AB, supra* n. 67.

goods and on the provision of advertising services of the impugned rules.[72] It is not clear whether this approach would be adopted more widely. There is an argument for suggesting that there is a distinction between the types of services provided by auctioneers and other retailers and those provided by advertising agencies. The former category deal in the goods themselves, whereas the latter category provide the services to the manufacturer or retailer and are only indirectly connected to the provision of the goods. Nonetheless, there seems to be a move towards considering such cases not just as they affect goods but also in relation to services. In the light of *Keck*,[73] this may be an attempt to introduce coherency between goods and services case law, or – more cynically – it may be an attempt to ensure that some measures, that would now lie outside Article 28, remain within the ECJ's consideration.

The result is that in the context of contracts requiring the provision of goods and services, there are three possibilities: that the matter will be viewed as a question only of services; that it will be viewed as goods alone; or that it will be viewed as both. In many cases the same test would seem to be relevant, that of whether the goods or services provided are purely ancillary or whether they have an economic value of their own. The exception seems to be advertising services, which only recently seem to be recognised as having an existence separate from the products advertised. Whether this means that both sets of provisions are to be deemed equally important in a given case, or whether one set of provisions will be considered more relevant is another question. Not only has the Court's jurisprudence been somewhat inconsistent, but any case will be determined on the facts. It should, of course, be noted that the four freedoms are mutually exclusive, though recent case law – such as that noted above – seems to have undermined this position. (See also Chapter 9.)

Problems also arise when we look at intangible items; should these be considered as goods or services? It was suggested above that tangibility is a hallmark of 'goods'. Supply of electricity seems, however, to be viewed as the provision of goods.[74] Advocate-General Jacobs suggested that this approach is 'perhaps justifiable by virtue of its function as an energy source and, therefore, its competition with gas and oil'.[75] The issue of competing products has not been considered in relation to other products as yet, although this idea might become more relevant should the market for electronic books, for example, develop. Broadcasting, by contrast to

72 In Case C-405/98 *GIP*, *supra* n. 67, it was also suggested, by contrast to *Keck*, *supra* n. 68, that the rules did fall within Article 28. See further Chapters 4 and 5.

73 Joined Cases C-267 and 268/91 *Keck*, *supra* n. 68.

74 Case C- 393/92 *Almelo* [1994] ECR I-1471.

75 Case C-97/98 *Jägerskiöld* v. *Gustafsson*, *supra* n. 35, Advocate-General's Opinion at paragraph 20.

electricity, has been held to fall within the services provision.[76] However, videos and films, which might contain the same programming that is broadcast via television (and which might therefore be considered to compete with broadcast material), are considered to fall within the goods provisions.[77] This distinction is somewhat fine, and has not gone without criticism. It has been suggested that this would be like characterising the act of selling goods as the provision of a retail service,[78] a position that the ECJ, in the context of auctions, seems to have rejected.[79] The problem in this instance seems to be that the ECJ focussed on the mechanism of transmission rather than considering the content – in the case of broadcasting, the programmes and films. Thus, the same product may be treated differently depending on the mechanism by which the consumer receives it. This problem looks likely to arise more frequently in respect of other intangible products such as software and music, as increasingly they are accessed, downloaded and bought via the Internet.

III Conclusions

Although in many cases the question of whether an item constitutes goods will be unproblematic, in some cases the matter will be far from clear. The issue has significance because the ECJ, on the whole, has taken the view that only one freedom should apply in any given case. It now seems as though technology is operating to exacerbate the difficulties in two main categories. The first relates to questions of morality and, in particular, whether some things, for example some biotechnological devices, should be the subject of trade. The second category concerns the potential overlap between the free movement of goods and other freedoms, notably services. This latter point is particularly significant, as there are some areas of divergence in the case law relating to Articles 28 and 29 on the one hand and Article 49 on the other. Categorisation is thus not merely about labels, but may have profound repercussions both on individual rights and the freedom of Member States to regulate some aspects of trade.

---

76 Case 155/78 *Sacchi supra* n. 36; Case 52/79 *Procureur du Roi* v. *Debauve* [1980]ECR 833.

77 Cases C-60 and 61/84 *Cinéthèque SA* v. *Fédération Nationale des Cinémas Français*, *supra* n. 13, See also *Debauve*, *supra* n. 76.

78 See March Hunnings, N., 'Case note on *Debauve* and *Coditel*' (1980) 17 *CMLRev* 560.

79 Case C-239/90 *SCP Boscher, Studer et Frometin* v. *SA British Motors Wright and Others supra* n. 10 at paragraphs 7–10.

Chapter 3

Whose Actions are Caught?

I Introduction

Articles 28–30 EC do not specifically refer to the actions of Member States,[1] although those actions of Member States which constitute quantitative restrictions (or measures having equivalent effect) clearly fall within the scope of Articles 28 and 29 EC. Given that these articles have direct effect,[2] individuals may rely on these provisions in their national courts; the case law identified in following chapters shows that many have done so – at least as against the actions of the Member States. Does Article 28, however, catch the actions of individuals? Initially there was some uncertainty on this point[3] but it now seems generally accepted that the goods provisions do not apply horizontally, the actions of individuals being caught by the competition provisions.[4] Recently though, the ECJ has

---

1 Old articles 31-33 EC, which specifically referred to the actions of Member States, were deleted as part of the tidying-up process carried out by the Treaty of Amsterdam, as they referred to the transitional period.

2 Case 74/76 *Ianelli* v. *Meroni* [1977] ECR 587.

3 Case 58/80 *Dansk Supermarked A/S* v. *A/S Imerco* [1981] ECR 181 at paragraph 17 seems to suggest that the actions of private individuals would be caught: see also the arguments in Quinn, M., and MacGowan., 'Could Art. 30 Impose Obligations on Individuals?' (1987) 12 *European Law Review* 163 and more recently the implications behind Case C-16/94 *Dubois and General Cargo Services* v. *Garonor Exploitation* [1995] ECR I-2421, paragraph 19.

4 The generally cited case for this proposition is Case 311/85 *Asbl Vereinigung van Vlaamse Reisbureaus* v. *Asbl Sociale Dienst van de plaatelijke en gewestlijke overheidsdiensten* [1987] ECR 3801 at paragraph 30 although in this case services rather than goods were in issue. In Case 8/74 *Procureur du Roi v. Dassonville* [1974] ECR 837, the ECJ in setting down its famous test for MEQR referred to 'All trading rules enacted by Member States ...' arguably implying that Article 28 was so limited. It should be noted, however, that the ECJ has not been consistent as to whether the *Dassonville* test only applies to trading rules: see further Chapter 5, thus undermining arguments based on the precise wording in the case. Advocate-General Lenz stated the limitation of Article 28 to state actions as being beyond contention in Case C-265/95

confirmed the horizontality of Article 39 in a judgment that re-emphasised the necessity of ensuring that obstacles to free movement through state action were not replaced by actions of individuals.[5] In the light of this judgment and of the *Angry Farmers* case,[6] which also erodes the distinction between public and private action, the issues under Articles 28 and 29 are worth revisiting. A couple of concerns arise. The first is the question of whether there should be a difference between goods and services in this regard. The second concerns the structure of the EC Treaty and its impact on the proper scope of EC law. The next section will identify the arguments for the proposition that Article 28 (and 29) should have horizontal effect that those against it, before outlining the case law on the nature of those bodies clearly caught by Articles 28 and 29 EC.

II Reasons why the Actions of Private Parties should or should not be caught by Articles 28 – 30 EC

One of the underlying justifications put forward by the ECJ as it developed the doctrine of direct effect was the need to ensure the effectiveness of Community law. Thus, Community law should have a legally binding quality irrespective of the actions (or omissions) of Member States in implementing and enforcing Community law. The ECJ took this approach initially with regard to negative obligations imposed on Member States by the Treaty, but subsequently extended it until, at least as far as Treaty articles and regulations were concerned, provisions that were sufficiently clear precise and unconditional would be binding on private parties as well as the Member States. In *Defrenne* v. *Sabena* (No 2), the ECJ, for example, argued:

> 'In fact, since Article 119 [new 141 EC] is mandatory in nature, the prohibition on discrimination between men and women applies not only to the action of public authorities, but also extends to all agreements which are intended to regulate paid labour collectively, as well as to contracts between individuals.'[7]

Similar statements can be found in case law relating to the provisions on free movement of workers, freedom of establishment and freedom to

---

Commission v. *France* (Angry Farmers) [1997] ECR I-6959 at paragraph 8, but he based his argument on former Articles 31 and 32 EC, see *supra* n. 1.

5 Case C-281/98 *Angonese* v. *Cassa di Rispamio di Bolzano SpA* [2000] ECR I-4139.

6 Case C-265/95 *Commission* v. *France*, *supra* n. 4.

7 Case 43/75 *Defrenne* v. *Sabena* (No. 2) [1976] ECR 455 at paragraph 39.

provide services,[8] although the precise extent of the obligation on non-State actors is the subject of some discussion.[9] The concern expressed by the Court, most recently in *Angonese*,[10] centres on the possibility of barriers created by state action being removed only to be replaced by those created by the actions of private parties, thus undermining the effectiveness and uniformity of Community law. Surely then, this type of reasoning would be applied to Articles 28 and 29 EC.

Some commentators have, however, suggested that the horizontal effect in the *Defrenne*[11] case arose out of the mandatory or foundational nature of the obligation contained in Article 141, that is the prohibition on discrimination, in the *Defrenne* context, on the grounds of gender. On this basis, only those actions of private bodies that contravene equally fundamental principles, notably discrimination on the grounds of nationality, would have horizontal effect. Assuming this to be the case,[12] Article 28 EC should not be excluded in principle from having horizontal effect, although questions might remain about the type of measure that would be affected by the horizontal prohibition. On the face of it, for private actions to be caught by Articles 28 or 29 EC, they must run contrary to the heart of the prohibitions in those articles, that is, by being discriminatory.[13]

---

8 Cases C- 415/93 *Union Royale Belge des Sociétés de Football (ASBL)* v. *Bosman* [1995] ECR I-4921 at paragraph 17; Case 36/74 *Walrave* v. *Union Cycliste Internationale* [1974] ECR 1405 at paragraph 17; Case 13/76 *Dona* v. *Mantero* [1976] ECR 455.

9 See for example Milner-Moore 'The Accountability of Private Parties under the Movement of Goods Principle' URL: http://www.law.harvard.edu/programs/Jean Monnet/papers/papers95.html suggesting that there is a difference between direct and indirect discrimination. The Advocate-General made such a distinction, albeit in a different context, in his Opinion in Case 249/81 *Commission* v. *Ireland* ('Buy Irish') [1982] ECR 4005 at p. 4030. Similar concerns underlie the point Advocate-General Caporti made in Case 82/77 *Openbaar Ministerie* v. *van Tiggele* [1978] ECR 25 at p. 47 concerning the distinction between the competition provisions and free movement provisions.

10 Case C-281/98 *Angonese* v. *Cassa di Rispamio di Bolzano SpA, supra* n. 5.

11 Case 43/75 *Defrenne* (No. 2), *supra* n. 7.

12 Whether all of the cases constitute examples of direct discrimination on grounds of nationality is debatable. In *Angonese, supra* n. 5, the matter was one of indirect discrimination and in *Bosman, supra* n. 8, the rules seemed to concern barriers to the market rather than the notion of discrimination itself.

13 See, for example, the Advocate-General's Opinion in Cases 60 and 61/84 *Cinéthèque SA* v. *Fédération Nationale des Cinémas Françaises* [1985] ECR 2605 at pp. 2609-2610.

Another argument put forward in support of the statement that Articles 28-30 should apply to private parties is the existence of the derogation in Article 30 for industrial and commercial property.[14] The argument is that intellectual property rights are held and exercised by private parties. The Treaty therefore envisages the involvement of private parties in intra-Community trade, as this exception to the general prohibition in Articles 28 and 29 would not make sense unless those general rules also applied to private parties. Certainly, there are many cases when private individuals have sought to rely on Article 30 (ex-36).[15] This argument is, however, countered by those who point out that Article 30 (ex-36) relates to the actions of Member States rather than those of private parties, as it is the Member States which have put into place the legislation without which the individuals' intellectual property rights would not exist. In *GEMA* the ECJ stated:

> 'It follows that national legislation whose application results in obstructing trade in sound recordings between Member States must be regarded as a measure having an effect equivalent to a quantitative restriction within the meaning of Article 30 [now Article 28].'[16]

Thus, in this case, it was not GEMA's action for damages, but the Member State's legislation that allowed GEMA to bring its claim, which was contrary to the EC Treaty.[17] This distinction between the existence of intellectual property rights and the exercise thereof lies at the heart of the ECJ's judgments on Article 30 and intellectual property rights. Whether it consistently supports the argument against Articles 28 and 29 encompassing the actions of private parties is another matter. In many of the judgments, the ECJ has been keen to emphasise that the Treaty does not affect the existence of property rights put in place by the Member States, as indeed would seem to be required by Article 295 EC (ex-222), but rather limits the way the rights themselves are exercised.[18] The consequence of this approach seems to be that it is the actions of private

14 The extent of this derogation is discussed further in Chapter 8.

15 See e.g. Case 78/70 *Deutsche Grammaphon* v. *Metro* [1971] ECR 487 at 500; Case 58/80 *Dansk Supermarked* v. *Imerco* [1981] ECR 181 and cases discussed in Chapter 8.

16 Cases 55 & 57/80 *Musik Vertrieb membran GmbH and K-Tel International* v. *GEMA* [1981] ECR 147 at paragraph 8.

17 See also Case 15/74 *Centrafarm BV and Adriaan de Peijper* v. *Sterling Drug Inc.* [1974] ECR 1147 at paragraph 24.

18 See e.g. Case 15/74 *Centrafarm BV* supra n. 17; Case 78/70 *Deutsche Grammaphon, supra* n. 15.

parties that are central rather than the underlying government measure, undermining the argument put forward in cases such as *GEMA*.

It has also been suggested that the existence of other Treaty articles, notably Articles 81 and 82 (ex-85 and 86), would catch any offending behaviour on the part of individuals. On this reasoning, not only is expanding Articles 28 and 29 unnecessary, but allowing both sets of provisions to apply to the same situations potentially exposes individuals to the risk of being caught by both sets of provisions. This problem would be exacerbated by the difference in scope which has developed between Articles 28–30 EC and the competition rules, notably the fact that Article 28 does not provide an exception for those provisions which have only a minimal or hypothetical impact on inter-state trade.[19] The institutions have, by contrast, incorporated a *de minimis* rule into Article 81. The distinction between the free movement provisions and the competition provisions seems to have been accepted by the ECJ, the ECJ noting that the two sets of provisions serve different functions. Certainly, Articles 81 and 82, as expressed in the Treaty, address only the actions of individuals, not those of states. The precise relationship between Articles 28 and 81 has not, however, always been clear, especially given the ECJ's expansion of Article 81 in conjunction with Article 10. These two provisions read together put Member States under a positive obligation not to undermine the competition provisions.[20] Indeed, despite the limitation on Articles 28 and 29, some situations may give rise to breaches of competition and free movement provisions.[21]

Although this division of labour between Articles 28-30 on the one hand and 81 and 82 on the other seems, on the surface, rational, a couple of points should to be noted. The first point relates also to the structure of the Treaty. If the existence of Articles 81 and 82 suggest that Articles 28 and 29 should not apply to the actions of private parties, should the same not also be true for the other freedoms, especially given the narrow boundary[22] between goods and services in some fields? As we know, Article 49 regarding services (as well as the freedom of establishment and free movement of workers provisions) does apply horizontally, yet the

---

19 Case C-184/96 *Commission* v. *France* (Foie Gras) [1998] ECR I-6197.

20 Case C-320/91 *Corbeau* [1993] ECR 1-2533; Case 66/86 *Ahmed Saeed Flugreisen & Silver Line Reiseburo GmbH* v. *Zentrale zur Bekampfung unlauteren Wettbewerbe e.V* [1989] ECR 803. See also comments of Advocate-General Caporti in Case 82/77 *van Tiggele supra* n. 9.

21 Case 82/77 *van Tiggele*, *supra* n. 9 at p. 48.

22 See Chapter 2.

competition provisions have also been applied in the field of services.[23] This asymmetry undermines any structural argument put forward to support the division of responsibility between free movement and competition, at least in terms of the type of person caught by a particular provision. It is difficult to argue that the Treaty operates as a coherent whole in respect to the free movement of goods, and then accept that it does not do the same as regards services.[24]

A second point questions whether there is any gap between the protection afforded by Articles 28 and 29 on the one hand and Articles 81 and 82 on the other. Given the wide definitions given to the competition provisions, particularly the terms, 'undertaking', 'association of undertakings' and 'agreement' in Article 81, most forms of action by more than one individual acting together will be caught. The same cannot be said for the actions of private parties acting alone. What about the actions, for example, of a sole trader who refuses to stock German goods?[25] This raises the question of the extent to which the actions of an individual *should* be caught by Articles 28–30 EC. Although the individual or company which discriminates on the grounds of nationality might seem to cause few doubts as to the appropriateness of Article 28's applicability, can we say the same, for example, when we consider the position of the individual consumer who chooses not to buy French goods as a protest against the testing of nuclear weapons in the South Pacific? This is surely a matter of individual conscience. In any event, how do we tell that this is what the consumer is doing? The consumer might choose to buy Cornish Yarg rather than Camembert merely because he or she prefers Yarg.[26] In general, there is a danger that conflicts may arise between individuals' civil rights and the characterisation of consumer action as a measure for the purposes of Article 28 and 29. For example, can protests against the export of live

---

23 See Case C-266/96 *Corsica Ferries France SA* v. *Gruppo Antichi Ormmeggiatori de Porto di Genova Coop arl* [1998] ECR I-3949 for the relationship between Article 49 and Articles 81 and 82.

24 Note, however, that there are some differences in the way the provisions relating to goods and services are structured. Competition within the service sphere might be particularly relevant because of the lack of any specific provisions relating to state monopolies.

25 Article 82 might catch the actions of a dominant undertaking; this provision is unlikely to be relevant to a sole trader.

26 The ECJ has expressed concerns about the crystallization of consumer habits. As regards discriminatory taxation, see e.g. Case 170/78 *Commission* v. *United Kingdom* [1980] ECR 417. The issue has also arisen in relation to Articles 28-30: Case 178/84 *Commission* v. *Germany* (Beer) [1987] ECR 1227, and discussed in more recent cases: see e.g. Case C-405/98 *Konsumentombusdmannen* v. *Gourmet International Products AB* [2001] ECR I-1795.

animals for slaughter not be seen as an exercise of the rights of freedom of expression and association?[27] Picketing imported goods, whilst constituting a barrier to trade, could in some circumstances be characterised as the exercise of trades' unions' rights.[28] It has been suggested trades union actions should not be caught by competition provisions.[29] This point is reinforced by the fact that Article 28 of the EU Charter specifically recognises the right to strike. Looking at the ECJ's jurisprudence, however, all these situations could fall within Article 28 were it to have horizontal effect, and would then have to be justified according to the Treaty scheme.[30]

From the earlier discussions, there are a number of possible approaches to the question of the appropriate scope of Articles 28-30 EC. One is to limit the liability of private parties to cases of overt discrimination. Although this may appear initially attractive, great difficulties remain in its practical application. Alternatively, one might argue that in the context of individuals at least, the free movement provisions should be required to have a certain minimum impact on intra-Community trade before be held to trigger the application of Articles 28 and 29. Unfortunately, the ECJ as has always rejected the possibility of a *de minimis* test as far as the free movement provisions are concerned.[31] This then brings us back to the distinction between the free movement provisions and the competition provisions. It may be that by virtue of their different focus, the most workable solution is to use competition to deal with the activities of private parties and the free movement to deal with those of governments and public bodies. This approach still leaves open the possibility that the completion of the internal market may be adversely affected by the actions of private persons; typically, however, the ECJ has sought to limit the gap in protection by taking a wide view of what constitutes a Member State.

---

27 *R.* v. *Chief Constable of Sussex, ex parte International Traders Ferry* [1999] 2 AC 418, [1999] 1 All ER 129, [1998] 3 WLR 1260, [1999] 1 CMLR 1320.

28 One counter argument would be to suggest that the Treaty provisions are interpreted in the light of the obligations of the Member States and the Union to respect, *inter alia*, the European Convention on Human Rights. Although the ECJ claims to uphold respect for human rights, it has been criticised on some occasions for prioritising economic or political considerations. See literature referred to in Chapter 1 and at n. 74.

29 Van Gerven, 'The Recent Case Law of the Court of Justice concerning Articles 30 and 36 of the EEC Treaty' [1977] *CMLRev* 5.

30 See Chapter 7.

31 See further Chapter 6.

III Governmental Actions

Given that Articles 28 – 30 EC will not necessarily catch the actions of all parties, it is important to define which fall within the scope of the free movement provisions. Clearly the actions of all forms of government will be caught as the ECJ illustrated in *Aragonesa de Publicidad.*[32] There, the ECJ stated that:

> 'Article 30 of the Treaty [now Article 28] may apply to measures adopted by all authorities of the Member State, be they central authorities, the authorities of a federal state, or other territorial authorities.'

The position of quangos and other private bodies which exercise some form of public function is less clear. The *Royal Pharmaceutical Society* case[33] is one of a series of cases in which the position of quasi governmental bodies were considered. In the earlier *'Buy Irish'* case,[34] a government sponsored programme for the promotion of Irish goods within Ireland through an advertising campaign was held to fall within the then Article 30, although the programme was run by the Irish Goods Council. The Advocate-General in this case emphasised the close link between the Council and the Irish government. The members of the Council were appointed by a minister, the government contributed to its budget and any change in its constitutional documents required ministerial approval. In the Advocate-General's words the Council had the 'same appearance as a public institution with auxiliary functions in an economic field.'[35] An advertising campaign run by such a body could not be likened to an advertising campaign run by an association of private individuals as it closely represented the Irish government's own policy. The ECJ had to decide another similar case the next year, this time involving the British Apple and Pear Development Council.[36] In this case, the Council was established by statutory instrument but was financed by a statutory levy imposed on domestic, but not imported, fruit. The majority of the income was spent on an advertising campaign, 'Polish up your English'. Drawing on its ruling in the *Irish* case,[37] the ECJ held that an advertising campaign

---

32 Case C-1/90 *Aragonesa de Publicidad* v. *Departmento de Sanidad* [1991] ECR I-4151.

33 Cases 226 & 227/87 *R.* v. *RPI ex parte Association of Royal Pharmaceutical Importers & Others* [1989] ECR 1295.

34 Case 249/81 *Commission* v. *Ireland* ('Buy Irish'), *supra* n. 9.

35 *Ibid.*

36 Case 222/82 *Apple and Pear Development Council* v. *K.J. Lewis Ltd and Others* [1983] ECR 4083.

37 Case 249/81 *Commission* v. *France* ('Buy Irish'), *supra* n. 9.

may fall within Article 28, 'where it is supported by the public authorities'.[38] Here the voluntary characteristic of the association's activities meant the scheme did not fall within Article 28.

In both these cases, the bodies in question had been set up by government. Bodies which are similarly approved by government, or derive their functions or special powers from state authority would seem similarly to be included within the definition of a public body for the purposes of the free movement provisions. In the *Royal Pharmaceutical Society* case,[39] this was the point at issue. The Royal Pharmaceutical Society was the governing body for all pharmacists in the UK and, as such, set up codes of conduct with which pharmacists had to comply. One such rule stated that pharmacists should not substitute generic drugs for those prescribed by name by the doctor, even if both drugs were therapeutically the same. This adversely affected the sale of drugs imported in parallel from other Member States, as doctors tended not to prescribe by generic name, but rather by the brand names that were known in the UK. The question was whether this rule constituted a 'measure' for the purposes of Article 28. Central to the issue was whether the rules of the RPI could be imputed to the government. In this case, there was no government intervention in the policy about the non-substitution of drugs. The ECJ held that,

> 'measures adopted by a professional body on which national legislation has conferred powers of that nature may, if they are capable of affecting trade between Member States, constitute 'measures' within the meaning of Article 30 of the Treaty.'[40]

The Advocate-General in coming to a broadly similar conclusion, emphasised that the private nature of the body would not take it outside the scope of Article 28 where such a body exercised compulsory supervision over a provision.[41] Thus, the form of a body is not conclusive for determining whether its actions may be imputed to the government. Instead, one must look to the nature of the powers exercised, in particular, where they are compulsory or backed up by legislation. In this approach we see similarities to the approach taken by the ECJ in relation to the

---

38 Case 222/82 *Apple and Pear Development Council, supra* n. 36 at paragraph 17. See also Case C-325/00 *Commission* v. *Germany* (Quality Label), judgment of 5 November 2002.

39 Cases 226 & 227/87 *R.* v. *RPI, supra* n. 33.

40 *Ibid.*, at paragraph 15.

41 *Ibid.* Advocate-General's Opinion at paragraph 14. See also Advocate-General Jacobs in Case C-325/00 *Commission* v. *Germany* (Quality Label), *supra* n. 38, Opinion at paragraphs 24–27.

boundary between public and private when directives are in question,[42] despite the fact that the reasons underlying the need for a distinction between public and private bodies in respect of the enforcement of directives are different from those put forward in respect of Articles 28–30 EC.[43]

Does the ECJ always take such a consistent view? It has been suggested that it does not, the scope of public body varying depending on whether a narrow or broad conception would most facilitate free movement. Given the supposed inter-relationship between the competition provisions and those relating to free movement of goods noted earlier,[44] it seems more important here that a coherent approach be taken in determining the boundary between public and private bodies. To fail to do so would put those bodies on the borderline between public and private (such as trade associations which also have regulatory functions) at risk of being penalised under both Article 28 and 81. Alternatively, a failure to co-ordinate these definitions might lead to a gap in the system created by the Treaty, allowing some measures, which discriminate against imports or which compartmentalize markets, to continue unhindered. Although the ECJ has considered the relationship between these provisions in a number of cases, the case law (and the approach of the institutions generally) determining the public private boundary, unfortunately, seems not to have been co-ordinated. From a number of decisions, it would seem that a trade association would fall within the definition of an association of undertakings for the purposes of Article 81.[45] Conversely, applying the approach in the *Royal Pharmaceutical Society* case[46] would indicate that equally some such bodies would constitute a public body for the purposes of Article 28.[47] The question of whether a trade association could simultaneously be both a public and a private body has not been addressed. Although the ECJ has indicated that the fact that a body has a status in

---

42 Case C-188/89 *Foster et al.* v. *British Gas plc* [1990] ECR I-3313.

43 Advocate-General Pergola when discussing the nature of the state for the purposes of Articles 23 and 25 EC in Case C-16/94 *Dubois and General Cargo Services* v. *Garonor Exploitation supra* n. 3, however, did refer to the test in *Foster* v. *British Gas, ibid.*, indicating that there was no distinction between the test for a state body in respect of directives and the provisions prohibiting tariff barriers.

44 Similar issues arise in relation to Articles 31(ex-37), 86 (ex-90), and 295 (ex-222).

45 See e.g. Case 123/83 *BNIC* v. *Clair* [1985] ECR 391 at paragraph 19, Case 127/73 *Belgische Radio en Televisie et al.* v. *SV SABAM et al.* [1974] ECR 313.

46 Cases 226 & 227/87 *R.* v. *RPI, supra* n. 33.

47 It seems likely that it would also satisfy the test set out in *Foster* v. *British Gas, supra* n. 42.

public law does not necessarily preclude it from falling within Article 81,[48] this would seem to be a reference to the relevant national law and not its status under EC law. Clearly this question is important for trade associations, especially those with statutory powers, but the issue of whether an action should be brought under the free movement provisions might well have significance for those seeking to challenge the actions of such bodies, as this may well impact on the range and scope of remedies available to them.

IV Actions of Private Parties and Governmental Failure to Act

The scope of Member State responsibility does not now end with bodies which have a quasi-governmental nature or function. The turning point came in *Commission* v. *France* (Angry Farmers).[49] The case concerned the protests by groups of French farmers against imported produce. The protests went on for a considerable period and involved damage to property, requirements on shops to purchase amounts of French food backed up by threats and intimidation. The French government took few steps to prevent such actions and to prosecute these groups. Clearly, if these actions were to be considered as constituting a barrier to trade, they were not the actions of the Member State, nor did the French government overtly support these actions. It would seem therefore that the farmers' actions did not come within the scope of the case law on public bodies. The question was could the actions nonetheless be imputed to French government? The ECJ commented that Article 28 is not limited to measures from Member States which in themselves create restrictions on trade between Member States, it also applies when action is required to deal with obstacles to trade. Basing its argument on Article 10 in conjunction with Article 28,[50] the ECJ held that Member States are required,

48 Case C-35/96 *Commission* v. *Italy* (Customs Agents) [1998] ECR I- 3851, at paragraph 40.

49 Case C-265/95 *Commission* v. *France, supra* n. 4.

50 The judgment is not entirely clear in its reasoning as in the previous paragraphs it seems as though the ECJ is basing its argument solely on Article 28, stating at paragraph 30 that Article 28 'does not prohibit solely measures emanating from the State which, in themselves, create restrictions on trade between Member states. It also applies where a Member State abstains from adopting the measures required in order to deal with obstacles to the free movement of goods which are not caused by the States.'

> 'to take all necessary and appropriate measures to ensure that [the fundamental freedom in Article 28] is respected on their territory.'[51]

This is a slightly different approach from that taken under the public bodies case law: there the bodies were considered to part of the state machinery. Here, this was clearly not the position of the farmers. The ECJ has thus de-coupled the responsibility of the Member State to take action from the notion of state control. Although the reasoning might be implicit in a previous case against France concerning fish quotas, in which France was found not to have taken action against fishermen for excessive fishing,[52] there is a crucial difference between the two cases. In that case, the secondary legislation in issue specifically required the governments to take action should overfishing occur. Here the obligation is derived from general treaty principles.[53] Consequently, not only does this ruling expand the potential scope of Articles 28 and 29 in quantitative terms, but also marks a qualitative difference in approach. Clearly, as a result of the reasoning in the *Angry Farmers* case,[54] Member States are under an obligation, not only to ensure that they themselves comply with the terms of Article 28, but that private parties within their jurisdiction do too. This change in approach is also implicit in the reasoning of both the Advocate-General and the ECJ: they emphasise the fundamental nature of the internal market project, referring to Articles 2, 3c and 14 (ex-7a) EC which do not refer to the actions of the Member States, but are more general in scope. Thus, with this ruling the ECJ has provided another possible way of avoiding the problematic situation of the horizontal effect of Articles 28–30 but has also implicitly confirmed that these provisions do not apply to the actions of private parties directly.[55]

The extent and consequences of this ruling are as yet unclear, although some points may be clarified in further cases currently pending before the ECJ.[56] The first question relates to which actions of private parties will be

---

51 *Ibid.*, at paragraph 32.

52 Case C-52/93 *Commission* v. *France* (Fisheries Regulation) [1995] ECR I-4443.

53 See also Case C-16/94 *Dubois and Général Cargo Services* v. *Garonor Exploitation supra* n. 3 regarding former Articles 9 and 12 regarding a levy imposed by a private undertaking on imports. There the ECJ held at paragraph 20 that the charges arose 'from the failure of the Member States concerned to fulfil its financial obligations under Articles 9 and 12 of the Treaty'. In the same case, Advocate-General Pergola found governmental liability for the charges but based his arguments on former Articles 9 and 12 in conjunction with former Article 5 (now 10).

54 Case C-265/95 *Commission* v. *France, supra* n. 4.

55 The Advocate-General made this point expressly - see *supra* n. 3.

56 See also Cases C-418 and 419/00 *Commission* v. *France* (Fisheries Policy) [2002] ECR 1-3969 on failure to take action to implement fisheries policy including failure to

imputed to the state. The situation in *Commission* v. *France* (Angry Farmers) was extreme and the relative inactivity of the French government was marked.[57] What level of action by individuals is required before the Member States' governments are obliged to take action, and what level of action will satisfy their obligations? As regards the former point, *Schmidberger*[58] may clarify some of the outstanding issues. It concerned the blocking of a motorway by protesters concerned about the impact of road traffic on the environment. The blockade was a one-off event, lasting a few days and carried out in accordance with the relevant national law. Further, the protest was not targeted at any particular category or nationality of goods. These factors distinguish the case from the *Angry Farmers* case. Nonetheless, Advocate-General Jacobs has suggested that Article 28 should apply, although the Austrian Government's decision may be justifiable. According to the Advocate-General, the assessment of whether there is a restriction of trade is an objective one; the level of impact and the motives of both the individuals involved and the relevant government are irrelevant at this stage of the enquiry. If the ECJ adopts a similar approach in its judgment in this case, and in particular accepts that any potential restriction arising from the actions of private parties deserves Governmental response, it could make the jurisprudence in the goods area unworkable in practice. The Advocate-General phrased the matter in terms of the obligation to keep transit routes open which does not seem too onerous. Taking an 'objective' stance, especially in the light of the *Dassonville* test,[59] is potentially far more wide reaching than that, covering the difficult issues, identified earlier, regarding the choices of private parties. How is a government to identify all the cases in which, under Articles 28 and 10, it has an obligation to take action? These issues gain further significance in the light of the 'sufficiently serious breach' test for the purposes of state liability actions.[60] At what point will governments

---

take penal action to prevent over fishing. This judgment was based, however, on a regulation containing specific obligations.

57 In Case C-52/93 *Commission* v. *France* (Fisheries Regulation), *supra* n. 52 the exhaustion of the fish quota was also very clear. Contrast the position in *R.* v. *Chief Constable of Sussex, ex parte International Traders Ferry*, which came before the English courts but which was not referred to the ECJ, *supra* n. 27.

58 Case C-112/00 *Eugen Schmidberger Internationale Transporte Planzüge* v. *Austria*, not yet decided, Opinion of the Advocate-General, 11 July 2002.

59 Case 8/74 *Procureur du Roi* v. *Dassonville et al.*, *supra* n. 4, discussed further in Chapters 4 and 5.

60 Joined Cases C-46 and 48/93 *Brasserie de Pêcheur SA* v. *Germany* [1996] ECR I-1029.

start to incur liability to individuals or companies who have suffered loss as a result of private party actions and governmental inaction?[61]

Furthermore, although this obligation falls on the Member States, and therefore cannot be considered as being horizontally directly effective, there is nonetheless a secondary impact on private parties' freedom of action. This issue brings us back to the questions identified earlier about the type of private action that should be caught within the Treaty prohibitions. It is not clear whether the impact of fundamental freedoms means that certain individual actions, such as the right to strike, do not trigger the Member State's responsibility in the first place or whether they may constitute justification for a Member State's failure to act under Article 30 or by virtue of the mandatory requirements rule in *Cassis de Dijon*.[62] *Schmidberger*[63] suggests this latter proposition to be the case. Nonetheless, this latter approach is still shifting the burden of proof on to the Member States to justify their action – or inaction.

Following the *Angry Farmers* case,[64] the Commission, at the request of the Amsterdam European Council, brought forward a proposal for a Council Regulation to create a mechanism whereby the Commission could intervene to remove certain obstacles to trade.[65] It was the subject of a relatively short but controversial legislative process[66] before a regulation (based on a Council re-draft of the original proposal) was agreed.[67] According to Article 1, the Regulation applies where obstacles to trade exist which originate in the action or inaction of the Member States. This would therefore cover the *Commission* v. *France* situation, as Article 1(2) clarifies: it defines inaction by tracking the wording of the judgment in the *Angry Farmers* case. In contrast to the Commission's draft, which gave the

61 This point was discussed in Case C-112/00 *Schmidberger*, *supra* n. 58.

62 Case 120/78 *Rewe* v. *Bundesmonopolverwaltung fur Branntwein* (Cassis de Dijon) [1979] ECR 649.

63 Case C-112/00 *Schmidberger*, *supra* n. 58.

64 Case C-265/95 *Commission* v. *France*, *supra* n. 4.

65 Proposal for a Council Regulation creating a Mechanism whereby the Commission intervene in order to remove certain obstacles to trade (COM (97) 619 final) OJ [1998] C 10/14.

66 Opinion of the Economic and Social Committee on the 'Proposal for a Council Regulation (EC) creating a mechanism whereby the Commission can intervene in order to remove certain obstacles to trade' [1998] OJ C 214/90; EP Report on the proposal for a Council Regulation (EC) creating a mechanism whereby the Commission can intervene in order to remove certain obstacles to trade, Document A4-0385/98 [1998] OJ C359.

67 Council Regulation 2679/98/EC of 7 December 1998 on the functioning of the internal market in relation to the free movement of goods among the Member States [1998] OJ L 337/8.

Commission the power to address a decision on a perceived breach of Member States' obligation to the Member State, Articles 3 and 4 establish an information exchange system. Article 3 relates to information regarding the obstacle to trade. Article 4 imposes on Member States the duty to take action against the measures of private parties and to notify the Commission of its action or intended action. Article 5 gives the Commission the power to 'notify' a Member State when it believes that there is an obstacle to trade in respect of which the Member State should take action. Ultimately, the final course of action for the Commission is to bring an action before the ECJ, which may lead to delays given the workload of the ECJ.

In the light of the limited of success of the Article 226 procedure,[68] it remains to be seen how successful this regulation will be in encouraging Member States to remove obstacles to trade. This problem is exacerbated by the relationship between the 'notification' procedure under Article 5 of the Regulation and the reasoned opinion under the Article 226 procedure; there is a danger that the Article 5 procedure will constitute an additional and time consuming step before the Commission could bring a successful action against a Member State under Article 226. The main benefit of the Regulation may not be to bring a speedy end to such infractions, one of its stated aims, but instead be the identification of the existence of a breach, potentially facilitating matters[69] in this regard for those seeking to bring state liability actions against the offending Member State.

Quite apart from the issue of the relationship between Article 226 and the procedure contained in the Regulation, there are a number of other issues concerning the Regulation that reflect the unanswered questions arising from the *Angry Farmers* case.[70] The Regulation covers 'obstacles' to the free movement of goods that are 'attributable to the Member State' whether it involves action on the part of the Member State or inaction.[71] The issue of attribution is not further elaborated: the focus is not on this issue – the responsibility of the state being taken for granted – but on the obstacle caused. The definition of 'obstacle' does, however, seek to limit the term's scope by listing three cumulative requirements: the serious disruption of the free movement of goods; serious loss to individuals affected; and the necessity of immediate State action. Presumably the *ad hoc* or one-off actions of individuals, especially those not acting in concert would not fall within the scope of the Regulation. In this, there would seem to be a divergence, following the Opinion of the Advocate-General in

68 Noted in the Recitals to Regulation 2679/98/EC, *supra* n. 3.

69 That is by making it more likely that a 'sufficiently serious breach' has occurred. Other difficulties, such as proving a causal link, may well still lie in the way of a potential applicant in such a situation.

70 Case C-265/95 *Commission* v. *France* (Angry Farmers), *supra* n. 4.

71 Article 1, Regulation 2679/98/EC, *supra* n. 67.

Schmidberger,[72] between the requirements to trigger the application of the Regulation and those triggering Articles 28 and 29. The Advocate-General seemed to suggest that there would be no *de minimis* requirement regarding the application of the Treaty provisions; by contrast under the Regulation there is a qualitative criterion of 'serious disruption'. Problematically, some co-ordinated action – such as industrial action – could still cause such results, raising the possibility of conflict between the free movement of goods and fundamental or constitutionally protected rights and threatening the distribution of competence between the EC and Member States.

Article 2 seeks to deal with this problem by stating that the 'Regulation may not be interpreted as affecting in any way the exercise of fundamental rights as recognised in Member States, including the right or freedom to strike.' As with the concerns over the scope of the *Angry Farmers* case,[73] at a conceptual level it is not clear whether Article 2 means that such actions are not attributable to Member States in the first place or whether they are but are also capable of justification. The latter approach does raise questions about the relationship between, for example, industrial relations policy, and the derogation from the free movement set out in Article 30 (ex-36). On this basis, the former approach seems preferable. Whether in practice there would be any noticeable difference between the two approaches is another question. It is difficult to delineate areas of policy which are the exclusive preserve of Member States as, ultimately, where there is an impact on trade Member State action must be compatible with Treaty requirements, thus bringing in review by reference to internal market objectives rather than necessarily social policy objectives or other similar considerations. Although the Union legal order claims to respect human rights,[74] the extent to which it has done so in practice has been the subject of some debate.[75] The Regulation may have been seen as a way of

72 Case C-112/00 *Schmidberger*, *supra* n. 58.

73 Case C-265/95 *Commission* v. *France* (Angry Farmers), *supra* n. 4.

74 See e.g. Case 29/69 *Stauder* v. *City of Ulm* [1969] ECR 419;Case 11/70 *Internationale Handelsgesellschaft mbH* v. *Einfuhr-und Vorratsstelle für Getriede and Futtermittel* [1970] ECR 1125; Article 6 TEU and most recently note the impact of Charter of Fundamental Rights annexed to the Treaty of Nice, already referred to in some cases, although not by the ECJ itself: Joined Cases C-122/99P and C-125/99P *D & Sweden* v. *Council*, judgment 31 May 2001. See also T-177/01 *Jégo Quéré*, judgment 3 May 2002.

75 Coppel, J., and O'Neill, A., 'The European Court of Justice: Taking Rights Seriously' (1992) 29 *CML Rev* 669; Weiler, J.H.H., and Lockhart, N.J.S. '"Taking Rights Seriously" Seriously?' (1995) 32 *CML Rev* 51, 579; Riley, A., 'Saunders and the Power to Obtain Information in European Community and United Kingdom Competition Law' (2000) 25 *El Rev* 264. The ECJ and the CFI have held that

clarifying the scope of *Commission* v. *France* (Angry Farmers) and identifying the extent to which individual action would trigger Articles 28 and 29, but in practice considerable uncertainties remain – and these difficulties reflect, not only problems arising from the *Angry Farmers* case, but also some of the difficulties relating to the horizontal effect of Articles 28 and 29.

---

restrictions on fundamental rights are acceptable provided that the restrictions do not interfere with the very substance of the rights: see e.g. Case C-62/90 *Commission* v. *Germany* [1992] ECR I-2575 at paragraph 23 and C 404/92P *X* v. *Commission* [1994] ECR I- 4737 at paragraph 18. This is a different and arguably lower standard than, for example, the 'necessary in a democratic society' test used in the European Convention on Human Rights.

Chapter 4

Article 28: Introduction to Quantitative Measures and MEQRs

Article 28 prohibits two types of measure: a quantitative restriction on imports and a measure having equivalent effect. Any measure falling within these articles and not justified by the terms of Article 30 is contrary to EC law and may not, therefore, be relied upon within the national legal system. Article 28 thus delineates the scope of Community law in this field. This chapter will outline the scope and inter-relationship of quantitative measures and measures having equivalent effect. It will then identify the type of measures likely to fall within Article 28. In outlining such measures, difficulties or inconsistencies in the jurisprudence will be identified briefly but not dealt with in detail. Instead, the following chapter will look at the issues raised by the notion of measures having equivalent effect, in particular, the difficulties raised by indistinctly applicable measures in relation to Article 28 and the development of the ECJ's jurisprudence since the infamous *Keck* judgment.[1]

I Relationship with Other Provisions Relating to Goods

As with many other terms in the Treaty, 'quantitative restriction' was not defined, although the article is clearly aimed at non-tariff barriers to trade; customs duties, discriminatory taxation and measures equivalent thereto are dealt with elsewhere in the Treaty. These forms of governmental actions are separate from quantitative measures and measures which fall under the provisions dealing with tariff barriers do not fall within the scope of Article 28. As the ECJ noted in *Iannelli* v. *Meroni*, a case concerning a levy payable on the import of paper goods,

1 Cases C-267 and 268/91 *Keck and Mithouard* [1993] ECR I-6097.

> '[h]owever wide the field of application of Article 30 [now Article 28] may be, it nevertheless does not include obstacles to trade covered by other provisions of the Treaty.'[2]

Therefore, as far as goods are concerned, the prohibition in Articles 28, especially that relating to measures having equivalent effect to quantitative restrictions, has the character of a fall-back provision, catching measures which are not caught by the more specific fiscal and tariff provisions. Although the concept of a fall-back provision might indicate a residual and consequently less important provision, Article 28 has in practice been used in many situations, perhaps including some that were not envisaged by those who framed the Treaty.[3] The proper scope of Article 28 has been the subject of much literature.[4]

II Meaning of Quantitative Restriction and Relationship with Measures having Equivalent Effect

The notions of quantitative restriction, quota and non-tariff barriers are well known in international law. Quantitative restrictions can be seen in two ways. In a broad sense it can viewed as 'any measure (other than a tariff or charge) which has the effect of reducing the flow of trade'. More narrowly, it can be used as a synonym for 'quota'.[5] From the drafting of Article 28, it seems as though the intention was that the provision would cover both possibilities but that the term 'quantitative restriction' would be seen in the narrow sense, with the term 'measures having an equivalent effect' (MEQRs) mopping up other types of non-tariff barriers.[6] This view is supported by the case of *Geddo*,[7] in which the ECJ defined quantitative restrictions as,

2 Case 74/76 *Iannelli* v. *Meroni* [1977] ECR 557, paragraph 9. See also Case 7/68 *Commission* v. *Italy* (Export Tax on Art Treasures) [1968] ECR 428.

3 The development of Article 28 and measures having equivalent effect is considered below at IV. Article 49 is also a 'fall-back' provision; it too has turned out to have a wide field of application.

4 See Chapters 3 and 5 and literature noted therein.

5 McGovern, E., *International Trade Regulation* (3rd ed.) (Globefield Press, 1995) at p. 5.11-1 discussing the matter in relation to Article XI of GATT. See similarly e.g. Mathews, C., 'Non-tariff Import Barriers and the Kennedy Round' (1964-5) 2 *CML Rev* 403.

6 Mathews, *ibid.*, at p. 406 suggests that this approach is the more usual one.

7 Case 2/73 *Riseria Luigi Geddo* v. *Ente nationale Risi* [1973] ECR 865.

'measures which amount to a total or partial restraint of, according to the circumstances, imports, exports or goods in transit.'[8]

Quantitative restrictions therefore include all measures that restrict imports (or exports) by reference to quantity, in effect a quota. Although it took the narrower view of 'quantitative restriction', the ruling in *Geddo* is still broad. It also looks to the effect (i.e. the restraint on trade) of the measure rather than its form or purpose. Thus quantitative measures include, for example, limitations by reference to a specific numeric amount; restrictions by reference to percentages of national production; and also total prohibitions.[9] The absolute nature of the prohibition in Article 28 has resulted in there being no possibility of a *de minimis* exception.[10] *Geddo* also makes it clear that the type of transaction involved is not a relevant consideration for the determination of whether or not there is a quantitative restriction. Normally, however, these types of restriction operate at the border[11] and tend by their nature to discriminate between imported and domestic products. More recently, the ECJ confirmed that a ban on imports may fall within Article 28 even if the prohibition extends to only part of a Member State's territory.[12] Finally, *Geddo* clarified that Article 28 extends to goods in transit, a point not explicit in the wording of the Treaty.[13]

The number of cases dealing specifically with the issue of quantitative restrictions is small,[14] especially compared with the number of cases dealt with as MEQR. This fact may be a result of the limited incidence of quotas

---

8 *Ibid.*, at p. 879.

9 See e.g. Case 7/61 *Commission* v. Italy (Ban on Pork Imports) [1961] ECR 317 and Case 34/79 *R.* v. *Henn and Darby* [1979] ECR 3795. The issue of bans raise difficult questions regarding justification; see Chapter 7 and contrast the approach with regard services discussed in Chapters 11 and 12.

10 Case 103/84 *Commission* v. *Italy* (Vehicles) [1986] ECR 1759.

11 The rules in the GATT distinguish also between 'border' restrictions and 'internal restrictions'. Within the latter category, dealt with by Article III, are matters such as discriminatory internal taxation as well as regulatory matters. See McGovern *International Trade Regulation, supra* n. 5. As noted in the text, discriminatory internal taxation is dealt with separately under the EC Treaty: Article 90 (ex-95) EC. See also confirmation that tariff and fiscal matters as regards goods do not fall within Articles 28 and 29: Case 74/76 *Iannelli* v. *Meroni supra* n. 2.

12 Case C-67/97 *Ditlev Bluhme* [1998] ECR I-8033.

13 Article 30 refers to goods in transit, a point which supports the ECJ's ruling in Case 2/73 *Riseria Luigi Geddo, supra* n. 7.

14 Many of the cases on import bans related to the transitional periods phasing out import bans contained in former Article 33 and the Acts of Accession: see e.g. Case 48/74 *Charmasson* v. *Minister for Economic Affairs and Finance* [1974] ECR 1383 and Case 231/78 *Commission* v. *United Kingdom* [1979] ECR 1447 respectively.

within the Member States of the EC even by the time of the Treaty of Rome, as a result of international law obligations such as the GATT (now encompassed within the World Trade Organisation) and OEEC (now the OECD) already prohibiting such measures. Partly, however, the relative lack of cases on quotas may be because MEQR is a wider category than that of quantitative restrictions. As noted, quantitative restrictions arise in limited circumstances. By contrast, MEQRs may arise in multitudinous guises, as shown below and in the next chapter.

Another factor which has operated to limit the number of cases considered as quantitative restrictions is the fact that the boundary between quantitative restrictions and MEQR is not completely clear, and it may be that some quantitative restrictions have been dealt with as MEQRs. In the early case of *Henn and Darby*,[15] the ECJ ruled that a total ban on importing a given product was still a restraint according to quantity, despite arguments from the UK government to the contrary. Similarly, albeit in the context of Article 29, the refusal by the authorities in *Hedley Lomas*,[16] to grant an export licence was considered to be a quota restriction.[17] The position is not always so clear-cut. In the *German Crayfish* case,[18] the Advocate-General discussed an absolute ban on the import of crayfish by reference to the *Dassonville*[19] test for MEQRs, whereas the ECJ viewed it as a quantitative restriction. The difficulty is that quantitative restrictions also satisfy the test for MEQRs as set down by the ECJ, effectively forming a sub-set of those measures. Thus, in other cases the ECJ has dealt with similar provisions as MEQRs.[20] Indeed, in *Commission* v. *Greece* (Banana Licensing),[21] the ECJ found it unnecessary to find whether the system in question constituted a quantitative measure or

---

15 Case 34/79 *R.* v. *Henn and Darby,* supra n. 9.

16 Case C-5/94 *R.* v. *Ministry of Agriculture, Fisheries and Food, ex parte Hedley Lomas (Ireland) Limited* [1996] ECR I-2552. See Oliver, P. 'Measures of Equivalent Effect: A Reappraisal' (1982) 19 *CMLRev* 217, who suggested that import licences could be viewed as quantitative restrictions. In his book, Oliver, P., *Free Movement of Goods* (3rd ed.), he suggests that a distinction, albeit narrow, can be drawn between the two categories.

17 See also Case 118/78 *C. J. Meijer BV* v. *Department of Trade* [1979] ECR 1387, Case 231/78 *Commission* v. *UK* [1979] ECR 1447, Case 34/79 *R.* v. *Henn and Darby, supra* n. 9.

18 Case C-131/93 *Commission* v. *Germany* (Crayfish) [1994] ECR I-3303.

19 Case 8/74 *Procureur du Roi* v. *Dassonville et al.* [1974] ECR 837.

20 See Case 41/76 *Donckerwolcke* v. *Procureur de la Republique* [1976] ECR 1921, Case 40/82 *Commission* v. *UK* (Newcastle Disease) [1982] ECR 2793, Case 261/85 *Commission* v. *UK* [1988] ECR 547, Case C-131/93 *Commission* v. *Germany, supra* n. 18.

21 Cases 194 and 241/85 *Commission* v. *Greece* (Banana Licensing) [1988] ECR 1037.

an MEQR, as it clearly fell within the terms of the prohibition in the Treaty. It may well be that at the European level the distinction between the two has little consequence because, at least as far as Article 28 is concerned, the significant distinction lies between distinctly and indistinctly applicable measures. With the possible exception of bans on products, a quantitative restriction is unlikely to be considered indistinctly applicable. For those measures which may be a quantitative restriction or an MEQR, the same approach applies; the measure will be prohibited unless it falls within the derogation from the free movement provisions found in Article 30 EC. It has, however, been suggested that the distinction between a quantitative restriction and MEQRs may have consequences for the way national courts deal with measures.[22]

III Meaning of MEQR

It should come as no surprise to discover that, despite the significance of this phrase in the development of the internal market, the Treaty provided no definition of the term 'measures having equivalent effect'. Much early literature was devoted to determining the scope of the then Article 30 (now 28), and this phrase in particular. During the 1960s some commentators argued that the phrase should be interpreted restrictively, to mean literally that only those measures which were equivalent in effect to quotas, i.e. that took effect at the border and were discriminatory, should be included. Others took a much wider view, suggesting that it was a measure's impact on trade rather than its form that was important. These different views reflect different conceptions of the treaty freedoms and, consequently, of the freedom left to Member States to regulate trade: the broader the interpretation given to the Treaty freedom, the greater the impact on Member States' internal regulatory competence. The discussion about Article 28 may then resolve itself into two linked questions: is Article 28 limited to prohibiting discrimination and what do we mean by discrimination anyway?[23] This focus on discrimination is in one sense odd, since Article 28 is not phrased in terms of a prohibition on discrimination.

The Commission put forward some guidance on the scope of Article 28 in the form of a Directive,[24] valid during the transitional period. It

22 Jarvis, *The Application of EC Law by National Courts: The Free Movement of Goods* (Oxford, 1998) at pp. 17-20.

23 Note the comments of Ulmer, cited by Oliver in 'Recent Case Law on Articles 30–36 EEC' (1980) 17 *CMLRev* 109 at 110, who criticises the test of discrimination on the basis that it was hard to determine what was meant by discrimination and then to apply it.

24 Directive 70/50 OJ Special English Edition 1970(I), p. 17.

suggested that Article 28 included certain measures that, whilst not overtly discriminatory, distinguish between imports and domestic products, making the importation of the former more difficult or costly than the disposal of domestic production. These measures could be categorised as being indirectly discriminatory. The Commission also made it clear that, in its view, such measures would be caught at whatever stage they applied, i.e. MEQRs were not limited to measures which applied on first import into the relevant Member State. Article 2(3) then set out a non-exhaustive list of types of MEQR which included: minimum or maximum prices applicable to imported products; the requirement of having an agent in the country of import; special conditions of payment applicable to imports; prohibition of publicity for domestic products; rules regarding stocking of products. Additionally, the Directive covered;

> 'measures governing the marketing of products which deal, in particular, with shape, size, weight composition, presentation, identification or putting up and which are equally applicable to domestic and imported products, where the restrictive effect of such measures on the free movement of goods exceeds the effects intrinsic to trade rules.'[25]

All of this clearly suggested a reasonably broad approach to the definition of MEQRs, although, given the Directive's legal status, the Commission's approach was not determinative. It was not until 1974 that the ECJ handed down what is still the primary test for MEQRs.

IV The *Dassonville* Test

To a certain extent following the Commission's views in Directive 70/50,[26] the ECJ in *Dassonville*[27] held that:

> '[a]ll trading rules enacted by Member States which are capable of hindering, directly or indirectly, actually or potentially, intra-Community trade are to be considered as measures having an effect equivalent to quantitative restrictions.'[28]

---

25 *Ibid.*, Article 3.

26 *Ibid.*

27 Case 8/74 *Dassonville, supra* n. 19.

28 *Ibid.*, p. 852.

This is a broad, effects-based test,[29] potentially including many national rules within its terms. This approach may be understandable given the centrality of the common market and the need for integration to the European project, especially when considered against the stagnation in the political sphere at the time of the *Dassonville* judgment. The process of harmonization through the enactment of European standards had progressed slowly, if at all.[30] The potential width of this ruling in conjunction with the direct effect of the provision (and the following case law) can be seen as a factor in encouraging Member States to take legislative action at Community level in fields relating to the free movement of goods,[31] as the result of a finding of a violation of Article 28 is that the offending measures will be struck down resulting in a regulatory gap that potentially leaves other societal considerations unprotected. The fact that the creation of the internal market takes priority over other considerations has given rise to some disquiet, as well as giving rise to concerns regarding the ability of Member States to legislate upon matters considered to be within their formal competence.[32] Nonetheless, there is clearly a link between the operation of Article 28 and the positive harmonization provisions: Articles 94 and 95.[33]

Before considering the substance of rules caught by the *Dassonville*[34] formula, a couple of points should be noted. The first concerns whether *Dassonville* has limited the notion of 'measure' by its reference to 'trading rules'. Despite the implication that the test requires the existence of rules regulating trade, the definition given to such rules has been very broad indeed, to the point of negating the requirement for trading rules in the first

29 The ECJ has on a number of occasions referred to the purpose of a measure. This point is discussed further in Chapter 5.

30 Weiler, J.H.H. 'The Transformation of Europe' (1991) 100 *Yale Law Journal* 2403, updated in *The Constitution of Europe* (Cambridge University Press, 1999). On harmonization see further Chapter 13.

31 In this we can see parallels to the approach the ECJ took with regard to the transitional period in respect of quotas: where there was legislative inactivity leading to lacunae and inequalities, this did not justify Member State action in violation of basic Treaty principles. Instead, it was, 'for the competent institutions and for them alone to adopt within the appropriate periods the requisite measures with a view to finding, in a community context, a comprehensive solution of the problem': Cases 232/78 *Commission* v. *France* (Mutton and Lamb) [1979] ECR 2729. See also Gormley, L. W. *Prohibiting Restrictions on Trade within the EEC* (Elsevier Science Publishers B.V., 1985), p. 26.

32 See discussion in Chapters 1 and 6 and associated literature.

33 Wils W.P.J., 'The Search for a Rule in Article 30 EEC: Much Ado About Nothing?' (1993) 18 *ELRev* 475.

34 Case 8/74 *Dassonville, supra* n. 19.

place. Although the Court frequently refers back to the *Dassonville* judgment in its decisions, it does not always follow precisely the same wording. In many cases the ECJ has not referred trading rules, either substituting a different phrase or leaving this requirement out completely.[35] The *Franking Machines* case[36] and the *Angry Farmers* case[37] show an extended notion even of the word 'measure' within the Treaty provision itself. These cases indicate that the *Dassonville* test would not be limited to rules which dealt with the act of trading alone. Instead, the concept had a broader ambit, including measures relating to the production of goods, or those which affect access to the market.

Furthermore, the notion of rules has been given an expanded meaning; it clearly is not limited to general legislative acts, despite the reference to the word 'enacted'. From the case law, administrative acts,[38] court decisions and non-binding or indirect expressions of government policy will all be included within the scope of the test. Thus, in the *Buy Irish* case,[39] the provision of funds for advertising national products was held to be contrary to Article 28.[40] Equally, in the *Dundalk Water Supply* case,[41] the inclusion of a term in the terms of a tender offer document, requiring the pipes to be used in the project under tender to comply with Irish standards, was also held to constitute an MEQR. Even when an offending law has been repealed, the administrative practices grown up around the old law can still constitute a barrier to trade. As the ECJ noted in the *Franking Machines* case:[42]

---

35 For example Case C-267 and 268/91 *Keck and Mithouard, supra* n. 1 refers to 'measures' whereas in Case C-265/95 *Commission* v. *France* (Angry Farmers) [1997] ECR I- 6959, the ECJ refers to barriers.

36 Case 21/84 *Commission* v. *France* (Franking Machines) [1985] ECR 1356.

37 Case C-265/95 *Commission* v. *France* (Angry Farmers), *supra* n. 35.

38 See e.g. Case 104/75 *De Peijper* [1976] ECR 613. Note that in this case the ECJ made no attempt to distinguish between the administrative acts and legislative measures; both were instances of intervention by authorities with binding effect.

39 Case 249/81 *Commission* v. *Ireland* (Buy Irish) [1982] ECR 4005.

40 There is a fine line here between the free movement of goods rules and those relating to state aid: Case 290/83 *Commission* v. *France* (Crédit Agricole) [1985] ECR 439: see Commission Guidelines on state aid for advertising agricultural produce.

41 Case 45/87 *Commission* v. *Ireland* (Dundalk Water) [1988] ECR 4929. See more recently Case C-325/00 *Commission* v. *Germany* (Quality Label), judgment 5 November 2002.

42 Case 21/84 *Commission* v. *France* (Franking Machines), *supra* n. 36, especially paragraphs 11–12.

> 'Under the cloak of a general provision permitting the approval of machines imported from other Member States, the administration might very well adopt a systematically unfavourable attitude towards imported machines, either by allowing considerable delay in replying to applications for approval on the grounds of various alleged technical faults for which no detailed explanations are given or which prove to be inaccurate.
>
> The prohibition on measures having an equivalent effect to quantitative restrictions would lose much of its useful effect if it did not cover protectionist or discriminatory practices of that type.'

It should be noted, however, that in the case of administrative practices 'a certain degree of consistency and generality'[43] is required. Although difficulties might arise in drawing a dividing line between an isolated act and a general practice,[44] the reasoning of the ECJ in this case is once again consistent with an approach that focusses on effect and not on form. Similar comments may be made about the *Angry Farmers* case:[45] there, the actions of the farmers and the failure of the authorities to take effective counter measures had carried for a significant period. Here was no isolated act – though the question of where the line should be drawn again arises. (This issue is discussed further in Chapter 3.)

A further point to note about the *Dassonville*[46] test is that, by contrast to the position regarding Article 81, there is no *de minimis* rule.[47] Advocate-General Caporti noted in *van Tiggele,*[48]

> 'That there is a distinction between Articles 30 and 34 [now 28 and 29] on the one hand and Articles 85 and 86 [now 81 and 82] on the other not only with regard to those subject to the prohibitions but also with regard to the nature of behaviour which is prohibited; we need only reflect that measures restricting trade between Member States are by their very nature incompatible with the Treaty because of the impediment which they cause to intra-Community trade …'

---

43 Case 21/84 *ibid.*, at p. 1364.

44 See the criticism of this approach by Arnull, A., *The European Union and Its Court of Justice* (Oxford University Press, 1999), p. 325.

45 Case C-265/95 *Commission* v. *France* (Angry Farmers), *supra* n. 35 discussed further in Chapters 3 and 7.

46 Case 8/74 *Dassonville, supra* n. 19.

47 See comments of Advocate-General Jacobs in Case C-379/98 *PreussenElektra AG* v. *Schleswag AG* [2001] ECR I-2099. The ECJ did not respond to his comments.

48 Case 82/77 *Openbaar Ministerie of the Kingdom of the Netherlands* v. *van Tiggele* [1978] ECR 25, at p. 47.

State measures, even those included through a broad definition have to have, by their nature, an undesirable impact on trade. This approach means that even those measures which are shown to have a negligible effect, or even no adverse effect, continue to be caught by Article 28. Thus, in the *Buy Irish* case,[49] the Irish government's campaign to encourage the Irish to buy Irish goods was shown to be unsuccessful; nonetheless Article 28 applied. Equally, in the *Sunday Trading* cases,[50] a change in trading patterns could be identified, but there was no proof of hindrance to inter-state trade. Again, the prohibition was held to apply (although this case law would now seem to be overturned by *Keck).*[51] The breadth of Article 28 was in fact articulated by the ECJ in the *Dassonville* formula, by its references to those measures which are capable either of hindering trade 'directly or indirectly' or of 'having an actual or potential effect on trade'.

Although there seems to be no quantitative prerequisite for the application of Article 28, the impact of some measures will be viewed as too remote to trigger Article 28. Thus rules relating to the seizure of goods to pay tax debts[52] and the duty to provide pre-contractual information in dealings between private parties[53] did not fall within Article 28. More recently, a rule requiring CPO patents to be translated into German before they would be recognised in Germany was similarly held to be too distant from Article 28.[54] This approach has been characterised as part of the rule that purely internal situations are outside the scope of Community law. It seems that the ECJ has divided trading rules into two categories: those that have an impact on trade; and those which do not and which therefore constitute an internal situation. For example, in *Blesgen*[55] the ECJ held that a Belgian provision prohibiting the sale of strong spirits for consumption on the premises in all places open to the public 'has in fact no connection with the importation of the products and for that reason is not of such a nature as to impede trade between Member States'.[56] Given the

---

49 Case 249/81 *Commission* v. *Ireland, supra* n. 39, at p. 4022.

50 Case 145/88 *Torfaen* v. *B & Q plc* [1989] ECR 3851, Case C-169/91 *Stoke on Trent* v. *B & Q plc* [1992] ECR I- 6635.

51 Cases C-267 and 268/91 *Keck and Mithouard, supra* n. 1.

52 Case C-69/88 *Krantz* [1990] ECR I-583.

53 Case C-93/92 *CMC Motorradcenter GmbH* v. *Baskiciogullari* [1993] ECR I- 5009.

54 Case C-44/98 *BASF* v. *Präsident des Deutschen Patentamts* [1999] ECR I-6269.

55 Case 75/81 *Blesgen* v. *Belgium* [1982] ECR 1211.

56 *Ibid.*, at paragraph 9. See also Case C-23/89 *Quietlynn* [1990] ECR I-3059, paragraph 11 and also Case C-350/89 *Sheptonhurst* [1991] ECR I-2387 but contrast Case 286/81 *Oosthoek Uitgeversmaatschappij* [1982] ECR 4575 at paragraph 15. These cases are discussed in more detail in Chapter 5.

broad scope of the *Dassonville*[57] test, it seems that there will be few internal situations.

It is clear that the discriminatory obstructions to trade identified by the Commission in Article 2 of Directive 70/50 fall within the scope of *Dassonville*. Import licences are caught, whether they are seen as quotas or MEQRs,[58] as are quality and health checks on imported goods.[59] In general the ECJ has taken a rigorous approach to the application of free movement rules to national measures which apply by virtue of the fact that goods cross a border. Thus even licences, the issuing of which is a pure formality, are caught by the prohibition in Article 28, since the operation of such an administrative system would impair the fundamental Community principle of unobstructed free movement and might even create uncertainty in the minds of traders, with a consequent adverse impact on intra-Community trade.[60] In taking this stance the ECJ seems to have gone beyond the approach of the Commission in Directive 50/70; the prudence of the Commission may reflect the fact the Directive related to the transitional period. By contrast, the case law dates from the time when Community law was in full vigour.[61]

Procedures that delay, make more complicated or more costly the sale of imported products are also caught. In *Commission* v. *Italy*,[62] for example, registration procedures and other requirements delayed the registration of imported cars. Similarly, in *Schloh*[63] the applicant had bought a car in Germany, which a Belgian dealer certified as being in conformance with vehicle types in Belgium. Nonetheless, Schloh was required to submit the vehicle to further roadworthiness tests, for which a fee was charged. Although ensuring that vehicles are roadworthy is a public interest aim, the ECJ held that the second set of tests was not justified as the vehicle had not been used in Germany and it carried a certificate of conformity.[64] Other restrictions, such as the requirement of

---

57 Case 8/74 *Dassonville, supra* n. 19.

58 Cases 51-54/71 *International Fruit Company* v. *Produktschap voor Groenten en Fruit* (No. 2) [1971] ECR 1107.

59 Case 4/75 *Rewe-Zentralfinanz* v. *Landwirtschaftskammer* [1975] ECR 515; Case 251/78 *Denkavit Futtermittel GmbH* v. *Minister für Ernährung* [1979] ECR 3369.

60 Case 124/81 *Commission* v. *United Kingdom* (UHT Milk) [1983] ECR 203.

61 See arguments of Advocate-General Caporti in Case 120/78 *Rewe-Zentral AG* v. *Bundesmonopolverwaltung fürBranntwein* (Cassis de Dijon) [1979] ECR 649 at 670.

62 Case 154/85 *Commission* v. *Italy* (Car Registration Procedures) [1987] ECR 2717.

63 Case 50/85 *Schloh* v. *Auto Controle Technique* [1986] ECR 1855.

64 For a more recent version of car registration problems see Case C-314/98 *Snellers Auto's BV* v. *Algemeen Directeur van de Dienst Wegverkeer* [2000] ECR I-8633, although this case concerned indistinctly applicable rules.

deposits, special credit conditions or the requirement of payment in cash[65] or restrictions on stock will all contravene Article 28.[66] Price fixing, as suggested by the Commission, also falls within the prohibition. For example, discriminatory rules setting the price of pharmaceuticals were found to be contrary to the EC Treaty in *Roussel*,[67] although it should be noted that in this case the effect of the rules on intra-Community trade was again taken into account as well as their discriminatory nature. Even rules which relate less directly to the distribution of goods may be caught by Article 28. *Allen and Hanburys* v. *Generics*[68] concerned a legal remedy that was available against an imported product that infringed a patent, but which was not available where the infringing product was domestic in origin. In striking down this rule, the ECJ referred also to the general principle of non-discrimination on grounds of nationality contained in Article 12 EC. Although not phrased as such (by contrast to the other free movement provisions in Articles 39, 43 and 49[69] and even, as regards goods, the provisions on non-discriminatory taxation in Article 90), Article 28 in this context can be seen as a variety of non-discrimination principle.

Member States are precluded from favouring national products, whether by engaging in an advertising campaign favouring the national product;[70] imposing origin marking requirements on imports[71] or via the public procurement rules[72]. In the *Irish Souvenirs* case,[73] the Irish government argued that requiring certain souvenirs of Ireland to be made in Ireland was acceptable, as the goods in question related to cultural

65 Case 95/81 *Commission* v. *Italy* [1982] ECR 2187, Cases 206/80 *Orlandi Italo e Figlio* v. *The Ministry for Foreign Trade* [1982] ECR 2147, Case 53/83 *Commission* v. *Greece* (Payments in Cash) [1984] ECR 2027.

66 Case 13/78 *Joh. Eggers Sohn & Co* v. *Freie Hansestadt Bremen* [1978] ECR 1935, [1979] 1 CMLR 562, Case C-323/93 *Société Civile Agricole de Centre d'Insemination de la Crespelle* v. *Co-operative d'Elevage et d'Insemination Artificielle du Departement de la Mayenne* [1994] ECR I-5077, Case C-189/95 *Franzén* [1997] ECR I-5909.

67 Case 181/82 *Roussel Labaratoria BV* v. *Netherlands* [1983] ECR 3849.

68 Case 434/85 *Allen and Hanburys* v. *Generics* [1988] ECR 1245.

69 On the role of Article 12 EC as regards the freedom to provide services and also free movement of people see e.g. Cases C-92 and 326/92 *Phil Collins* v. *Imtrat Handelsgesellschaft mbH* [1993] ECR I-5145 and Case C-122/96 *Stephen Austin Saldhana & MTS Securities Corporation* v. *Hiross Holding AG* [1997] ECR I-5325.

70 Case 249/81 *Commission* v. *Ireland* ('Buy Irish'), *supra* n. 39. Note that the Commission has issued guidelines on state funded advertising of farm products, but this relates to state aid rules rather than Articles 28–30.

71 Case 113/80 *Commission* v. *Ireland* (Irish Souvenirs) [1981] ECR 1625.

72 Case 45/87 *Dundalk Water*, *supra* n. 41.

73 Case 113/80 *Commission* v. *Ireland* (Irish Souvenirs), *supra* n. 71.

individuality.[74] The ECJ disagreed; souvenirs are essentially reminders of the place visited and it was therefore unnecessary for them to have been manufactured in that place. This somewhat harsh assessment is certainly open to criticism given the nature of the goods in question. The judgment is typical, however, of the ECJ's tough stance against discriminatory measures. Any attempt to structure public buying so as to favour domestic goods is clearly incompatible with Article 28. Thus, requirements to buy certain proportion of public supplies from a given region, even if that area is economically depressed, are contrary to the Treaty.[75] Similarly, any public tendering process should not disadvantage imported goods, for example, by a requirement to use national products or national standards.[76] Preferential tax treatment[77] and other measures to encourage the use of local products are unacceptable.[78] Storage and minimum stock requirements have been found equally objectionable.[79] Some local grab measures, particularly those motivated by environmental concerns, have, however, given rise to certain inconsistent rulings.[80]

A linked problem to that of origin marking, is that of special product designations, reserved to particular products from particular areas.[81] The problem arose in *Commission* v. *Germany*,[82] which concerned national rules reserving given terms, Sekt, Prädikatssekt and Weinbrand, to German produced drinks, or to drinks of foreign origin provided that German was an official language throughout the whole of the country of production. Imported products, which might have had the same characteristics, were required to adopt other designations, less familiar to the consumer. In principle, such appellations are acceptable, but only if the product were in

74 This idea was introduced in Case 12/74 *Commission* v. *Germany* [1975] ECR 181.

75 See for example Case C-21/88 *Du Pont de Nemours Italiana Spa* v. *Unita Sanitaria Locale No. 2 Di Carrara* [1990] ECR I-889, Case 72/83 *Campus Oil* v. *Minister for Industry and Energy* [1984] ECR 2727.

76 Case 45/87 *Dundalk Water*, *supra* n. 41.

77 Case 18/84 *Commission* v. *France* (Tax Breaks for Newspapers) [1985] ECR 1339 – this case involved preferential tax treatment to encourage industry to establish itself in France.

78 Case C-30/90 *Commission* v. *UK* (Compulsory Plant Breeders Licence) [1992] ECR I-829.

79 Case 13/78 *Joh. Eggers Sohn & Co* v. *Freie Hansestadt Bremen*; Case C-189/95 *Franzén*, both *supra*, n. 66.

80 See Chapters 5 and 6.

81 Issues relating to proof of origin such as the requirement to provide a certificate of authenticity have, on the whole been treated similarly to other certificates, such as those for health inspection requirements: see Case 251/78 *Denkavit Futtermittel GmbH* v. *Minister für Ernährung*, *supra* n. 59.

82 Case 12/74 *Commission* v. *Germany*, *supra* n. 74.

fact to possess qualities arising from the fact that it originated in a specific geographic area such as to distinguish it from other products.[83] This was a very narrow formulation and one that, outside natural products (i.e processed products), was criticised as unworkable.[84] More recent cases in this area indicate a more sensitive approach on the part of the ECJ. In *Exportur SA* v. *LOR SA and Confiserie du Tech*,[85] which concerned French rules reserving the designations in question to a type of nougat produced by Spanish producers, the Court accepted that the designation of origin provides important information about the quality of the product to the consumer that is not necessarily linked to geographic conditions. To a certain extent this case law has been replaced by Community secondary legislation,[86] although there will always be questions about the scope of the protection afforded by the legislation.[87]

One question, which was not expressly resolved by *Dassonville*, was whether MEQRs would include rules which on the face of it applied to domestic products just as much as imports. This possibility remained open. One might distinguish here between rules which were expressly to apply equally but were in practice applied unequally and those which by their nature affect imports. An example of the former approach can be seen in the *Franking Machines* case, in which administrative practice operated neutrally phrased rules to the detriment of imports.[88] There the ECJ held that Article 28 applied. What about rules which by their nature adversely affect imports? In a number of cases on price fixing, where the rules were expressed to apply without distinction, the ECJ found that, because price levels (or profit margins) were fixed at such a level,

> 'imported products are placed at a disadvantage in relation to identical domestic products either because they cannot profitably be marketed in the

---

83 Case 12/74 *Commission* v. *Germany, ibid.*, at paragraph 7.

84 Mathies, Beier. The reasoning in the case was more generally criticised: Meij and Winter, 'Measures having an Equivalent Effect' (1976) 13 *CMLRev* 79.

85 Case 3/91 *Exportur SA* v. *LOR SA et al.* [1992] ECR I- 5529.

86 Regulation 2081/92 OJ [1992] L 208/1 and Regulation 1107/96 OJ [1996] L 148/1.

87 See e.g. Joined Cases C-321-324/94 *Jacques Pistre* [1997] ECR I-2343 concerning the use of the word 'montagne' (mountain), which fell neither within the protection offered by Regulation 2081/92, *ibid.*, nor that set down in Case 3/91 *Exportur, supra* n. 85 and Case C-87/97 *Conzorzio per la Tutela del Formaggio Gorgonzola* v. *Käserei Champignon Hormeister GmbH & Co KG, Eduard Bracharz GmbH* [1999] ECR I-1301, which concerned the rights of a German soft cheese manufacturer to produce Cambozola, a Gorgonzola-like cheese.

88 Case 21/84 *Commission* v. *France* (Franking Machines), *supra* n. 36 especially paragraphs 11–12.

conditions laid down or because the competitive advantage conferred by the lower cost prices is cancelled out.'[89]

Although the ECJ in *van Tiggele* seemed to emphasise the discriminatory nature of the measure,[90] it can be seen as being non-discriminatory – at least in its form, as it applies to all products. It is in its effect that it discriminates against imports, a point the ECJ also emphasised. What is in issue here is arguably another form of discrimination; that of treating dissimilar products alike.[91] In these cases, the Member States failed to take into account the special characteristics as imports.[92] Thus, the ECJ argued that, although such rules relating to selling prices do not in themselves constitute an MEQR, such rules could have the same effect on trade, contrary to Article 28.[93] These price fixing cases illustrate the fine line between discriminatory and non-discriminatory measures. They have also been criticised: the reasoning in some of the case law is contradictory,[94] and there appeared to be a lack of clarity as to whether the ECJ was concerned with discrimination in law, in fact or with access to the market.[95] Further, these rulings may have the consequence that price restrictions continue to apply to domestic products but not to imports, thus placing the domestic products at a disadvantage. In this context the ECJ has pointed out that the aim of Article 28 is not to ensure equal trading conditions but to ensure that obstacles to intra-Community trade are removed.[96] Reverse discrimination, as with the other Treaty freedoms, is permitted.

Although *Dassonville*,[97] by emphasising effect rather than form and by its specific reference to 'directly or indirectly', implied that Article 28 could catch indistinctly applicable measures, the issue of whether Article

---

89 Case 82/77 *Openbaar Ministerie* v. *van Tiggele*, *supra* n. 48.

90 Indeed the ECJ approved Article 2 of Directive 70/50, that is the provision that refers to measures other than equally applicable measures.

91 See e.g. Weatherill and Beaumont *EU Law* (3rd edition) Penguin.

92 See also Case C-152/78 *Commission* v. *France* (Advertising of Alcoholic Beverages) [1980] ECR 2299.

93 Case 13/77 *N.V. GB-INNO-BM* v. *Vereiniging van de Kleinhandelaars in Tabak* [1977] ECR 2115.

94 Case 65/75 *Tasca* [1976] ECR 291 and Case 127/73 *Belgische Radio en Televisie et al.* v. *SV SABAM et al.* [1974] ECR 313.

95 Gormley, *supra* n. 31. This issue will be discussed in more detail in Chapter 5, as it remains at the heart of disputes regarding the proper approach to Article 28.

96 Cases 80 and 159/85 *Nederlandse Bakkerij Stichting* v. *Edah BV* [1986] ECR 3359, [1988] 2 CMLR 113 regarding bread prices and Case 355/85 *Ministère Public* v. *Cognet* [1986] ECR 3231 regarding fixed prices for books.

97 Case 8/74 *Dassonville*, *supra* n. 19.

28 catches measures that are expressed neutrally was clarified in the famous *Cassis de Dijon* case.[98] The case involved national rules relating to the content of liqueurs, which applied to all liqueurs to be sold in Germany. French Cassis, however, made in accordance with traditional French standards, did not conform to the German requirements and the German authorities therefore prohibited its import into Germany. Clearly the rule was indistinctly applicable; it was expressed to apply to all liqueurs, not just imports. Nonetheless, it created a particular problem for the non-domestic product; the effect of the rule was to prohibit the sale of the imported product. The ECJ confirmed that, although in the absence of harmonization 'it is for the Member States to regulate all matters relating to the production and marketing of alcohol and alcoholic beverages on their own territory',[99] Article 28 could catch such provisions and that the interests served by the national rules in question were not 'such as to take precedence over the requirements of the free movement of goods'[100]. The *Cassis* judgment[101] is significant because it makes clear that differences between legal systems can create barriers to trade that are not the fault of one particular Member State, but arise from the different approach to regulation taken in the various Member States.

There have been many cases in which traders sought to challenge such rules. For example, recipe rules, such as those in the *Cassis de Dijon* case,[102] have been the subject of much litigation. In *Gilli and Andres*,[103] an Italian rule specified that apple vinegar must be made from the fermentation of wine and was found to be contrary to Article 28. Similarly, in *Deserbais*,[104] an importer of German cheese fell foul of a French rule requiring Edam cheese to have a specified minimum fat content. Again the rule constituted an impediment to the marketing of cheese in France, which had been lawfully marketed in Germany. *Drei Glocken* concerned the content of pasta.[105] Packaging and labelling requirements have been an

98 Case 120/78 *Cassis de Dijon, supra* n. 61, especially paragraph 14.

99 *Ibid.,* at paragraph 8.

100 *Ibid.*, at paragraph 14. The fact that the ECJ refers to the public interest is discussed further below.

101 Case 120/78 Cassis *de Dijon, supra* n. 61.

102 Case 120/78 *Cassis de Dijon supra* n. 61. As to alcohol, see also Case 182/84 *Miro BV* [1985] ECR 3731, concerning Jenever, Case 94/82 *De Kikvorsch* v. *Groothandel Import- Export BV* [1983] ECR 947, Case 176/84 *Commission* v. *Germany* [1987] ECR 1193, and Case 178/84 *Commission* v. *Germany* [1987] ECR 1227, concerning beer.

103 Case 788/79 *Italy* v. *Gilli and Andres* [1980] ECR 2071.

104 Case 286/86 *Ministère Public* v. *Deserbais* [1988] ECR 4907.

105 Case 407/85 *Drei Glocken GmbH* v. *USL Centro-Sud & Provincia Autonoma di Bolzano* [1988] ECR 4233, see also Case 90/86 *Zoni* [1988] ECR 4285.

equally fertile source of case law. *Rau* concerned a requirement that margarine be sold in cube-shaped packages,[106] whilst a number of cases concerned language requirements.[107] All these rules were found to fall within the ambit of Article 28, as did rules regarding the information that may or must be included on packaging.[108] Again, origin marking, even if non-discriminatory, may fall with the definition of MEQR, because its effect is to allow consumers to discriminate between products on grounds of nationality.[109] Not only does the origin marking requirement add costs to the imported products, but it also makes them more difficult to sell, thus 'slowing down economic interpenetration in the Community'.[110] Restrictions on advertising, which indirectly disadvantage imports by prohibiting advertising of product types that typically tended to have been imported, have also been found to be contrary to EC law.[111] Similarly, rules relating to place and time of sale were considered in principle to be MEQRs.[112] The extent to which, post-*Keck*,[113] such rules will still fall within the prohibition in Article 28 is not clear.[114]

---

106 Case 261/81 *Walter Rau Lebensmittlwerke* v. *de Smedt Pvba* [1982] ECR 3961.

107 Case 27/80 *Fietje* [1980] ECR 3839; Case 369/89 *Piageme et al.* v. *BVBA Peeters* [1991] ECR I-2971; Case C-85/94 *Groupement des Producteurs Importateurs et Agents Généreaux d'Eaux Minérales Etrangères, VZW (Piageme) et al.* v. *Peeters NV* [1995] ECR I-2955.

108 Case C-293/93 *Houtwipper* [1994] ECR I- 4249; Case C-470/93 *Verein gegen Unwesen in Handel und Gewerbe Koln eV* v. *Mars GmbH* [1995] ECR I-1923; Case C-315/92 *Verband Sozialer Wettbewerb eV* v. *Clinique Laboratories SNC et al* [1994] ECR I- 317. Language requirements are considered in more detail in Chapters 7 and 12.

109 Case C-47/90 *Ets Delhaize Frères et Compagnie Le Lion SA* v. *Promalvin SA et al.* [1992] ECR I-3669; and Case 207/83 *Commission* v. *United Kingdom* (Origin Marking) [1985] ECR 1201.

110 Case 207/83 *Commission* v. *United Kingdom* (Origin Marking), *ibid.*, at paragraph 17.

111 Case 152/78 *Commission* v. *France* (Advertising of Alcoholic Beverages) [1980] ECR 2299. In doing so it took an approach similar to that adopted in respect of discriminatory taxation, referring to the fact that the products were similar and in competition: see Case 168/78 *Commission* v. *France* (Tax on Spirits) [1980] ECR 347. See also Case 286/81 *Oosthoek Uitgeversmaatschappij* [1982] ECR 4575.

112 The Sunday Trading Cases: Case 145/88 *Torfaen BC* v. *B&Q plc* [1989] ECR 3851, Cases C-306/88, 304/90 and 169/91 *Stoke on Trent CC* v. *B&Q plc* [1992] ECR I-6457 but contrast rules requiring registration of sex shops: case C-28/89 *Quietlynn* [1990] ECR I-3059. See also Case 75/81 *Blesgen, supra* n. 55.

113 Cases C-267 and 268/91 *Keck and Mithouard, supra* n. 1.

114 See Case C-405/98 *Gourmet International Products* [2001] ECR I-1795, discussed in more detail below and in Chapters 5 and 7.

V The Impact of Keck

Keck[115] concerned indistinctly applicable rules prohibiting certain sales techniques. Following on from previous case law, notably the *Sunday Trading* cases,[116] it would have seemed as though these rules would have fallen within the scope of the *Dassonville* test. The ECJ expressly overturned some of its previous rulings and held that rules relating to selling arrangements, provided that they applied equally in law and in fact, would not fall within the scope of the *Dassonville* test for an MEQR, as they would not hinder inter-state trade.[117] By contrast, requirements to be met by goods, such as requirements as to designation, form, size, weight, composition, presentation, labelling or packaging that result in obstacles to free movement, continued to be caught.[118]

Keck[119] therefore seems to divide indistinctly applicable measures into two[120] mutually exclusive categories: 'selling arrangements' and 'product requirements'. Advocate-General Lenz in the *Infant Milk* case[121] suggested that there was a third category: selling arrangements that fell outside paragraph 16 and falling per se within Article 28. The ECJ, however, refrained from following this approach, implicitly approving the approach based on just two categories. One could argue that there is a difference between categorisation of rules by type and categorisation by effect and, from the ruling in the *Infant Milk* case, it seems that the ECJ adopted the former approach. Although product requirements are not necessarily directly discriminatory, by their nature they would seem to subject imports to added burdens and therefore need to be scrutinised by reference to Article 28 principles. Thus, recipe rules and those relating to quality or size of a product are unaffected by *Keck*.[122] Selling arrangements, by contrast, benefit from a rebuttable presumption that they are too remote from trade to fall within Article 28.

---

115 Cases C-267 and 268/91 *Keck and Mithouard, supra* n. 1.

116 Case 145/88 *Torfaen BC* v. *B&Q plc, supra* n. 112; Cases C-306/88, 304/90 and 169/91 *Stoke on Trent CC* v. *B&Q plc, supra* n. 112.

117 Cases C-267 and 268/91 *Keck and Mithouard, supra* n. 1, paragraph 16.

118 *Ibid.*, paragraph 15.

119 Cases C-267 and 268/91 *Keck and Mithouard, supra* n. 1.

120 The possibility that price fixing constituted a separate category seems to have been rejected by the ECJ: Case C-63/94 *Groupement national des négotiants en pommes de terre de Belgique* v. *ITM Belgium* [1995] ECR I-2467.

121 Case C-391/92 *Commission* v. *Greece* (Infant Milk) [1995] ECR I- 162.

122 A relatively recent example is Case C-123/00 *Criminal Proceedings against Christina Bellamy and English Shop Wholesale SA* [2001] ECR I- 2795.

Keck[123] left some unanswered questions, in particular that of what constitutes a selling arrangement. Although none have attempted a comprehensive definition, *Keck* has been followed in a number of cases from which it seems as if rules relating to some sales technique legislation, as well as local regulation of socio-economic concerns, will no longer been seen as falling within Article 28. Thus, in *Hünermund*,[124] the ECJ held that rules prohibiting pharmacists from advertising para-pharmaceutical products outside their premises did not constitute MEQRs. Similarly, rules relating to Sunday trading and shop opening hours now seem, contrary to the *Sunday trading cases*, not to fall within Article 28.[125] Even rules which limit where goods may be sold now fall outside Article 28, seemingly overturning cases such as *Delattre*[126] and *Monteil*[127] which, in line with the ECJ's reasoning in *Dassonville*[128] itself, condemned the channelling of sales through certain categories of traders.[129]

Note that although 'selling arrangements' is a broad category, there are limits to the rules which, as a consequence of the ECJ's ruling in *Keck*,[130] do not fall within Article 28. Although television advertising and even point of sale arrangements constitute selling arrangements, as *Keck* itself pointed out, advertising rules which go to the packaging or get up of the product are still capable of being considered MEQRs. Thus in *Clinique*,[131] German rules forbidding the use of the term "Clinique" on cosmetic products on the basis that the use of the term was likely to confuse consumers as to the products' nature, were considered to fall within Article 28. Other consumer protection rules precluding Mars from using more than a certain percentage of the packaging area to announce an increase in the product's size similarly constituted an MEQR.[132]

---

123 Cases C-267 and 268/91 *Keck and Mithouard, supra* n. 1.

124 Case C-292/92 *Hünermund* v. *Landesapothekerkammer Baden-Württemberg* [1993] ECR I-6787.

125 Cases C-69 and 258/93 *Punto Casa SpA* v. *Sindaco del Commune di Capena* [1994] ECR I-2355.

126 Case C-369/88 *Delattre* [1990] ECR I-4747.

127 Case C-60/89 *Monteil et al* [1991] ECR I-1547.

128 Case 8/74 *Dassonville, supra* n. 19.

129 Contrast the position as regards services discussed in Chapter 11. See also the approach taken by the EFTA Court in Case E-1/97 *Gundersen* v. *Oslo Kommune* [1997] *EFTA Court Reports* 110 and Case E-9/00 *EFTA Surveillance Authority* v. *Norway*, judgment of 15 March 2002.

130 Joined Cases C-267 and 268/91 *Keck and Mithouard, supra* n. 1.

131 Case C-315/92 *Verband Sozialer Wettbewerb eV* v. *Clinique Laboratories SNC et al, supra* n. 108.

132 Case C-470/93 *Verein gegen Unwesen in Handel und Gewerbe Koln eV* v. *Mars GmbH, supra* n. 108.

In *Familiapress*,[133] the Austrian government argued that rules prohibiting prize competitions in magazines constituted a selling arrangement because the competitions were only included in the magazine as a marketing device. The ECJ dismissed this argument: the prize competition was part of the content of the magazine and the Austrian rules thus related to product characteristics and fell to be considered under Article 28.

Even when rules do concern selling arrangements, they must 'apply to all affected traders operating within the national territory' and apply equally in law and in fact. This latter point is an issue to be determined by the national court.[134] In *Punto Casa*,[135] it was argued that the Sunday trading rules affected large stores more severely than other categories of trader. The ECJ did not expressly address this argument but it seems implicitly to have rejected it: the ECJ found the rule to be a *Keck* selling arrangement and therefore outside Article 28. The Advocate-General did address the point, suggesting that the concern was that traders from outside the importing Member State should not be disadvantaged by comparison with domestic traders, rather than being worried about whether various categories of domestic traders were treated differently.[136] In *Keck*[137] itself, for example, the prohibition on resale at a loss applied to retailers but not to manufacturers. If this interpretation is correct, there seems to be a very close link (if not an overlap) between this requirement and the requirement that a rule relating to a selling arrangement should apply equally in law and in fact. The *Keck* judgment would also seem to indicate that when assessing the equality of application of the national rule, the ECJ would take into account the overall position, rather than look at individual cases.

In *Gourmet*,[138] concerning Swedish rules restricting the advertising of alcoholic beverages, the ECJ took the opportunity to refine this second point still further and, in doing so, it drew on previous rulings, notably *Keck*[139] and *de Agostini*.[140] The Court started by emphasising that *Keck*,

---

133 Case C-368/95 *Vereinigte Familiapress Zeitungsverlags- und vertriebs GmbH* v. *Heinrich Bauer Verlag* [1997] ECR I- 3689.

134 Joined Cases C-34-36/95 *Konsumentombudsmannen* v. *de Agostini* and *TV Shop i Sverige* [1997] ECR I-3843.

135 Cases C-69 and 258/93 *Punto Casa SpA*, *supra* n. 125.

136 See the Opinion of the same Advocate-General in Cases C-401 and 402/92 *Criminal Proceedings against Tankstation 't Heukste vof and J. B. E. Boermans* [1994] ECR I-2199 at paragraph 21.

137 Cases C-267 and 268/91 *Keck and Mithouard*, *supra* n. 1.

138 Case C-405/98 *Konsumentombudsmannen* v. *Gourmet International Products AB*, *supra* n. 114.

139 Joined Cases C-267 and 268/91 *Keck and Mithouard*, *supra* n. 1.

although it drew a distinction between selling arrangements and requirements to be met, was also concerned with ensuring that measures 'must not be of a kind as to prevent access to the market by products from another Member State or to impede access any more than they impede the access of domestic products'. Thus, as *de Agostini* had recognised, a prohibition on types of sales promotion might have a greater impact on imported products than on domestic goods.[141] Although it re-emphasised that the national courts should make the assessment of whether this was so in the cases before them, the ECJ itself remarked:

> 'the Court is able to conclude that, in the case of alcoholic beverages, the consumption of which is linked to traditional social practices and to local habits and customs, a prohibition on all advertising aimed at consumers in the form of advertisements in the press, on the radio, and on television, the direct mailing of unsolicited material or the placing of posters on the public highway is likely to impede the products from other Member States more than it impedes access by domestic products, with which consumers are instantly more aware.'[142]

Gourmet[143] can be seen as somewhat of a retreat from the position in *Keck*,[144] or at least confirmation that the selling arrangements approach cannot provide all the answers. The ECJ seems keen to limit the effect of its ruling in *Gourmet*, however, in two ways. The ECJ makes its comments applicable to a limited category of goods – those 'the consumption of which is linked to traditional social practices and to local habits and customs'. Nonetheless, this approach could extend quite widely, for example to include all foodstuffs.[145] Secondly, the ECJ delineate particular types of rules that are affected by the ruling. Again, advertising rules generally constitute a wide category, but it would seem that other rules, for example dealing with shop opening hours, remain unaffected by *Gourmet*.

---

140 Joined Cases C-34-36/95 *Konsumentombudsmannen* v. *de Agostini and TV Shop i Sverige* [1997] ECR I-3843. The question of whether this constitutes discrimination or access to the market is discussed further in Chapter 5.

141 *Ibid.*

142 Case C-405/98 *Konsumentombudsmannen* v. *Gourmet International Products AB*, *supra* n. 114, paragraph 21.

143 *Ibid.*

144 Joined Cases C-267 and 268/91 *Keck and Mithouard*, *supra* n. 1.

145 See for example the comments of the Advocate-General in Case 407/85 *Drei Glocken GmbH* v. *USL Centro-Sud & Provincia Autonoma di Bolzano, supra* n. 105.

VI Rule of Reason and the Principle of Mutual Recognition

Many of the rules described above were enacted for public interest reasons, such as consumer protection, rather than in an attempt to limit access to the domestic of imported products. In the absence of a Community harmonized approach, responsibility for regulation falls to the Member States, resulting in a patchwork approach to regulation throughout the Community. The operation of different rules is likely to make it more difficult to export goods through more than one territory, potentially resulting in such rules being seen as MEQRs and being struck down as contrary to Article 28. The original *Dassonville*[146] ruling, however, implicitly recognised that some areas require regulation, a point which was developed in *Cassis de Dijon*.[147] Providing the rule in question satisfied what became known as the rule of reason, indistinctly applicable national rules would not be struck down despite initially seeming to fall within the definition of an MEQR. As the ECJ held in *Cassis de Dijon:*

> 'In the absence of common rules relating to the production and marketing of alcohol ... it is for the Member States to regulate all matters relating to the production and marketing of alcohol and alcoholic beverages on their own territory.
>
> Obstacles to movement within the Community resulting from disparities between the national laws relating to the marketing of the products in question must be accepted in so far as those provisions may be recognised as being necessary in order to satisfy mandatory requirements relating in particular to the effectiveness of fiscal supervision, the protection of public health, the fairness of commercial transactions and the defence of the consumer.'[148]

Thus, one can see the ECJ attempting to provide a mechanism for balancing the needs of the common market against the needs of other general interests, such as the environment, human health and consumer protection. Article 30 (originally 36) provided some limited exceptions to Article 28 (originally 30). Following the expansion of Article 28 to cover indistinctly applicable measures, the rule of reason can be seen as an attempt not to tip the balance too far towards a deregulated environment.

Initially there were some concerns that the *Cassis* rule of reason undermined the role of Article 30 EC, the Treaty derogation from Article 28.[149] The rule of reason, however, has two crucial differences from Article 30, apart from being judge-made. It applies only in the case of

146 Case 8/74 *Dassonville*, *supra* n. 19.

147 Case 120/78 *Cassis de Dijon*, *supra* n. 61.

148 *Ibid.*, at paragraph 8.

149 Oliver, P., *supra* n. 16, at p. 112.

indistinctly applicable measures,[150] thus a distinction between these and distinctly (or overtly discriminatory) rules continues to be necessary.[151] Further, the judgment in *Cassis de Dijon* does not give a complete list of the 'mandatory requirements' that trigger the operation of the rule of reason. One reason for the difference in approach is that distinctly applicable rules are overtly discriminatory, and therefore contravene one of the fundamental principles of the EC Treaty, that of non-discrimination. It is not surprising that any exception to this rule would be narrowly construed. Indistinctly applicable measures by contrast are less offensive, as they only have a discriminatory effect (to the extent that they are discriminatory) as a by-product of other policy goals. The relationship between the grounds for derogation from Article 28 set out in Article 30 and the mandatory requirements is considered in Chapter 7.

The ruling in *Cassis de Dijon* also introduced another Community law principle, that of mutual recognition.[152] The Court argued that,

> '[t]here is therefore no valid reason, provided they have been lawfully produced and marketed in one of the Member States, why alcoholic beverages should not be introduced into any other Member State ...'[153]

This ruling was subsequently clarified by the Commission in a Communication as meaning '[a]ny product lawfully produced and marketed in one Member State must, in principle, be admitted to the market of any other Member State.' This raised the question of what 'lawfully produced and marketed' meant. Subsequent case law confirmed that the principle applied to goods that had been produced outside the EC and placed in free circulation, despite the specific wording of the Communication and the reference to the goods having been marketed in one of the Member States.[154] The condition should be therefore seen as operating in the alternative rather than constituting, as phrased, a cumulative test. This does not, however, address the position of goods produced for export only. Although adopting the approach in *Peureux*[155]

---

150 Note, however, the environmental cases, discussed further in Chapters 6 and 7.

151 Case 119/78 *S.A des Grandes Distilleries Peureux* v. *Directeur des Services Fiscaux de la Haute-Saône et du Territoire de Belfort* [1979] ECR 975. See further Chapters 5 and 7.

152 The precursor to this principle had already been seen in the pharmaceutical sphere: see e.g. Case 104/75 *De Peijper, supra* n. 38 and was implicit in *Dassonville, supra* n. 19.

153 Case 120/78 *Cassis de Dijon, supra* n. 61, at paragraph 14.

154 Case 119/78 *S.A des Grandes Distilleries Peureux, supra* n. 151; Case 59/82 *Schutzverband gegen Unwesen in der Wirtschaft* v. *Weinvertriebs GmbH* [1983] ECR 1217.

155 *Ibid.*

would suggest that lawful production would suffice, this could lead to a gap in protection in the situation in which the Member State of production did not permit the marketing (but permitted the production)[156] of the products in question. In that instance, would the Member State of origin bother to provide the national standards upon which the principle of mutual recognition is based?

The introduction of mutual recognition is interesting for a number of other reasons. Firstly, it operates, in theory, to introduce the idea of one-stop regulation; goods which have satisfied one Member State must not be forced to satisfy a second (or more) set of hurdles in respect of the same public interest concern.[157] Mutual recognition therefore assumes that the standards in the lowest of the Member States are acceptable. Whether this is true or not, the reasoning assumes, and imposes, a certain commonality between the Member States. At a more conceptual level, therefore, it also operates to suggest a level of community and trust amongst the Member States (subject to the operation of the rule of reason). Mutual recognition also constitutes a form of choice of law clause,[158] in that it produces a preliminary presumption as to which Member State's rules will apply to a given product. It thus co-ordinates the horizontal relationship between the various Member States' legal systems. Further, the approach introduced by *Cassis de Dijon* in theory allows national and regional idiosyncrasies to continue, and would seem to protect against excessive standardisation. Whether this has proved to be the case or whether there has in practice been a race to the bottom in terms of standards is another question.[159] Finally, mutual recognition forms the basis of an approach that was to be used in respect of the other freedoms, notably services, and underpins much of the Community harmonizing legislation.[160]

---

[156] Of course Article 28 could not be used to challenge a ban on manufacture; though whether a ban in respect of goods manufactured for export is capable of being challenged under the Treaty is another matter. See test for application of Article 29 discussed in Chapter 6.

[157] See e.g. comments of ECJ in Case 261/81 *Walter Rau, supra* n. 106 in which the ECJ held that if a product '"suitably and satisfactorily" fulfils the legitimate objective of a Member State's own rules ... the importing country cannot justify prohibiting its sale in its territory by claiming that the way it fulfils the objective is different from that imposed on national products.'.

[158] This is not choice of law in a private international law sense.

[159] See further Chapter 7 and 13.

[160] See further Chapter 13.

VII Conclusions

Although on the face of it, the approach of the ECJ in *Dassonville*[161] and *Cassis de Dijon*[162] may seem to be a noble attempt to reconcile the conflicting pressures between Member State and Community competence and policy; and even between different Member State interests, problems have arisen out the way in which *Dassonville* has been interpreted over the years. The ECJ has not taken the approach of identifying each element in the test and applying them (contrast the position for early Article 81 case law), instead focussing on one element of the test to justify its conclusion in each case. Unsurprisingly, this has lead to confusion and criticism of an overly broad and often inconsistent body of cases, resulting in the ECJ seeking to limit the scope of Article 28 in *Keck.*[163] Although mutual recognition may seem a flexible tool by which the differences between Member States may be reconciled, it too has given rise to concerns. It essentially operates to ensure that the lowest standard of protection is acceptable throughout the Community. Such a principle also operates to undermine Member States' freedom of regulatory choice. The difficulties surrounding the scope of Article 28 and MEQRs are discussed in the following chapter. The scope of the derogation from Articles 28 and 29 are discussed in Chapters 7 and 8.

---

161 Case 8/74 *Dassonville, supra* n. 19.

162 Case 120/78 *Cassis de Dijon, supra* n. 61.

163 Cases C-267 and 268/91 *Keck and Mithouard, supra* n. 1.

Chapter 5

What is the Proper Scope of Article 28?

I Introduction

Much has been written about the proper scope of Article 28.[1] The issue is significant because of its impact on Member States' competence and regulatory freedom. As Wils famously remarked, 'Article [28] is the tool for policing the borderline between legitimate and illegitimate national regulation.'[2] Article 28 has perhaps received so much attention because the case law on this area was relatively well-developed at an earlier stage in the Community's development than the other freedoms; certainly this is so if Article 28 is compared with Article 49. Equally one might suggest that so much attention has been paid to Article 28, at least by academics, because the jurisprudence in this area has been perceived as problematic. It has been seen as inconsistent;[3] as including within the scope of Article 28 too many Member States' rules;[4] more recently, of looking to the form of a measure rather than its impact; and, in some instances, of being of poor quality, with far reaching judgments being drafted in sweeping terms rather than closely reasoned logical steps.[5]

---

1 See e.g. Steiner, J., 'Drawing the Line: Uses and Abuses of Article 30 EEC' (1992) 29 *CMLRev* 749; Mortelmans, 'Article 30 of the EEC Treaty and Legislation relating to Market Circumstances: Time to Consider a New Definition?' (1991) 28 *CMLRev* and White 'In Search of Limits to Article 30 of the EEC Treaty' (1989) 26 *CMLRev* 235 who suggested that the then Article 30 had been overextended. Gormley, L., 'Commentary on *Torfaen BC* v. *B&Q*' (1990) 27 *CML Rev* and Wils, W. 'The Search for the Rule in Article 30 EEC: Much Ado About Nothing?' (1993) *ELRev* 475 express views in favour of a broad interpretation of Article 28 (ex-30).

2 Wils, *ibid.*, at p. 478.

3 Steiner, *supra* n. 1, p. 750.

4 See e.g. Weatherill, S., 'After *Keck*: Some Thoughts on how to Clarify the Clarification' (1996) 33 *CMLRev* 855.

5 Joined Cases C-267 and 268/91 *Keck and Mithouard* [1993] ECR I-6097 received much adverse comment. More recently, Case C-379/98 *PreussenElektra AG* v. *Schleswag AG* [2001] ECR I-2099 in terms of its section on Article 28 contains very

This chapter will provide an overview of the main criticisms and seek to identify to what extent the problems in the jurisprudence have been resolved. In doing so, it will be broken down into three sections. The first section will deal with the early criticism concerning the over-extension of Article 28, whilst the second part will focus on the ECJ's response in the case of *Keck*[6] and the post-*Keck* case law. The third section will consider a slightly different problem: the notion of indistinctly applicable measures as opposed to discriminatory measures.

II From *Dassonville* to the *Sunday Trading* Cases

As noted in Chapter 4, the starting point for determining the scope of Article 28 was the test laid down in *Dassonville,*[7] as clarified by *Cassis de Dijon.*[8] The test is broad and effects-based[9] and may catch not only overtly discriminatory measures, but also those which apply to both imports and domestic products. The problems in this area have not tended to concern the former category of rule, as they clearly lie at the heart of Article 28. Their potential for discouraging intra-state trade is obvious, although it should be noted that the issue of what constitutes a discriminatory measure is not always clear. This point will be discussed further below. The issue under consideration here is which of the range of 'indistinctly applicable' measures should be caught by Article 28. The problem is that once we have accepted that indistinctly applicable measures can fall within Article 28, a boundary between those measures that properly fall within the scope of the Treaty and those which should be considered as falling within Member State general regulatory competence needs to be identified, as otherwise virtually all Member State rules could be challenged under Article 28.

The Commission in Directive Article 3 of 70/50[10] adopted an approach which included within Article 28 those 'measures which are equally applicable to domestic and imported goods', but limited the scope of the prohibition by the inclusion of a proviso; that is, 'where the restrictive effects of such measures on the free movement of goods exceeds the

---

little reasoning and its lack of clarity is exacerbated by the fact that the transcript still used old Treaty numbers rather than the post-ToA numbering.

6 Joined Cases C-267 and 268/91 *Keck and Mithouard, supra* n. 5.

7 Case 8/74 *Procureur du Roi* v. *Dassonville et al.* [1974] ECR 837.

8 Case 120/78 *Rewe* v. *Bundesmonopolverwaltung fur Branntwein* (Cassis de Dijon) [1979] ECR 649, itself confirmed by Case 788/79 *Italy* v. *Gilli and Andres* [1980] ECR 2071.

9 On the notion of effects-based test, see further Case C-379/98 *PreussenElektra AG, supra* n. 5 discussed below.

10 OJ [1970] Sp. Ed. 17.

effects intrinsic to trade rules'. Effectively, this would seem to introduce a proportionality element to the test used to identify whether Article 28 should apply in the first place, even before there could be any question of assessing the national measures by reference to mandatory requirements. It would therefore seem to tilt the balance of the test, albeit only slightly, in favour of national measures. The ECJ, however, rejected this approach.[11] How then would the ECJ determine the boundary between those indistinctly applicable measures, non-discriminatory in form, which are inimical to inter-state trade and those that are not? Van Gerven put forward the suggestion that there were two types of cases in which Article 28 would be engaged as regards indistinctly applicable measures.[12] The first situation involves a rule that operates to the advantage of the domestic product;[13] the second where a measure does not necessarily confer an advantage on the domestic product but still operates to undermine the existence of the single market.

There are numerous examples of van Gerven's first category of rules. For example, rules which prohibit the marketing of the imported product in the host Member State because the product (marketed lawfully in the Member State of origin) does not comply with a national measure in the host Member State would fall within this category,[14] as do the German beer purity laws[15] or those at issue in *Cassis de Dijon* itself.[16] Even rules that do not prohibit the marketing of an imported product may make the import of that product more difficult or costly, for example by duplicating public interest measures that have been provided for in the Member State of origin. An example of a rule of this sort is a provision that requires information different from that required by the Member State of origin to be included on the label in the interests of consumer protection or a rule that requires a certain type of container to be used.[17] These measures are discriminatory, even if only indirectly, as they require a producer to take extra steps to market the product thereby incurring extra costs. In some instances it may not be possible to market the product at all; many of the

---

11 Case 190/73 *Van Haaster* [1974] ECR 1123.

12 Case 145/88 *Torfaen BC* v. *B & Q plc* [1989] ECR 3851. See also Steiner, *supra* n. 1, pp. 754-5.

13 The focus on an advantage to the domestic product is central to the case law on Article 29, see Chapter 6.

14 See also Case 407/85 *Drei Glocken GmbH* v. *USL Centro-Sud & Provincia Autonoma di Bolzano* [1988] ECR 4233 regarding the content of pasta and Case 788/79 *Gilli and Andres, supra* n. 8 regarding vinegar.

15 Case 176/84 *Commission* v. *Germany* [1987] ECR 1193.

16 Case 120/78 *Cassis de Dijon, supra* n. 8.

17 See e.g. Case 302/86 *Commission* v. *Denmark* (Danish Bottles) [1988] ECR 4607.

national 'recipe' rules, such as those in issue in *Cassis de Dijon*, have this effect.

The second category of rules identified by Advocate-General van Gerven was slightly more contentious. It did, however, receive judicial recognition. The turning point in this respect was *Cinéthèque*,[18] which concerned a French rule prohibiting the marketing of films on video for a specified period after the relevant film's release in French cinemas, the aim of the rule being to protect the film industry. The rule did not single out imported products, applying to domestic and imported products alike. The marketing of the product was not prohibited – just delayed – and the ultimate marketing was not rendered more expensive or burdensome for imports than for domestic products. Advocate-General Slynn in *Cinéthèque* suggested that the measure in issue did not trigger Article 28, arguing that indirect discrimination of the kind identified above would be necessary to bring a measure within the scope of the Treaty, even if the rule led to a restriction or reduction in imports.[19] The ECJ, however, took a different approach. Notwithstanding the fact that the rule applied to both domestic and imported goods and did not have the purpose of regulating trade patterns, it created barriers to trade as a result of the disparities in the regulatory systems in each Member State. In principle, therefore, it fell within the scope of Article 28. This case consequently removed the link between application of Article 28 and discrimination, albeit discrimination that operated indirectly. The justification for the approach here was that the ECJ was concerned to ensure that individual national markets were not partitioned off from intra-Community trade. The judgment can therefore be categorised as one based on the goal of creating the internal market.[20]

Not all case law can be neatly ascribed to a particular category of case, however, even before *Cinéthèque*.[21] In *Blesgen*,[22] a national rule restricted the sale of alcoholic drinks above a certain percentage. The rule did not require the imported product to satisfy any extra requirements to market the product by comparison with the domestic product. Nonetheless, the

---

18 Cases 60 and 61/84 *Cinéthèque SA* v. *Fédération Nationale des Cinémas Françaises* [1985] ECR 2605.

19 Cases 60 and 61/84 *Cinéthèque*, *ibid.*, at p. 2611. Steiner, *supra* n. 1, criticises this approach as it blurs the distinction between the competition rules and those relating to free movement. As the discussion in Chapter 3 shows, the relationship between the competition rules and the free movement rules is complex and to a certain extent has already been blurred.

20 Thus rules that permit the reliance on intellectual property rights would equally undermine the single market; Case 158/86 *Warner Bros.* v. *Christiansen* [1988] ECR 2605. On intellectual property rights generally, see Chapter 8.

21 Cases 60 and 61/84 *Cinéthèque*, *supra* n. 18.

22 Case 75/81 *Blesgen* v. *Belgium* [1982] ECR 1211.

rule might discourage the import of alcoholic beverages of the requisite percentage, and thus the divergence in regulatory system could be seen, as it was in *Cinéthèque*, as creating a barrier to trade. The ECJ, however, dismissed any argument that the rule fell within Article 28, merely stating that the national rule 'had no connection with the importation of such products' and that it 'was not of such a nature as to affect trade between Member States'. Similarly, the rules in *Oebel*,[23] which prohibited the delivery of bakery products to retail outlets or to consumers during night hours, were not contrary to Article 28 as, 'trade remained possible at all times'.[24] Thus, even after *Cinéthèque*, the ECJ found that some national rules which might discourage traders from importing products were too remote from inter-state trade.[25] Notably, in *Quietlynn*,[26] the ECJ held that a measure, which prohibited the sale of sex articles save from specifically licensed premises, was 'merely a rule regarding the distribution' of the goods in question.[27] Given that trade between Member States remained possible at all times and the products could be marketed within the United Kingdom through the licensed premises, the rule was 'not of such a nature as to impede trade between Member States'. Further, planning rules fell outside the scope of the then Article 30, although the ECJ did not explain why.[28]

By contrast, barriers to trade were found to exist in other cases involving marketing and distribution of imported goods. In a series of

---

23 Case 155/80 *Oebel* [1981] ECR 1993.

24 Case 155/80 *Oebel, supra* n. 23 could also been seen as part of the ECJ's reluctance to find measures that form part of the Member State policies aimed at achieving public good objectives. See for example, Case 238/82 *Duphar* v. *The Netherlands* [1984] ECR 523, which concerned a Dutch insurance scheme whereby a patient would be refunded the cost of a medicine only if it was approved by the State. This had an impact on trade – particularly because a large percentage of medicines in Holland were imported. Contrast more recently the approach taken in Case C-120/95 *Nicholas Decker* v. *Caisse de Maladie des Employés Privés* [1998] ECR I-1831, discussed in Chapter 9.

25 Case 148/86 *Direction Générale des Impôts and Procureur de la République* v. *Forest* [1986] ECR 3449 regarding a quota for the milling of flour, where millers were free to fill their quota by imported wheat; and Case C-69/88 *Krantz* v. *Ontvanger der Directe Belastingen* [1990] ECR 583 regarding the right of tax authorities to seize goods against tax debts.

26 Case C-23/89 *Quietlynn* [1990] ECR I-3059.

27 Contrast the approach taken with regard to satellite dishes in the field of services, discussed in Chapters 2 and 11.

28 Case 20/87 *Ministère Public* v. *Gauchard* [1987] ECR 4879 and see also the discussion about planning rules in the Communication regarding Satellite Dishes, Chapter 2.

cases, rules which did not relate to the product, or even the way the product was packaged, were held to constitute MEQRs – although such rules were found to be justifiable. Thus, a rule restricting the use of free gifts was held to fall within the scope of Article 28,[29] as was door-to-door selling of encyclopaedias.[30] A rule requiring the registration of auctioneers was also held to fall within the scope of MEQR.[31] Provisions restricting certain types of advertising were held to constitute an MEQR as the restriction 'affect[ed] marketing opportunities for the imported products' and consequently could affect the overall volume of sales.[32] A similar concern was found in the *Sunday Trading* cases, when British rules which prohibited the sale of most types of goods on Sundays was held to have an impact on trade.[33] One could argue that in the free gifts case and the door-to-door selling case, the national rules required, at least to a certain degree, a potential amendment to the product's advertising and distribution arrangements, a point the ECJ made in both cases. In the third case, however, the auctioneers' case, the ECJ eschewed that line of reasoning, merely asserting that the restrictions on certain types of advertising did not directly affect imports but might have an indirect effect on volume of sales. Finally, in the *Sunday Trading* cases, a negative impact on the overall volume of sales was assumed. Nonetheless, in principle Article 28 could apply. Actual impact on trade seemed not to be necessary to trigger the application of Article 28. Indeed this reflects the ECJ's approach in *Dassonville,* which referred to potential effect.

Although in each case it is possible to rationalise the ECJ's decision, the problem is that the Court did not adopt a consistent approach to the cases and that for any argument identifying a general rule that might be put forward, it seems possible to find an exception. The ECJ variously focussed on the issue of whether trade was possible; whether there was a barrier and finally the issue of remoteness between a measure and any impact on inter-state trade. It is consequently difficult to reconcile the cases. For example, if some rules concerning where and when products may be sold are contrary to the Treaty, how do *Blesgen*[34] and *Oebel*[35] fit in? If *Quietlynn*[36] is a rule regarding distribution, then surely so is *Torfaen*.[37]

---

29 Case 286/81 *Oosthoek Uitgeversmaatschappij* [1982] ECR 4575.

30 Case 382/87 *Buet* v. *Ministère Public* [1989] ECR 1235.

31 Case C-239/90 *SCP Boscher, Studer et Frometin* v. *SA British Motors Wright and Others* [1991] ECR I-2023.

32 Case C- 362/88 *GB-Inno-BM* v. *Confederation du Commerce Luxembourgois* [1990] ECR I-667.

33 For example, Case 145/88 *Torfaen BC, supra* n. 12.

34 Case 75/81 *Blesgen, supra* n. 22.

35 Case 155/80 *Oebel, supra* n. 23.

36 Case C-23/89 *Quietlynn, supra* n. 26.

These cases also illustrated the difficulty in determining the boundary between what the ECJ has termed 'an internal situation' and those having an impact on trade. Although the potential relevance of Article 28 is clear when imported goods are in issue, what is the position when the goods originate from the same Member State as the rules which are the subject of the challenge? The issue has been discussed quite recently in *Pistre.*[38] There, a French rule limiting the marketing of products with the designation of 'montagne' to those originating from certain areas in France was held to have a Community dimension. In *Pistre*, the ECJ seemed to consider the question of whether there is a Community element from an objective stance. In the ECJ's view, it did not matter that all the relevant facts arose in France, it was sufficient that the rule could affect intra-Community trade.[39] In *Pistre*, however, it could be argued that the fact that the rule was categorised as discriminatory (it effectively precluded the marketing of mountain cheese from other Member States) was a relevant factor. The subsequent case of *Guimont*[40]concerned a rule that would apply equally to both domestic and imported products. The ECJ held that such a rule would fall within Article 28 'only in so far as it applies to situations that are linked to the importation of goods in intra-Community trade'.[41] Despite the fact that, again, all the relevant facts arose in France, the ECJ went on to find that the rule in question fell foul of Article 28.

Following these two cases, it seems that an internal situation is limited to the circumstances where the rule in question could *never* affect goods originating from other Member States. Where the rule is of a type that could affect such goods, notwithstanding the fact that the rule in question does not actually affect any such goods in the case in issue, it would seem that Article 28 could apply. The ECJ has thus turned the question of the internal situation into an abstract, objective test rather than a test that relates to the facts in the case. Internal situations are now rare indeed. Moreover, it seem that the determination of an internal situation has now become entangled with the question of whether there should have been an Article 234 reference in the first place.[42] In any event, the lack of clarity in this area contributed to the volume of criticism that the ECJ's case law

---

37 Case 145/88 *Torfaen BC, supra* n. 12.

38 Joined Cases C-321-324/94 *Jacques Pistre* [1997] ECR I-2343.

39 *Ibid.*, at paragraph 48.

40 Case C-448/98 *Criminal Proceedings against Jean-Pierre Guimont* [2000] ECR I-10663.

41 *Ibid.*, at paragraph 21, citing Case 286/81 *Oosthoek Uitgeversmaatschappij, supra* n. 29.

42 See reasoning in Case C-448/98 *Guimont, supra* n. 40 at paragraph 22. See also Case C-254/98 *TK-Heimdienst* [2000]ECR 1-151 in which the Advocate-General and the ECJ took different approaches as regards *Pistre, supra* n. 38.

attracted during the late 80s and early 90s, and it does not seem that the position now is much clearer.[43] It should be noted that this concern is not limited to questions relating to goods but arises in relation to all the four freedoms.[44]

Clearly, the *Dassonville* test is wide – arguably too wide if it is to includes rules which are both non-discriminatory and which have only hypothetical effects on trade. The ECJ's restrictive approach to the rule of reason and the derogation in Article 30 compounds the difficulties in this area. Even for indistinctly applicable measures, once the *prima facie* case of an MEQR had been successfully raised, then the burden of proof would fall on the Member State to justify the rule. Given that in some instances the rule of reason would be assessed by national courts, there was a real risk that there would an unequal assessment as to whether the national rule was justified – as the different approaches in the *Sunday Trading* cases[45] before a variety of British courts illustrated. Equally problematical was the lack of certainty in this area. Arguably these latter problems might have been at least mitigated by clearer (and earlier) guidance by the ECJ.[46]

The question remains, to what extent – if we are talking about non-discriminatory rules – does the rule have to have an affect on the internal market to fall within the definition of MEQR and if so, what level of effect? Arguably, the ECJ failed to produce a satisfactory solution to these questions because it did not consistently address the question of what Article 28 was trying to achieve, despite the fact that numerous Advocates-General raised this question. The problem is this: in talking about the creation of the market, are we concerned with the removal of discrimination between imported and domestic goods or about the creation of what is effectively a domestic market writ large? As a linked question, in identifying potential barriers, should the ECJ be concerned with the structure of the internal market or with individuals' freedom to trade?[47]

At the end of the eighties and beginning of the nineties, a considerable amount of time was devoted to trying to develop a coherent rule to identify the appropriate limits to Article 28, most of which seemed to hinge on discrimination in its various forms. There are, however, exceptions to

---

43 For a more recent discussion see Arnull, A., *The European Union and its Court of Justice* (Oxford, 1999) at pp. 56-60.

44 See e.g. Case C-281/98 *Angonese* v. *Cassa di Rispamio di Bolzano SpA*, [2000] ECR I-4139 and contrast Case C-264/96 *Imperial Chemical Industries* (ICI) v. *Hall Colmer* [1998] ECR I-4695, especially paragraph 35.

45 *Supra* n. 12.

46 Gormley, *supra* n. 1, though he noted the risk that in doing so the ECJ might have overstepped the boundaries of its own jurisdiction and offended the national courts.

47 See e.g. comments of Advocate-General Tesauro in Case C-292/92 *Hünermund* v. *Landesapothekerkammer Baden-Würrtemburg* [1993] ECR I-6787.

every rule. Gormley, for example, suggested that the most appropriate course of action was a broad application of the *Dassonville* test with rules to be saved, as appropriate, by the application of the rule of reason.[48] In his view, the cases to be criticised were *Krantz*[49] and *Quietlynn*,[50] in which the ECJ found no impact on inter-state trade. Gormley's approach might have relieved some of the uncertainty about the scope of Article 28, but this could have resulted in more inconsistent assessments of the rule of reason by national courts. Further a 'mechanical' application of *Dassonville* would be the one most likely to blur the boundaries between the situations that were internal and those that were not, thus allowing cases with 'little integrationist merit' to be brought before the courts.[51] Crucially, Gormley's approach fails to resolve tensions about Member States' freedom to legislate in areas that might incidentally affect the internal market.

One proposed solution to limit the scope of Article 28 was based on the distinction between the characteristics of the product and the measures that regulate the circumstances in which products are sold.[52] It could be argued that this is broadly a distinction between those rules which impose extra burdens on producers to ensure that the product is marketable (i.e. indirectly discriminatory or dual burden) and those which require no such changes. Thus, rules relating to content of the product would remain within the scope of Article 28, whereas rules that regulate who may sell the products and when and where, such as those in *Blesgen*[53] and *Quietlynn*,[54] would not be caught by Article 28. This approach was not entirely consistent with the Court's jurisprudence. Adopting this categorisation would have suggested that *Buet*[55] and *GB-INNO*[56] should fall outside Article 28, whereas the ECJ held they did not. Nonetheless, the proposal was refined by Mortelmans, who suggested that the 'market circumstances' category needed to be sub-divided into those rules which have 'a territorial element' and those which do not, applying more generally.[57] Thus rules that require the sale of a product through a specific location, such as

---

48 See also Arnull, (1991) 16 *ELRev* 112.

49 Case C-69/88 *Krantz, supra* n. 25.

50 Case C-23/89 *Quietlynn, supra* n. 26.

51 This is a point Gormley subsequently seemed to recognise: Gormley, L.,'Recent Case Law on the Free Movement of Goods' (1990) 27 *CMLRev* 825.

52 White, *supra* n. 1.

53 Case 75/81 *Blesgen, supra* n. 22.

54 Case C-23/89 *Quietlynn, supra* n. 26.

55 Case 382/87 *Buet* v. *Ministère Public, supra* n. 30.

56 Case 362/88 *GB-Inno-BM, supra* n. 32.

57 Mortelmans, *supra* n. 1.

Blesgen,[58] would remain outside the definition of MEQR; whereas those which are not linked to a particular location, such as *Buet*,[59] pose a greater threat to the creation of the internal market and therefore should fall within Article 28 (subject to the rule of reason). Although this approach seems to match the approach taken by the ECJ in the cases cited, it is problematic in that the boundary between the different categories might sometimes be hard to identify.

Another approach[60] put forward at this time suggested avoiding categorising rules by type, instead proposing a return to *Dassonville*.[61] Such an approach would be significant in two respects: the first is that it is the effect of the national measures that would be determinative; secondly, although *Dassonville* refers to potential and indirect consequences for the market, it should not be satisfied by *any* change. Rather the consequence must constitute – or have the potential to constitute – a *hindrance*.[62] A number of the judgments (and commentaries) instead refer to 'an effect', which could be positive or even neutral, as well as negative. Referring to an effect is clearly much broader than referring to a hindrance and would leave little room for measures that might change patterns of trade but not adversely affect them. An approach that does not distinguish between hindrance and effect means that there are only two possible responses to the *Dassonville* question. Either there is an internal situation or there is an MEQR. Focussing on hindrance allows a third possibility: a rule which does not satisfy the stringent requirements of an internal situation but which is not sufficiently damaging to trade to constitute an MEQR. A hindrance is likely to occur when traders 'are forced to adapt their production or marketing methods to meet the demands of the importing State'.[63] Even when extra cost is not involved, however, where markets in the host Member State are in some way limited, the rules may act as deterrent, as Slynn noted in *Cinéthèque*.[64] Moving into the market of the Member State in such a case would not be an attractive business proposition. Of course, taking such a broad view of hindrance could itself blur the distinction between hindrance and effect. This would be the case where no objective criteria, such as extra costs, could be identified but where the more subjective assessment of whether there was a deterrent in

58 Case 75/81 *Blesgen*, *supra* n. 22.

59 Case 382/87 *Buet* v. *Ministère Public*, *supra* n. 30.

60 Steiner, *supra* n. 1.

61 Case 8/74 *Dassonville*, *supra* n. 7.

62 This was certainly the approach in some of the case law: see e.g. the reasoning of the Advocate-General in Case 207/83 *Commission* v. *United Kingdom* (Origin Marking) [1985] ECR 201.

63 Steiner *supra* n. 1 p. 769.

64 Cases 60 and 61/84 *Cinéthèque*, *supra* n. 18.

the eyes of a trader was instead used. This would then return us to the possible danger of an over-extension of Article 28.[65]

III *Keck*

To some extent the arguments outlined above are of historic importance only, as the ruling in *Keck* sought to limit the scope of Article 28. Given the judgment's limited success in this regard, however, the concepts and difficulties identified may still have relevance. *Keck*[66] concerned a French rule that prohibited resale at a loss. The applicants, who operated in Strasbourg, claimed that the rule constituted an MEQR. In a somewhat surprising decision, the ECJ expressly overturned some of its previous case law and introduced a new test, which seems to have some resemblance to the test proposed by White,[67] noted earlier. Famously, the ECJ – after complaining somewhat querulously about 'the increasing tendency of traders to invoke Article 30 [now Article 28] of the Treaty as a means of challenging any rules whose effect is to limit their commercial freedom' – suggested the following boundary for Article 28.

> 'However, contrary to what has previously been decided, the application to products from other Member States of national provisions restricting or prohibiting certain selling arrangements is not such as to hinder directly or indirectly, actually or potentially, trade between Member States within the meaning of the *Dassonville* judgment ... provided that those provisions apply to all affected traders operating within the national territory and provided that they affect in the same manner, in law and in fact, the marketing of domestic products and of those from other Member States.'[68]

By contrast, 'requirements to be met' by goods, such as designation, form size, weight composition, presentation, labelling and packaging, in principle remain to be judged by *Cassis de Dijon* and the rule of reason.[69] In reaching its conclusion, the ECJ also underlined three basic elements constituting the free movement of goods, elements that can be discerned also in its approach in the much earlier *Cassis de Dijon* case.[70] The three

---

65 Similar problems arise in connection with Article 49. See Chapter 11.

66 Cases C-267 and 268/91 *Criminal proceedings against Keck and Mithouard, supra* n. 5.

67 White, *supra* n. 1.

68 Cases C-267 and 268/91 *Criminal proceedings against Keck and Mithouard, supra* n. 5, paragraph 16.

69 *Ibid.*, paragraph 15.

70 Case 120/78 *Cassis de Dijon, supra* n. 8.

elements are that a legally marketed product from one Member State should not, in the absence of some overriding public interest, be required to conform to standards in the host Member State – in effect the principle of mutual recognition; that imports should not be discriminated against, either in formal terms or in fact; and that the access of imports to the market of the host Member State should be ensured.[71]

The judgment seems to be based on a distinction between those rules which are perceived to impose an additional burden on imports and those which do not. Paragraph 15 of *Keck*[72] refers back to the *Cassis de Dijon* case when discussing 'requirements to be met' and the fact that the goods would have to comply with the requirements imposed in the public interest by the Member State of origin. Rules from the importing state therefore duplicate any necessary regulation. On this reasoning, such rules are by their very nature likely to create some level of hindrance to inter-state trade.[73] By contrast, 'selling arrangements' are perceived not to constitute an extra burden: the ECJ noted[74] that the purpose of such rules was not to regulate inter-state trade directly.[75]

The ECJ's ruling has been subject to a certain amount of criticism. Despite its express statement that some of the previous case law would be overruled, there is no guidance in *Keck*[76] as to which judgments are no longer good law. It would seem, for example, that the Sunday trading rules would not now be caught by Article 28.[77] Other rules relating to licensing of premises and restricting where goods may be sold or advertised, some of which were not caught under the old case law, in any event, would equally seem to constitute 'selling arrangements'.[78] What, however, of cases such

---

71 See Chalmers, D., 'Re-packaging the Internal Market – the Ramifications of the *Keck* Judgment' (1994) 19 *ELRev* 385, p. 391.

72 Cases C-267 and 268/91 *Keck, supra* n. 5.

73 Case C-401 and 402/92 *Criminal Proceedings against Tankstation 't Heukste vof and J. B. E. Boermans* [1994] ECR I-2199, p. 2215.

74 Cases C-267 and 268/91 *Keck, supra* n. 5 at paragraph 12.

75 This point was also noted in some of the earlier judgments, for example: Case 155/80 *Oebel, supra* n.23, Case 75/81 *Blesgen, supra* n. 22, Case C-23/89 *Quietlynn, supra* n. 26, Case 69/88 *Krantz, supra* n. 25 and Case C-93/92 *CMC Motorradcenter* [1993] ECR I-5009. Contrast Case C-405/98 *Konsumentombudsmannen* v. *Gourmet International Products AB* [2001] ECR I-1795.

76 Cases C-267 and 268/91 *Keck, supra* n. 5.

77 Case C-401 and 402/92 *Tankstation 't Heukste, supra* n. 73: rules relating to closing hours for petrol stations; Cases C-69 and 258/93 *Punto Casa SpA* v. *Sindaco del Commune di Capena* [1994] ECR I-2355: closure of retail outlets on Sundays.

78 Case C-292/92 R. *Hünermund* v. *Landesapothekerkammer Baden-Würrtemburg, supra* n. 47; Case C- 391/92 *Commission* v. *Greece* (Infants Milk) [1995] ECR I-1621. See, however, the approach of the EFTA court in Case E-9/00 *EFTA Surveillance Authority*

as *Cinéthèque*?[79] Would the rule in issue in that case constitute a selling arrangement or requirements to be met? The Advocate-General in that case had suggested that the measures, which in his view did not discriminate, fell outwith Article 28, a view that is restated by at least one Advocate-General's Opinion in post-*Keck* case law.[80]

The notion of 'selling arrangement' was also unclear, as 'selling arrangements' is a term that has no particular meaning in any of the Member States' legal orders. One particular issue was whether the notion of selling arrangements would include all rules that affect the marketing and distribution of products, or whether there was there a distinction between rules that were not product-specific (such as shop opening hours) and those that related to a particular product?[81] Thus, initially, it was not clear whether advertising would be held to fall within the ambit of selling arrangement. It shortly became clear from a number of cases that advertising would be so considered.[82] This position in itself is not without difficulty: in particular, what do we mean by advertisement? In *Mars,*[83] the ECJ held that national legislation relating to an advertising campaign could not take advantage of the selling arrangement rule: the labelling of the product itself would have been affected by the rule. In *Familiapress*,[84] a question arose as to whether Austrian rules prohibiting the inclusion of prize competitions in journals fell outside the terms of Article 28 by virtue of the *Keck* ruling. Although prize competitions can be seen as a marketing device, the ECJ held that the Austrian rule was concerned with the content of the magazine and the rule dealt therefore with product requirements.[85] To this extent the purpose behind the measure is irrelevant. The central distinction between the rules in these cases and those cases where rules affecting advertising were held to constitute selling arrangements is that

---

v. *Norway*, judgment of 15 March 2002, based on Case E-1/97 *Gundersen* v. *Oslo Kommune* [1997] *EFTA Court Reports* 110: it seems from recent case law that the EFTA Court has rejected Keck as regards limitations on where products may be sold.

79 Cases 60 and 61/84 *Cinéthèque, supra* n. 18.

80 See the views of Advocate-General van Gerven in Cases C-401 and 402/92 *Tankstation, supra* n. 73.

81 See Mortelmans' suggestion, *supra* n. 1, discussed at pp. 77-78.

82 See e.g. Joined Cases C-34-36/95 *Konsumentombudsmannen* v. *de Agostini* and *TV Shop i Sverige* [1997] ECR I-3843; Case C-405/98 *Konsumentombudsmannen* v. *Gourmet International Products AB, supra* n. 75.

83 Case C-470/93 *Verein gegen Unwesen in Handel und Gewerbe Koln eV* v. *Mars GmbH* [1995] ECR I-1923.

84 Case C-368/95 *Vereinigte Familiapress Zeitungsverlags- und vertriebs GmbH* v. *Heinrich Bauer Verlag* [1997] ECR I-3689.

85 Case C-368/95 *Vereinigte Familiapress, supra* n. 84, paragraph 11.

the legislation 'bears on the actual content of the product'.[86] It thus seems that the immediate packaging of the goods has been equated to the content itself. Certainly, in the case of hallmarks the indelible nature of the mark on the product itself was emphasised.[87]

The lack of certainty following *Keck*[88] could be argued to be no more than that which follows any new development in the law. The difficulties arising out the *Keck* judgment were widely perceived to go beyond the inherent, however. In addition to the definitional issues, a number of linked criticisms were put forward. Initially, it was not considered clear whether the *Keck* test was an answer to the *Dassonville*[89] question, or whether *Keck* advocated an entirely different route for those rules that were considered to be selling arrangements.[90] It would seem more straightforward, as well as in line with the reference to *Dassonville* in paragraph 16 of the *Keck* judgment, to suggest that a common test be adopted in the first instance, that of *Dassonville*, and that *Keck* suggests that the effect of selling arrangements on trade is to indirect or too uncertain for those rules to fall foul of Article 28. *Keck* is on this view a form of remoteness test.

This view of *Keck*[91] is supported by some subsequent case law. In *DIP SpA*,[92] the refusal of municipalities to grant licences to shops to trade was challenged under Article 28. The ECJ held, after noting that the rules did not discriminate and nor was their intention to regulate trade, that,

> 'the restrictive effects which [the rules] might have on the free movement of goods are too uncertain and indirect for the obligation which they impose to be regarded as being capable of hindering trade between Member States.'[93]

A similar approach was also taken in other Article 28 cases more recently: in *BASF*,[94] the company tried to challenge a rule which required patents

86 Case C-368/95 *Vereinigte Familiapress*, *supra* n. 84. See also the opinion of the Advocate-General in the Spanish Chocolate case: Case C-12/00 *Commission* v. *Spain*, not yet decided, Opinion of 6 December 2001 at paragraph 32.

87 Case C-30/99 *Commission* v. *Ireland* (Hallmarking) [2001] ECR I-4619.

88 Cases C-267 and 268/91 *Keck*, *supra* n. 5.

89 Case 8/74 *Dassonville*, *supra* n. 7.

90 See for example the discussion of the Advocate-General in Case C-401 and 402/92 *Tankstation 't Heukste* , *supra* n. 73, especially paragraph 19.

91 Cases C-267 and 268/91 *Keck*, *supra* n. 5.

92 Joined Cases C-140-2/94 *DIP SpA* v. *Commune di Bassano del Gruppa*, *LIDL Italia Srl* v. *Commune di Choggia* and *Lingral Srl* v. *Commune di Choggia*, [1995] ECR I-3257; See also Case C-387/93 *Giorgio Domingo Banchero* [1995] ECR I-4663; and Case C-134/94 *Esso Española* v. *Communidad Autónoma* [1995] ECR I-4223.

93 Joined Case C-140-2/94 *DIP SpA*, *supra* n. 92.

94 Case C-44/98 *BASF AG* v. *Präsident des Deutschen Patentamts* [1999] ECR I-6269.

granted by the European Patent office in respect of Germany, to be translated at the cost of the patentee, into German. BASF argued that the high translation costs meant that patent holders would choose in which States they could afford to have patent protection, with a consequent impact on the States in which the product would be marketed.[95] The ECJ rejected this argument summarily.[96] Interestingly, though, in neither of these two cases did the ECJ introduce the *Keck* formula.[97]

More significantly, it is commonly suggested that by looking at the category of rules rather than the rules' effect, the ECJ has adopted an unnecessarily formal approach[98] that could mean that Member States shape their rules so as to fall outside the scope of Article 28 by being deemed to be 'selling arrangements'. Even were Member States to indulge in no such manipulative behaviour, rules that fell within the notion of selling arrangements might still have an impact on inter-state trade. This would be particularly true of rules which could operate so as to segregate national markets. This point has been made forcefully by Advocate-General Lenz, who was critical of the position ultimately adopted in the *Infant Milk* case.[99] He argued that,

> 'Article 30 [now 28] goes beyond a mere prohibition of discrimination ... The aim of Article 30 continues to be to prohibit such measures in order to establish and maintain an internal market. ... [W]hat should be determinative is the hindrance to the access to the market of imported goods.'[100]

Is the distinction between product requirements and selling arrangements in reality a discussion about dual burden rules? In *Clinique*,[101] *Mars*[102]

---

95 On the ECJ's approach to patent protection see Chapter 8.

96 The ECJ has rejected other convoluted arguments in respect of both Article 29, Case C-412/97 *ED Srl* v. *Fennochio* [1999] ECR I-3845, and Article 39, Case C-190/98 *Graf* [2000] ECR I-493, though it accepted that a tax on the installation of satellite dishes would have an impact on services. See further Chapter 11.

97 Contrast Case C-368/95 *Familiapress, supra* n. 84 and Case C-405/98 *Gourmet, supra* n. 75 both of which started from *Keck* and found Article 28 in principle applicable.

98 See comments of Advocate-General Jacobs in Case C-412/93 *Leclerc-Siplec* v. *TF 1 Publicité* [1995] ECR I-179.

99 Case C-391/92 *Commission* v. *Greece* [1995] ECR I-1621. See also Gormley, L., 'Two Years After *Keck*' (1996) 19 *Fordham International Law Journal* 866 at 879.

100 *Ibid.*, at 1628–29. See also comments of Advocate-General Jacobs in Case C-412/93 *Leclerc-Siplec*, *supra* n. 105.

101 Case C-315/92 *Verband Sozialer Wettbewerb eV* v. *Clinique Laboratories SNC et al* [1994] ECR I-317.

102 Case C-470/93 *Verein gegen Unwesen in Handel und Gewerbe Koln eV* v. *Mars GmbH, supra* n. 83.

and *Familiapress*,[103] producers would have been required by the national law in issue to change the product, thus incurring added costs. Arguably the distinction between 'selling arrangements' and 'requirements to be met' could be seen as shorthand for a rule based on discrimination. Alternatively, it could be argued that the distinction here is between two types of impact on the producer – one where the producer is required to take steps to comply with a rule, the second is where a producer is required to discontinue an existing strategy.[104] According to this distinction, the former would remain unacceptable whilst the second category would constitute a selling arrangement. A difficult boundary between the two categories remains: as the Advocate-General in *Leclerc* noted,

> 'if traders had to modify their publicity brochures in accordance with the legislation of each Member State, they would incur the same sort of additional burden that is imposed when the goods themselves have to be modified.' [105]

Certainly, the requirement in *Keck* that the rules should apply equally in law and in fact suggests the traders in imported goods cannot be affected to a greater degree than those dealing in domestic products. This would certainly match the approach in cases such as *Tankstation*,[106] where the rules concerned opening hours. As Weatherill suggested, the reason that the rules fell outside Article 28,

> 'was not that they were rules affecting selling arrangements applied equally in law and in fact, but that they were measures applying equally in law and in fact and exercising no direct impediment to access to markets of a Member State.'[107]

As regards the fact that there was no direct impediment, it should be noted that the ECJ, in discussing the law in issue in *Keck,* accepted that,

> '[s]uch legislation may, admittedly, restrict the volume of sales in so far as it deprives traders of a method of sales promotion.'[108]

---

103 Case C-368/95 *Vereinigte Familiapress, supra* n. 84.

104 Both these possibilities were noted by the ECJ in Case C-126/91 *Yves Rocher* [1993] ECR I-2361 at paragraph 15, though it then found both to be objectionable.

105 Case C-412/93 *Leclerc-Siplec* v. *TF 1 Publicité, supra* n. 98.

106 Case C-401 and 402/92 *Tankstation 't Heukste, supra* n. 73.

107 Weatherill, S., 'After *Keck*: Some thoughts on how to clarify the clarification', *supra* n. 4 at p. 895.

108 Cases C-267 and 268/91 *Keck, supra* n. 5, paragraph 13.

In paragraph 16 of *Keck*, however, the ECJ then went on to comment that a national rule prohibiting a selling arrangement 'is not such as to hinder, directly or indirectly, actually or potentially, trade between Member States'. A restriction in the volume of sales would seem to constitute such a hindrance. On one reading this might indicate an internal contradiction in the *Keck* reasoning. Alternatively, one could argue that, implicitly, it seems that the ECJ has accepted that some degree of accommodation to marketing in more than one Member State is acceptable.[109] In this position, we see reflections of the early Commission position that indistinctly applicable measures may have some impact on trade provided that those effects were proportional.

More concerns in this context arose with respect to rules prohibiting or limiting advertising. As even *Keck*[110] noted, such limitations may have an impact on trade, even if they do not prevent or hinder trade. When we consider the position of a trader trying to break into a new market, however, we can see that advertising is crucial. Thus rules that severely restrict the possibilities of advertising – or preclude it altogether – may well operate so as to partition the market. Thus in *de Agostini*,[111] the Swedish national rules that prohibited advertising aimed at children and were considered to be selling arrangements effectively precluded the producer of the goods from advertising the product.[112] The response to this point would be that selling arrangements are only excluded from the scope of Article 28 if they apply equally in law and in fact. The ECJ made this point in *de Agostini*, but referred the question – without guidance – to the national court to assess. Such an approach, of course, opens up the possibility of an unequal approach to the question between the different courts of the Member States – as occurred with the *Sunday Trading* cases.[113] As Advocate-General Jacobs noted in *Leclerc-Siplec*, the impact of advertising regulation on trade would become more acute in the case of advertising linked to direct sales.[114] The difficulty was recognised again in *Gourmet*,[115] which concerned Swedish rules prohibiting alcohol

---

109 See also the reasoning of the ECJ in Case C-391/92 *Commission* v *Greece* (Infant Milk), *supra* n. 78 at paragraph 12.

110 Joined Cases C-267 and 268/91 *Keck*, *supra* n. 5.

111 Joined Cases C-34-36/95 *de Agostini*, *supra* n. 82.

112 Note that Case C-34-36/95 *de Agostini*, *supra* n. 82 was not only concerned with the free movement of goods, but also concerned the application of the Television without Frontiers Directive and raised certain considerations about the freedom to provide services.

113 See e.g. Case 145/88 *Torfaen BC* v. *B&Q*, *supra* n. 12.

114 Case C-412/93 *Leclerc-Siplec*, *supra* n. 105.

115 Case C-405/98 *Konsumentombudsmannen* v. *Gourmet International Products AB*, *supra* n. 75.

advertising save in trade magazines and at the point of sale. There the ECJ again raised the question of whether the limitations on advertising applied equally, suggesting in this instance that they could not. The ECJ argued that the special nature of alcohol and its links to traditions in the social sphere rendered it more likely that advertising would be needed so as to counter the force of tradition.

Although the ECJ's response might seem to solve the problem in the case in issue, its approach does undermine the *Keck*[116] 'solution', suggesting that those who had criticised it for being the wrong answer – or perhaps the answer to the wrong question – may have been justified. An alternative assessment is that those who criticised *Keck* on this basis oversimplified the position somewhat. The *Keck* judgment referred to '*certain* selling arrangements',[117] which could be seen as implying that other rules which were in principle still selling arrangements nonetheless fell within the scope of Article 28, a contention which the earlier post-*Keck* case law could support. In any event, following *de Agostini*[118] and more particularly *Gourmet*,[119] it is clear that the issue to be addressed is whether the measure has an equal effect or not. This brings us back to the question of discrimination and what we mean by it. How direct must the discriminatory impact on trade be for Article 28 to come into play, and do we accept, as *Tankstation* and paragraph 13 of *Keck* seem to suggest, a certain level of constraints inherent in the notion of trading rules? Although these issues are likely to remain uncertain for the time being, what now seems beyond dispute is that the *Keck* test is not determinative. Rather than providing a solution to the perceived over-extension of Article 28, it now seems to constitute a detour in the route that rules must take to be justified under EC law. For some national measures, though not all, it constitutes a 'short cut'.

One further issue, that was indicated in but not developed by *Keck*,[120] is the question of whether the purpose of the national rule that is the subject of challenge is relevant for determining whether Article 28 is applicable or not. *Dassonville*[121] is usually explained as being an effects-based test, which means that purpose is irrelevant, yet in a number of cases, *Keck* included, the ECJ has referred to the intention of the relevant Member State – or rather the fact that the Member State had not intended

---

[116] Joined Cases C-267 and 268/91 *Keck, supra* n. 5.

[117] Joined Cases C-267 and 268/91 *Keck, supra* n. 5, author's emphasis.

[118] Joined Cases C-34-36/95 *de Agostini, supra* n. 82.

[119] Case C-405/98 *Konsumentombudsmannen* v. *Gourmet International Products AB, supra* n. 75.

[120] Cases C-267 and 268/91 *Keck, supra* n. 5.

[121] Case 8/74 *Dassonville, supra* n. 7.

to regulate trade.[122] In each of these cases the rules were held to be indistinctly applicable and the statement regarding the purpose of the measure was usually linked to the fact that the measure's effects on the internal market were too indirect and uncertain to bring the measure within Article 28. In *Tankstation*, the Advocate-General suggested that where the purpose of an indistinctly applicable measure is to regulate trade, the Court will assume that such a measure does have an impact on trade.[123] The ECJ has, however, been silent on this point. One might suggest that although the lack of intention supports a determination that a rule should not fall within the prohibition in Article 28, on its own it is not conclusive.

The position seems to have changed somewhat in the more recent case of *PreussenElektra*.[124] There, the ECJ had to consider German rules about the supply of electricity that required electricity suppliers where possible to purchase, at minimum costs, electricity produced by renewable energy schemes. The ECJ accepted that, according to previous case law,[125] rules requiring traders to purchase products from a given source prevent those traders from obtaining the products from traders in other Member States.[126] *Prima facie*, this measure would seem to fall within Article 28. In an unusual piece of reasoning, running contrary to the Opinion of the Advocate-General, the ECJ then went on to hold:

> 'However, in order to determine whether such a purchase obligation is nevertheless compatible with Article 30 of the Treaty [now Article 28], account must be taken, first, of *the aim of the provision* in question, and, second, of the particular features of the electricity market.'[127]

The ECJ then identified the purposes of a policy seeking to stimulate the use of renewable energies by reference to a number of Community acts, and specifically referred to the former Article 130r(2) and Article 6 both as amended and renumbered by the Treaty of Amsterdam, which required that environmental protection policies must be integrated into the definition and implementation of other Community policies. This point was not expanded further. Finally, the ECJ concluded that the German legislation was not incompatible with Article 28.

---

122 See cases cited at n. 75.

123 Case C-401 and 402/92 *Tankstation 't Heukste, supra* n. 73.

124 Case C-379/98 *PreussenElektra AG* v. *Schleswag AG, supra* n. 5.

125 Case 72/83 *Campus Oil* [1984] ECR 2727 at paragraph 16; Case C-21/88 *Du Pont de Nemours Italiana Spa* v. *Unita Sanitaria Locale No. 2 Di Carrara* [1990] ECR I-889 at paragraph 11.

126 Case C-379/98 *PreussenElektra, supra* n. 5 at paragraph 70.

127 *Ibid.*, at paragraph 72, author's emphasis.

This case is significant because for the first time the ECJ expressly stated that the aim of the national measure should be taken into account; in earlier cases the purpose was referred to in a much weaker way.[128] The Court also did not refer to the *Dassonville* test,[129] which is the case in which the effects-based test was first clearly expressed. Further, *PreussenElektra*[130] clearly deals with a discriminatory measure that will have a direct impact on the cross-border sale of electricity. In the earlier cases in which motive was considered indistinctly applicable measures were concerned.[131] The ECJ, in accepting a motive-based argument in relation to a discriminatory measure, has extended the sphere in which the notion of intention may be relevant. It is not longer limited to indistinctly applicable measures having only a peripheral impact on intra-Community trade. Clearly, then, there is a difference here between *PreussenElektra* and the earlier case law.

It should be noted that the purpose of the measure was in line with specified Treaty objectives, environmental protection, which following ToA have a high ranking within the Community legal order, rather than individual Member State interests. One might suggest on this basis that the effect of *PreussenElektra*[132] is limited. It still constitutes a development in the Court's jurisprudence. Although the ECJ has previously interpreted the notion of indistinctly applicable measure expansively in the light of environmental objectives,[133] it now seems that the interpretation of Article 28 itself will be subject to interpretation in the light of other Community policies. It is a little early to tell whether this approach is an isolated case or an approach limited to the environmental sphere: there are a number of areas where Treaty amendment has highlighted the importance of other policy goals – for example consumer protection[134] and public health.[135] The obligations to take these policies into account are not, however, as expressly worded as is the case for protection of the environment, a point

---

128 In Case C-391/92 *Commission* v. *Greece* (Infants Milk), *supra* n. 78, paragraphs 11-12, for example, the ECJ referred to the measure's purpose but then implied that what would matter is the measure's actual effect.

129 Case 8/74 *Dassonville*, *supra* n. 7.

130 Case C-379/98 *PreussenElektra*, *supra* n. 5.

131 See cases cited at n. 25.

132 Case C-379/98 *PreussenElektra*, *supra* n. 5.

133 Case C-2/90 *Commission* v. *Belgium* (Walloon Waste) [1992] ECR I-4431, see further below.

134 Discussed in Chapter 7.

135 Discussed in Chapter 12.

that might justify treating the position of environmental policies as exceptional.[136]

IV Boundary between Distinctly Applicable and Indistinctly Applicable Rules

One final issue relates to the question of what constitutes discrimination. It may seem that the bulk of this chapter has been spent considering whether the ECJ is concerned with discrimination or with access to the market. The question of discrimination has another consequence: indistinctly applicable measures may be justified by reference to mandatory requirements whereas distinctly applicable rules, or discriminatory rules, may be justified by reference only to the grounds set out in the Treaty.[137] The question then of where the boundary between the two classes of rules lies is of some importance. Clearly an import ban that is not reflected in a similar ban for domestic products will be discriminatory, but what about dual burden rules which have a discriminatory effect on imports? Such a rule was not considered 'discriminatory' in the *Cassis de Dijon* case.[138] The classic distinction between discriminatory measures and indistinctly applicable measures relates to their form; that is, are the measures discriminatory in law?[139]

Despite the apparent simplicity of this approach, some difficulties arise. There are, for example, questions as to whether rules that affect only imported rules (for example because there is no domestic production of the product in question) should be considered discriminatory. Although the

---

136 The impact of Treaty amendments on the ECJ's jurisprudence has been argued before the ECJ before, albeit in different contexts, but to little effect. In Case C-9/99 *Échirolles Distribution SA* v. *Association du Dauphiné* [2000] ECR 1-8207, the applicants argued that the ECJ should re-visit its case law on the fixing of book prices on the basis of completion of the internal market and the amendments introduced by TEU. The ECJ's argument was that the general principles set out in for example in Article 3 EC are to be understood in the light of the provisions designed to implement them; in this instance Articles 28-30. Since there had been no Treaty amendment of these provisions, there was no need to call the ECJ's jurisprudence into question. See paragraph 24.

137 Case 113/80 *Commission* v. *Ireland* (Souvenirs) [1982] ECR 1625 at paragraph 11; Case 207/83 *Commission* v. *United Kingdom* (Origin Marking) [1985] ECR 1201 at paragraph 22; and Cases C-1 and 176/90 *Aragonesa* [1991] ECR I-4151 at paragraph 13.

138 Case 120/78 *Cassis de Dijon*, *supra* n. 8.

139 See Case C-401 and 402/92 *Tankstation 't Heukste*, *supra* n. 73, Opinion of the Advocate-General at paragraph 15.

point is not entirely clear in the judgment, the ECJ seemed to regard French rules which limited advertising of alcohol by reference to beverage types to be discriminatory, as the rules tended to favour beverages traditionally made in France.[140] Contrast the post-*Keck Infant Milk* case.[141] There the ECJ rejected as irrelevant the argument that the national rule in issue must be discriminatory since there was no Greek production of the product in question, arguing that the rule constituted a general regulation and that the non-production within Greece of the product could change over time. The Advocate-General, however, considered the matter as a question of whether a selling arrangement applied equally in law and in fact and suggested that the fact that there was no domestic production meant that the rule did not apply equally.

Further, the ECJ does not seem to have taken a consistent approach towards the determination of discriminatory and indistinctly applicable measures, and it certainly does not seem to be based on whether the rules are phrased in an indistinctly applicable manner or not. Price fixing rules may operate to put imports at a disadvantage[142] but they can be phrased in a neutral way.[143] Generally, however, they are seen as discriminatory.[144] Equally origin marking rules which are required of both domestic and imported products would seem, on the face of it, to be an indistinctly applicable rule relating to packaging. They have, however, been treated as discriminatory rules.[145] In the UK case, which required all products irrespective of whether they constituted domestic products or imports to show their origin, the ECJ held that,

> 'the purpose of origin or origin marking is to enable consumers to distinguish between domestic and imported products and that this enables them to assert any prejudices which they have against foreign products.'[146]

The purpose was therefore discriminatory. It would appear that similar

---

140 Case 152/78 *Commission* v. *France* (Advertising of Alcohol) [1980] ECR 2299.

141 Case C-391/92 *Commission* v. *Greece*, *supra* n. 78.

142 Case 181/82 *Roussel Labaratoria BV* v. *the Netherlands* [1983] ECR 3849 concerned price fixing which distinguished between domestic and imported products.

143 Case 82/77 *Openbaar Ministerie* v. *van Tiggele* [1978] ECR 25 concerning minimum selling prices.

144 See e.g. Craig and de Burca, *EU Law: Text, Cases and Materials* (2nd ed.) (OUP, 1998), p. 591-592 although the Advocate-General in See Case C-401 and 402/92 *Tankstation 't Heukste, supra* n. 73, in footnote 36 to the Opinion seems to have taken a different approach.

145 Case 207/83 *Commission* v. *UK*, *supra* n. 137.

146 *Ibid.*, at paragraph 17.

considerations underpin the recent *Irish hallmarking* case.[147] All precious metals to be sold as such were required to be hallmarked. The Irish law recognised Irish hallmarks, certain British hallmarks and hallmarks that complied with the terms of an international convention on hallmarks. Goods manufactured outside Ireland but being hallmarked by the Irish Assay Office had a different hallmark applied to them than that applied to Irish products undergoing the same hallmarking procedure. This requirement the Court held to be discriminatory. On one view, however, the goods were being subject to the same process as domestic goods, at the same cost; it was just that the design of the hallmark that was different.

On the other side of the equation, the *Irish Origin Marking* case[148] was discriminatory in that the rules applied only to imported products. Despite the fact that the ECJ in that case noted that mandatory requirements could consequently not be relied upon, implying that the measure was discriminatory, the Court then held that it was 'necessary to consider whether the contested measures are indeed discriminatory or whether they constitute discrimination in appearance only'. Again, the ECJ was looking beyond the form of a measure to its potential effect. In a subsequent case, a rule that only wines from certain parts of Germany could be marketed in a specified shape of bottle was held to be indistinctly applicable.[149] This put imports at a disadvantage expressly by reference to place of origin. One could seek to justify this on the basis that German producers in other regions of Germany are also affected by the rule. This comparison has not, however, been adopted in other cases, such as the local grab cases,[150] also found under Article 29.[151] The approach there was that a measure is discriminatory if *some* national producers benefit from the measure. In the more recent case of *Aher Waggon*,[152] which distinguished on the face of it between aeroplanes from one Member State and all the others, the ECJ did not consider whether the measure was indistinctly applicable but focussed on whether the measure was justifiable as a mandatory requirement for the protection of the environment. Given that mandatory requirements may be used to justify indistinctly applicable measures only, it would seem as though the ECJ assumed the measure in this case to be indistinctly applicable.

---

147 Case C-30/99 *Commission* v. *Ireland* (Hallmarking), *supra* n. 87.

148 Case 113/80 *Commission* v. *Ireland*, *supra* n. 137.

149 Case 16/83 *Prantl* [1984] ECR 1299.

150 See e.g. Case C-21/88 *Du Pont de Nemours Italiana*, *supra* n. 125, at paragraph 12.

151 The question of whether discriminatory rules on the export of waste in the interests of the environment could be justified by mandatory requirements was left open in *Dusseldorp*: Case C-203/96 *Chemische Afvalstoffen Dusseldorp* v. *Minister van Volkshuisvesting* [1998] ECR I-4075.

152 Case C-389/96 *Aher-Waggon* v. *Germany* [1998] ECR I-4473.

Part of the problem in this area seems to arise from the fact that two issues are not clearly identified. The first issue is whether the measure comes within the scope of Article 28 in the first place. Much of the discussion regarding the proper scope has focussed on which indistinctly applicable measures should fall within Article 28 and whether the matter can be resolved by reference to indirect discrimination (or dual burden rules) or whether the appropriate test is based on access to the market. Whatever the answer to this question, a separate issue is which measures should be justifiable by reference to mandatory requirements and the heads of derogation in the Article 30, and which measures may only be justified by reference to Article 30. For the first question, the impact on the imported goods is crucial; for the second it is – or should be – irrelevant. What is relevant is the form, or possibly the clear purpose, of the rule.

Whatever attempt is made to rationalise the case law in one area, the *Walloon Waste* case[153] stands out. It concerned a ban on the imports of waste into Wallonia from other Member States. The Belgian Government sought to rely on a mandatory requirement, the protection of the environment, to justify the rule. The ECJ effectively ruled that the effect of what was then Article 130r(2) (now 174(2)) was to render the national measure indistinctly applicable so that it could be justified on environmental grounds. This approach was unique. The issue of discriminatory measures in the interests of the environment was raised again in *PreussenElektra.*[154] In his opinion, the Advocate-General specifically raised the difficulties on this point and suggested that the ECJ should clarify its position on whether directly discriminatory measures in general are capable of justification by mandatory requirements.[155] Rather than rely on disingenious reasoning to show that a measure is not discriminatory in the view of the Advocate-General, such an approach should be taken in relation to environmental concerns at the very least, given the importance of environmental protection.[156] As we have seen, the ECJ took a different approach leaving the issues relating to the scope of discriminatory measures unresolved.[157]

Although treating environmental rules as a special case might deal with the majority of problem cases, it does not deal with all of them. Perhaps a way forward would be, as has been suggested, to remove the distinction between discriminatory and indistinctly applicable measures; Article 30 and the mandatory requirement case law do contain safeguards against

---

153 Case C-2/90 *Commission* v. *Belgium* (Walloon Waste), *supra* n. 133.

154 Case C-379/98 *PreussenElektra, supra* n. 5.

155 *Ibid.*, Opinion of the Advocate-General at paragraph 229.

156 Note the introduction of Article 6 EC following the ToA discussed in Chapter 1.

157 Case C-379/98 *PreussenElektra, supra* n. 5, discussed pp. 91-93.

abuse and so widening the potential scope of the mandatory requirements should not result in protectionist national measures being saved.[158]

V Conclusions

Despite the volume of jurisprudence in this area and the ECJ's attempts to clarify the law in this area, the proper scope of Article 28 remain uncertain. Although the ECJ has adopted a number of different approaches to resolving this issue, fundamentally the problem remains the same: to what extent may Member States regulate in policy areas affected by trade? Recent case law indicates another issue, a point raised by Wils albeit in a different context. The question is the degree to which the completion of the internal market and the amendments to the EC Treaty, extending the scope of Community concerns, affect the interpretation of Article 28. Wils[159] suggested that, as the internal market project progressed, there would be a greater emphasis on removing the remaining barriers. Arguably the reverse is the case. We might wonder whether the introduction of provisions such as Article 6 EC signals an era in which the Community institutions, including the ECJ, will have to give greater weight to wider societal issues, whether this be in the Community policies themselves or by allowing Member States greater freedom to regulate within the scope of Community law.

---

158 See further Chapter 6.

159 Wils, *supra* n. 1.

Chapter 6

Article 29: Restrictions on Exports

I Introduction

Article 29 bears a striking similarity to Article 28; it prohibits quantitative restrictions and measures having equivalent effect, but in relation to exports rather than imports. Given the commonality between the two articles, it would seem logical to expect that there would be a similarity in terms of the manner in which the ECJ has interpreted them. To a certain extent this is indeed so, but there are also some marked differences between the two. The difference between the approaches to import and export of goods is especially noteworthy when Article 49 is considered: there is no such difference in approach between import and exports in relation to the services.[1]

II Type of Action Caught

As with Article 28, Article 29 is addressed to the actions of Member States, including regional and local authorities, and those bodies for which Member States are liable.[2] These are discussed in Chapter 3. Although the ECJ has not ruled on this point, the House of Lords[3] following the *Angry Farmers* decision[4] has accepted that measures for the purposes of Article 29 will include omissions, when Article 29 is read in conjunction with Article 10. It would seem likely that were such a matter to come before the ECJ, it would take a similar line. Certainly, Advocate-General Jacobs, in the context of a road blockade, which prevented road haulage both into and out of Austria, accepted that the failure of the Austrian authorities

---

1 See further Chapters 10 and 11. Note in the draft Constitutional Treaty Article III-42 consolidates Article 28 and 29 into one provision.

2 Contrast the position regarding services discussed in Chapter 9.

3 *R.* v. *Chief Constable of Sussex, ex parte International Traders Ferry* (HL) [1999] 2 AC 418, [1999] 1 All ER 129, [1998] 3 WLR 1260, [1999] 1 CMLR 1320.

4 Case C-265/95 *Commission* v. *France* (Angry Farmers) [1997] ECR I-6959.

constituted a restriction.[5] Further, legislative acts and administrative acts, where there is an accepted practice, will also constitute measures.[6]

III Overview of Article 29 Jurisprudence

What of the scope of Article 29; has the ECJ taken the same very expansive view of export restrictions as it has with regard to imports? From the wording of the article absolute prohibitions on exports would seem to be prohibited, as would quotas[7] – with the exception of fish conservation quotas under the common organisation for fish.[8] Export monopolies are also caught by Article 29.[9] The boundary between export quotas and export licences is not always clear,[10] but whether classified as a quantitative restriction or an MEQR, it would seem that export licences would fall foul of Article 29. This parallels the approach in Article 28. Restrictions relating to quality that are applied to goods for export, but not to those for domestic consumption, would also seem to fall foul of Article 29.[11] Article 29 applies to inspections carried out within the Member State's territory, as well as at the frontier, provided they are conducted with a view to the subsequent export of goods.[12] Article 29 thus seems to have a reasonably broad scope.

The examples given so far have, however, all been examples of discriminatory rules. The ECJ has excluded the possibility of using the indistinctly applicable approach developed in respect of Article 28. Indeed, rather than apply the *Dassonville*[13] and *Cassis de Dijon*[14] approach,[15] despite the fact that the *Dassonville* test is certainly wide enough to cover

5 Case C-112/00 *Eugen Schmidberger Internationale Transporte Planzüge* v. *Austria*, not yet decided, Opinion of the Advocate-General, 11 July 2002.

6 See further Chapter 4.

7 Case 68/76 *Commission* v. *France* (Potato Export Licence) [1977] ECR 515; Case 53/76 *Procureur de la République* v. *Bouhelier* [1977] ECR 197.

8 Cases 3, 4 and 6/76 *Kramer* [1976] ECR 1279.

9 Case C-110/89 *Commission* v. *Greece* (Maize) [1991] ECR I-2659. In this Article 29 seems more similar to Article 49 than Article 28, as state monopolies for the sale of goods are caught by Article 31.

10 This matter is discussed in more detail in Chapter 4.

11 Case 53/76 *Procureur de la République* v. *Bouhelier, supra* n. 7.

12 Case C-272/95 *Bundesanstalt für Landwirtschaft and Ernährung* v. *Deutsches Milch-Kontor GmbH* [1997] ECR I-1905.

13 Case 8/74 *Procureur du Roi* v. *Dassonville et al.* [1974] ECR 837.

14 Case 120/78 *Rewe* v. *Bundesmonopolverwaltung fur Branntwein* (Cassis de Dijon) [1979] ECR 649.

15 Discussed in Chapters 4 and 5.

exports,[16] the ECJ has adopted a more restrictive view of Article 29, focussing on discriminatory measures.[17] In the leading case in this area, *Groenveld,* the ECJ held that Article 29,

> 'concerns national measures which have as their specific object or effect the restriction of patterns of exports and thereby the establishment of a difference in treatment between the domestic trade of a Member State and its export in such a way as to provide a particular advantage for national production for the domestic market of the State in question.'[18]

This is a point which has been confirmed in a number of cases.[19]

The accepted test can be seen to have two stages:

1) the object or effect of restricting of exports; and
2) the requirement that the measure is discriminatory in that it favours the domestic market.

The first part of this test is potentially broad. It not only covers those measures that intend to restrict exports, such as directly discriminatory measures, but also those which have that effect. The inclusion of an effects-based element meant that Article 29 could apply to indistinctly applicable measures and, referring to this aspect of the *Groenveld* test alone, one could argue that there are similarities to the effects-based approach to *Dassonville*. It is the second element of the test that operates to limit the scope of Article 29, as it requires a discriminatory effect. On the

---

16 Indeed the Advocate-General in Case 15/79 *Groenveld* v. *Produktschap vooR. ee en Vlees* [1979] ECR 3409 examined whether the restriction on horse meat fell within the *Dassonville* test before applying the *Cassis* rule of reason. See also White, E., 'In search of the Limits to Article 30 of the EEC Treaty' (1989) 26 *CMLRev* 235 at pp. 278-9.

17 See Case 155/80 *Oebel* [1981] ECR 1993 in which the ECJ held that rules 'which are part of economic and social policy and apply by virtue of objective criteria to all undertakings in a particular industry which are established within the national territory without leading to any difference in treatment whatsoever on the ground of nationality of traders and without distinguishing between the domestic trade of the State in question and the export trade' fell outside Article 29, see p. 2009.

18 Case 15/79 *Groenveld, supra* n. 16, paragraph 7.

19 The ECJ applied Case 8/74 *Dassonville, supra* n. 13, in Case 53/76 *Procureur de la République* v. *Bouhelier et al., supra* n. 7. Further examples of cases where the ECJ has followed Case 15/79 *Groenveld, supra* n. 16, include: Case 237/82 *Jongeneel Kaas* [1984] ECR 483; Case 141/81 *Holdijk* [1982] ECR 1299; Case C-322/89 *André Marchandise* [1991] ECR I-1027; Case C-209/98 *FFAD* v. *Københavns Kommune* [2000] ECR I-3743.

face of it, this second requirement is a relatively narrow view of discrimination. It is not sufficient that products for the domestic market and those for the export market are being treated differently, but the test also requires that the national rule must lead to an advantage for the domestic market. It is arguable that this second requirement could result in a limited scope for Article 29 with very few export restrictions conferring an advantage to the domestic market. On the contrary, export restrictions might be seen as tending to have the opposite effect from benefiting the domestic market, limiting the markets to which domestic products can sell.

This argument depends, however, on what such an advantage in practice means.[20] Local grab measures are perhaps the clearest example of national rules where the exporting state gives its home market a special advantage. In *Inter-Huiles*[21] French rules on the recovery of waste oils provided that collectors of such oils had to deliver them to approved disposal sites where the oils would be treated. In practice this meant that there was no export of waste oils. The ECJ held that rules relating to the processing of waste would not fall foul of Article 29 where exports were still possible.[22] This statement suggests that the notion of a restriction is narrower here than it is in the context of imports and services (see further below at IV). The notion of 'advantage' was, however, not so limited. According to the judgment in *Inter-Huiles*, the advantage gained by the domestic market was the ability to acquire waste oil for disposal at a low price, an advantage unavailable to foreign waste oil collectors.[23] A similar approach can be seen regarding rules restricting the disposal of offal[24] and also as regards a prohibition on the export of live sheep.[25] Similarly in *Promalvin*, a regional bottling requirement for Rioja wine, which limited by reference to quantity the amount of wine which could be sold in bulk outside the region but which permitted bulk sales within the region, was held to fall foul of Article 29.[26]

---

20 This point is discussed further below: see Section IV.

21 Case 172/82 *Syndicate national des Fabricants raffineurs d'huile de graissage et al.* v. *Groupement d'intérêt économique 'Inter-Huiles'* [1983] ECR 555.

22 Case 172/82 *'Inter-Huiles', supra* n. 21, paragraph 11 confirmed in Case C-208/98 *FFAD, supra* n. 19, paragraph 37.

23 In this context it is difficult to reconcile the concept of discrimination used here with that adopted by the ECJ in Case C-2/90 *Commission* v. *Belgium* (Walloon Waste) [1992] ECR I-4431in respect on a prohibition on the import of waste from abroad.

24 Case 118/86 *Openbaar Ministerie* v. *Nertsvoederfabriek Nederland* [1987] ECR 3883.

25 Case C-5/94 *R.* v. *Ministry of Agriculture, Fisheries and Food, ex parte Hedley Lomas (Ireland) Limited* [1996] ECR I-2552.

26 Case C-47/90 *Établissements Delhaize Freres et Compagnie Le Lion SA v. Promalvin and AGE Bodegas Unidas* [1992] ECR I-3669.

The corollary of an approach as adopted in relation Article 29 which catches only discriminatory measures, is that export restrictions cannot be justified by rule of reason mandatory requirements. Indistinctly applicable measures would fall outside Article 29 in the first place and therefore stand in no need of justification, whether this be by reference to mandatory requirements or Article 30. This apparently clear statement is more complex than it initially looks, because it also depends to a great degree on the meaning attributed to 'indistinctly applicable measures' and 'discrimination'. As the discussion in Chapter 5 suggests, these matters are not entirely clear.[27] In any event, the limitation of Article 29 makes the determination of discrimination perhaps more significant than it might be in relation to Article 28.[28]

IV Problems with the *Groenveld* Test

It has been suggested that in taking this approach, the ECJ has been influenced by the American courts' approach to the Commerce Clause in the US Constitution and attacks on State legislation that, although phrased in general terms, actually affected out of state buyers adversely.[29] On this analysis, the US courts are seen to distinguish between the situation where the adverse consequence is merely incidental to the need to regulate the state market, such regulation being acceptable as it has little to do with inter-state trade, and the situation where the purpose behind the regulation is discriminatory. If this is the case, arguably Articles 28 and 29 would have different motivations. Other commentators have suggested that, to the contrary, a discrimination based approach reflects the fact that Articles 28 and 29 are about ensuring equal treatment of domestic and imported products and that there is a problem with dual burdens as far as imports are concerned which does not necessarily arise with regard to exports.[30] This argument works, provided always that the evil at which the free movement provisions are aimed are dual burden rules. Arguably, however, the real concern of the EC Treaty has been access to the market, as the approach towards Articles 28 and 49 illustrates.[31] Further, neither of these views deal fully with the criticism of Advocate-General Caporti in *Oebel*, who commented 'that the abandonment of a single concept of what constitutes

27 See also discussion in relation to services, especially state monopolies, in Chapter 11.

28 It has been suggested in relation to Article 28 and the justification of MEQRs that the distinction between the two categories be abandoned. See also Chapter 7.

29 See Gormley, L., *Prohibiting Restrictions on Trade within the EEC* (TMC Asser Institut, The Hague, 1985) at p. 102.

30 See Oliver, P., 'Recent Case Law on Articles 30–26 EEC' (1980) 17 *CMLRev* 109.

31 See Chapters 1, 5 and 11.

measures having an effect equivalent to quantitative restrictions is likely to give rise to confusion'.[32]

It is submitted that any such confusion has worsened as the ECJ has developed case law that is not entirely consistent. In particular, there is uncertainty as regards the key issue of whether, if the distortion of trade element of the *Groenveld* test is satisfied but the advantage to the domestic trade element is not, Article 29 applies. It has been suggested that the ECJ's approach to early case law adopted a cumulative approach to the *Groenveld* test, requiring both a restriction on exports and an advantage to the national market.[33] This issue is linked to a second point; that is, how do we determine the existence of an advantage to the domestic market? This case law in this area is confused. Certainly, from the 'local grab' cases, it is clear that the benefit to the same product or service market is not necessary; the *Groenveld* test will be satisfied if another national market receives a benefit. Nonetheless, there are cases in which the operation of the contested measure brings only dubious advantage to the domestic market. One of the earlier cases on Article 29, *Jongeneel Kaas*,[34] concerned a quality stamp relating to cheese, which was applied only to cheese for export. The measure distinguished between domestic and goods for export, but the measure brought no advantage to the domestic market. More recently, in the *Compassion in World Farming*[35] the prohibition on the export of veal calves for rearing in veal crates could not advantage the domestic market as the veal crate system had already been abolished in the UK. The ECJ did not explain its reasoning on this point, although the fact that there was relevant Community secondary legislation in this area may have affected the decision.[36] One possibility is that there is a distinction in the case law between those measures, such as those in *Jongeneel Kaas,* that formally distinguish between domestic products and those destined for exports and other rules, which do not do so. Arguably, it is only in the latter situation that a benefit for the domestic market is needed. Such an approach would match the position sometimes put forward in relation to Article 28 where distinctly applicable measures would be caught by the prohibition on MEQRs, as would any indistinctly applicable rules that imposed a dual burden.[37]

If we accept that some advantage for the domestic market is necessary, we need to look at how much advantage the domestic market receives.

---

32 Case 155/80 *Oebel, supra* n. 17, at p. 2016.

33 Gormley, L., *Prohibiting Restrictions on Trade within the EEC, supra* n. 29, at p. 106.

34 Case 273/82 *Jongeneel Kaas* v. *Netherlands, supra* n. 19.

35 Case C-1/96 *R.V. Minister for Agriculture, Fisheries and Food, ex parte Compassion in World Farming Ltd* [1998] ECR I-1251.

36 Case C-1/96 *Compassion in World Farming, ibid.*, paragraph 21.

37 See further Chapter 5.

Following *Promalvin*,[38] the Spanish government brought in rules which stated that the Rioja denominación de origen calaficada could be applied only to those wines which had been bottled at specified bottling plants within the region. Although some bottling plants in the region would benefit, some would not. These Spanish bottling plants would be in the same category as other Spanish bottling plants outside the Rioja region and those operations outside Spain altogether. The wine in question had never been prohibited from export; it was the form in which the wine was shipped that was restricted. The Belgium government brought an action against Spain for failure to comply with the *Promalvin* judgment. The ECJ considered the *Promalvin* judgment, emphasising that the bottling rules in that case,

> 'had the specific effect of restricting patterns of exports of wine in bulk and in particular, of procuring a special advantage for bottling undertakings situated in the region of production.'[39]

In assessing the facts in the second *Rioja* case, the ECJ then noted that, although the new requirements restricted the amount of bottling within the region, as well as affecting bottling outside it, the measure was nonetheless one,

> 'which has the effect of specifically restricting patterns of exports of wine eligible to bear the "denominación de origen calaficada" and thereby of establishing a difference of treatment between trade within a Member State and its export trade.'[40]

Arguably, the rule in this instance was indistinctly applicable; it certainly adversely affected Spanish bottling plants, including some bottling plants even within the Rioja region, as well as bottling plants abroad. It would seem that even a limited advantage to some operators, with a corresponding (or greater) disadvantage to other domestic operators is sufficient to trigger the second element of the test in *Groenveld*.

Contrast the approach taken in *FFAD*.[41] It concerned Danish environmental regulations that granted the rights to establish a system for the collection of building waste for recovery with a limited number of operators. Other operators were precluded from operating in that market. One of them sought to challenge the Danish regulations on a number of

---

38 Case C-47/90 *Promalvin, supra*, n. 26.

39 Case C-388/95 *Belgium* v. *Spain*, judgment 16 May 2000, at paragraph 21 referring to Case C-47/90 *Promalvin, supra* n. 26 paragraphs 12–14.

40 Case C-388/95 *Belgium* v. *Spain, ibid.*, at paragraph 41.

41 Case C-209/98 *FFAD* v. *Københavns Kommune, supra* n. 19.

grounds, including Article 29. The national rule disadvantaged those other operators in Denmark that had not acquired the exclusive right, as well as affecting the transport of waste to those outside Denmark. In this sense, the rule did not overtly discriminate because domestic operators were disadvantaged too. Certain players in the domestic market did benefit, however, from the rule. Referring to its earlier decision in *Rhône-Alpes Huiles*,[42] the ECJ re-affirmed that national rules, which precluded qualified intermediaries from participating in the collection of waste to export, would constitute an obstacle to exports contrary to Article 29.[43] The ECJ then re-iterated its ruling in *Inter-Huiles*:[44] the grant of an exclusive right in itself does not create a barrier to exports provided that the domestic regulations in question do not preclude operators from exporting their goods, or in this case, the waste for processing.

This case shows the ECJs accepting some restrictions on export trade providing such trade remains possible. In this, *FFAD*[45] is different from the *Rioja* cases.[46] In the more recent *Rioja* case the export of wine in bulk was impossible, in *FFAD* the export of waste was just more difficult. Despite the advantage to the home market, the rules in the Danish case did not necessarily contravene Article 29. *FFAD* therefore highlights a difference in approach between Articles 29 and 28, and between Articles 29 and 49. As the discussion in Chapters 5 and 11 illustrate, even a hypothetical restriction could trigger the application of Articles 28 and 49. Following *FFAD*, this is not the case for Article 29. The Advocate-General in *FFAD* raised this point. His argument was that a waste producer thinking about exporting waste could be put off exporting it because the producer would have to contract with a larger number of intermediaries than if the producer disposed of the waste within Copenhagen to the licensed companies. The ECJ did not follow the Advocate-General's argument. Its reasoning seemed to focus on the existence of a ban, the Advocate-General on the existence of a hindrance.[47]

One might question the assumption that the approach to exports has been noticeably different in practice from the *Dassonville* approach to imports. The case law can be used to highlight certain points. Certainly, the rule in the *Rioja* cases[48] suggest there is a parallel between the Court's approach to Article 29 in respect of measures that apply to both domestic

42 Case 295/82 *Rhône-Alpes Huiles* [1984] ECR 575.

43 Case C-209/98 *FFAD* v. *Københavns Kommune*, *supra* n. 19, paragraphs 42-43.

44 Case 172/82 *Inter-Huiles*, *supra* n. 21.

45 Case C-209/98 *FFAD* v. *Københavns Kommune*, *supra* n. 19.

46 Case C-388/95 *Belgium* v. *Spain*, *supra* n. 39; Case C-47/90 *Promalvin*, *supra* n. 26.

47 Case C-209/98 *FFAD* v. *Københavns Kommune*, *supra* n. 19, Opinion, paragraphs 115-6.

48 Case C-388/95 *Belgium* v. *Spain*, *supra* n. 39.

and imported products with an advantage to some players in the domestic market, and that taken in respect of indistinctly applicable measures which have a discriminatory effect under both Article 28 and 49. It would seem that the difference regarding indistinctly applicable rules arises when hindrances or 'access to the market' style issues are considered, which both Article 28 and 49 to varying degrees cover but which would not seem, according to cases such as *FFAD*,[49] to fall within Article 29.[50] More questions arise, however, when cases such as *Compassion in World Farming*[51] are concerned. *Belgium* v. *Spain* indicates that the advantage to the domestic market need only be slight to contravene Article 29, but where was the advantage, however slight, in *Compassion in World Farming*? Does the fact that the measure directly affected imports justify this distinction? If this were to be the case, there would again seem to be parallels between Article 29 and the other freedoms, in that directly discriminatory measures are treated more harshly than indistinctly applicable measures.

One other suggestion is that the difference between FFAD and Compassion in World Farming arises from the nature of the national rules in each case. FFAD condescend protection of the environment, which receives a high level of protection within the two. The ECJ made no express reference to environmental concerns in its judgment, however. It is at best abate whether the ECJ has protected and environmental considerations in other cases, especially those involving 'local grab' measures.[52] In the case law, an environmental perspective, the Court's decision might be seen as unreliable.[53] Concern for the environment has also led to anomalous case law in respect to Article 28, as can be seen in Chapter 5. In this, there are again parallels between the jurisprudence on Articles 28 and 29.

V Conclusions

There has been a certain amount of criticism of the ECJ's case law in the field of exports, as regards its internal consistency and its consistency with Article 28. Despite this, there seem to be reasonably clear parallels between the jurisprudence on the two articles, in practice if not in terms of

49 Case C-209/98 *FFAD* v. *Københavns Kommune*, *supra* n. 19.

50 See Chapters 5 and 11, especially Case C-384/93 *Alpine Investments BV* v. *MinisteR. an Financiën* [1995] ECR I-1141 in relation to services.

51 Case C-1/96 *Compassion in World Farming*, *supra* n. 35.

52 Case C-203/96 *Chemische Afvalstoffen Dusseldorp* v. *Minister van Volkshuisvesting* [1998] ECR I-4075.

53 See Chapter 7 and literature cited therein.

the wording of the test used. It is therefore misleading to suggest that Article 29 only applies to discriminatory measures without clarification, as the impact of this statement depends on how discrimination is interpreted. Of course, the danger with removing this second element of *Groenveld* and moving overtly to a *Dassonville/Cassis de Dijon* approach is that national regulation which was not intended to affect exports but which may do so to some degree would be capable of challenge under Article 29, raising again the possibility of over-extension of this article, in a similar way to the over-extension of Article 28.[54] Problematically, the ECJ has not yet considered whether Article 29 may be tempered by a rule of reason approach, as found in both Article 28 and 29. This omission may go back to the view that Article 29 affects only (directly) discriminatory measures and that a rule of reason is inappropriate in such circumstances. Nonetheless, such a view may leave some public interest concerns, notably protection of the environment, without adequate protection. Further, a distinction between the jurisprudence on Articles 28 and 29 may no longer be appropriate given the draft Constitutional Treaty currently consolidates the provisions regarding imports and exports into one article.

54 If, however, Article 29 is restricted domestic traders might be in the strange position of being able to challenge national rules under Article 28 because of their potential impact on imported goods: see e.g. wide definition of 'internal' in Joined Cases C-321-324/94 *Jacques Pistre* [1997] ECR I-2343 discussed in Chapter 4.

Chapter 7

Derogation from the Free Movement of Goods

The scope of the free movement provisions has always defined and constrained the freedom of Member States to take action. Derogation, in principle, provides the counterbalance by permitting some, albeit limited, retention of Member State sovereignty. In the Treaty derogation and through mandatory requirements we also see the tension between different policy choices highlighted. We might ask to what extent is it possible for changing policy concerns to be reflected within the grounds of derogation, whether these be express Treaty provision or the judge made justifications. Further, in assessing the interplay between free movement and other policies, it is questionable whether adequate concern is addressed to those competing policy objectives. This issue has become particularly interesting in the light of treaty revisions affecting the EC's fundamental objectives, notably environmental concerns, consumer protection and public health.

I General Rules Relating to the Interpretation of the Derogation

The ECJ has consistently held that any derogation from a Treaty freedom, whichever that freedom may be, must be interpreted restrictively.[1] This principle applies to Article 30 and manifests itself in a number of ways. The scope of the heads of derogation themselves have, on the whole, been interpreted narrowly – passing off, for example, was held not to fall within the scope of commercial and industrial property.[2] Further, the ECJ has also held that the list of grounds for derogation in Article 30 is exhaustive.[3] Thus, over the years the ECJ has held that the fairness of commercial transactions[4] and consumer protection,[5] economic policy[6] and cultural

1 See e.g. Case 7/68 *Commission* v. *Italy* (Export Tax on Art Treasures) [1968] ECR 423 at p. 430 and Case 113/80 *Commission* v. *Ireland* (Souvenirs) [1981] ECR 1625 at p. 1638.

2 Case 6/81 *Beele* [1982] ECR 707.

3 Case 95/81 *Commission* v. *Italy* [1982] ECR 2187.

4 Case 95/81 *Commission* v. *Italy*, *supra* n. 3.

5 Case 177/83 *Theodor Kohl KG* v. *Ringelhan & Rennett SA* [1983] ECR 3651.

diversity[7] all fall outside the scope of Article 30. Treaty amendment would be required to extend this list.

In the light of this approach it may initially appear surprising that the ECJ then developed a separate set of justifications which might be applied in respect of MEQRs; the *Cassis de Dijon* mandatory requirements. A number of comments may be made, however. The first is that mandatory requirements relate, with rare exceptions, to indistinctly applicable measures which, given the ECJ's interpretation of the *Dassonville* test, is a broad category including national rules which may have but little, if any, effect on intra-state trade. Further, since the *Dassonville* test itself was so wide, some form of counterbalance to an excessively deregulatory force would seem (politically) necessary. At a more technical level, mandatory requirements are not strictly a form of derogation from Article 28; they operate instead to determine its field of application. Therefore, the use of mandatory requirements means that the measure in question never contravenes Article 28 in the first place.[8]

Whether the case law supports this distinction is another question. The ECJ has held that the two types of exception are separate and that, when considering whether a national rule falls within a head of derogation, one must consider Article 30 before considering mandatory requirements.[9] Such an approach reflects a respect for the terms of the Treaty itself, in that the express treaty derogation should be used in preference to judge made rules. It, however, does not correspond with the view that indistinctly applicable rules that are protected by a mandatory requirement do not contravene Article 28 in the first place. Further, following *Familapress*,[10] it could be argued that the ECJ confirmed that mandatory requirements do constitute a derogation from Article 28, after a finding of a *prima facie* breach of that provision. The argument is based on the fact that the ECJ referred to the European Convention on Human Rights ('ECHR') which it would only have power to do were the national measures within the scope

---

6 Case C-324/93 *R.* v. *Secretary of State, ex parte Evans Medical Ltd and Macfarlan Smith Ltd* [1995] ECR I-563 at paragraph 36.

7 Case 229/83 *Association des centres distributeurs Edouard Leclerc et al. v. Sàrl 'Au blé Vert' et al.* [1985] ECR 1. On the subject of culture see further below and Chapter 12.

8 Case 177/83 *Theodor Kohl KG* v. *Ringelhan & Rennett SA, supra* n. 5, paragraph 19. For a discussion of this issue see Gormley, L., *Prohibiting Restrictions on Trade within the EEC*, pp. 51-57.

9 Case C-1/90 *Aragonesa de Publicidad* v. *Departmento de Sanidad* [1991] ECR I-4151.

10 Case C-368/95 *Vereinigte Familiapress Zeitungsverlags- und vertriebs GmbH* v. *Heinrich Bauer Verlag* [1997] ECR I-3689.

of Community law; that is, by derogating from a Community law rule. In taking this approach, the ECJ certainly departed from its earlier ruling in *Cinéthèque*,[11] in which it held that it could not refer to fundamental rights in similar circumstances.[12] In practice, however, the mandatory requirements tend to be used as a form of derogation, irrespective of the precise legal position. Certainly, it has been noted that the distinction between the two is slight and has little significance.[13]

Despite this difference, there are a number of similarities in the structure of the Article 30 derogation and the mandatory requirements, just as there are certain similarities in the ECJ's approach to the two issues.[14] There are three basic requirements in the case of both mandatory requirements and Article 30 heads of derogation: there should be no harmonizing legislation occupying the field;[15] the national rule must fall within one of the heads of derogation or constitute a mandatory requirement, as appropriate (and a Member State cannot rely on mandatory requirements in respect of matters arising in other Member States as regards restrictions on exports);[16] and the rule must, in effect, be proportional and not constitute arbitrary discrimination or a disguised restriction on trade. In both instances, the burden of proof falls upon the Member State[17] to show that the measure lies within the scope of the

---

11 Cases 60 and 61/84 *Cinéthèque SA* v. *Fédération Nationale des Cinémas Françaises* [1985] ECR 2605.

12 *Ibid.*, at p. 2627 when the Court held 'Although it is true that it is the duty of this Court to ensure observance of fundamental rights in the field of Community law, it has no power to examine the compatibility with the European Convention of national legislation which concerns, as in this case, an area which falls within the jurisdiction of the national legislators'.

13 Case C-1/90 *Aragonesa de Publicidad* v. *Departmento de Sanidad, supra* n. 9, at p. 4177.

14 Case C-1/90 *Aragonesa de Publicidad* v. *Departmento de Sanidad, ibid.*

15 Case C-39/90 *Denkavit* [1991] ECR I-3069, paragraph 19. Harmonization is discussed in Chapter 13.

16 See e.g. Case C-5/94 *R.* v. *Ministry of Agriculture, Fisheries and Food, ex parte Hedley Lomas (Ireland) Limited* [1996] ECR I-2552, but contrast Case C-384/93 *Alpine Investments BV* v. *Minister van Financien* [1995] ECR I-1141 regarding services.

17 See e.g. Case 227/82 *Leendert van Bennekom* [1983] ECR 3883, paragraph 40 and Cases C-13 and 113/91 *Criminal Proceedings against Michel Debus* [1992] ECR I-3617, paragraph 18. Note that sometimes in a preliminary reference situation national authorities will not be involved: see e.g. Case C-368/95 *Familiapress, supra* n. 10. As regards an Article 226 action, the burden of proof falls on the Commission: Case C-55/99 *Commission* v. *France* (In Vitro Devices) [2000] ECR I-11499, paragraph 30.

derogation. Finally, in all cases derogation from free movement principles must be assessed in the light of the rights guaranteed by the ECHR.[18]

II Arbitrary Discrimination, Disguised Restrictions on Trade and Proportionality

Before looking at the individual grounds that justify derogation from Article 28, we shall consider the requirements contained in the second sentence of Article 30, which have much in common with the ECJ's approach to mandatory requirements. It must also be borne in mind that sometimes the boundary between the head of derogation and the second sentence of Article 30 prohibiting disguised restrictions and arbitrary discrimination has become blurred, especially as the ECJ has interpreted into Article 30 a test of proportionality when considering whether the ground of derogation is made out.[19] It is insufficient that the measure satisfies one of the concerns identified in Article 30.[20] The measure must achieve the desired goal and go no further than is necessary to do so:[21] these are commonly referred to as the test of necessity[22] and proportionality and are also found in the case law on mandatory requirements. Arguably the tests of proportionality and necessity fulfil the same role as the prohibitions in the second sentence of Article 30; certainly the appropriateness of national measures can be assessed from both perspectives.

Despite some blurring of boundaries between the elements of Article 30, and the suggestion that at least one or other of the requirements of 'disguised restriction on trade' and 'arbitrary discrimination'[23] set out in the second sentence of Article 30 is superfluous, there is some case law specifically on the second sentence of Article 30. In *Commission* v.

18 See Case C-260/89 *ERT* v. *DEP* [1991] ECR I-2925 and Case C-288/89 *Stichting Collective Antennevoorziening Gouda* v. *Commissariaat voor de Media* [1991] ECR I-4004, albeit in the context of services, returning to the position suggested by Case 36/75 *Rutili* v. *Minister for the Interior* [1975] ECR 1205. Contrast the approach with that taken in the case of Cases 60 and 61/84 *Cinéthèque SA* v. *Fédération Nationale des Cinémas Françaises, supra* n. 11, in which the ECJ rejected an argument based on the ECHR. This case is discussed above.

19 Case C-55/99 *Commission* v. *France* (In Vitro Devices), *supra* n. 17, paragraph 29.

20 Case 132/80 *United Foods* v. *Belgium* [1981] ECR 995 regarding controls imposed on imported fish.

21 Case 104/75 *Officier van Justitie* v. *De Peijper* [1976] ECR 613.

22 Case 13/78 *Eggers* v. *Freie Hansestadt Bremen* [1978] ECR 1935.

23 This phrase seems to have been borrowed from Article XX of GATT.

France,[24] although the ECJ accepted that restrictions on the advertising of alcoholic beverages might serve a public health purpose, it held that the rule in question constituted arbitrary discrimination because the goods principally affected by the rule were imported products.[25] It has been suggested that it is possible to find the purpose, if not the definition, of the prohibition on disguised restriction in the ECJ's statement in *Henn and Darby*[26] to the effect that restrictions on trade that might be justifiable under Article 30 should not be diverted from their proper purpose.[27] This approach is supported by the ruling in *Commission* v. *UK* (Newcastle Disease),[28] which concerned a suddenly imposed ban on the import of turkeys that coincidently operated to protect the British turkey market in the period prior to Christmas. The ECJ stopped short of suggesting that the justification for a measure which addressed a legitimate concern could be vitiated purely because there was additionally an 'improper' motive on the part of a Member State. Instead, the ECJ suggested that there was a rebuttable presumption that the measure was in contravention of the second sentence of Article 30. Although this reasoning seems to make sense, it contradicts the relevant wording of the Treaty.

Proportionality raises more difficult questions. The first concern is whether the ECJ requires the same level of proportionality in all cases. It has been suggested that the ECJ has imposed a tougher approach in determining whether a measure is proportional or not in some cases than in others. Arguably, the ECJ will take a more relaxed view of proportionality where the challenged national measure has a relatively remote impact on trade. Alternatively, it may be that the ECJ views some grounds of derogation as being more sensitive than others: the ECJ has typically given a high value to the protection of human health; public morality and public security are areas where the ECJ has recognised that Member States have a certain margin of appreciation. Conversely, some grounds of derogation are potentially too broad, so that there is a risk that Member States may stretch them so that they become overused. Arguably, one could see consumer protection in this light. On the current case law, it is difficult to put any of these proposals forward as anything more than unproven hypotheses. Further, the scope of the individual categories of mandatory requirement and the assessment of whether the Member State measure is

---

24 Case 152/78 *Commission* v. *France* (Alcohol Advertising) [1980] ECR 2299.

25 For a similar approach see Case 121/85 *Conegate Ltd* v. *Commissioners of Customs and Excise* [1986] ECR 1007, discussed further below and regarding exports Case 53/76 *Bouhelier* [1977] ECR 197.

26 Case 34/79 *R.* v. *Henn and Darby* [1979] ECR 3795, discussed further below.

27 See Oliver, P. *Free Movement of Goods in the European Community* (3rd edition) (London, Sweet and Maxwell, 1996).

28 Case 40/82 *Commission* v. *UK* (Newcastle Disease) [1982] ECR 2793.

proportional in a given case is somewhat unpredictable: the line between proportional and disproportional is fine.[29]

One way of seeing proportionality is to see it as a mechanism for balancing competing interests. On this basis, the proportionality test asks whether the measure for the protection of the public interest has a disproportionate effect on the free movement of goods. Another conception asks whether the measure is disproportionate in relation to the public interest goal the measure itself seeks to protect. The former conception subordinates the ability of the Member States to set the appropriate level of public interest protection to internal market aims. The latter leaves the determination of the public interest to the Member State. The difference is whether the measure is to be assessed as proportional or whether the public interest goal itself must be proportional in internal market terms. Clearly, the approach taken will determine the freedom left to the Member States. Unfortunately, as the discussion below shows, it seems as though the ECJ has not necessarily taken a consistent view as to which of these two conceptions it wishes to adopt. Unless we wish to see a world in which free trade constitutes the ultimate value, the proportionality of a measure should be judged by reference to its own goals.

III Grounds for Derogation in Article 30

As a general rule, it seems as though the grounds for derogation in Article 30 are treated as distinct categories, although clearly there are potential overlaps between the categories[30] and attribution of a case to one or other category may well depend on the analysis that the ECJ adopts in each case. Even where a national rule supports a Community policy, a Member State cannot derogate from the principle of free movement unless that rule falls

---

29 Jarvis gives the example of Case 238/82 *Duphar BV and Others* v. *Netherlands* [1984] ECR 523 and Cases 266 and 267/87 *R.* v. *Pharmaceutical Society of Great Britain and Secretary of State for Social Services, ex parte Association of Pharmaceutical Importers* [1989] ECR 1295, noted Weatherill, S., (1990) 53 *MLR* 699. In the former case a limit placed on expenditure for medicinal products was held not to violate the then Article 30 (now 28), whereas the Advocate-General thought that there was a violation but that it was justified. In the latter case similar measures were found by the ECJ to violate then Article 30 but to be justified, whereas the Advocate-General thought the measures fell outside then Article 30 altogether.

30 See e.g. Case 72/83 *Campus Oil Ltd et al* v. *Minister for Industry and Energy et al* [1984] ECR 2727 which was discussed in relation to both public policy and public security. Public order in many instances could be ascribed to either of the two categories.

within the scope of one of the grounds for derogation.[31] Economic grounds cannot be used as justification for a restriction contrary to Article 28,[32] as this would run contrary to ideas underpinning the creation of the common market. If such a goal is to be achieved, Member States cannot protect their individual national markets. Sometimes, however, the link between the heads of derogation and economic concerns are close indeed.[33] The creation of the internal market necessitates some limitation on Member States' individual economic considerations. Nevertheless, some concerns that are closely linked to economic considerations, such as intellectual property rights, are specifically included and consequently stand out.

a) Public Morality

The proper scope of public morality is a difficult and contested issue, even within individual Member States. When taken to the Community level, these difficulties are compounded. The ECJ has held in a number of cases that Member States remain free to determine their own standards of public morality.[34] A uniform approach across the Community is not anticipated, although in the *Biotechnological Inventions* case recently, Advocate-General Jacobs suggested that some harmonization of morality has taken place.[35] There are, however, limits to the freedom: a Member State must regard the public policy issue as sufficiently serious to justify an exception to one of the fundamental Treaty freedoms and ultimately the ECJ remains free to review the scope of Member State action. Despite some of the earlier judgments, which suggested that Member States enjoy exclusive and unlimited competence in the field of public morality, the approach of Article 30 is not to reserve to Member States a sphere of action in which national measures are immune from review by reference to Community objectives.[36] *Henn and Darby*,[37] which concerned the UK rules regarding the sale of pornographic materials, was criticised for the scope it seemed to give Member States as regards the scope of public morality and, in particular, for its approach towards the division of competence between Member States and the Community in the sphere of public morality. The

---

31 Case 216/84 *Commission* v. *France* (Substitute Milk Powder) [1988] ECR 793.

32 Case 174/82 *Sandoz* [1983] ECR 2445.

33 See notably Case 72/83 *Campus Oil* v. *Minister for Industry and Energy, supra* n. 30 and discussed below.

34 Case 34/79 *R.* v. *Henn and Darby, supra* n. 26.

35 Case C-377/98 *Netherlands* v. *European Parliament and Council* (Biotechnological Inventions) [2001] ECR I-7079, Opinion, paragraph 20.

36 This approach matches that taken in relation to other policy areas too, such as social security and public health.

37 Case 34/79 *R.* v. *Henn and Darby, supra* n. 26.

concern was that viewing areas of derogation as lying outside Community competence altogether might lead to Member State abuse. It now seems that the approach in *Henn and Darby* on this particular point is no longer good law.

Given the potentially wide scope of the public morality exception, how might one identify what properly falls within it? In *Conegate*,[38] the ECJ held that evidence for such seriousness, or rather the lack of it, would be found in the fact that the Member State in question did not prohibit the manufacture or marketing of the imports the subject of the prohibition. The ECJ further held that it was a question of fact for the national court to decide whether, in a given case, there was such a prohibition, before stating that in this case restrictions on the sale of the goods in question would not constitute such a prohibition. This case can be contrasted with the earlier case of *Henn and Darby*[39] where the ECJ held that, although there was not an absolute ban on the domestic production and circulation of the goods in question, the various pieces of national legislation taken as a whole limited the relevant domestic industry as, in effect, there was no lawful trade in such material in the UK.

In some fields, such as the protection of health, there are at least some objective standards against which to verify Member State behaviour. In the field of morality, there are no such standards. As a result, the approach taken at the European level to the determination of the proper scope of the public morality exception is especially important but, also, equally sensitive. Whilst one might consider that a Member State could seek to 'hide' protectionism under the cloak of public morality, it is important that genuine moral and ethical questions are not ignored or dismissed on purely economic grounds. Arguably, morality is what distinguishes humans from animals. As a separate point, morality is often based on religion and freedom of religion is a generally recognised fundamental human right, which goes beyond membership of an established church.[40]

The approach taken in the cases outlined above match that taken in similar cases in respect of the other Treaty freedoms,[41] for example the position of prostitutes under provisions relating to the free movement of persons, and are perhaps some mechanisms for identifying in the Member State's concerns are genuine. Nonetheless, one might question the extent to which there must be absolute parity of treatment between the national

38 Case 121/85 *Conegate Ltd, supra* n. 25.

39 Case 34/79 *R.* v. *Henn and Darby, supra* n. 26.

40 Indeed the European Court of Human Rights has extend the freedom of religion to non-theistic beliefs.

41 Cases 115 and 116/81 *Adoui and Cornaille* v. *Belgium* [1982] ECR 1665, discussed further in Chapter 12.

goods and the imported products.[42] For example, even in *Henn and Darby*[43] there was not an absolute UK-wide ban on the goods in question, despite the imposition of an absolute ban on imports. Indeed, the proportionality test could be used to determine the bona fides of a national measure, identifying whether it instead constituted an attempt at disguised protectionism. Whilst Member States should remain free to identify where issues of public morality arise, the ECJ would remain free to assess whether the measures taken by the Member State are necessary and proportional to the importance of that societal goal.[44]

Although in general terms, the ECJ has refrained from determining whether there is in reality an issue of public morality, some limitations to the substantive scope of this derogation have however now crept in. Public morality could encapsulate a wide range of religious and ethical concerns. It seems that concerns regarding animal welfare, even if based on ethical concerns, do not fall within public morality but are issues of animal health.[45] The subject matter on which ethical concerns are based would seem to need to be distinct from those on which other heads of derogation are based. The ECJ's reasoning was as follows:

> 'It remains to be examined whether a Member State may rely on Article 36 [now Article 30] in order to restrict the export of calves to other Member States for reasons relating to the protection of public policy or public morality, which are not the subject of the Directive.
>
> CIWF supports recourse to those justifications simply by drawing attention to the views and reactions of a section of national public opinion that believes that the system put in place by the Directive does not adequately protect animal health. So, in reality, public policy and public morality are not being invoked as a separate justification but are an aspect of the justification relating to the protection of animal health, which is the subject of the harmonising directive.
>
> In any event, a Member State cannot rely on the views or the behaviour of a section of national public opinion, as CIWF maintains, in order unilaterally to challenge a harmonising measure adopted by the Community institutions.'[46]

---

42 There is a crucial difference between goods and people: under international law, a Member State could not 'ban' (or expel) its own nationals. A similar limitation does not arise in relation to goods.

43 Case 34/79 *R.* v. *Henn and Darby*, *supra* n. 26.

44 On the question of whether the ECJ always assesses proportionality by reference to the goal to be achieved to by reference to the national measure's impact on trade, see the discussion of public health.

45 Case C-1/96 *R.* v. *Ministry of Agriculture, Fisheries and Food, ex parte Compassion in World Farming Ltd* [1998] ECR I-1251.

46 Case C-1/96 *Compassion in World Farming*, *supra* n. 45, paragraphs 65–67.

Although the ECJ's approach has a certain logic, it is questionable whether CIWF's concerns were only about animal health. It is submitted that the CIWF were not merely concerned with the animals' welfare but with the standards of treatment that society should be prepared to condone. Just because an animal is healthy does not mean that a proposed course of treatment is right. Seen this way, the argument is about society's values (including the minimum level of rights that members of society are prepared to accord animals) – which surely equates to public morality or public policy – rather than just animal welfare. To transpose the argument to a different arena; should the EC agree public health conditions for medical research on foetuses, does this mean that there can be no discussion about whether such research is ethically right or wrong?

Compassion in World Farming[47] concerned an export restriction and as such also illustrates a difficulty in this field generally, that of the extraterritoriality of a Member State's competence. If a Member State imposes a rule on products for export, is this an attempt to impose its morality on other Member States? If we accept this reasoning, is there not a danger that Member States' ability to regulate within their own territory will be undermined in respect of producers of products for export?[48] Presumably, a distinction must be drawn between prohibiting a product absolutely and permitting a product but limiting what you can do with it. The former would seem to be acceptable; the latter much more problematic. In *Compassion in World Farming*, trade in calves was not the problem; the difficulty arose out of the treatment of the animals.

The ECJ's reasoning in *Compassion in World Farming*[49] raises another question; how are Member States to determine what constitutes public morality? The ECJ in that case discounted the possibility of referring to 'a section of national public opinion'. Although the Court made the point in the context of a challenge to a directive, the underlying point is surely worrying, especially in an area in which Member States are particularly free to determine their own standards. Even were the ECJ making the point that only a small proportion of the British public held this view, surely the weight that that group's opinions should carry is a matter for the domestic constitutional order. Despite the early criticisms that the public morality derogation would be too broad, it now seems that Member States' political choices in areas in which ethical questions arise are being foreclosed.

---

47 Case C-1/96 *Compassion in World Farming, supra* n. 45.

48 On the difficulties regarding exports see also Chapters 6 and 13.

49 Case C-1/96 *Compassion in World Farming, supra* n. 45.

b) Public Policy

The public policy exception is potentially very broad and seems, by virtue of its general nature, to come into play only when the other reasons listed in Article 30 are not applicable. Although the ECJ has accepted that the particular circumstances justifying recourse to public policy will vary between the Member States,[50] and that Member States enjoy a certain margin of appreciation in this area,[51] it is clear that the public policy exception cannot be used as a general exception to the right to free movement. The limits on its use are defined by reference to Community law rather than the Member States' various understandings of public policy. To have held otherwise would have had the potential to undermine the freedom of goods to a significant degree, as Member States would have been able to resort to a broad exception from the internal market. How then could a balance be struck between the needs of the individual Member States and the internal market? In a judgment on public policy relating to the free movement of people, the ECJ held that reliance on that exception presupposed the existence 'of a genuine and sufficiently serious threat to the requirements of public policy affecting one of the fundamental interests of society.'[52] Although there may well be some differences between the interpretation of public policy in respect of goods and people,[53] it would seem likely that the main thrust of the exception will remain the same. Thus Member States must point to some important interest that is directly threatened. It should be noted that the fact that a Member State reinforces a measure by penal sanctions does not mean that the measure in question constitutes public policy for the purposes of Article 30.[54] Further this heading is not just a collective noun for the concerns covered by mandatory requirements. Indeed, the types of policy concern dealt with under this heading in Article 30 seem narrower than those protected by mandatory requirements. Thus public policy here has nothing to do with the rule of reason.[55]

---

50 Case 41/74 *van Duyn* [1974] ECR 1337, paragraph 18 concerning the free movement of workers.

51 Case C-265/95 *Commission* v. *France* (Angry Farmers) [1997] ECR I-6959.

52 Case 30/77 *R.* v. *Bouchereau* [1977] ECR 1999, discussed in Chapter 12.

53 This would arise for two reasons: that Articles 30 and 46 are drafted differently; and that there are inherent differences between people and goods which will affect how rules are applied to them.

54 Case 16/83 *Prantl* [1984] ECR 1299 at p. 1329.

55 Case 113/80 *Commission* v. *Ireland* (Souvenirs) [1981] ECR 1625 at p. 1638 and Case 177/83 *Theodor Kohl KG* v. *Ringelhan & Rennett SA*, *supra* n. 5 at p. 3663.

As noted, the ECJ has held that Member States may not rely on the public policy exception in Article 30 in respect of economic interests.[56] It is, however, sometimes hard to draw the line between public policy and economic considerations, as can be illustrated by a number of cases. In *R.* v. *Thompson*,[57] a case concerning rules limiting the importation of coins, a public policy argument was successfully put forward based on the integrity of coinage. Similarly, public policy was relied on in relation to speculative transactions in *Commission* v. *Italy*.[58] Given that money and the stability of money is at the base of economic policy, could we not argue that these cases concerned economic policy? It has, however, been suggested that what was at issue – at least in *Thompson* – was some more general proprietary right in the currency itself. The import of currency would therefore affect one of the central attributes of a sovereign state.

Often there is a clear link between an economic concern and another policy objective, although the ECJ has not always been sympathetic to such arguments. In *Chemische Afvalstoffen*,[59] the ECJ dismissed the Dutch government's argument that a restriction on waste transportation was necessary for the viability of Dutch waste management companies whose existence would of course be beneficial to the environment.[60] Similar difficulties arise when dealing with the allocation or management of scarce or finite resources, such as national health care provision and social security.[61] It has been suggested that the public policy argument may be acceptable when the economic consideration is not the primary

---

56 Case 188/83 *Commission* v. *Ireland* [1985] ECR 1761 at p. 1776, re-iterated more recently in Case C-120/95 *Nicholas Decker* v. *Caisse de Maladie des Employés Privés* [1998] ECR I- 1831, paragraph 39.

57 Case 7/78 *R.* v. *Thompson et al* [1978] ECR 2247.

58 Case 95/81 *Commission* v. *Italy, supra* n. 3, but contrast with Case 206/80 *Orlandi Italo e Figlio* v. *Ministry for Foreign Trade* [1982] ECR 2147 and note comments of Advocate-General Warner in Case 30/77 *Bouchereau, supra* n. 52 at pp. 2025-2026.

59 Case C-203/96 *Chemische Afvalstoffen Dusseldorp* v. *Minister van Volkshuisvesting* [1998] ECR I-4075.

60 Although C-203/96 *Chemische Afvalstoffen Dusseldorp, ibid.*, does not concern public policy generally, similar concerns as regards the relationship between economic policy and the other heads of derogation arise. As regards the position regarding economic policy and environmental policy see: G. van Calster 'Court criticises Restrictions on Free Movement of Waste' (1999) 24 *ELRev* 170.

61 Case C-120/95 *Nicholas Decker* v. *Caisse de Maladie des Employés Privés, supra* n. 56 and, in the context of establishment, Case C-204/90 *Bachmann* v. *Belgium* [1993] ECR I-249. The scope of this exception has been interpreted increasingly restrictively in more recent cases: Case C-80/94 *Wielockx* v. *Inspecteur der Directe Belastingen* [1995] ECR I-2493; Case C-484/93 *Svensson and Gustavsson* v. *Ministre du Logement et de L'Urbansme* [1995] ECR I-3955.

consideration. This point is illustrated by the House of Lords' judgment in *International Traders Ferry.*[62] In that case budgetary limitations constrained the Chief Constable's ability to release police personnel to ensure that exports of live animals were not disrupted by demonstrators. Although this decision had its roots in constraints imposed by economic considerations, the House of Lords accepted that what the Chief Constable was really doing was balancing the competing public interests within the framework of resources open to him. The balance between economic and other considerations is fine however, as the ECJ case law shows, and it is far from clear that an argument by a Member State that it did not have the resources to take action against protesters would always be successful. Certainly, Member States pleas regarding internal political and financial difficulties have not been sympathetically received in the context of enforcement actions by the Commission under Article 226.

The need to take action by a Member State and the scope of the public policy exception when public order is in question, especially where there is unrest relating to the import of foreign products, has been the subject of some litigation before the ECJ. The French government sought to rely on the need to deal with public unrest in *Cullet.*[63] This argument was rejected by both the Advocate-General and the ECJ, but for seemingly different reasons. The Advocate-General pointed to that fact that were civil disturbance to be accepted as a general ground for non-compliance with Treaty provisions, it could undermine the four freedoms totally. Further, the determination of policy would be a matter for private interest groups rather than national (and supranational) institutions. The ECJ, however, merely remarked that the French government had not proved its point that it would be unable to deal with the consequences of allowing the imports. Whereas the Advocate-General seemed to refuse the argument based on public unrest as a matter of principle, the ECJ's reasoning seems to suggest that in some circumstances Member States would be able to rely on public unrest as a reason for not fulfilling Treaty obligations.

In the subsequent *Angry Farmers* case,[64] the ECJ agreed that Member States were obliged to take action to ensure the free movement of goods under Article 28 read in conjunction with Article 10. In this case, the French government had failed to fulfil its obligation by taking insufficient action against demonstrations and destruction carried out by groups of French farmers. The French government sought to argue that its failure to take sufficient action had been rooted in public order difficulties. Without

---

62 *R.* v. *Chief Constable of Sussex, ex parte International Traders Ferry* [1995] 3 WLR 802; [1998] Q.B. 477 (CA); [1999] 2 A.C. 418, [1998] 3 W.L.R. 1260, [1999] 1 All E.R. 129 (HL).

63 Case 231/83 *Cullet* v. *Centre LeClerc* [1985] ECR 305.

64 Case C-265/95 *Commission* v. *France* (Angry Farmers), *supra* n. 51.

going into great detail as to its reasoning, the ECJ simply held that Article 30 might apply in specific cases, thus reaffirming its approach in *Cullet*,[65] but that there was no justification for a global non-intervention policy. As the Advocate-General in *Cullet* implied, accepting this principle might lead to some worrying consequences. The concern can be seen in relation to the freedoms relating to the movement of individuals, for example, tensions arising from the arrival of immigrant workers particularly during periods of recession. Equally, seeking to block the protests of groups of individuals completely is worrying from the perspective of freedom of speech and freedom of association, both of which are fundamental principles in a democratic society. Should *all* protests be stopped to ease international trading links?[66]

c) Public Security

As noted above, this head of derogation has strong links with public policy. It covers matters of national security both internal and external[67] but is still a somewhat vague concept. The leading authority, *Campus Oil*,[68] has been particularly criticised for its unconvincing reasoning.[69] *Campus Oil* concerned an Irish rule that required importers to buy 35 per cent of their oil requirements from the state owned refinery at prices set by the Irish government, a rule that the ECJ held to be an MEQR. The Irish government sought to justify the rule on the basis of importance of oil for the life of the country and the need for Ireland to maintain refining capacities of its own. The ECJ, in considering whether there was a need to maintain oil flows, emphasised the exceptional importance of oil as an energy source, not only to a country's economy, but also to its essential public services. An interruption could thus, according to the ECJ, seriously affect public security. This judgment comes very close to accepting that some economic interests may fall within the scope of Article 30, although the impact of an oil crisis would be likely also to affect public services, including the police and security services. *Campus Oil* raises additional difficulties because, even if one accepted that the ECJ was seeking to protect 'essential services', in its judgment the Court did not attempt to define such services.

---

65 Case 231/83 *Cullet, supra* n. 63.

66 The issue of public protest arose in Case C-112/00 *Eugen Schmidberger Internationale Transporte Planzüge* v. *Austria*, not yet decided, Opinion of the Advocate-General, 11 July 2002.

67 Case C-367/89 *Richardt et al.*, [1991] ECR I-4621.

68 Case 72/83 *Campus Oil Ltd* v. *Minister for Industry and Energy, supra* n. 30.

69 See e.g. Gormley, L., in Vaughan (ed.) *Law of the European Communities Service* (London, loose leaf since 1990), pp. 134-9.

Subsequent case law has, however, interpreted public security narrowly, perhaps reflecting some judicial disquiet with *Campus Oil*. Even in *Cullet*,[70] which concerned similar rules to those in *Campus Oil*, [71] the Advocate-General went to great pains to distinguish the circumstances in *Cullet* from those in *Campus Oil*. Furthermore, in *Commission* v. *Greece*,[72] although the ECJ confirmed that the maintenance of oil supplies in principle could fall within the scope of the public security exception, on the facts the measure was held to be disproportionate. More recently, the ECJ has clarified that *Campus Oil* is limited to a narrow type of product: not all types of energy are so central to the running of the country as oil and they would therefore not get benefit of the *Campus Oil* approach.[73] It would therefore seem that *Campus Oil*, rather than being the leading authority, is really the exception to the rule in this area.[74]

d) Protection of Health and Life of Humans, Animals or Plants

In its case law, the ECJ does not seem to distinguish between health and life, although it has stated that the health and life of humans is more important than the health and life of animals. Indeed, it has held that 'the health and life of humans rank foremost among the property or interests protected by Article [30]'.[75] This would suggest that in determining whether there is a risk to life or health, the risk in the case of humans need not be so severe of immediate as would required with respect to animals or plants, though the actual level of risk required in a given case remains unclear.[76] As with the other heads of derogation, in the absence of harmonization, it is for the Member State to select the level of protection it wishes to adopt,[77] although it has been suggested that a Member State has

---

70 Case 231/83 *Cullet, supra* n. 63.

71 Case 72/83 *Campus Oil, supra* n. 30.

72 Case C-347/88 *Commission* v. *Greece* [1990] ECR I-4747.

73 Case C-379/98 *PreussenElektra AG* v. *Schleswag AG* [2001] ECR I-2099.

74 See particularly the view of Advocate-General Ruiz-Jarabo Colomer in Case C-398/98 *Commission* v. *Greece* (Oil Refineries) [2001] ECR I-7915, paragraphs 42–49, distinguishing Case 72/83 *Campus Oil, supra*, n. 30. The ECJ seems to imply that *Campus Oil* could still apply but held that in the case in issue the Greek Government was concerned with economic questions, see paragraphs 29-31.

75 Case C-473/98 *Kemikalieninspektionen* v. *Toolex Alpha AB* [2000] ECR I-5681, paragraph 38.

76 Oliver suggests a risk of one case in 20 years would justify Member State action: Oliver, P. *Free Movement of Goods in the European Community*, *supra* n. 27 paragraph 8.40, at p. 204.

77 Case C-400/96 *Harpegnies* [1998] ECR I-5121, paragraph 33.

a wider discretion with regard to human health and life than animal and plant health and life.[78]

i) Health and life of humans Much of the case law in this area concerns food and other products that humans consume. As a general rule, where a Member State has a concern about the risk to health or life posed by products originating in another Member State, it may take steps to deal with the concern. To do so, however, there must be a legitimate concern and the Member State of import must take into account tests and controls carried out in the Member State of origin. In particular, the importing State may not systematically duplicate controls.[79] Spot checks are acceptable, as are checks to identify subsequent damage, provided that they do not turn into *de facto* border controls.[80] Re-treatment and import licences (as opposed to import declarations of compliance) will rarely be acceptable. Requirements for health certificates will usually be justified, provided the concern itself is well grounded.[81]

One area in which there has been significant case law has been that of additives.[82] It seems that in the absence of medical proof and where the effects or safe intake of an additive are uncertain, a Member State may take action.[83] Where another Member State permits the use of the additive, the recipient Member State must authorise the use of the additive if: the international scientific data shows the additive to be harmless bearing in mind the dietary habits of the population of the Member State of import; and the inclusions of the additive meets a genuine technical need. As regards the first of these two elements, it is interesting to note that the ECJ in principle was prepared to take account of differences between the habits

78 See comments of Advocate-General Fennelly in Case C-55/99 *Commission* v. *France* (In Vitro Devices), *supra* n. 17, paragraph 39 and contrast approach regarding Member State discretion where animals are concerned in Case C-350/97 *Monsees* [1999] ECR I-2921, paragraph 30.

79 Case 124/81 *Commission* v. *UK* (UHT) [1983] ECR 203; Case C-228/91 *Commission* v. *Italy* (Fish) [1993] ECR I-2701.

80 Case C-128/89 *Commission* v. *Italy* (Grapefruit) [1990] ECR I-3239.

81 Case C-205/89 *Commission* v. *Greece* (Certificate of Health) [1991] ECR I-1361.

82 Contrast the approach with regard to food additives to that taken regarding pesticides, where the ECJ's approach differed markedly. Arguably, since the pesticide cases predated the additive cases, the earlier cases may be no longer seen as good law. Certainly the ECJ also seemed to take a similar approach with regard to dangerous chemicals. Where the Member State has raised the possibility of there being a medical concern but the precise impact was not known, it was not inappropriate for that Member State to take measures: Case C-473/98 *Toolex*, *supra* n. 75.

83 Case 53/80 *Officier van Justitie* v. *Koninlijke Kaasfabriken Eyssen* [1981] ECR 409; Case 178/84 *Commission* v. *Germany* (Beer) [1987] ECR 1227.

of the populations of the Member States, an approach it has not always been prepared to take in other areas, such as consumer protection.[84] The difference can be seen as further evidence of the high value ascribed to human health reaffirmed by the Treaty itself in Article 152(1). The case law provides further detail on the meaning of 'technical need'. It may be nutritional, as in *Sandoz*,[85] or economic. Furthermore, a Member State may not argue that because it is possible to make the product without the additive, there is no technical need for its incorporation in the product.[86] The Member State must take into account the way the product is actually made. In addition, the Member State must make available a procedure for obtaining the authorisation and provide an appeal mechanism should the authorisation not be granted. Although Member States may impose labelling requirements, these obligations should be aimed at providing the consumer with information rather than making the supervision of imports by the importing State easier.[87]

The ECJ has generally been sensitive to Member States' concerns about maintaining public confidence in pharmaceuticals and medical devices. It accepted that a rule prohibiting the substitution of generic pharmaceuticals for brand name products was necessary in the interests of public health.[88] The need to maintain the supply of prescription drugs has also fallen within Article 30.[89] At the same time, national rules restricting the import of prescription drugs have been held not to fall within the health justification.[90] The distinction between these cases is unclear. The provision of public health care is discussed under services,[91] although many of the rules limiting who can sell certain types of product[92] may now not fall within Article 28 as a result of *Keck*.[93] Some uncertainty has been

---

84 Consumer protection is discussed at III (a) below.

85 Case 174/82 *Sandoz, supra* n. 32.

86 Case 178/84 *Commission* v. *Germany* (Beer), *supra* n. 83.

87 Case 217/99 *Commission* v. *Belgium* (Notification Numbers) [2000] ECR I-10251.

88 Cases 226 & 227/87 *R.* v. *RPI ex parte Association of Royal Pharmaceutical Importers & Others, supra* n. 29.

89 Case C-324/93 *R.* v. *Secretary of State, ex parte Evans Medical Ltd and Macfarlan Smith Ltd, supra* n. 6.

90 Case 215/87 *Schumacher* v. *HZA Frankfurt* [1989] 617; Case C-62/90 *Commission* v. *Germany* (Prescription Drugs) [1992] ECR I-2575.

91 See further Chapter 9.

92 Case C-271/92 *Laboratoire de Prothèses Oculaires* v. *Union Nationale des Syndicates d'Opticiens de France* [1993] EC4R I-2899; Case C-369/88 *Delattre* [1991] ECR I-1487, but contrast the reasoning in Case C-108/96 *MacQuen, Pouton, Godts and Grandvision* [2001] ECR I-837 concerning services and establishment.

93 Joined Cases C-267 and 268/91 *Keck and Mithouard* [1993] ECR I-6097.

introduced as to the scope of the derogation despite the importance of the interest protected.

Other types of concern have been found to fall within the health and life of humans: rules regarding wood working machines,[94] roadworthiness checks for second hand cars;[95] and concerns about public health arising from alcohol consumption.[96] The scope of the derogation is therefore not limited to diseases and drugs. More recently, noise emissions insofar as they were severe enough to have an impact on health were also held to fall within this category.[97] This broad approach would seem to reflect the definition of health set down by the World Health Organization, recognised by the ECJ in the social policy field, that health constitutes 'a state of complete psychic, mental and social well-being'.[98] Nonetheless, there must be some link between the rule and the need to protect public health. The genuineness of the risk is therefore not just relevant to questions of proportionality, as discussed above, but also for the making out of the life and health ground in the first place. This point can be illustrated in a number of cases. A minimum alcohol requirement was not found to fall within Article 30[99] nor was a prohibition on the sale of bread concerning more than a certain quantity of dry matter.[100] Some of these issues were, however, analysed as matters of consumer protection, discussed further below.

Despite the wide view of health accepted by the Court,[101] it should be noted that the health of humans has not been used to protect concerns regarding the living environment generally; there must be an additional direct risk to health,[102] although recent case law was thought to illustrate a potential change in the ECJ's emphasis. In *Chemische Afvalstoffen Dusseldorp*,[103] the ECJ rejected the Dutch government's attempts to

---

94 Case 188/84 *Commission* v. *France* (Woodworking Machines) [1986] ECR 419.

95 Case 50/85 *Schloh* v. *Auto Controle Technique* [1986] ECR 1855.

96 Case C-1/90 *Aragonesa de Publicidad* v. *Departmento de Sanidad, supra* n. 9.

97 Case C-389/96 *Aher-Waggon GmbH* v. *Germany* [1998] ECR I-4473.

98 Case C-84/94 *UK* v. *Council* (Working Time Directive) [1996] ECR I-5755.

99 Case 120/78 *Rewe* v. *Bundesmonopolverwaltung fur Branntwein* (Cassis de Dijon) [1979] ECR 649.

100 Case 130/80 *Kelderman* [1981] ECR 527.

101 Case C-84/94 *Working Time Directive, supra* n. 98.

102 Case C-2/90 *Commission* v. *Belgium* (Walloon Waste) [1992] ECR I-4431, although note that earlier case law implied the possibility of taking a broader approach: Case 125/88 *Nijman* (Improsol) [1989] ECR 3533 where ECJ noted that pesticides 'present significant risks to the health of humans and animals and to the environment'. See also Case 94/83 *Albert Heijn* [1984] ECR 3263.

103 Case C-203/96 *Chemische Afvalstoffen Dusseldorp* v. *Minister van Volkshuisvesting, supra* n. 59.

justify a rule controlling the export of waste shipments on the basis that the rule was based on economic concerns, but in doing so it did seem to leave open the possibility that, were economic policy not involved, a measure could in principle be justified on general environmental grounds.[104] This issue arose again in *FFAD* v. *Københavns Kommune*, in which the ECJ returned to a narrower view, linking the protection of the environment to the need to show some sort of risk to health.[105] This development is slightly unexpected as, in general, the ECJ seems, in the light of the amendments brought in by the ToA, to be according the protection of the environment higher protection.[106] The issue of environmental protection is consider further at (ii) and III (b) below.

ii) Animal life and health There are three main themes that run through the case law in this area: first, the need to protect the health of the animals and plants from diseases and disease control. This is usually linked to persons with an economic concern in the animals. Broadly speaking, rules similar to those on health checks and other inspections in respect of food and drugs apply here too. Secondly, it now seems that Article 30 extends to cover animal welfare;[107] this was a precursor to the developments at Treaty level. The Treaty of Amsterdam replaced the Maastricht Declaration on animal welfare with a protocol on the same subject. Finally, health and life of animals has been used to protect rare or endangered species,[108] and it is in here that we see links with the mandatory requirement of protection of the environment. The ECJ, reflecting its approach to environmental questions and the health and life of humans, *FFAD* notwithstanding, seems recently to have been taking a more expansive approach. In the *Danish Bees* case[109] the ECJ accepted that the protection of biodiversity would justify reliance on the health and life of animals. Thus, there is less emphasis on the immediate risk to life or health of the animal. Interestingly, in making this judgment the ECJ did not really investigate the necessity of the measure for the purposes of the proportionality test; instead it accepted that the approach taken by the

---

104 See Denys, C., 'Note on Case C-203/96 *Chemische Afvalstoffen Dusseldorp*' [1999] *European Environmental Law Review* 21.

105 Case C-209/98 *FFAD* v. *Københavns Kommune* [2000] ECR I-3743.

106 See Article 6 EC and consider approach in Case C-379/98 *PreussenElektra AG*, *supra* n. 73 discussed in Chapter 6.

107 Cases 141-3/81 *Holdijk* [1982] ECR 1299.

108 Case C-169/89 *Gourmetteries* [1990] ECR I-2143. There is now Community secondary legislation dealing with plants and animals under threat of extinction, discussed in Case C-510/99 *Tridon* v. *Fédération Départmentale des Chasseurs de l'Isère and FRAPNA* [2001] ECR I-7777.

109 Case C-67/97 *Ditlev Bluhme* [1998] ECR I-8033.

Danish Government was in accordance with principles accepted in international law.

e) Protection of National Treasures Possessing Artistic, Historic or Archaeological Value

There is no case law in this area, although – or perhaps because – there is now Community secondary legislation on concerning cultural goods.[110] The secondary legislation, however, is not so much focussed on the protection or development of culture[111] but on the need to ensure that stolen works of art are retrieved. Given the lack of jurisprudence in this area, there is some uncertainty as to what would constitute a national treasure.[112]

Arguing from the ECJ's case law in respect of the other grounds for derogation, it can be assumed that it is in principle for each Member State to determine its own scale of values as to what may be termed a 'national treasure'. Part of the difficulties in this area arise from the fact that there are textual differences between the different language versions of the Treaty. Whereas the English and French language text refer to national treasures, other language versions refer to 'artistic heritage'. This difference in wording may have some consequence for the type of works found to be within Article 30. National treasures need not have the same level of artistic merit that is implied by 'artistic heritage'. Of course, items with historical and archaeological value need have no artistic merit; their value comes from their antiquity. Similarly, 'treasure' seems to imply that the work in question is of special importance; arguably 'heritage' is more general and does not carry this connotation. It is in any event clear that the goods covered by Article 30 cannot be seen as all cultural goods: the reference to national treasure would seem to require a link with the cultural history of a particular country, however widely that is defined. Questions in this context relate to whether works of value only to a specific region may be included within the scope of Article 30, and whether the requirement that the work be national limits a Member State to taking action in respect of works which have been produced within that Member

110 Council Regulation 3911/92 on the Export of Cultural Goods to Third Countries [1992] OJ L 395/1 and Directive 93/7 on the Return of Unlawfully removed Cultural Objects [1993] OJ L 74/74. See Biondi, A. (1997) 34 *CMLRev* 1173. The directive has been amended, most recently by Directive 96/100/EC [1997] OJ L 60 and both pieces of legislation are currently under review: see COM (2000) 845 and COM (2000) 844 [2001] OJ C 120. See also the UNIDROIT Convention of 24th June 1995.

111 See development of case law on the function of copyright, Chapter 8.

112 The preambles to Directive 93/7 specifically state that the items listed in the Directive should not be used as guidance by the ECJ in interpreting Article 30.

State. Such a reading is somewhat parochial and could operate to deprive Europe as a whole of some valuable works.

It is interesting to note that the ECJ has specifically excluded cultural diversity from the scope of Article 30,[113] suggesting that in any event the notion of the items protected are restricted to those of 'high culture'. Some caution should be exercised in this context, however, as this judgment predated the introduction of the Community's formal cultural competence contained in Article 152. Nonetheless, the Treaty still does not define what is meant by culture for these purposes. A wider view of culture might have been implied by Article 152, but the ECJ has specifically refused to review its judgment in the French book prices case, despite the completion of the internal market and the changes introduced by TEU, because there have been no relevant changes to Article 28–30.[114] If this is the case, this approach applies equally to other rules within the cultural sphere. Arguably, the express widening of EC policies by the TEU and subsequent treaties would seem to have little effect,[115] despite the obligation in Article 152(4) requiring the Community to take cultural aspects into account in its action under other provisions of the Treaty. As the Community institutions themselves seem to be aware, heritage items seem to constitute a very limited sense of daily culture.[116] Nonetheless, it seems that less highbrow cultural works remain to be protected by the mandatory requirements.[117]

f) The Protection of Industrial and Commercial Property

This is the area in which there has been, perhaps, the most case law as it goes to the heart of many business activities. Since there are differences in structure between the head of derogation and the other grounds set out in Article 30, the questions relating to industrial and commercial property are dealt with separately in Chapter 8.

---

113 Case 229/83 *Association des centres distributeurs Edouard Leclerc et al.* v. *Sàrl 'Au blé Vert' et al*, *supra* n. 7.

114 Case C-9/99 *Échirolles Distribution SA* v. *Association du Dauphiné* [2000] ECR I-8207.

115 Note the ECJ did refer to Article 151 in the context of copyright: discussed in Chapter 8.

116 See policy documents on television policy and Harrison and Woods 'European Citizenship: Can European Audio-visual Policy make a Difference?' (2000) *Journal of Common Market Studies* 471-94.

117 Cases 60 and 61/84 *Cinéthèque*, *supra* n. 11. Contrast the position with regard to services Chapter 12.

IV Mandatory Requirements

As noted earlier, mandatory requirements are a judge-made development based on the *Cassis de Dijon* ruling.[118] Mandatory requirements and the rule of reason cannot be relied on in relation to export restrictions for the purposes of Article 29. In contrast to the position under Article 30, the list of mandatory requirements is not exhaustive, a point which may be deduced from the use of the phrase 'in particular' when the ECJ first enumerated its list of examples.[119] This point has been confirmed by subsequent case law with the protection of the working environment;[120] environmental protection;[121] plurality of the media;[122] protection of national socio-cultural characteristics:[123] and protection of cultural expression[124] all being found worthy of protection in addition to the original list of 'effectiveness of fiscal supervision, the protection of public health, the fairness of commercial transactions and the defence of the consumer'. Despite the fact that there is obvious overlap between the ECJ's original list of mandatory requirements and the heads of derogation in Article 30 in that public health occurs in both mandatory requirements and the Article 30 justifications are, as noted earlier, normally taken to be mutually exclusive. It is also accepted that mandatory requirements may be used only when the measure in question is indistinctly applicable,[125] although there are some difficulties in determining this boundary.[126] As with Article 30, the ECJ interprets mandatory requirements restrictively and subjects them to an assessment of proportionality. Difficulties with the ECJ's assessment of proportionality have already been noted. Sections a) and b) will consider two of the potential mandatory requirements more closely: consumer protection and environmental protection. These areas

---

118 Case 120/78 *Cassis de Dijon, supra* n. 99.

119 Case 120/78 *Cassis de Dijon, supra* n. 99, at paragraph 8.

120 Case 155/80 *Oebel* [1981] ECR 1993.

121 Case 302/86 *Commission* v. *Denmark* (Danish Bottles) [1988] ECR 4607.

122 Case C-368/95 *Familiapress, supra* n. 10 .

123 Case 145/88 *Torfaen BC* v. *B & Q plc* [1989] ECR 3851.

124 Cases 60 and 61/84 *Cinéthèque, supra* n. 11 .

125 Case 207/83 *Commission* v. *UK* (Origin Marking) [1985] ECR 1201, paragraph 22 Joined Cases C-1 and 176/90 *Aragonesa, supra* n. 9, paragraph 13, although the Advocate-General in his Opinion in Case C-379/98 *PreussenElektra AG* v. *Schleswag AG, supra* n. 73, stated at paragraph 220, that this position was until recently well established but suggested that the ECJ should revisit this point. In its judgment the ECJ avoided the issue.

126 See e.g. Case C-2/90 *Walloon Waste, supra* n. 102; Case C-389/96 *Aher-Waggon GmbH* v. *Germany, supra* n. 97. This matter is discussed further in Chapter 5. See also discussion of services at Chapters 11 and 12.

are highlighted as they are fields in which there has been a considerable amount of jurisprudence and so some trends in the ECJ's jurisprudence may be discernable.

a) Consumer Protection

Although early statements by the ECJ indicated that consumer protection and prevention of unfair competition were one and the same mandatory requirement, it seems clear that they are now regarded as two separate issues, albeit closely linked in terms of the circumstances that give rise to them. Consumer protection arguments have arisen in many circumstances to do with the sale of goods and thus could have a significant impact on the free movement of goods and the creation of the internal market. This is especially the case because the justification for many consumer protection measures is based on an assumption of what the consumer in a given Member State is likely to think of as normal.

Although in many areas the ECJ has left it to the relevant Member State to identify where mandatory requirements need protecting, it has constrained Member States' freedom in this field somewhat by introducing some elements of a Community definition of the consumer who needs protecting, particularly in the field of misleading advertising. Jurisprudence during the nineties has outlined the level of consumer protection that will be acceptable; that aimed at protecting the reasonably well-informed and reasonably observant and circumspect consumer.[127] It would also seem that the risk of confusion to the consumer must be significant, although to a certain extent the assessment of these factors lies in the hands of the national courts.[128]

Even where the ECJ accepts the principle of consumer protection, it still takes a stringent test towards the assessment of whether the measure is necessary and proportional. As a general rule, as the *Cassis de Dijon*[129] case itself illustrates, a prohibition on the sale of a product will not be permissible when labelling will suffice to convey relevant information to the consumer. This point has occurred frequently with respect to what may be termed 'recipe laws', that is the rules that regulate the content of foodstuffs and beverages.[130] Not all labelling is, however, acceptable:

---

127 Case C-210/96 *Gut Springenheide and Rudolf Tusky* v. *Oberkreisedirector des Kreises Steinfurt-Amt für Lebensmittel Überwachung* [1998] ECR I-4657, paragraph 31.

128 Save where the facts are obvious; see Case C-210/96 *Gut Springenheide, supra* n. 127, paragraph 30, confirmed in e.g. Case C-366/98 *Yannick Geffroy* [2000] ECR I-6579, paragraph 19.

129 Case 120/78 *Cassis de Dijon, supra* n. 99.

130 For example see Case 120/78 *Cassis de Dijon, supra* n. 94 relating to liqueurs; Case 788/79 *Italy* v. *Gilli and Andres* [1980] ECR 2071 (vinegar); and Case 407/85 *Drei*

some labelling requirements may merely add to producers' costs without providing any more information than that which was already available.[131]

Language requirements, which are another aspect of labelling, are subject to limitations. In *Geffroy*[132] the ECJ outlined the basic criteria. A Member State may not require the use of a specific language for the labelling of foodstuffs without taking into account the possibility that another language could be understood by the purchaser,[133] nor may the Member State require the labelling to be in the language most widely spoken in the area where the product is offered for sale, even if the use of other languages is not excluded.[134] By contrast, where a specific language is prescribed but the national rule also permits, as an alternative, the use of a language easily understood by consumers, such a rule is acceptable.[135] The distinction between these situations is fine and it is not immediately obvious how to reconcile them, especially when the matter is viewed from a consumer protection perspective. The ECJ seems to have prioritised the concerns of producers not to incur extra costs over the need to ensure that consumers in a given locality are likely to be able to understand the information that is provided on product labels.

The case law in the area of consumer protection has not been without its critics. As with the other grounds of derogation, in principle it is for the Member State to determine the level of protection it thinks appropriate, however the principle of proportionality limits this significantly. Clearly, as in *Cassis de Dijon*,[136] where less intrusive mechanisms are available, such mechanisms should be used. The ECJ seems to have gone further than this, though, in its jurisprudence on misleading advertising. Through the introduction of the notion of the reasonably well-informed and reasonably observant and circumspect consumer, termed the 'average consumer' (though this is not necessarily the case), the ECJ has limited the Member States' scope for determining which consumers to protect, and when. Further, the requirement that risk of consumer confusion be significant further limits Member States' freedom of action. The ECJ seemingly favours consumer protection through choice and integration rather than

---

Glocken GmbH v. *USL Centro-Sud & Provincia Autonoma di Bolzano* [1988] ECR 4233 (pasta).

131 See e.g. Case C-217/99 *Commission* v. *Belgium* (Notification Number), *supra* n. 87.

132 Case C-366/98 *Geffroy, supra* n. 128. Labelling requirements have to a certain extent been harmonized: see Directive 79/112/EEC of 18 December 1978 on the approximation of the laws of the Member States relating to the labelling, presentation and advertising of foodstuffs [1979] OJ L 33/1, as amended.

133 Case C-369/89 *Piageme* v. *Peeters* [1991] ECR I-2971.

134 Case C-85/94 *Piageme* v. *Peeters* [1995] ECR I-2955.

135 Case C-385/96 *Goerres* [1998] ECR I-3341.

136 Case 120/78 *Cassis de Dijon, supra* n. 99.

consumer protection by means of national integration and this is a position that has been subject to some criticism.[137] It may well be that the consumer best able to take advantage of increased choice may not be the consumer most in need of consumer protection legislation. In this context, it should be noted that the ECJ in its earlier jurisprudence had accepted that certain groups may need particular protection: the less intelligent; the less well-informed; and even those who are simply very busy.[138] It is not clear how this earlier line of jurisprudence relates to the jurisprudence introducing the circumspect and well-informed consumer and, in particular, whether the earlier jurisprudence has simply been superseded by the approach in subsequent cases.

Beyond this, the ECJ has adopted a Community notion of the consumer, and in doing so has not always paid full attention to differences between Member States.[139] The '*Clinique*' case[140] is one example of this problem: the German authorities sought to prevent the use of the word 'Clinique' because of risk of confusion to the German language speaker with the work 'Klinik', meaning hospital. Although the peculiarities of a particular group of consumers had previously been advanced before the ECJ before to justify some particular need for regulation, the ECJ in this case did not accept the argument and found the national measure unjustified. More worrying, it reasoned by analogy with the approach in other Member States, which undermines the entire point that only German speakers were at risk from this particular misunderstanding.[141] Admittedly the ECJ has not always disregarded linguistic diversity,[142] but the differences in approach between the various cases introduce a lack of certainty in this area.

In the *Estée Lauder* case,[143] which concerned the allegedly misleading use of the wording 'lifting' in respect of a face cream, the ECJ stated that

---

137 Weatherill, S., 'Recent Case Law concerning the Free Movement of Goods: Mapping the Frontiers of Market Deregulation' (1999) 36 *CMLRev* 51.

138 Case 382/87 *Buet* v. *Ministère Public* [1989] ECR 1235.

139 Contrast the approach with regard to trade marks in Cases C-317/91 *Deutsche Renault A.G.* v. *Audi AG* [1993] ECR I-6227, discussed in Chapter 8.

140 Case C-315/92 *Verband Sozialer Wettbewerb eV* v. *Clinique Laboratories SNC et al* [1994] ECR I-317.

141 It also misses the point that each Member State is free to choose its own standards and the fact that something is acceptable in one Member State does not mean is has to be acceptable in another.

142 Case C-313/94 *Fratelli Graffione SNC* v. *Ditta Fransa* [1996] ECR I-6051, which concerned the Cotonelle trade mark.

143 Case C-220/98 *Estée Lauder Cosmetics GmbH & Co OHG* v. *Lancaster Group GmbH* [2000] ECR I-117.

to apply the 'average consumer' test, the national court should bear in mind,

> 'whether social, cultural or linguistic factors may justify the term "lifting", used in connection with a firming cream, meaning something different to the German consumer as opposed to consumers in other Member States.'[144]

This approach introduces an element of subjectivity into the European definition of consumer, thus allowing for some differences between the Member States. Additionally in this case, the ECJ specifically stated that, as a fall-back position a national court could commission a survey to determine whether the term is in fact misleading. How this possibility of actual consumer perceptions will operate within the framework of a theorized, objective European notion of consumer is not clear. There is a concern that, as happened in the *Sunday Trading* cases,[145] there will be a variety of national court reactions.

Since Maastricht, consumer protection has expressly been introduced as a Community concern. Following the changes made to the EC Treaty by the Treaty of Amsterdam,[146] the Community is under an obligation to protect 'the health, the economic interests of consumers, as well as promoting their right to information, education and to organise themselves in order to safeguard their interests.' Further Article 153(2) EC as amended by the ToA requires consumer protection requirements to be taken into account in defining and implementing other Community policies. Although the precise consequences of Article 153 are as yet unclear, it could require the ECJ to take the need for a high level of consumer protection into account when interpreting Articles 28-30.[147] It is submitted that the test of the reasonable circumspect and well-informed consumer is not wholly consonant with such an obligation.

---

144 *Ibid.*, paragraph 29.

145 See e.g. Case 145/88 *Torfaen BC* v. *B & Q plc* [1989] ECR 3851, discussed in Chapter 5.

146 The changes introduced by the ToA strengthened the former Article 129a EC considerably by making explicit reference to specified consumer rights. Consumer rights have also been incorporated into the EU Charter of Fundamental Rights, although these are expressed to be based on ex-129a, now 153 EC.

147 Contrast the approach taken with regard to culture: Case C-9/99 *Échirolles Distribution SA* v. *Association du Dauphiné*, *supra* n. 114, where the ECJ suggested that a change in Articles 2 and 3 would be required with Case C-379/98 *PreussenElektra*, *supra* n. 73, which concerned the protection of the environment. The relationship between the four freedoms and Treaty general principles is discussed in Chapter 1. See also Chapter 13 for a discussion of the interrelationship of the specific treaty base for flanking policies with Article 95.

b) Protection of the Environment

The ECJ accepted that the protection of the environment could constitute a mandatory requirement in the *Danish Bottles* case.[148] Given the potential for protection of the environment via concerns for health and life of humans, plants and animals, environmental concerns in this context have been more addressed to quality of environment rather than issues that pose a specific, immediate threat. Thus, recycling[149] and waste management[150] cases have played a significant role in the development of this area of law.[151]

The ECJ's case law in this area has, however, been the subject of some criticism: although in principle Member States, in the absence of harmonization,[152] remain free to set their own standards, in practice this freedom has been diluted by reference to proportionality and the impact of the measures on the free movement of goods. The ECJ has adopted a similar approach to its interpretation of other grounds for derogation and seeks to identify if the measures taken are appropriate, i.e. necessary to achieve the policy aim – here environmental protection.[153] More worryingly the ECJ sometimes conflates the question of necessity with the issue of proportionality, in its narrow sense. It seems as if the Member State's freedom to assess the level of protection is subject to the impact the measure will have on inter-state trade. Thus, the Commission in *Danish Bottles*[154] suggested that the Member State's aims should not be excessively high and that less intrusive means should be used even if they are less effective than the means chosen. Even more problematically, the ECJ itself seems undecided as to whether proportionality should be

---

148 Case 302/86 *Commission* v. *Denmark* (Danish Bottles), *supra* n. 121.

149 *Ibid.*

150 Case C-2/90 *Walloon Waste*, *supra* n. 102, Case C-203/96 *Chemische Afvalstoffen Dusseldorp*, *supra* n. 59.

151 Noise pollution as well as being a health risk could be seen as affecting the environment: Case C-389/96 *Aher-Waggon GmbH* v. *Germany*, *supra* n. 97 and Advocate-General Jacobs suggested that renewable energy policy was similar capable of falling within protection of the environment: Case C-379/98 *PreussenElektra*, *supra* n. 73.

152 This issue is not always the most clear-cut: see the differing approaches of the Advocate-General and the ECJ in Case C-1/96 *Compassion in World Farming*, *supra* n. 45. Harmonization is discussed further in Chapter 13.

153 Although it has not always been the most consistent; it seems to take a more rigorous approach when mandatory requirements are under consideration than health and life issues. Contrast approach in Case 169/89 *Gourmetterie*, *supra* n. 104 and Case C-67/97 *Ditlev Bluhme*, *supra* n. 109 with Case 302/86 *Danish Bottles*, *supra* n. 121.

154 Case 302/86 *Danish Bottles*, *ibid.*

decided by reference to the impact on free movement or to the public interest goal, a point which can be illustrated by the case of *ABDHU*.[155] The ECJ first held that,

> 'the principle of freedom of trade is not to be viewed in absolute terms but is subject to certain limits justified by the objectives of general interest pursued by the Community provided that the rights in question are not substantially impaired.'

It continued, however, that the measures should not 'go beyond the inevitable restrictions which are justified by the pursuit of the objective of environmental protection'.

There are a number of difficulties with the jurisprudence in this area. It is confused. Further, by referring to the impact on trade, the ECJ has cut down Member States' freedom of choice as to the level of protection to be afforded in this area. There has consequently been an impact on the attribution of competence between the Community level and the Member States. Finally, one might question whether a narrow approach to the protection of the environment is consistent with the changes introduced by the ToA.

As we have already seen, a number of flanking policies now expressly state that they should be taken into account within general Community policy and in each instance that there should be a high level of protection.[156] Environmental policy, however, receives a higher degree of emphasis. Article 174 refers to the need for a high level of protection in this area, Article 176 provides that Member States may, within the scope of the EC Treaty, take more stringent measures than the harmonized Community standards and Article 6 provides that environmental protection requirements must be integrated into the definition and implementation of Community policies. Although these provisions may seem similar to those introduced in relation to other flanking policies, the fact that the requirement to take environmental protection into account is contained in the general provisions section of the Treaty is suggestive of the fact that this goal has attained a fundamental status with the Community legal order. Furthermore, and by contrast to the other flanking policies, an express reference to sustainable development is found in Article 2 EC. The ECJ seems, at least on one instance, to have taken these concerns into account

---

155 Case 240/83 *ADBHU* [1985] ECR 531, paragraphs 12 and 15.

156 See e.g. Article 152(1) regarding health discussed in Chapter 12 and see also discussion of Cases C-267-8/95 *Merck* v. *Primecrown* [1996] ECR 1-6285, discussed in Chapter 8 and Article 153(2) concerning consumer protection discussed at (2) above).

when considering the free movement provision.[157] Nonetheless, the general approach as regards mandatory requirements still does not seem fully to reflect the political institutions' concerns in the environmental field. It is hoped that this is be purely because the ECJ has not yet had much opportunity to development new lines of jurisprudence post ToA.

V Themes and Conclusions

The case law indicates that the scope of mandatory requirements and Article 30 have developed over time, responding to changing societal concerns. The development of these principles is important because they constitute the judicial mechanisms by which policy clashes may be resolved and also a mechanism by which the competence over such issues may be determined. Underlying the positive aspects of this development is a concern about the interpretation of the scope of the grounds of derogation in practice and the application of the proportionality principle. A rule of thumb in this area which balances Member States' concerns about societal issues with the need to ensure free trade is that the Member States are free to identify when there is an issue worthy of protection whilst the ECJ tests the relevant measures' appropriateness and proportionality. This division seems to have been blurred. The ECJ has repeatedly held that any derogation from Treaty freedom should be interpreted narrowly; worryingly this means that not only the measures themselves are tested for necessity and appropriateness, but the policy goals themselves may be judged by reference to the internal market and the goal's impact on that market – although even the ECJ seems unsure as to when and how this test applies. The concern about competing policies is underscored by the repeated Treaty amendments that have introduced formal recognition of the higher value to be placed on issues such as consumer protection and environmental protection, which have not always received the attention that they merit from the ECJ.

---

157 See Case C-379/98 *PreussenElektra, supra* n. 73.

Chapter 8

Protection of Commercial and Industrial Property Rights

I Introduction

The protection of industrial and commercial property, a term which is equated here with intellectual property rights (IPRs), is one of the heads of derogation identified in Article 30 EC.[1] It is discussed separately because in some crucial respects it differs from the other grounds of derogation in Article 30. Whereas the case law on the latter concerns the interplay between EC freedoms and Member State policy choices, in the field of intellectual property rights the tension is different. The challenge is not, in general, to the policy choice itself. The granting and protection of intellectual property rights and the national rules underlying them seem to be accepted, although questions might arise regarding their scope. This question of the rights' scope means that tension arises at a later stage, between private actions and the need to ensure the free movement of goods concerning the field in which they exercise such rights and how they are exercised. This statement itself is not without difficulty, however, as the ECJ in many cases involving intellectual property rights has stated that it is not concerned with the exercise by private parties of their rights. Apparently, the express concern is the underlying legislative base for those rights. Whether this is really the case or not is another issue; the ECJ's rulings in this area have been inconsistent.[2] Certainly the line between the two positions is fine.

This area is, in any event, problematic. It contains a basic contradiction between the fundamental principle of the free movement of goods and the fact that, according to Article 295 EC, the systems of property ownership within the Member States are expressed to be unaffected by Community rules. Although it appears that this provision was originally intended to make clear that nationalisation was not inconsistent with the Treaty,[3] industrial and commercial property is clearly a form of property right

1 The categories of 'industrial and commercial property' are not closed.

2 See discussion in Chapter 3.

3 Written Question 346/80 OJ [1980] C 123/6.

within Article 295 and therefore the potential conflict between that provision and Article 28-30 was an issue which the Court had to resolve. These rights are granted because they are perceived as a way of encouraging technical development and product improvement and therefore may also result in economic growth. Equally, however, their main function is to give their holder certain rights in relation to a particular territory which can create monopolies and partition the market, for example through exclusive distribution rights. Ambivalence about the desirability and scope of intellectual property rights, given their potential impact on competition and the market structure, are not unique to the EU; similar concerns have arisen in the field of public international trade law also.[4] The derogation in Article 30 does not explain how this tension is to be resolved; it merely states that industrial and commercial property rights can constitute an exception to the free market principle.

The ECJ has sought to solve the problem by interpreting the scope of both Article 295 and Article 30 narrowly. In the *Compulsory Plant Breeders Licence* case,[5] the ECJ commented:

> 'Article 222 [now 295] cannot be interpreted as reserving to the national legislature, in relation to industrial and commercial property, the power to adopt measures which would adversely affect the principle of free movement of goods within the Common Market as provided for and regulated by the Treaty.'[6]

As regards Article 30, the ECJ has sought to distinguish between the existence of the right and the exercise of the right.[7] The question of existence or scope of the intellectual property right has been left to the Member States: as suggested above, the ECJ has fought shy of holding that national legislation does not fall within the scope of Article 30.[8] The ECJ thus seems to assume that the grant of the right is in accordance with the first sentence of Article 30, although the grant of any such rights must always respect the principle of non-discrimination on the grounds of

---

4 U. Joos and R Moufang 'Report of the second Ringberg Symposium' in *GATT or WIPO?*, Beier and Schricker (eds) (1989, IIC Studies, VCH) at p. 31.

5 Case C-30/90 *Commission* v. *UK* (Compulsory Plant Breeders Licence) [1992] ECR I-829.

6 Case C-30/90 *Compulsory Plant Breeders Licence*, *ibid.*, at p. 865.

7 Cases 56 and 58/64 *Établissements Consten SA* v. *Commission* [1966] ECR 299; Case 24/67 *Parke, Davis & Co.* v. *Probel* [1968] ECR 55.

8 Case 144/81 *Keurkoop* v. *Nancy Kean Gifts* [1982] ECR 285; Case 53/87 *Maxicar* v. *Renault* [1988] ECR 6039.

nationality contained in Article 12 EC.[9] Ironically, given the ECJ's reluctance to recognise economic considerations within other grounds of derogation, the Treaty itself, in its focus on intellectual property rights, seems to encapsulate reasoning with could be considered to be linked to such concerns.

By contrast, the exercise of the right has been the subject of much case law under Article 30.[10] This issue is essentially about the scope of the freedom allowed to the holders of intellectual property rights. The ECJ has sought to limit the exercise of the relevant right to its 'specific subject matter',[11] which presumably will need to be defined in relation to each type of intellectual property right. Indeed, in some cases the ECJ has referred to the essential function of the right in question to determine the rights' scope.[12] Seeking to go beyond the protection of the essential subject matter of the right will constitute abuse of the right, rather than constituting its normal use.[13] In terms of the wording of Article 30, although the national rule has fallen within one of the heads of derogation in the first sentence, it has failed the test in the second sentence. That is, the effect is disproportionate or constitutes 'a means of arbitrary discrimination or a disguised restriction on trade'. The approach taken by the ECJ can be reduced thus: a right holder has the right to market a product for the first time,[14] but once the holder has placed the goods on the

---

9 Cases C-92/92 and 326/92 *Phil Collins* v. *Imtrat Handellsgesellschaft mhH* [1993] ECR I-5145. See also the discussion of the rental right in Case C-200/96 *Metronome Musik GmbH* v. *Musik Point Hokamp GmbH* [1998] ECR I-1953 as not being disproportionate.

10 See e.g. Case 119/75 *Terrapin* v. *Terranova* [1976] ECR 1039.

11 Whether the different types of intellectual property right deserve different levels of protection is another questions: see comments of Advocate-General Dutheillet de Lamothe in Case 40/70 *Sirena* [1971] ECR 69: 'Both from the economic and from the human point of view the interests protected by patent legislation merit greater respect than those protected by trade marks ... From the human point of view, the debt which society owes to the 'inventor' of the name 'Prep Good Morning' is certainly not of the same nature, to say the least, as that which humanity owes to the discoverer of penicillin.'

12 See e.g. Case C-10/89 *SA CNL-Sucal NV* v. *Hag GF AG* (Hag II) [1990] ECR I-3711. In some cases the ECJ refers to the essential function of the right which somewhat confusingly seems to be a slightly different concept from the right's specific subject matter.

13 This approach seemingly subjects the actions of private parties to the Treaty rules; see Chapter 3 for further discussion.

14 Although the ECJ has tended to characterise this right in a positive manner, this is not always the case: the right holder of an patent improving on an earlier patent may be reliant on the holder of the earlier rights to be able to market the subsequent product.

market within the EC, it can not rely on intellectual property rights to limit the further sale of those products. These principles are known as the doctrines of consent and exhaustion. They limit the right holders' ability to prevent parallel imports and thus to partition the market, because such rights would not form part of the specific subject matter of the right.[15] Of course, when the value of a type of property lies in the exercise of such rights, by limiting those rights it would seem as though at least part of the existence of the right is being challenged. The key question therefore is, when has the right in question been exhausted?

The ECJ's case law has been subject to criticism on the grounds that its jurisprudence is inconsistent and that the ECJ's perceived view of the specific subject matter of the intellectual property right in question does not necessarily relate to the usually accepted function of the right. To a certain extent it may be that, in the absence of harmonization, some differences are inevitable: intellectual property rights are based in the national legal systems of the Member States and therefore may vary both as the circumstances in which rights will be granted and as to the scope of the right under national law. The criticism goes further than this. According to one author,

> '... the concept of specific subject matter is often redefined in order to justify the outcome of the case, whereas the principle of exhaustion will not automatically be applied when the intellectual property owner consents to putting the protected products on the EC market.'[16]

The result is, however, that in the absence of a clear analysis by reference to the function ascribed to the rights,[17] the distinction between existence and exercise becomes unclear, as does the distinction between use and abuse. Equally, the notion of 'consent' is somewhat opaque. Consequently, although broad themes can be identified within the jurisprudence, in some instances the Court's rulings have been unpredictable. Further, it is case

---

15 This reasoning first appeared in Case 78/80 *Deutsche Grammaphon* v. *Metro* [1971] ECR 487 and developed in Case 15/74 *Centrafarm* v. *Sterling Drug* [1974] ECR 1147 and the point is re-iterated in many cases: see for example Case 144/81 *Keurkoop* v. *Nancy Kean Gifts, supra* n. 8, regarding industrial designs, especially at 2873.

16 I. Govaere, *The Use and Abuse of Intellectual Property Rights in E.C. Law* (1996, Sweet and Maxwell: London) at p. 4.

17 Contrast the approach of the Advocate-General in Cases 56 and 58/64 *Consten and Grundig, supra* n. 7, with that taken by the ECJ and the ECJ's failure to distinguish between different intellectual property rights in Case 58/80 *Dansk Supermarked A/S* v. *A/S Imerco* [1981] ECR 181. It would seem that function and specific subject matter are not the same things: F-K Beier, 'Industrial property and the free movement of goods in the Internal Market' [1990] *IIC* 131 at p. 148.

law that might be seen as skewing the balance in favour of the internal market rather than the protection of intellectual property holders' rights, despite statements in the jurisprudence regarding the need to respect national systems of property ownership. As far as IPRs are concerned, we see the same issue arising as occurs in relation to other heads of derogation: the relative strength of the internal market in the Community scale of values. The difference is that here other actors are affected: private parties' actions are the subject matter of review rather than those of the Member States.

II Patents

The leading case in this area is that of *Centrafarm* v. *Sterling Drug*,[18] which concerned the patent for a drug that was owned in both the United Kingdom and in the Netherlands by Sterling Drug. The drug was on sale at a much lower price in the UK than in the Netherlands. Centrafarm sought to import into the Netherlands drugs which had been legally marketed in the UK, undercutting the Dutch price set by Sterling Drug. The ECJ acknowledged the essential function of a patent: 'to reward the creative effort of the inventor' by giving the inventor,

> 'the exclusive right to use an invention with a view to manufacturing industrial products and putting them into circulation for the first time ... as well as the right to oppose infringements.'[19]

Creative effort is rewarded therefore by the right to obtain monopoly profits. Although this approach was in line with that taken by the internal systems of the various Member States, at the EC level there was a proviso. These rights were limited and, in particular, could not be used to prevent parallel imports,

> 'where the product has been put onto the market in a legal manner, by the patentee himself or with his consent, in the Member State from which it has been imported ...'.[20]

In this case, we see the beginning of the doctrine of exhaustion of rights.

One reading of *Sterling Drug*[21] suggests that the exhaustion doctrine depends on the existence of parallel patent protection in the Member States

---

18 Case 15/74 *Centrafarm* v. *Sterling Drug*, *supra* n. 15.

19 Case 15/74 *Centrafarm* v. *Sterling Drug*, *supra* n. 15, at p. 1162.

20 Case 15/74 *Centrafarm* v. *Sterling Drug*, *supra* n. 15, at p. 1163.

21 Case 15/74 *Centrafarm* v. *Sterling Drug*, *supra* n. 15.

from which the parallel imports originate. On this basis, the patent-holder has already obtained his monopoly profits when the products are marketed in that Member State.[22] This reasoning proved not to be the case. *Merck* v. *Stephar*[23] concerned parallel imports originating from Italy, a country in which no patent protection for the relevant product was available under national law. Despite the fact that the patentee was not able to derive monopoly profits, or obtain the other benefits usually attributable to patents, in respect of the parallel imports from Italy, the ECJ still held that exhaustion had occurred. In particular, it held that,

> '[t]hat right of first placing a product on the market enables the inventor, by allowing him a monopoly in exploiting his product, to obtain the reward for his creative effort, without, however, guaranteeing that he will obtain such a reward in all such circumstances.'[24]

The ECJ based this conclusion on the fact that it is for the patentee to decide where and when to market the product for the first time, bearing in mind all the implications of that choice. The patentee in this case had made an informed commercial choice and had to take the consequences of that choice. This approach seems inconsistent with the view which assumes that the patent-holder is entitled to exercise its patent rights, albeit only once; in *Merck* v. *Stephar*, the patent rights had not been exercised at all. The emphasis in the ECJ's case law seems to be moving from an emphasis on the function of the patent to reward the patentee for its inventiveness, noted in *Centrafarm* v. *Sterling Drug*, to a focus based on the issue of the patent-holder's consent instead.[25]

The centrality of consent was re-emphasised in *Pharmon* v. *Hoechst*.[26] The case concerned a medicinal product for which Hoechst held patents in three Member States. In one of these countries, the UK, the product was subject to compulsory licensing. Despite the ruling in *Merck*, which would have indicated that Hoechst had chosen to market in the UK knowing of the compulsory licensing system for this type of product and therefore could not rely on its patent rights to prevent parallel imports from the UK, the ECJ held here that there had been no exhaustion of rights. The ECJ

---

22 W. Alexander 'Intellectual Property and the Free Movement of Goods – 1996 Case Law of the European Court of Justice' [1998] *IIC* 16 at p. 23.

23 Case 187/80 *Merck* v. *Stephar* [1981] ECR 2063.

24 Case 187/80 *Merck* v. *Stephar*, *ibid.*, paragraph 10, p. 2081, see also Advocate-General's Opinion at p. 2090.

25 The ECJ had the opportunity to overrule Case 187/80 *Merck* v. *Stephar, supra* n. 23 in Case C-267-8/95 *Merck* v. *Primecrown* [1996] ECR I-6285, but, contrary to the suggestion of the Advocate-General, chose not to.

26 Case 19/84 *Pharmon* v. *Hoechst* [1985] ECR 2281.

held that the compulsory nature of the licence meant that the patent-holder could not be said to have been able 'to determine freely the conditions under which he markets his products'.[27] Although the ECJ's approach in this case may seem to have much to commend it from a right holder's perspective, it is somewhat difficult to reconcile the approach of the ECJ in *Pharmon* and in *Merck*. It may be that the ECJ simply revised its view of consent,[28] or that *Pharmon* is limited to the compulsory licence situation. One point seems clear. Despite the ECJ's references to the specific subject matter of the patent, and even its essential function, the rights of the patent-holder are not always protected from the imperatives of the single market. Consent and the doctrine of exhaustion are the vehicles used to define the limits of protection conferred by patents and consequently the scope of patent-holders' permissible behaviour.

III Copyright

The ECJ confirmed in *GEMA*[29] what had been implicit in the earlier *Deutsche Grammaphon* case:[30] that copyright fell within the scope of Article 30. Some had felt that while 'industrial and commercial property' clearly covers intellectual property, the same was less obvious with regard to artistic property.[31] In *GEMA* the matter at issue was the importation into Germany of records and cassettes from other Member States, where they had been marketed with the copyright holder's consent. The royalties received were set at the level of the Member State of origin, often lower than the rate applicable in Germany. The copyright management society, GEMA, sought to recover the difference in royalties payable in Germany and in the other Member States, but the ECJ, adopting a similar stance to that which it adopted in *Merck* v. *Stephar*,[32] held that the copyright holders had agreed to distribution in the light of the knowledge of the different levels of remuneration throughout the Community. The fact that the royalty rate in the UK was set via the imposition of a statutory licence, and was not

27 Case 19/84 *Pharmon* v. *Hoechst, ibid.*, at paragraph 25.

28 See also developments in copyright: Joined Cases 55 and 57/80 *Musik-Vertieb GmbH & K-Tel International* v. *GEMA* [1981] ECR 147; and Case 341/87 *EMI Electrola* v. *Patricia* [1989] ECR 79, and the difficulties for trade marks arising from common origin. See further below.

29 Joined Cases 55 and 57/80 *Musik-Vertieb GmbH & K-Tel International* v. *GEMA, supra* n. 28.

30 Case 78/70 *Deutsche Grammaphon* v. *Metro, supra* n. 15.

31 See the comments of Advocate-General Warner in Case 62/79 *Coditel SA* v. *Ciné Vog Films SA* [1980] ECR 878, at p. 878-9 and 881.

32 Case 187/80 *Merck* v. *Stephar, supra* n. 23.

agreed commercially, was irrelevant. Thus, the doctrine of exhaustion based on consent was introduced into copyright. The function of copyright, or even its specific subject matter, was not considered. The point that consent is crucial was re-emphasised in *EMI Electrola*.[33] There, *GEMA* was distinguished on the ground that the marketing in the Member State from which the parallel imports originated was due to the expiry of the protection period rather than as a result of an act or the consent of the copyright holder. Thus, in *EMI Electrola*, the copyright holder could enforce its national law rights. *EMI Electrola* can be seen as a move away from implied consent, or consent under compulsion, to actual consent. A similar approach can be seen in relation to patents in *Pharmon* v. *Hoechst*.[34] Whether the ECJ maintains this approach is another question.

GEMA[35] was also distinguished in *Warner Bros* v. *Christiansen*.[36] *Warner* concerned rental rights for videos. Under Danish law the consent of the copyright holder was required before a video could be hired out; in the UK this was not the case. Christiansen bought a video in the UK and imported it into Denmark, intending to rent it out without the consent of Warner Bros. The matter came before the courts and was referred to the ECJ. Christiansen sought to rely on *GEMA*, but the ECJ rejected this argument. It took the view that the specific right to authorise video rentals would be rendered worthless were that right to be considered exhausted by the sale of the video in a Member State that did not have specific rules regarding video rental. The facts in *Warner Bros* are different from the normal parallel import situation. The difference arises from the nature of videos, in that an individual video permits many viewers to enjoy the artistic work from the same physical manifestation of that work. This point was re-emphasised in *Laserdisken*,[37] when the ECJ held that the placing of a film or other such recordings out for rental does not exhaust the author's rental rights; the exclusive right to hire out copies can by its very nature be exploited repeatedly.[38] On this reasoning, *Warner Bros* seems to have an application beyond video and films. In *Metronome Musik*,[39] the goods at issue were music compact discs and, following the logic in *Warner Bros*,

33 Case 341/87 *EMI Electrola* v. *Patricia, supra* n. 23.

34 Case 19/84 *Pharmon* v. *Hoechst, supra* n. 26.

35 Joined Cases 55 and 57/80 *Musik-Vertieb GmbH & K-Tel International* v. *GEMA, supra* n. 28.

36 Case 158/86 *Warner Bros.* v. *Christiansen* [1988] ECR 2605. Rental rights are now dealt with in a Directive: Council Directive 92/100 [1992] OJ L 346/61.

37 Case C-61/97 *Forenigen af Danske Videogramdistributører* v. *Laserdisken* [1998] ECR I-5171.

38 Case C-61/97 *Forenigen af Danske Videogramdistributører* v. *Laserdisken, ibid.*, especially paragraph 18.

39 Case C-200/96 *Metronome Musik GmbH* v. *Musik Point Hokamp GmbH, supra* n. 9.

the ECJ accepted that there was a separate and valuable market for the renting out of the discs.[40] Presumably given the different ways in which recorded works may now be accessed, the principle in *Warner Bros* and *Metronome Musik* would extend to cover those situations, even were the issue to be discussed as a derogation from Article 49.[41]

These cases are all phrased in terms of consent, although the ECJ's careful attention to the type of marketing to which the copyright holders have consented determines the ultimate ruling as to whether this constitutes respect for copyright. Does consent, as understood within the ECJ's jurisprudence, protect all aspects of copyright? Copyright seeks to protect innovative endeavour in the field of creative or artistic activity. Creators can control the use of their work, thus potentially providing remuneration for that work. It should also be noted that copyright protects other interests besides the financially motivated: those of moral rights. Copyright recognises that the author of a work might have artistic pride in his or her achievement, which also justifies some control on what people can do with that work. Therefore, unlike the position for patents, the point that a creator of a work has sold that work does not conclude all the debates about the creator's interests in the work.[42] Whether the exhaustion doctrine protects this element of copyright is far from clear. Certainly it seems that the main focus of the ECJ's attention in *Metronome Musik* was to protect authors' economic rights rather than to take into account other considerations, such as moral rights.[43] Interestingly, however, the ECJ in this case referred also to Article 151 and the obligation of ensuring the flowering of cultures by promoting artistic creativity, suggesting that the ECJ was reading Article 30 in the light of the new Treaty provisions. Certainly, it seemed to indicate that copyright seen within Article 30 was not purely about economic motivations.

It is, however, difficult to develop a general rule relating to the relationship between Article 30 and the new Treaty provisions. In the

---

40 Case C-200/96 *Metronome Musik GmbH* v. *Musik Point Hokamp GmbH*, *supra* n. 9, paragraph 15 see also Opinion of the Advocate-General, paragraph 14. This reasoning is drawn from Case 195/87 *Ministère Public* v. *Tournier* [1989] ECR 2521.

41 The ease of copying music was noted by the ECJ: Case C-200/96 *Metronome Musik GmbH* v. *Musik Point Hokamp GmbH*, *supra* n. 9, paragraph 24.

42 See also Directive on Resale Rights for the Benefit of the Authors of Original Works of Art, 3 July 2001.

43 Moral rights include the right to be identified as the author of a work (paternity right); and the right to object to derogatory treatment of a work (integrity right). On the subject of moral rights and free movement see L. Ubertazzi 'Copyright and the Free Movement of Goods' [1985] *IIC* 46 and the comments of Advocate-General Tesauro in Case C-200/96 *Metronome Musik GmbH* v. *Musik Point Hokamp GmbH*, *supra* n. 9, paragraph 12.

Merck v. *Primecrown* case,[44] concerning patents, the ECJ rejected an argument based on Article 152 and the obligation to take steps towards ensuring 'a high level of human health protection', which might have been considered an analogous obligation, albeit in a different field.[45] One way to rationalise this distinction is to return to the respective justifications for copyright and patents; whereas the subject matter of patents exist *only* in the economic sphere the subject matter of copyright tends to have another aspect – those of social and cultural values. Nonetheless, the inter-relationship between this aspect of Article 30 and the new Treaty provisions remains unclear. In this lack of clarity, there are parallels between the jurisprudence on intellectual property rights and the case law in respect of the other heads of derogation.

IV Trade Marks

Trade marks do not confer exclusivity in the relevant product. They are therefore different from the other forms of intellectual property right discussed here. Instead, trade marks relate to the brand name and are a designation of origin.[46] They prevent third parties trading on any good name that the owner of the brand name has built up through producing quality products. Trade marks, and other designations of origin, can also be seen from a consumer protection perspective:[47] the mark gives the consumer information about the quality of the product via the identification of the manufacturer or the place of manufacture and some designations of origin (including 'indirect' indications such as specific packaging shapes),

44 Case C-267-8/95 *Merck* v. *Primecrown, supra* n. 25.

45 Indeed, one might argue that the terms of Article 152(2) EC impose a stronger obligation on the institutions than those of Article 151.

46 Designations of geographical origin have also been held to fall within the scope of Article 30, although to a certain extent Community law on this subject has been harmonized: Case 3/91 *Exportur SA* v. *Lor Sa and Confiserie du Tech* [1992] ECR I-5529. Nonetheless, there remains a significant body of case law on the subject: see e.g. Case 12/74 *Commission* v. *Germany* [1975] ECR 181; Case C-47-90 *Ets Delhaizes Frères et Compagnie Le Lion SA* v. *Promalvin SA et al* [1992] ECR I-3669; Joined Cases C-321-324/94 *Pistre* [1997] ECR I-2343, some of which has been subject to heavy criticism e.g. Beier in *Protection of Geographic Denominations of Goods and Services* Cohen Jehoren (ed) (Alphen aan den Rijn, 1980); Beier, 'Note on Case 3/91 *Exportur SA*' (1994) 25 *IIC* 73.

47 See for example the reasoning in Case 9/93 *IHT International Heiztechnik* v. *Ideal Standard* [1994] ECR I-2789; more traditional views of the trade mark see it as protecting the right of the proprietor, as the submissions of the Commission and the Opinion of the Advocate-General at paragraph 101 in *Ideal Standard* illustrate.

for example the *Bocksbeutel* case,[48] have been discussed as such under the rule of reason.[49] Designations of origins should in any event be considered separately. Since by their nature they cannot be exhausted, they are therefore subject to different rules from intellectual property. This section will deal with trade marks that do not fall within designation of origin rules.

The leading case relating to trade marks and the internal market is *Centrafarm* v. *Winthrop,*[50] which again involved the parallel importation of pharmaceuticals but which this time related to an infringement of the trade mark under which the drug was sold. The ECJ took a similar approach to that in the *Sterling Drug* case[51] regarding patents, looking to identify the specific subject of a trade mark. The ECJ focussed on the element of the trade mark that makes it valuable to its owner: the goodwill associated with that mark. The ECJ concluded that the mark granted the trade mark proprietor (or to some other person/entity with the proprietor's consent) the right to first marketing of the product bearing the trade mark. Note that the doctrine of exhaustion elaborated by the ECJ in respect of trade marks relates to goods placed on the market in the EC and not those marketed elsewhere: there is no doctrine of international exhaustion of rights.[52]

The approach in *Winthrop*[53] would suggest a parallel approach to the other intellectual property rights based on consent. A consent-based approach may protect the producer's rights, at least to some degree, but is the sole function of trade marks the protection of the manufacturer's goodwill? The Court took the opportunity in *Hoffmann-La Roche*[54] to develop its ruling in *Winthrop.* In particular, the ECJ held that the function of the trade mark is to guarantee the identity of the trade marked product to the consumer or end user.[55] If considerations of confusion and consumer protection are introduced, a number of other related issues arise. The first relates to the scope of the trade mark right as regards trade marks that are not the same but are similar. More difficult questions arise when the same

---

48 Case 179/85 *Commission* v. *Germany* [1986] ECR 1201.

49 Perhaps the most famous example would be the *Dassonville* case: Case 8/74 *Procureur du Roi* v. *Dassonville* [1974] ECR 837.

50 Case 16/74 *Centrafarm* v. *Winthrop* [1974] ECR 1183.

51 Case 15/74 *Centrafarm* v. *Sterling Drug, supra* n. 15.

52 Case C-355/96 *Silhouette International Schmied* v. *Hartlauer Handelsgesellschaft* [1998] ECR I-4799.

53 Case 16/74 *Centrafarm* v. *Winthrop, supra* n. 50.

54 Case 102/77 *Hoffmann-La Roche* v. *Centrafarm* [1978] ECR 1139.

55 See e.g. Case 102/77 *Hoffmann-La Roche* v. *Centrafarm, supra* n. 54; Joined Cases C-417, 429 and 436/93 *Bristol-Myers Squib and Others* v. *Paranova* [1996] ECR I-3457. Consider also the approach in the cases on common origin discussed below.

trade marks have been used in relation to goods which have a different origin or which have been affixed by parties other than the trade mark proprietor without the proprietor's consent. In each of these cases, there is a particular risk of consumer confusion and consequently a tension between one of the perceived functions of a trade mark and the free movement of goods. This is particularly problematic given that a strict definition of the consent and exhaustion doctrines may not operate so as to minimise risk of consumer confusion as to origin.[56] It leaves the question of whether the Court takes a consistent view towards the importance and meaning of consent or the function of the trade mark.

Looking at the first point, the trade mark right now includes not just the same mark but also confusingly similar marks.[57] Thus, in *Terrapin* v. *Terranova*,[58] the ECJ held that a trade mark owner may use his right to prevent the import of goods bearing such a similar mark. The question of whether a mark is confusingly similar or not is, subject to harmonization, a matter for national law,[59] although in some earlier cases the ECJ appears to suggest that a mutual recognition approach should be taken.[60] The Court has emphasised, however, that the confusingly similar argument may be used in relation to similar products,[61] although it is again for the national courts to assess the similarity of the products. This approach can be seen as re-affirming the point that the ECJ is hesitant to become involved in a discussion as to whether the right in question falls within the scope of the first sentence of Article 30.[62]

One area in which there is a lot of case law is that relating to the re-packaging of goods. This issue tends to arise where a company markets the same product in different Member States, under different names or in different packaging, at differential pricing. A profit may be made by importing the goods sold more cheaply into the Member State where the relevant goods are sold at a higher price. Such a scheme would work only if the goods could be sold lawfully, for example by complying with

56 The re-packaging cases are a clear example of this problem – see e.g. Case 102/77 *Hoffmann-La Roche* v. *Centrafarm, supra* n. 54.

57 The 'likelihood of confusion' point is now covered by Articles 4 and 5 of the First Trade Mark Directive.

58 Case 119/75 *Terrapin* v. *Terranova* [1976] ECR 1039.

59 Cases C-317/91 *Deutsche Renault A.G.* v. *Audi AG* [1993] ECR I-6227, especially paragraphs 29-39, concerning the use of 'Quadra' and 'Quattra' as names for cars.

60 Case 16/83 *Prantl* [1984] ECR 1299, especially paragraphs 34–38.

61 See Case C-10/89 *Hag II, supra* n. 12; Case 9/93 *IHT International Heiztechnik* v. *Ideal Standard, supra* n. 47.

62 Contrast the views of Advocate-General Jacobs in *Hag II, supra* n. 12, at p. 3740 and p. 3743. His suggestions were either avoided, as the Court decided *Hag II* on other grounds, or rejected, as in Case C-317/91 *Deutsche Renault, supra* n. 59.

relevant national laws regarding packaging, and the consumer could recognise the product. This could mean changing the name from that used in the Member State of origin to that used in the Member State of import. Obviously, the packaging of the product and the affixing of the trade mark fall within the area protected by the trade mark, but would allowing the trade mark proprietor to exercise the trade mark so as to preclude parallel imports constitute an abuse of the right? This issue arose in *Hoffman-La Roche*.[63] There the goods had been re-packaged and the Hoffman-La Roche trade mark re-affixed without the consent of the trade mark proprietor. Had the ECJ merely adopted the standard exhaustion approach and focussed on the first marketing of the product, the function of the trade mark as consumer protection through a guarantee of identity would have been undermined.[64] The trade mark proprietor was allowed to exercise the rights, but on limited conditions, discussed further below. Arguably, the ECJ prioritised concerns relating to function over arguments based on consent. A similar approach was taken in *Centrafarm* v. *American Home Products,*[65] but this time in relation to the affixing of the proprietor's trade mark used in the Member State to which the goods were being imported. In *American Home Products,* the ECJ confirmed that the,

> 'right granted to the proprietor to prohibit any unauthorised affixing of his mark to his product accordingly comes within the specific subject matter of the trade mark.'

The fact that the trade mark proprietor had chosen to market the products in the other Member States was irrelevant, although ultimately the ECJ will still act to ensure that parallel trading remains possible.

Although in principle the exercise of a trade mark to protect the specific subject matter will not be considered an abuse of the right protected by Article 30, it can still in some circumstances constitute a disguised restriction on trade within the meaning of the second sentence of Article 30. It now seems that re-packaging will not be permitted unless it is established that the use of the trade mark right by the owner will contribute to the artificial partitioning of the market; the re-packaging cannot adversely affect the product (i.e. the produce inside the package); the owner of the trade mark receives advance notice that the re-packaged product is to be put on sale; and the new packaging identifies the person by

---

63 Case 102/77 *Hoffman-La Roche* v. *Centrafarm*, *supra* n. 54.

64 For a discussion of the ECJ's approach, see Govaere, I., 'The Use and Abuse of Intellectual Property Rights in E.C. Law' *supra* n. 16, at pp. 90-92. See also the ECJ's approach in respect of industrial designs; Case 144/81 *Keurkoop BV* v. *Nancy Kean Gifts BV*, *supra* n. 8.

65 Case 3/78 *Centrafarm BV* v. *American Home Products Corporation* [1978] ECR 1823.

whom the product has been re-packaged.[66] The Court has refined its guidance on when trade mark proprietors' actions would be found to be partitioning the market and when the quality of the trade marked products is likely to be affected within the terms of the *Hoffman-La Roche* test.[67] Unsurprisingly, the ECJ held that a parallel importer did not need to show that the intention of the trade mark owner was to partition the mark; instead the ECJ referred back to the function of the trade mark. Where reliance on the trade mark protected the essential function of the trade mark, the resultant partitioning of the market could not be considered as artificial,[68] although this does raise the question of what precisely the function of a trade mark now is.

Looking at specific examples, the Court held that if the trade marked goods were packaged in different types of packaging in different Member States, for example as a result of Member State requirements regarding packaging, the trade mark owner would not be justified in relying on its rights to prevent repackaging. The owner could oppose re-packaging, however, where the importer could achieve packaging permissible in the Member State of importation by adding extra labels to comply with the requirements of that Member State. The rights of the trade mark owner are thus limited to changes necessary to allow the parallel importer to market the products.[69] A similar approach will be taken in the situation where a different trade mark is affixed to the product.[70] As regards the condition of the product, this should be assessed in the light of the products itself and the nature of the re-packaging. Where inner packaging is left intact, the mere substitution of new outer layers of packaging is unlikely to affect the condition of the goods. Similarly, the addition of extra labels, the insertion of extra items or new instructions, for example in the language of the Member State of importation, would be equally unlikely to affect the product. The ECJ did accept, however, that where new instructions were incomplete or inaccurate or where the extra article inserted did not comply with the means of usage envisaged by the manufacturer, then the product

---

66 Case 102/77 *Hoffman-La Roche* v. *Centrafarm, supra* n. 54; Case 1/81 *Pfizer* v. *Eurim-Pharm* [1981] ECR 2913 – this case concerned the re-packaging of blister strips which were re-packaged in such a way that the original trade marks were still visible.

67 Joined Cases C-427, 429 and 436/ 93 *Bristol-Myers Squibb, supra* n. 55.

68 Joined Cases C-427, 429 and 436/93 *Bristol-Myers Squibb, supra* n. 55, paragraph 40.

69 Joined Cases C-427, 429 and 436/93 *Bristol-Myers Squibb, supra* n. 55, paragraph 56. See Cases C-443/99 and 143/00 *Merck, Shap and Dohme GmbH* v. *Paranova Pharmaceutika Handels GmbH* and *Boehringer Ingelheim KG and Boehringer Ingelheim Pharma KG* v. *Swingward Ltd*, judgment 25 April 2002.

70 Case C-379/97 *Pharamacia & Upjohn SA* v. *Paranova A/S* [1999] ECR I-6927. See new reference on this issue: *Glaxo Group* v. *Dowelhurst* (No. 2) [2000] FSR 529.

condition might be considered to be affected for the purposes of the *Hoffman-La Roche* test.

Although much of the case law in this area has been generated in the field of pharmaceuticals, it seems that the ECJ's jurisprudence on trade marks, re-packaging and re-labelling is of more general application. In *Frits Loendersloot*,[71] a case concerning the re-labelling of alcoholic drinks by an importer, the ECJ confirmed that proprietors could oppose re-labelling in the circumstances it had identified in the pharmaceutical cases. Given the nature of the product, however, the ECJ held that it was not necessary that the re-labelled bottle identified the person responsible for the re-labelling and that the trade mark proprietor did not have the right to request a specimen label. It has been suggested that, in taking this approach, the ECJ was not entirely in accordance with its previous jurisprudence in which it had recognised that the consumer should not be misled as to whether the importer is the manufacturer of the product and owner of the trade mark.[72]

By contrast to the position regarding the re-packaging of the product itself, the ECJ has held that a trade mark proprietor does not have the right to object to advertising in a way which is customary in the re-seller's sector, where the re-seller habitually markets articles of the same kind but not necessarily of the same quality, unless it seriously damages the reputation of the mark.[73] In considering such damage, the ECJ held that in the case of luxury goods, the re-seller should not act unfairly in relation to the legitimate interests of the trade mark proprietor: in particular the re-seller should not detract from the image of luxury products as prestigious. Whether this proviso adequately protects the trade mark is another question, especially given the importance of the advertising function of a trade mark. Certainly in the case law there is a marked difference in the approach regarding the distribution of the product and advertising of the product. In the former situation, a trade mark proprietor may act when there is a risk of damage to the trade mark, whereas in the latter case *serious* damage is required before the trade mark proprietor may act. It would seem that what is being protected by the trade mark is not necessarily its reputation but the exclusive rights to first marketing which itself is seen to protect the reputation.[74] In this line of cases, we see the approach of the ECJ being much closer to the notion of exhaustion

---

71 Case C-349/95 *Frits Loendersloot* v. *George Ballantine* [1997] ECR I-6227.

72 See Walsh, Treacy and Feaster, 'The Exhaustion and Unauthorised Exploitation of Trade Mark Rights' (1999) 24 *ELRev* 259 referring to Joined Cases C-427, 429 and 436/93 *Bristol-Myers Squibb, supra* n. 55, paragraph 74.

73 Case C-337/95 *Parfums Christian Dior* v. *Evora BV* [1997] ECR I-6013, see Article 7(2) of the Trade Mark Directive, Directive 89/104 [1989] OJ L 40/1.

74 See Case 16/74 *Centrafarm BV* v. *Winthrop BV, supra* n. 50, at pp. 1162.

expounded in cases such as *Winthrop*[75] than it was in the re-packaging cases.

Damage to a mark may similarly occur when consumers are confused as to the link between the trade mark proprietor and the re-seller. This concern was raised in *BMW*, where BMW sought to prevent a specialist car repair mechanic from using the BMW trade mark in his advertising.[76] The ECJ accepted that the exhaustion of rights doctrine should not preclude the trade mark proprietor from opposing the use of the trade mark where there were legitimate grounds for doing so. These grounds included the existence of a risk of misconception as to the economic link between the proprietor and the re-seller.[77] Where there is such a risk, then the trade mark proprietor can act even though there is no risk to the reputation of the mark because the re-seller is competent. Where there is no risk of consumer confusion as to the link between proprietor and re-seller, then the proprietor cannot prevent the use of the trade mark, save where there is a risk of serious damage to the mark. Here, the emphasis of the ECJ's approach seems to be on the potential damage to the public rather than to the damage to the trade mark proprietor. In its jurisprudence, the ECJ has attempted to balance the competing interests of the trade mark owners, the consumers and the principle of free movement, although it seems that the balance of concerns might be shifting. The approach taken, particularly in the advertising cases, would seem either to undermine the trade mark's function of protecting business goodwill, or to redefine it as mainly a consumer protection issue. As we have seen, if consumer confusion is the main concern of a trade mark then the traditional doctrine of consent and exhaustion is less helpful in determining the appropriate boundary between the various interests at play.

The doctrine of consent has also had a troubled development as far as trade marks and the doctrine of common origin is concerned. The case where the question originally arose, *Hag I*,[78] concerned the Hag trade mark that was lawfully owned in two different Member States by two separate companies. This situation arose because the Belgian company (a subsidiary of the German company) had been sequestered as enemy property after the war. Despite the fact that there were now no links between the two companies, the ECJ held that the Luxembourg holder of the Hag mark could not oppose import bearing the Hag mark of the Belgian company. The ECJ justified this approach on the grounds that the result was

75 Case 16/74 *Centrafarm BV* v. *Winthrop BV*, *ibid*.

76 Case C-63/97 *BMW* v. *Deenik* [1999] ECR I-905.

77 On the issue of 'confusion' see also Case C-251/95 *Sabel* v. *Puma* [1997] ECR I-6191 and Case C-39/97 *Canon* v. *Pathe Communications* [1998] ECR I-5507.

78 Case 192/73 *Van Zuylen* v. *Hag* [1974] ECR 731.

necessary to unite the national markets of the Member States in a single market.[79]

The case was heavily criticised and the judgment was eventually reversed in *Hag II*,[80] in which the ECJ focussed on the need for consumers to be able to distinguish between products and services and thereby allowing a company to trade on the quality of its products. For this to be the case, the company had to be able to guarantee that all the goods bearing its trade mark had been produced under the control of a single entity responsible for the quality of the product. Thus, in this case, in so far as there were identical marks there remained a risk of confusion. As the Advocate-General commented, '[t]he consumer is not interested in the geneology of trade marks; ... he is interested in knowing who made the goods that he purchases'.[81] The ECJ restricted its ruling in *Hag II* to the facts before it and expressly refrained from dealing with the situation where a mark has been subdivided contractually, an issue dealt with more recently in *IHT International Heiztechnik* v. *Ideal Standard*.[82]

In *Ideal Standard*[83] the ECJ, again emphasising the need for accountability for product quality, confirmed the *Hag II* approach. The Court argued that what was in issue was control over the manufacture of the goods, rather than the ability to limit the marketing of sub-standard goods. A licensor could take action under the licence agreement to ensure the quality of the goods produced by the licensee. If the licensor failed to do so, the consequences of that failure would rest with the licensor. Similar arguments would apply in relation to the use of trade marks devolved through group companies. This argument would not apply when, as here, a trade mark had been assigned outside to a completely different company in respect of a different geographic area. Where there is no such link by which the original licensor can exert control over quality, a trade mark proprietor may oppose the import of trade marked goods. The Advocate-General suggested that in voluntarily assigning the trade mark, the trade mark proprietor should be viewed as having consented to the marketing of the goods within the meaning of the doctrine of exhaustion; certainly the consequences for the proprietor were insufficient to outweigh the creation of the single market.[84] The ECJ took a different approach, arguing that the

79 The ECJ subsequently restated its argument in Case 119/75 *Terrapin* v. *Terranova*, *supra* n. 10, as an aspect of the doctrine of exhaustion, see paragraph 6, and suggested that any consumer interest in the origin of the products was undermined by the fact that the mark had already been divided.

80 Case C-10/89 *Hag II*, *supra* n. 12.

81 Case C-10/89 *Hag II*, *ibid.*, paragraph 26 of the Opinion.

82 Case 9/93 *IHT International Heiztechnik* v. *Ideal Standard*, *supra* n. 47.

83 Case 9/93 *Ideal Standard*, *ibid.*, paragraph 37.

84 Case 9/93 *Ideal Standard*, *ibid.*, Opinion paragraph 102.

'consent implicit in any assignment is not the consent required for the application of the doctrine of exhaustion of rights'.[85] Thus, in *Ideal Standard,* a French company assigning its trade mark to an American company was not impliedly consenting to the company placing products on the French market.

Ideal Standard[86] has received a certain amount of criticism.[87] Although the ECJ has addressed the issue of consent, it seems to have changed the basis of its reasoning. Rather than focus on consent as it was understood in the earlier cases, it re-defined consent to be linked to the notion of quality control, which is linked to concerns about the protection of the consumer. Whether one accepts this argument depends on your view of consumer protection. The Advocate-General suggested that consumers would benefit from greater choice or lower prices as a result of parallel imports. This argument is based on the assumption that the consumer will know that he or she is buying goods manufactured by somebody else; a point the Advocate-General emphasised in *Hag II.*[88] As discussed in Chapter 7 in relation to the consumer protection cases, this might not be the case. Nevertheless, the case is unusual as the Court's reasoning clearly puts the internal market at some risk. It would seem, however, that *Ideal Standard* is limited to the case of assigned trade marks. It would not seem to apply to other intellectual property rights, as their functions have little relevance to quality control, the concern which forms the basis of this judgment. Furthermore, subsequent case law dealing with other aspects of trade marks do not seem to have focussed to the same degree on the link between entities and control, although in some cases the guarantee of product identity remains important. Nonetheless, questions remain in this area. The solution, of course, would be a Community trade mark – and the current Community trade mark, although it creates a unitary right, does not replace the national trade mark systems.

The Trade Mark Directive[89] has to some extent replaced this case law. Article 7 can be seen as a basic restatement of the principle of exhaustion.[90] Article 7(2) provides an exception to that principle, stating that a trade mark proprietor may oppose the further commercialisation of the products where there is a legitimate reason for doing so. Although the ECJ has held that Article 7 regulates trade mark questions in respect of

85 Case 9/93 *Ideal Standard, ibid.*, paragraph 43.

86 Case 9/93 *Ideal Standard, ibid.*

87 See e.g. case notes by Alexander (1995) *CML Rev* 327; Tritton (1994) 10 *EIPR* 422.

88 Case C-10/89 *Hag II, supra* n. 12.

89 Directive 89/104 [1989] OJ L 40/1.

90 Article 7 states 'The trade mark shall not entitle the proprietor to prohibit its use in relation to goods which have been put on the market in the Community under that trade mark by the proprietor or with his consent.'

products traded within the Community, it has also held that the directive must be interpreted in the light of the Treaty rules on the free movement of goods and in particular Article 36 [now Article 30].[91] The case law in this area therefore remains relevant.

V Conclusions

In developing the doctrine of exhaustion and consent, the ECJ has taken a broadly similar approach to each of the main intellectual property rights. Given the similarity or areas of overlap underlying justifications for the different rights, the introduction of a similar approach to the rights regarding the introduction exhaustion and consent seems to be sensible, even if the ECJ has not sought to argue that the convergence in case law in this area is a matter of policy. Although consistency is in general terms laudable, such an approach may underplay some essential differences in the functions of the various rights. Alternatively, one might argue that the ECJ has not always seemed clear as to what the functions of the respective rights are. Although it seems that the ECJ does not seek to interfere with the Member States' policy choices as to when intellectual property rights occur, which is different from the general trend regarding the other Article 30 heads of derogation, the ECJ's approach is restrictive in terms of the scope allowed to such rights, with some exceptions that occur somewhat unpredictably depending on the perceived function of the right and the Court's approach to consent. As the case law illustrates in respect of each of the intellectual property rights discussed, there are some inconsistencies. Whether the Court's view towards intellectual property rights is viewed as a limitation on Member States or on the rights of the individual right holder, it seems clear that the ECJ in many instances emphasises the needs of the internal market over an extensive view of the rights of the proprietor. In this, one can see parallels to the Court's approach in respect of other heads of derogation.

---

91 Joined Cases C-427, 429 and 436/93 *Bristol-Myers Squibb*, *supra* n. 55.

Chapter 9

Scope of Services I: Definitions

I Introduction

The freedom to provide services is governed by Articles 49 and 50 EC, with Article 56 establishing the derogation from this freedom. Articles 49 and 50 identify the scope of the freedom to provide services, both in terms of the nature of the services themselves and as regards those who may benefit from the right. This chapter will discuss these two issues in more detail as they, in particular, have the possibility of affecting the division of competence between Member States and the EC, especially in relation to the provision of public service. Succeeding chapters will focus respectively on the question of whose actions are caught; the nature of the prohibition in Article 49; and the scope of the derogation therefrom.

II The Nature of Services

Services are an amorphous concept. Insofar as they are capable of a general definition, they tend to be perceived as being intangible and incapable of being stored.[1] Services are therefore consumed at the time of production, with a consequent lack of a distinction between wholesale and retail. These points were however, not specifically addressed by the drafters of the EC Treaty in the definition of services in Articles 49 and 50. Although, in contrast to the position for goods,[2] there was some attempt to define services in the Treaty, the definition is not exhaustive.[3]

Article 50 states that services for the purposes of the Treaty are those that are provided for remuneration, insofar as they are not governed by the

---

1 See Chapter 2 and literature cited therein.

2 *Ibid.*

3 Contrast the position with regards to GATS. In that agreement there is a general definition of services in Article I:2 GATS but despite this GATS will only cover services listed by the signatory in their individual schedules. States therefore have control over the definition of services covered, if not the notion of services at an abstract level. See further: Trebilcock, M.J., and Howse, R., *The Regulation of International Trade*, 2nd ed. (New York: Routledge, 1999).

provisions relating to the other treaty freedoms on goods, capital and persons. A list of examples states that activities of an industrial or commercial character are caught, as are the activities of professionals or craftsmen. Thus, although it gives examples, the Treaty does not outline the characteristics of services as a general concept and it seems implicit from this open definition that the precise scope of services is not precise, being defined almost by what they are not.[4] Certainly, the question of what a service is has never been answered particularly clearly and in some instances the Community institutions have had difficulty identifying the scope of a service in a given case.[5] Given the universality of the EC Treaty, however, it seems that the potential category of services is wide indeed.[6] Certainly it seems that, in principle, no specific category is excluded from the potential ambit of the Treaty[7] and it is generally accepted that the morality and desirability, or otherwise, of the provision of a particular service will not affect its categorisation for purposes of EC law as a service.[8]

This latter point requires clarification. There are two possible arguments on this point. The first is that the activities do not fall within the scope of Article 49 in the first place and therefore cannot claim the benefit of Community law principles; the second that, although the activities may constitute services, the function of Article 49 is not to prevent Member States from banning certain activities but to ensure that such prohibitions operate without discrimination between domestic providers of services and

---

4 Eeckhout suggests that the difficulty of defining services is not limited to the EC: GATS has raised its own problems: see Eeckhout, P., *The European Internal Market and International Trade: A Legal Analysis* (Clarendon Press: Oxford, 1994), Chapter 1 and literature cited therein.

5 See Case 352/85 *Bond van Adverteerders* [1988] ECR 2085.

6 This point was noted early in the Community's life: see Van Gerven, W., 'The Right of Establishment and Free Supply of Services within the Common Market' (1965-6) 3 *CMLRev* 344 at p. 160.

7 See Case C-159/90 *Society for the Protection of Unborn Children* v. *Grogan* [1991] ECR I-4685 at 4739, Case C-275/92 *H.M. Customs and Excise* v. *Schindler et al.* [1994] ECR I-1039 at 1089-1090, Case 36/74 *Walrave and Koch* v. *Association Union Cycliste Internationale et al.* [1974] ECR 1405 at 1417 and also Case C-158/96 *Kohll* v. *Union des Caisses de Maladie* [1998] ECR I-1931, Case 263/86 *Belgian State* v. *René and Marie Thérèse Humbel* [1988] ECR 5365, Case C-415/93 *Union Royale Belge des Sociétés de Football Association ASBL* v. *Jean-Marc Bosman* [1995] ECR I-4921, [1996] 1 CMLR 645 and Joined Cases C-51/96 and C-191/97 *Christelle Deliège* v. *Ligue Francophone de Judo et Disciplines Associées ASBL et al.* [2000] ECR I-2549.

8 See discussion in Case 15/78 *Société Générale Alsacienne de Banque SA* v. *Koestler* [1978] ECR 1971.

those from another Member State. The crucial distinction between the reasoning is that in the second approach a Member State would have to justify its position *vis-à-vis* the service. In both *Grogan*,[9] which concerned the advertisement of medical services in respect of termination of a pregnancy, and *Schindler*,[10] which concerned the provision of gaming services, the service in question was legal within at least one Member State and that state was the state from which the service was to be provided. What is the position of activities that are legal in none of the Member States? The Community institutions are currently endeavouring to prohibit tobacco advertising: would the theoretical provision of advertising services in relation to tobacco products still constitute a service within Article 49?[11] Further, is there a distinction between this situation, where in principle advertising services are permissible and clearly within the scope of Article 49 although certain products may not be advertised, and, for example, the case of trafficking in human beings for the provision of sexual services? There is no ruling on this particular point but it would seem unlikely, despite the ECJ's desire not to distinguish between different conceptions of morality, that the ECJ would use free movement principles to challenge a prohibition found in all Member States and it is, in any event, questionable whether the ECJ should take such a stance. The free movement provisions do not mean that all possible services are permissible without any restriction. The test for behaviour contrary to Article 49 and the scope of the derogation there from will be discussed in Chapters 10-12.

Although the original scope of Article 49 seemed to be aimed primarily at service providers who sought to move to another Member State to provide their service, with consequently clear links to the freedom of establishment,[12] the ECJ extended the provision's scope to include a person who sought to move from one Member State to another to receive services.[13] In part, this approach was based on the need to create the common market and eliminate all restrictions on grounds of nationality in respect of all economic activity. The ECJ argued that the right to provide

---

9 Case C-159/90 *Society for the Protection of Unborn Children* v. *Grogan*, *supra*, n. 7.

10 Case C-275/92 *H.M. Customs and Excise* v. *Schindler et al.*, *supra* n. 7.

11 On tobacco advertising see further Chapter 13.

12 Indeed, van Gerven, *supra* n. 6, questions the utility of the distinction between services and establishment, at p. 344.

13 This possibility was addressed by the Advocate-General in Case 118/75 *Watson and Belmann* [1976] ECR 1185, but it was not until Joined Cases 286/82 and 28/83 *Luisi and Carbone* [1984] ECR 377 that the ECJ expressly addressed the issue. See also Case 186/87 *Cowan* v. *French Treasury* [1989] ECR 195, Case C-158/96 *Kohll* v. *Union des Caisses de Maladie*, *supra*, n. 7.

services as its corollary clearly covered the receipt of services, as the recipient is 'a necessary party to the transaction'.[14] Thus,

> '... the freedom to provide services includes the freedom, for recipients of services, to go to another Member State in order to receive a service there, without being obstructed by restrictions, even in relation to payments ... tourists, persons receiving medical treatment and persons travelling for the purpose of education or business are to be regarded as the recipients of services.'[15]

The service recipients need not themselves be migrants to rely on Article 49. Provided there is a cross-border element, a recipient may rely on that provision against the Member State in which the service recipients are located.[16]

This does, however, raise the question of whether Article 49 can be used to force a service provider into offering and providing a service to a particular person to whom the service provider would not have chosen voluntarily to provide that service. The British government raised this concern in the context of education, but as the Advocate-General noted, the refusal to provide a service to a migrant EC national in the context of public service is questionable given a government's public duties and in the light of the prohibition on the grounds of nationality.[17] The position is slightly more problematic where the service provider is not a public body: should private parties be forced to provide services? It could be that the more appropriate way to deal with the issue is to consider the competition provisions, notably Article 82 and its case law. Certainly this has been the approach taken regarding goods, as Article 28 and 29 do not seem to apply horizontally.[18] It should be noted, however, that Article 49 may be relied on against private parties in contrast to the position as regards goods.[19]

In extending Article 49 to allow a service recipient to rely on the freedom to provide services, a third possibility is opened up: that of both service provider and recipient moving to another Member State. Indeed,

---

14 Case 186/87 *Cowan* v. *Trésor public, ibid.*, Advocate-General's Opinion at paragraph 17, p. 207.

15 *Ibid.*, at paragraph 16.

16 Case C-294/97 *Eurowings Luftverkehr* [1999] ECR I-7447, paragraph 34. The difficulty with this approach is that is may lead to circumstances in which the boundary between Community law and an internal situation may be difficult to identify. See further Chapter 11.

17 Case 263/86 *Humbel, supra* n. 7.

18 See further Chapter 3.

19 Case 36/74 *Walrave, supra* n. 7 and Chapter 10. See also Chapter 3 regarding goods.

the Advocate-General in *Cowan* highlighted this possibility.[20] One question that should be noted here is whether the service provider and the recipient must be resident in different Member States, which seemed to be the assumption the Advocate-General made in identifying this category of services. It would appear that this requirement has, however, not proved necessary: the paradigm situation for recipient and provider both moving is in the leisure industry, when people go on touring holidays, complete with guide.[21] Although in this instance it may be that provider and recipient are established in different Member States, it is more likely that the company offering the service and the holiday-maker will be established in the same Member State. This position has been confirmed, for example in *Bent Vestergaard*, where the ECJ identified the relevant criteria for the application of Article 49 as being that they are 'provided to nationals of a Member State on the territory of another Member State, irrespective of the place of establishment of the provider or recipient of the services.'[22]

A possibility which seems not to have occurred initially to the drafters of the Treaty, nor to the ECJ in its early jurisprudence, was that the services themselves might be seen to move, as illustrated by the examples of insurance,[23] broadcasting[24] or telecommunications.[25] Indeed, the examples given in the Treaty focus on a traditional view of services, seeing services as linked to persons – for example craftspersons and liberal professions – rather than identifying any of the services associated with the new economy, such as information technology and telecommunications

---

20 Case 186/87 *Cowan* v. *Trésor public, supra* n. 13, at paragraph 17, p. 207.

21 Common problems relate for example to a host Member State requirement that local guides or drivers must be used: e.g. Case C-154/89 *Commission* v. *France* (Tour Guides) [1991] ECR I-659 at 685. Some limitations remain in this area: see WQ P-0360/01 of 8 February 2001 [2001] OJ C-174E/260. See also Case C-20/92 *Hubbard* v. *Hamburger* [1993] ECR I-3777 at p. 3794, which concerned a German law regarding the non-German executor of a will to lodge security for costs in an action before the German courts. Presumably the facts underlying Case 36/74 *Walrave and Koch, supra* n. 7 where cyclists and pacemakers both travelled to other Member States to compete in competitions would also fall within this category although it does not seem to have been discussed as such.

22 Case C-55/98 *Skattenministeriet* v. *Bent Vestergaard* [1999] ECR I- 7641, paragraphs 18–19 citing Case C-381/93 *Commission* v. *France* (Maritime Transport Services) [1994] ECR I-5145, paragraphs 14 and Case C-398/95 *Syndesmos ton en Elladi Touristikon kai Taxidiotikon Grafeion* (*SETTG*) v. *Ypourgos Ergasias* [1997] ECR I-3091, paragraph 8.

23 Case 205/84 *Commission* v. *Germany* (Insurance Services) [1986] ECR 3755.

24 Case 155/78 *Sacchi* [1974] ECR 409.

25 E.g. Case C-353/89 *Commission* v. *Netherlands* [1991] ECR I-4069.

services. Nonetheless, in the light of the broad view of services suggested above, the concept of services is now,

> 'no longer rigidly dependent on the crossing of frontiers but is geared to the intrinsic content of the service as an activity which is useful also for the citizens of Member States other than the Member State in which the supplier of the service resides.'[26]

Thus, such activities fall within the definition of services just as much as hairdressing or dentistry and must be allowed to circulate throughout the Community freely. It is in this view of services that we see the most similarity to the free movement of goods and the position furthest away from the free movement of people.

Broadly then, there are four categories in which services can fall:

1) service provider moves to another Member State;
2) service recipient moves to another Member State;
3) both provider and recipient move to another Member State; and
4) the service itself moves.

One might question whether a similar approach to identifying the existence of a service and the nature of restrictions on services will be used in all these categories, even before considering the congruence of the services jurisprudence with that relating to goods. In this context it should be noted that these four categories cover the possibility of both 'import' and 'export' situations.[27] This approach can be contrasted with that adopted in relation to goods, where imports and exports are dealt with by separate provisions and where the jurisprudence on imports and exports differs in crucial respects.[28]

Despite these questions, Articles 49 and 50 illustrate certain points: the category of services is a residual one (i.e. it is defined as not being the other four freedoms) and, as well as having the nature of a service, services must be economic in nature. Furthermore, according to the consistent case law of the ECJ, there must be a cross-border element before a case can fall within the scope of Community law. Individuals, who have not exercised their EC law rights to migrate, cannot rely on EC law to challenge national

---

26 Case 352/85 *Bond van Adverteerders*, *supra* n 5, Opinion of the Advocate-General at p. 2114.

27 See e.g. Case C-384/93 *Alpine Investments BV* v. *Minister van Financiën* [1995] ECR I-1141.

28 See Chapter 6.

rules.[29] Indeed, this point is implied by the wording in Article 49: the provision relates to nationals established in a Member State other than that where the intended recipient is, though the cross-border element is limited to this situation. As is the case in the context of a similar point concerning goods, there is some overlap between this issue and the nature of the hindrance triggering the application of Article 49. The matter will be more fully discussed in Chapters 10 and 11. The economic requirement and the inter-relationship between services and the other freedoms will be discussed below.

a) Economic Nature of Services

Article 49 EC states that services must be provided for remuneration. This requirement reflects the fact that the internal market, which the free movement of goods, persons, services and capital aims to achieve, is concerned with economic questions.[30] The ECJ has not addressed the question of whether the remuneration must be monetary or whether some other form of consideration would suffice. Presumably, given the broad manner in which the treaty freedoms are interpreted, it may be assumed that at least other forms of consideration which have some value will be sufficient to satisfy the remuneration requirement. Certainly the ECJ, borrowing from its jurisprudence in respect of workers and Article 39, has held that remuneration need not be of a particular value, and certainly need not be assessed by reference to the making of a profit, provided it is 'genuine and effective' and not 'purely marginal or ancillary'.[31] Although there must be some sort of economic link between service provider and recipient,[32] the payment in respect of the service need not be direct; it is not necessary that the recipient of the service pays the provider of the service for it. Free-to-air commercial television, such as the ITV companies in the UK, exemplifies this point. Viewers do not pay the television company for the programmes they watch (the licence fee is in respect of

---

29 See e.g. Cases C-330 and 331/90 *López Brea* [1992] ECR I-323, Case C-60/91 *Batista Morais* [1992] ECR I-2085 at 2105-6, Case C-70/95 *Sodemare SA, Anni Azzurri Holding SpA, Anni Azzurri Rezzato Srl* v. *Regione Lombardia* [1997] ECR I-3395 at 3435-6. This point is well established: in its 3rd Annual Report to the European Parliament, the Commission stated that there must be a 'cross-frontier link'.

30 Articles 2 and 3c EC.

31 See Joined Cases C-51/96 and 191/97 *Christelle Deliège* v. *Ligue Francophone de Judo et Disciplines Associées ASBL et al.*, *supra* n. 7. at paragraph 54, citing Case 53/81 *Levin* v. *Staatssecretaris van Justitie* [1982] ECR 1035, paragraph 17 and Case 196/87 *Steymann* v. *Staatssecretaris van Justitie* [1988] ECR 6159, at paragraph 13.

32 For an example of a case where there was held to be no such link see Case C-159/90 *Society for the Protection of Unborn Children* v. *Grogan*, *supra* n. 7.

the BBC's services);[33] the broadcaster receives income from advertisers, although the value of the advertising slot is affected by the anticipated number of viewers it attracts.

Although this proposition appears unproblematic and, in the majority of cases, most likely is, there are a number of issues that require further attention. Two particular areas highlight difficulties relating to the remuneration requirement or the economic link, both as regards the existence of the remuneration in the first place and the directness of the payment. The first of these areas is the right to receive services, especially public services; the second concerns sport, particularly in conjunction with broadcasting. There is a preliminary point, however, which will affect any assessment of questions raised in these areas. In the context of goods, it is clear that what is important in determining the scope of the term is that the items in question are of the *type* to be goods, irrespective of whether the goods in question are the *immediate subject matter* of a contract.[34] The question to be discussed is whether this is also true of services?

The Treaty itself would indicate that in determining this question we should be looking at the type of services and ask whether they are the sort that are 'normally provided for remuneration'.[35] This point is addressed, albeit indirectly, in *Humbel* where the Advocate-General in the course of his argument stated that '[s]tate education, however, like health care, is *largely* financed from State taxes'.[36] It is implicit in this statement that such services are not normally provided for remuneration and therefore fall outside the scope of Article 49, even were such a service to be paid for individually. The Advocate-General did not, however, develop this point further, but, like the Court, focussed on the nature of the remuneration.[37]

A slightly different aspect of this question was discussed by the Advocate-General in *Cowan*.[38] The case concerned the claim of a British tourist in France for compensation, in respect of damage suffered as a result of a mugging, from a French fund set up for this purpose. Cowan argued that as a tourist, he was a recipient of tourist industry services in France and therefore within the scope of the Treaty. Discussing the question of defining the recipient of services, the Advocate-General noted that two main approaches could be identified, which he defined as *ex ante* (i.e. looking at a generalised notion of the type of services likely to be

---

33 The position of the BBC is arguably comparable to that of the other public service providers, discussed below, although the BBC now has responsibility for collecting the licence fee itself and could therefore be seen as being paid directly.

34 See Chapter 2.

35 Article 49 EC.

36 Case 263/86 *Humbel*, *supra*, n. 7, at p. 5379, author's emphasis.

37 Case 263/86 *Humbel*, *ibid.*, at p. 5387-8.

38 Case 186/87 *Cowan* v. *Trésor public*, *supra* n. 13.

provided) and *ex post* (looking at whether services had actually been received). The Advocate-General suggested that, although the latter would effectively preclude the improper reliance by a migrant on the status of a recipient of services which might not actually be received, the *ex ante* approach would be preferable to avoid unregulated areas and confusion.[39] Although the Advocate-General was not looking at the issue of remuneration in this case but the question of whether the service had been provided, the point is that the Advocate-General suggests the focus should be on the *type* of service in question, rather than on the individual facts of a given case. Arguably, on this approach the person claiming to be a recipient of services need not be economically active. The ECJ did not expressly address this point, although it held that tourists were recipients of services within the scope of Article 49.

In the more recent case of *Bickel*,[40] which also concerned the rights of tourists, the ECJ held that Article 49 covers all EC nationals who 'visit another Member State where they intend or are likely to receive services'.[41] This definition would seem to support the *ex ante* approach originally suggested by the Advocate-General in *Cowan*.[42] Indeed, it would seem to take a very broad view of that test, because as well as considering what is objectively likely, it takes into account the hypothetical visitors' intentions, however unlikely. In reality, however, it is doubtful whether there would be many cases where the objective and subjective elements of this test do not coincide.

Equally, however, there are a number of cases in which it seems that the ECJ has looked at the particular instance of service provision. One example is found in the Opinion of the Advocate-General in *Wirth*, where, adopting the argument of the UK, he stated that, 'the possibility that a provision of services is involved cannot be ruled out when the tuition or studies are financed entirely or essentially out of contributions from the students...',[43] a point accepted by the ECJ.[44] Thus, although some educational services may fall within Article 49, others may not, depending on the circumstances of their provision. The distinction relied on in *Wirth* has become more pronounced as the case law in this area has developed. Indeed, the distinction between amateur (non-economic) sport and

---

39 Case 186/87 *Cowan* v. *Trésor public*, *supra* n. 13, at paragraphs 28–34, pp. 209-210.

40 Case C-274/96 *Criminal Proceedings against Horst Otto Bickel and Ulrich Franz* [1998] ECR I-7637.

41 Case C-274/96 *Bickel and Franz*, *ibid.*, at paragraph 13, p. 7655.

42 Case 186/87 *Cowan* v. *Trésor public*, *supra* n. 13.

43 Case C-109/92 *Stephan Max Wirth* v. *Landeshauptstadt Hannover* [1993] ECR I-6447 at paragraph 12, p. 6456.

44 Case C-109/92 *Wirth*, *ibid.*, at paragraph 17, p. 6469.

professional (sport for remuneration) has become the basis of the jurisprudence in the area of sport.[45]

The possibility of non-economically active individuals migrating on the basis of the hypothetical receipt of services is consequently limited. An underlying concern seemed to be that left unconstrained, such an approach would lead to 'tourism' for social advantage. Certainly, this concern underlay a series of cases in which the argument that students could claim the benefit of Article 49 by claiming to be the recipients of services was put forward. Member States were worried about the impact such claims would have on their systems for the provision of public services. The ECJ put an end to such claims to education by making the twofold argument that state education was not provided for remuneration in that the students were not paying directly for it and that education was provided by the state that was not intending to make a profit but instead operating to secure social solidarity.[46] One might have argued that the *Bond van Adverteerders*[47] approach to indirect remuneration might have worked in such circumstances, but this point does not seem to have been expressly considered in the education cases. It could have been that the indirect payment argument was seen to apply only in relation to the provision of services rather than their receipt, although this point seems disproved, at least as far as medical cases are concerned.[48] In any event, the ECJ in *Wirth* introduced an extra element to the issue of remuneration – that of the service provider's motive. The ECJ thus seemingly put a full stop to claims to receive public services, at least until recently.

The problem cases now are in the medical field and the relationship between national provision for health care and free movement provisions. The issues have arisen not only in the context of services, but also in the

---

45 Case 13/76 *Donà* v. *Mantero* [1976] ECR 1333; at paragraphs 14 and 15, Case C-415/93 *Union Royale Belge des Sociétés de Football Association et al* v. *Bosman*, *supra* n. 7 at paragraph 76 and 127; and Joined Cases C-51/96 and 191/97 *Christelle Deliège* v. *Ligue Francophone de Judo et Disciplines Associées ASBL et al.*, *supra* n. 7 at paragraph 43. This approach is now supported by the Declaration on Sport (Declaration 29) annexed to the Treaty of Amsterdam.

46 Case 263/86 *Humbel*, *supra* n. 7 at paragraph 18 – see also Case C-109/92 *Wirth*, *supra* n. 43.

47 Case 352/85 *Bond van Adverteerders*, *supra* n 5.

48 Case C-158/96 *Kohll* v. *Union Caisses de Maladie*, *supra* n. 7; Case C-157/99 *Geraets-Smits* v. *Stichting Ziekenfonds VGZ* and *Peerbooms* v. *Stichting CZ Groep Zorgverzekeringen* [2001] ECR I-5473; Case C-368/98 *Abdon Vanbraekel and Other* v. *Alliance nationale des mutualités chrétiennes (ANMC)* [2001] ECR I-5363. See also another case currently pending before the ECJ: Case C 8/02 *Ludwig Leichtle* v. *Bundesanstalt für Arbeit* OJ [2002] C-84/50.

area of goods.[49] *Kohll*[50] concerned the Luxembourg health care system, which is set up on an insurance basis. Individuals who wished to be reimbursed for their medical expenses were not permitted under the scheme's terms to receive treatment abroad without prior authorisation, which was granted only in limited circumstances. This rule was challenged as contrary to Article 49. It was argued by Member States that the rules fell within the terms of social security provisions rather than the provisions relating to the free movement of services. Although the ECJ agreed in principle that it is for Member States to organise their own social security systems, the Court then stated that, as the orthodontist's treatment was a professional activity for remuneration, it was a service for the purposes of Article 49.[51] Consequently the rules regarding medical treatment had to comply with the free movement principles.

This approach is clearly different from that taken in *Humbel*[52] and *Wirth*:[53] a number of differences between the cases might be put forward to account for the change. Is it, for example, to do with the different sectors involved? Although education and health services clearly are different, does this justify such a difference in approach? The acceptance of this proposition would undermine any consistency in determining what constitutes a service, especially as regards the receipt of public services. Furthermore, such an approach would not fit in with the terms of the ECJ's earlier judgments which suggest that any rule should be applied generally, rather than focussing on a sector specific approach. Another suggestion is that the difference relates to the fact that in *Humbel* and the other education cases, the cost of providing the service claimed would be met by the host state, whereas in *Kohll*[54] the cost of the treatment would be repatriated were Kohll successful. A distinction based on the requirement that the costs be repatriated would, however, run contrary to *Cowan*,[55] in the sense that Cowan sought compensation from a public fund in the host Member State which would not be reimbursed by his State of origin, albeit as a claim ancillary to the receipt of tourist services.

The most crucial distinction is perhaps that of payment mechanism. Most educational systems are provided directly by the state free of charge, at least to their own citizens, and therefore any payment to educational

---

49 Case C-120/95 *Decker* v. *Caisse de Maladie des Employés Prives* [1998] ECR I-1831.

50 Case C-158/96 *Kohll* v. *Union Caisses de Maladie*, *supra* n. 7.

51 Medical services have been seen as falling in principle within the concept of services before: see e.g. Case C-159/90 *Society for the Protection of Unborn Children* v. *Grogan*, *supra* n. 7.

52 Case 263/86 *Humbel*, *supra* n. 7.

53 Case C-109/92 *Stephan Max Wirth* v. *Landeshauptstadt Hannover*, *supra* n. 43.

54 Case C-158/96 *Kohll* v. *Union Caisses de Maladie*, *supra* n. 7.

55 Case 186/87 *Cowan* v. *Trésor public*, *supra* n. 13.

establishments tends to be indirect. Health care systems are funded in a variety of ways across the EU and in Luxembourg an insurance-based system is used. Thus, Kohll had to pay directly for the treatment received and then seek reimbursement from his insurance company. Accepting that the distinction between the cases is based on payment mechanisms raises a number of questions and it is unsurprising that the issue of the relationship between public health care and the rights of free movement have arisen again.

In *Smits-Peerbooms*,[56] nationals of one Member State were seeking to have treatment in another Member State, the cost of which was to be covered by their home state health system. Unlike the Luxembourg system, this was not a case of straight re-imbursement by the insurance company of sums paid out to medical practitioners by the patient. Instead, the cost was to be defrayed directly by the health insurance system. In contrast to *Kohll*,[57] the Advocate-General in each of these cases referred to the approach taken in *Humbel*,[58] in particular emphasising the Member State's motive in providing health care as well as the indirect link in the payment by the patient to the medical service provider. Were the ECJ to have adopted the Advocate-General's approach in its judgments, it would have been possible to justify the difference between *Smits-Peerbooms* on the one hand and *Kohll* on the other by reference to the mechanism of payment; questions of Member State motive would then arise only in the case of an indirect payment situation. By accepting this solution, however, the ECJ would have created divisions between the Member States, subjecting the health care systems of some to the free movement principles, whilst excluding others on formal grounds relating to how Member States chose to structure their national health care systems.

When the matter came before the ECJ, it disregarded the suggestions of the Advocate-General. Instead, the ECJ chose to follow reasoning similar to that it adopted in *Kohll*.[59] It began by emphasising that social security falls within Member State competence, but that this power must be exercised in conformity with Community law. The ECJ then dismissed arguments put forward by various Member States based on *Humbel*[60] and *Wirth*,[61] without explaining why the approach in these cases would not be applicable. Instead the ECJ stated that medical activity falls within the Treaty and that no distinction can be made between care provided in a

56 Case C-157/99 *Geraets-Smits, supra* n. 48.

57 Case C-158/96 *Kohll* v. *Union Caisses de Maladie, supra* n. 7.

58 Case 263/86 *Humbel, supra* n. 7.

59 Case C-158/96 *Kohll* v. *Union Caisses de Maladie, supra* n. 7.

60 Case 263/86 *Humbel, supra* n. 7.

61 Case C-109/92 *Wirth, supra* n. 43.

hospital and that provided outside the hospital environment.[62] It then went on to hold:

> 'It must be accepted that a medical service provided in one Member State and paid for by the patient should not cease to fall within the scope of the freedom to provide services ... merely because the reimbursement of the costs of the treatment involved is applied for under another Member State's sickness insurance legislation which is essentially of the type which provides for benefits in kind.'[63]

The ECJ then went on to refer to *Bond van Adverteerders*[64] and made the point that had not been raised in *Kohll*,[65] that indirect payment would constitute remuneration for the purposes of Article 49.

It would seem that there is, in this context, no difference between the arguments relating to the provision of services and those related to their receipt. Further, the payment under the scheme undoubtedly constituted consideration as far as the hospital was concerned. Consequently it would appear that, in this case at least, the ECJ focussed on the perspective of the provider of the service rather than the recipient to determine whether there had been payment. The relevant point seems to be that somebody is paying for the service, and not the link between service provider and recipient. This approach clearly is in line with that taken in *Bond van Adverteerders*, where the television company received payment from the advertisers. It is, however, questionable whether the ECJ put the same emphasis on the provider of the service when it considered the same question in *Deliège*,[66] discussed below, and which the ECJ cited as authority for its ruling in *Smits-Peerbooms*.

Although *Smits-Peerbooms*[67] avoids the difficult distinctions thrown up by the approach of the Advocate-General in this case, it does have huge implications for the Member States' ability to arrange their national health systems as they see fit, despite the fact that, according to the Treaty, notably Article 152(5), and jurisprudence of the ECJ, social security (including health care provision) falls within Member State competence. One might question whether the jurisprudence in this area is fully in line with the terms of the Treaty as regards division of competence.

---

62 Case C-157/99 *Geraets-Smits, supra* n. 48 paragraph 53.

63 *Ibid.*, at paragraph 55. The ECJ took a similar approach in Case C-368/98 *Vanbraekel, supra* n. 48.

64 Case 352/85 *Bond van Adverteerders, supra* n. 5.

65 Case C-158/96 *Kohll* v. *Union Caisses de Maladie, supra* n. 7.

66 Cases C-51/96 and 191/97 *Christelle Deliège* v. *Ligue Francophone de Judo et Disciplines Associées ASBL et al., supra* n. 7.

67 Case C-157/99 *Geraets-Smits, supra* n. 48.

Furthermore, questions must now arise as to the status of the public education cases. Is it possible to distinguish between the health care system and the educational system? Although medical services can be provided privately, so can education. It could well be argued that *Wirth*[68] and *Humbel*[69] are no longer good law and that it is now irrelevant that the state might be acting to ensure social solidarity. Although the applicants in *Smits-Peerbooms* seem on the facts sympathetic, it is somewhat shocking that state provision of health and education are now to be judged by reference to free movement concerns, especially given the emphasis awarded to public service following the introduction of Article 16 EC by the ToA. The discussion of Member States' ability to provide public services, and particularly services within the context of social security, is not over. Other cases have been referred to the ECJ in the field on public health care[70] and a case concerning the provision of pensions, which raises similar issues about the nature of services for the purposes of Article 49, is currently under consideration by the Court.[71]

The issue of the boundary between the economic and non-economic, in particular when we consider the possibility of indirect payment and linked services, arises again in the context of cases involving sports people. Although sport is accepted as having cultural and social values,[72] the ECJ has long held that sporting activity could fall within the scope of the EC Treaty where an economic activity is involved.[73] The situation is more complex when we consider the position of amateur sports people, especially high ranking ones. The issue was discussed in the case of *Deliège*,[74] which concerned a Belgian competitor's attempts to challenge the judo association's rules regarding selection for international competition. In contrast to the position in the earlier cases, Deliège was classed as an amateur sportswoman by the judo association, although she received a small grant from the Belgian authorities and some sponsorship. She was denied entry to certain competitions, participation in which was a prerequisite to being considered for selection for the national Olympic team. Deliège sought to challenge the national judo association's ruling on

68 Case C-109/92 *Wirth, supra* n. 43.

69 Case 263/86 *Humbel, supra* n. 7.

70 E.g. Case C-08/02, *supra* n. 48.

71 Case C-136/00 *Rolf Dieter Danner*, judgment 3 October 2002.

72 Case C-415/93 *Union Royale Belge des Sociétés de Football Association et al* v. *Bosman, supra* n. 7 at paragraph 106, reaffirmed by the Declaration on Sport annexed to the Treaty of Amsterdam.

73 Case 36/74 *Walrave and Koch, supra* n. 7.

74 Cases C-51/96 and 191/97 *Christelle Deliège* v. *Ligue Francophone de Judo et Disciplines Associées ASBL et al., supra* n. 7.

the basis that the national association's rules constituted a hindrance to the possibility of her competing abroad.

Unsurprisingly, the ECJ held that the association's amateur classification was not determinative for the purposes of identifying whether Deliège was providing a service for remuneration within the terms of Article 49. Equally, the fact that those competitions in question were precursors for Olympic selection did not itself exclude the competitions from the ambit of Community law. The issue was the actual economic status of the individual providing the service and, as noted earlier, the amount of the remuneration was not important provided that such remuneration was not marginal or ancillary. Here it would seem that the sponsorship and the grant brought Deliège within Article 49, although the assessment of facts in this case, and thus the determination of this point, was left to the national court. The fact that Deliège might represent her country, until this point an issue accepted as falling within the 'cultural' aspect of sport, was here seen to have little relevance in affecting the question of whether she fell within the scope of the EC Treaty or not. This ruling might thus have repercussions on some national teams which receive sponsorship or which pay team members a fee for participating, particularly if the matches do not form part of a major tournament.

The ECJ, however, went further, making a statement of potentially much broader application. After reiterating the possibility of services being remunerated indirectly, the ECJ held that there may be a series of services provided within the context of sporting events.

> 'For example, an organiser of such a competition may offer athletes an opportunity of engaging in their sporting activity in competition with others and, at the same time, the athletes, by participating in the competition, enable the organisers to put on a sports event which the public may attend, which television broadcasters may retransmit and which may be of interest to advertisers and sponsors.'[75]

Thus, it seems that the athlete in performing in the competition is an essential component in the creation of an event that is the subject matter of a commercial transaction, especially where the event is broadcast. In contrast to the position of the hospital in *Smits-Peerbooms*,[76] it is hard to see that the athlete in this circumstance (i.e. the service provider) is being remunerated, although the organiser clearly would be providing a service and obtaining an economic benefit. It would seem that, where indirect payment is concerned, the ECJ does not always focus on the view of the

75 Cases C-51/96 and 191/97 *Christelle Deliège* v. *Ligue Francophone de Judo et Disciplines Associées ASBL et al.*, *ibid.*, paragraph 57.

76 Case C-157/99 *Geraets-Smits*, *supra* n. 48.

service provider or, in the case of linked transactions, all the service providers. What seems to be important is that there is a commercial transaction.[77] On this approach, the category of athletes who would not be considered to be in principle within the economic scope would be small indeed. 'Pure sport' would seem to exclude any athlete who participates in any event that people pay to watch or which is televised (or, presumably broadcast on radio).

By tying its statement in *Deliège* to a reference to *Bond van Adverteerders*,[78] the ECJ seems to suggest that the approach here is no more than an application of that doctrine. One crucial difference, however, is that in *Bond van Adverteerders*, the material broadcast and retransmitted was made for that purpose. Here, the athlete's primary purpose is to compete in a competition, not to create the economic event. This approach does not therefore fit well with the ECJ's repeated statement that the individual's economic activity should not be ancillary to another purpose. It would seem that the ECJ's approach to the relevance of motive for determining the existence of economic activity is equivocal where the notion of remuneration is concerned. Although this may be of importance only in marginal cases, it is ironic that the ECJ has taken such a broad view in an area where the limited competence of the Community and the importance of non-economic issues has so recently been emphasised.

b) Distinction between Services and Other Treaty Freedoms

As has already been noted, the treaty freedoms are mutually exclusive, the provisions relating to services constituting the residual category.[79] In effect, this means that the other freedoms need to be ruled out before Article 49 may come into play. Whether the ECJ jurisprudence consistently reflects this position remains to be seen. The boundary between goods and services, perhaps the central distinction in this work, has already been discussed in Chapter 2. This section will therefore consider the distinction between services and persons (contained in the right of establishment and the right of workers to move in Articles 43 and 39 respectively) and the free movement of capital. Article 51 excludes the transport sector from the scope of Article 49. Special provisions applying to this sector, contained in Articles 70-80 EC, although in some cases Article 49 has also been relevant.

77 Contrast the position taken in regard to goods, discussed Chapter 2.

78 Case 352/85 *Bond van Adverteerders* v. *Netherlands*, *supra* n. 5.

79 Article 50 EC.

i) Establishment There are close links between the freedom to provide services and the rights of establishment. One aspect of the right to provide services is linked to the free exercise of a trade or profession other than in the course of employment; equally so does the right of establishment, which can be characterised as the right of the self-employed to move from Member State to Member State. This connection is re-emphasised by the structure of the Treaty itself: not only are these rights dealt with successively, but certain provision apply to both.[80] Furthermore, it seems that common themes run through the jurisprudence, particularly regarding the prohibition on discrimination contained in both Articles 43 and 49.[81] How then do we define establishment, and how do services differ from it?[82]

The Court has assumed that the distinction between establishment and services lies not necessarily in any qualitative difference between the types of service provided, but in respect of the permanency of the link with the host Member State. In *Factortame*, the ECJ held that establishment required 'the actual pursuit of an economic activity through a fixed establishment in another Member State for an indefinite period'.[83] A permanent link means that an individual or corporate body has exercised the right to freedom of establishment, even where the establishment in the host Member State does not constitute an official branch or agency. In the earlier case law, it would suffice that an office was organised by the individual or company, or that someone had authority to act for the company.[84]

By contrast, the Court in *Gebhard* commented that the temporary element of service providers' relationship with a host Member State did not mean that they could not provide themselves with the infrastructure, such as office space, to enable them to provide services, provided this were necessary for the provision of the services concerned.[85] Furthermore, an individual receiving services may remain in the host Member State for the

---

80 Article 55 EC states that Articles 45 *et seq.* apply to services as well as to establishment.

81 See Case 415/93 *Union Royale Belge des Sociétés de Football Association ASBL et al.* v. *Bosman, supra*, n. 7, especially the comments of the Advocate-General at paragraph 196 *et seq.*.

82 The question is phrased thus because services will only apply if establishment does not: Case C-55/94 *Gebhard* v. *Consiglio dell'Ordine degli Avvocati e Procurati di Milano* [1995] ECR I-4165 at p. 4194.

83 Case C-221/89 *R.* v. *Secretary of State for Transport, ex parte Factortame Limited* [1991] ECR I-3905 at p. 3965.

84 Case 205/84 *Commission* v. *Germany* (Insurance Services), *supra* n. 23 at p. 3801.

85 Case C-55/94 *Gebhard* v. *Consiglio dell'Ordine degli Avvocati e Procurati di Milano*, *supra* n. 81, confirmed in Case C-3/95 *Reisebüro Broede* [1995] ECR I-6511.

duration of the time that he is receiving the services.[86] Given that, for example, private education could cover a period of years, it is possible that a service provider, or service recipient, might be resident in a host Member State longer than someone who establishes themselves there.[87] This would seem to suggest temporal issues are not determinative. In *Sodemare*,[88] however, which concerned an old people's home, what seemed crucial was the indefinite nature of the stay, rather than its actual duration. This point is picked up elsewhere. The *Gebhard* judgment pointed out key elements to the provision of services related 'not only to the duration of the provision of services, but also its regularity, periodicity or continuity'.[89] Establishment now seems to require 'a minimum degree of stability derived from the permanent presence of both the human and technical resources necessary' to supply the relevant services. This requirement would seem to narrow the scope of establishment.

The *Gebhard*[90] judgment and its characterisation of services may be criticised. The criteria are vague. The impact of the respective relevant factors has not been made clear and are open to different interpretations, especially where different weight is attributed to the various criteria. These factors might cause particular problems should national courts be called on to assess the boundary between establishment and services, as there is a risk of divergent interpretations between the courts of different Member States. The difficulty here may be less significant than it first appears, however, as Article 49 only applies when the other freedoms do not. The more recent test for establishment seems more precise than that in *Gebhard*, suggesting it might be easier to determine the scope of establishment and, consequently, that of services. Problematically, however, there is some evidence that the ECJ is moving towards a view of the four freedoms that is cumulative rather than seeing them apply in the alternative, as illustrated by the reasoning in *Donatella Calfa*.[91] After

---

86 See Directive 73/148, Article 4(2).

87 See Advocate-General Slynn's comments in Case 263/86 *Humbel*, *supra* n. 7 at p. 5378, when he commented that 'I do not think that the fact that Frédéric received this service for a period of some six years necessarily takes the matter outside the scope of the Treaty provisions on services, which some would say must be of a transitory nature given the contrast with the more permanent nature of "establishment".'

88 Case C-70/95 *Sodemare*, *supra* n. 29. See also Case C-221/89 *Factortame*, *supra* n. 83.

89 Case C-55/94 *Gebhard* v. *Consiglio dell'Ordine degli Avvocati e Procurati di Milano*, *supra* n. 81, paragraph 27. Note the use of the word 'or' indicates that these criteria are alternative, not cumulative.

90 Case C-55/94 *Gebhard* v. *Consiglio dell'Ordine degli Avvocati e Procurati di Milano*, *supra* n. 81.

91 Case C-349/98 *Donatella Calfa* [1999] ECR I-11.

discussing the case from the perspective of Article 49, it then concluded that the national rules in question were contrary not only to Article 49 but also 43 and 39. Discussing services first hardly seems to suggest that Article 49 is a residual category. Further, the boundary between the establishment and the provision of services is blurred and, bearing in mind earlier judgments, has altered over the years. As a consequence, the determination of the question of whether a person is exercising the right of establishment or to provide services will depend on the facts in each case.

Quite apart from questions about the position of the boundary between these two freedoms, one might consider whether the view of services as irregular, short term or intermittent properly describes *all* services. Telecommunications and broadcasting are both clearly seen as services,[92] but the cross-frontier transmission of programming need not be intermittent, temporary or short term.[93] Perhaps we see a difference in approach between those services where the provider or recipient moves, and those in which the service itself moves.

Although there are parallels between the Court's approach towards the two freedoms enshrined in Articles 43 and 49, one significant difference between the two lies in the fact that the Member State in which a person, legal or natural, is established takes greater responsibility for the regulation of that person than a host does to a service provider.[94] This can have great significance in the situation where one Member State's rules are more favourable than another's regulatory regime in respect of a particular activity. Thus in *van Binsbergen*,[95] a case concerning professional rules which precluded a lawyer from representing clients in the Netherlands once he had moved to Belgium, the ECJ held:

> 'a member State cannot be guaranteed the right to take measures to prevent the exercise, by a person providing services whose activity is entirely or principally directed towards its territory, of the freedom guaranteed by Article 59 [now Article 49] for the purpose of avoiding the professional rules of conduct which would be applicable to him if he were established within that state …'[96]

---

92 Case 155/78 *Sacchi, supra* n. 24, Case C-260/89 *ERT* v. *DEP* [1991] ECR I-2925, Joined Cases C-34-36/95 *Konsumentombudsmannen* v. *de Agostini* and *TV Shop* [1997] ECR I-3843.

93 A number of broadcasters are established in the UK (under the Television without Frontiers Directive (89/552), OJ [1989] L 298/15, as amended), yet broadcast on a regular basis to other Member States.

94 See e.g. Case 279/80 *Webb* [1981] ECR 3305. See also Chapter 12.

95 Case 33/74 *JHM Van Binsbergen* v. *Bestuur van de Bedrijfsvereniging voor de Metaalnijverheid* [1974] ECR 1299.

96 *Ibid.*, at paragraph 13.

The issue has continued to arise, notably in a number of broadcasting cases. Each of these cases involved a broadcaster which had established itself in one Member State and broadcast back to another Member State. In some instances this manoeuvre seems to have been carried out for the purposes of avoiding restrictions on broadcasting, such as prohibitions on advertising, in the recipient Member State.[97] In a number of these cases, it was suggested that individuals should not be entitled to 'abuse' Community law in this way.[98] The scope of the 'anti-avoidance' principle was further explored in *TV10*,[99] where the ECJ held that the television company was held to be established in the Member State at which it directed its broadcasts. In doing so, the ECJ held that there were two pre-requisites to the application of the anti-avoidance principle:

1) the foreign broadcaster must be broadcasting wholly or principally to the Netherlands; and
2) it must have been set up in the country where it was so as to avoid the relevant mandatory rules in the receiving country.[100]

It thus seems that the company must have been set up from the very beginning to avoid the recipient state rule, rather subsequently taking advantage of this possibility. The cases caught by this principle would consequently seem only to be the most blatant cases of abuse of Community law.

Although a desire to ensure that Community law was not abused,[101] might be laudable, certain difficulties arise in its operation and it seems that subsequently the ECJ has sought to limit the scope of this doctrine's operation. The matter was again raised in *VT4*,[102] another case concerning the cross-border transmission of broadcasts. Although the ECJ did not address the issue, the Advocate-General did and in so doing suggested an arguably narrower conception of the anti-avoidance principle: in addition to the intention to evade, the company must be acting abusively. The question is, how do we identify abuse? One cannot assume that just

97 Case C-288/89 *Stichting Collectieve Antennevoorziening Gouda* v. *Commissariaat voor de Media* [1991] ECR I-4007; Case C-148/91 *Vereniging Veronica Omroep Organisatie* v. *Commissariaat voor de Media* [1993] ECR I-487; Case C-23/93 *TV10 SA* v. *Commissariaat voor de Media* [1994] ECR I-4795. See also Case C-56/96 *VT4 Ltd.* v. *Vlaamse Gemeenschap* [1997] ECR I-3143.

98 See for example Case C-148/91 *Veronica, ibid.*

99 Case C-23/93 *TV10, supra* n. 97.

100 *Ibid.*, at paragraph 26.

101 This concern was seen elsewhere in the ECJ's jurisprudence at the same time: Joined Cases C-267 and 268/91 *Keck and Mithouard* [1993] ECR I-6097.

102 Case C-56/96 *VT4 Ltd.* v. *Vlaamse Gemeenschap, supra* n. 97.

because a broadcaster is established in one Member State but targeting another, such behaviour constitutes abuse. To do so would accept a variety of assumptions about where companies should be based and where their natural markets are, assumptions which are contrary to the idea of a common market. Advocate-General Lenz raised a further point concerning the determination of abuse: that it is dangerous to look at the nationality of the employees in a company (the Belgians had pointed out that the majority of the employees based in Luxembourg were Belgian), as to do so would, again, be tantamount to discrimination on the grounds of nationality.[103] The Advocate-General also suggested, in contrast to the ECJ's approach in *TV10*, that the anti-avoidance principle should be relied on only when the legislation being evaded protected 'important legal interests that are recognised in Community law'.[104]

Although the case law on this point is not entirely clear, particularly as to the nature of the national rule being avoided and how abuse is proved, it seems indisputable that any anti-avoidance principle will be interpreted narrowly. A narrow approach, for example, is central to the interpretation of the derogations to all of the Treaty freedoms (discussed further in Chapter 7, 8 and 12). More particularly here, a narrow view of the anti-avoidance principle would be supported by the ECJ's approach to abuse and establishment: the anti-avoidance principle cannot be used in relation to the rules governing establishment itself.

In *Centros*[105] a company incorporated under English law made no attempt to trade in the United Kingdom but sought to establish a branch in Denmark. Although the company satisfied English requirements as to capital, the company had insufficient capital under Danish rules. For this reason the authorities refused to register the branch, arguing that this was an attempt to avoid its rules on company minimum capital. The ECJ rejected this argument, distinguishing the situation from the cross-border provision of services, and holding that the very purpose of the Treaty was to allow companies to set up subsidiaries and branches throughout the Community and therefore the choice of a national of one Member State to incorporate a company under the less restrictive rules of another Member State could not constitute an abuse of the right to establishment. Whether one might now not put forward the same argument with respect to the right

103 *Ibid.*, Advocate-General's Opinion, paragraphs 54-68.

104 *Ibid.*, Advocate-General's Opinion, paragraph 30. In so doing he returned to the approach adopted in Case C-148/91 *Veronica, supra* n. 97.

105 Case C-212/97 *Centros* v. *Erhvervs-og Selskabsstyrelsen* [1999] ECR I-1459.

to provide services is another question.[106] The precise scope of any anti-avoidance principle is therefore far from settled.[107]

ii) Capital The point made generally that the freedom to provide services is a residuary right is emphasised by Article 61, which provides that banking and insurance services connected with capital movement are to be dealt with in line with the Treaty provisions on capital, Articles 56–60 EC. The boundary between services and capital has been the subject of some judicial consideration, although the boundary between the two is still not clear. Despite Article 49's character as a residual provision, it seems to have been again treated on an equal footing, in this context with the free movement of capital, supporting the proposition that there is a more general move towards a cumulative approach to the application of the four freedoms. In *Svensson and Gustavsson*[108] the ECJ held that the rules that stated that the approval of a credit institution based in Luxembourg was required before an interest subsidy would be granted by the state were contrary to the provisions on capital as well as those regarding services. This view would seem inconsistent with the Treaty structure. It was an approach that was subsequently criticised by Advocate-General Tesauro in *Safir*.[109] His counter suggestion was to classify rules into those to which the provisions on capital would apply and those to which the rules on services were applicable. The distinction between the two lies in whether the impact on the free movement of capital is direct or indirect: if the former, the rules on capital apply; if the latter, Article 49 is more appropriate. The Advocate-General did accept that both sets of free movement rules might apply, 'but only in relation to the provisions restricting simultaneously, although from different angles, both provision

---

106 See comments of Advocate-General Jacobs in Joined Cases C-34-36/95 *de Agostini*, *supra* n. 92 on this point.

107 New cases covering similar points continue to come before the courts: note a new case has been referred to the ECJ: C-447/00 *Holto Limited*: ref Art. 43: national restrictions on the establishment of a branch without carrying on any economic activity and currently before the House of Lords is a case concerning a broadcasting company which based in England and Wales, but broadcasting to Denmark, thereby not being subject to the Danish rules regarding the need to ensure that certain sporting events are broadcast free-to-air. In its judgment, the House of Lords did not discuss the issue of avoidance: *R.* v. *ITC, ex parte TV-Danmark* over ruling the Court of Appeal's decision at [2000] E.C.C. 11, p. 103.

108 Case C-484/93 *Svensson and Gustavsson* v. *Ministre du Logement et de l'Urbanisme* [1995] ECR I-3955.

109 Case C-118/96 *Safir* v. *Skattemyndigheten i Dalarnas Lan* [1998] ECR I- 1897, at pp. 1903–07.

of services and the movement of capital'.[110] The ECJ did not comment on whether it was necessary to classify a case as falling within the rules on services or capital but did seem to follow the Advocate-General's suggestion that the case in question would fall within Article 49. The issue of whether the capital provisions could also apply was not addressed.

Safir[111] is not exceptional. The same approach was subsequently adopted in *Ambry*.[112] This dual approach may have more significance when a provision is found not to contravene the provisions relating to capital, but which still falls foul of the rules relating to services, because the exceptional restrictions permitted in relation to Article 49 are narrower than those in relation to capital. In particular, Article 58 permits Member States to discriminate on the basis of residence in fiscal matters. With some rare and increasingly narrowly drawn exceptions relating to tax,[113] discrimination on the basis of residence is seen as the negation of the freedom to provide services.[114] There is a danger that the specific derogation regarding capital could be undermined by the application of Article 49 in such circumstances.[115]

III Beneficiaries of the Right

Article 49 is expressed in terms of the abolition of discrimination against nationals of one Member State who provide services in another Member State. The key to relying on the right in Article 49, as far as natural persons who seek to provide services are concerned, is the possession of the nationality of one of the Member States. Nationality is an issue to be determined by the relevant Member State. This approach, common to the free movement of persons provisions, is a contrast to the approach taken in respect of goods where, once the goods have satisfied customs formalities, they may circulate freely irrespective of their point of origin or the nationality of their owner. The Council does have the power, under Article 49(2), to extend the services provisions to third country nationals who are established in the Community, although it has not yet done so. An additional requirement on service providers imposed by the wording of Article 49 is that anyone seeking to rely on this provision must also be

110 Case C-118/96 *Safir*, *ibid.*, at p. 1907.

111 Case C-118/96 *Safir*, *ibid.*

112 Case C-410/96 *Criminal Proceedings against André Ambry* [1998] ECR I-7875.

113 See e.g., Case C-204/90 *Bachmann* [1992] ECR I-249.

114 See Chapter 10.

115 Similar concerns have arisen in respect of the potential overlap between Articles 28 and 29 on the one and hand and the competition provisions, notably Article 81, on the other. See Chapter 3.

established within the EC. Thus, a British national resident in the United States of America could not rely on Article 49 to provide services in France – although Article 43 (right of establishment) would seem to permit such a person to rely on Article 43 to establish herself in France.

Since the ECJ extended the scope of Article 49 to include the right to receive services, the question arises of whether here, too, the right is limited to EC nationals. It would seem, however, that third country nationals who are already established within the Community may rely on Article 49 to cross borders to receive services.[116] The provision may not, however, be used by a third country national as a means of entering the Community in the first place; that would encroach on the sensitive area of Member States' immigration policies.

As with the right of establishment, the right to provide services is extended to companies and firms,[117] such legal persons are therefore to be treated on the same footing as natural persons. Companies for the purposes of Articles 49 and 43 are defined in Article 48. To obtain the benefit of the provision a legal person must satisfy two requirements. The first concerns their form and objectives. Article 48 states that 'companies or firms' are those 'constituted under civil or commercial law, including co-operative societies, and other legal persons governed by public or private law, save for those which are non-profit making'. It seems from this that the form of the legal person is not crucial – certainly they do not have to constitute a company as such. What is central, however, is the profit element.[118] In this requirement we see a reflection of the fact that the EC Treaty has been primarily concerned with the economic and that the purely charitable and the amateur fall outside the scope of the Treaty. It is presumed that this element relates to the legal person's motive rather than an objective assessment of its bank balance. To interpret this otherwise would exclude not only the insolvent, but also viable businesses that are in their start-up phase and not yet making a profit. Such an approach would seem inconsistent with the test adopted by the ECJ in respect of workers[119] and, which is, seemingly, now used in respect of establishment and the right to provide services:[120] that there is no specified minima in respect of income and profit generation, but the activities undertaken must be genuine rather than ancillary or marginal. What this means in practice is another

---

116 See Case C-180/89 *Commission* v. *Italy* [1991] ECR I-709 at 738-9.

117 Article 55 EC.

118 Case 182/83 *Fearon* v. *Irish Land Commission* [1984] ECR 3677 at paragraph 8.

119 Case 53/81 *Levin* v. *Staatssecretaris van Justitie, supra* n. 31, and Case 196/87 *Steymann* v. *Staatssecretaris van Justitie, supra* n. 31.

120 Joined Cases C-51/96 and 191/97 *Christelle Deliège* v. *Ligue Francophone de Judo et Disciplines Associées ASBL et al., supra* n. 7.

question.[121] It should be noted that Article 48 merely seeks to define a class of legal persons; therefore national rules reserving the provision of certain types of activities to non-profit making companies are not incompatible with Article 48, although they may constitute a violation of Articles 43 or 49.[122]

The second element required by Article 48 relates to the nationality of the legal person, reflecting similar concerns to those exhibited regarding natural persons. Thus, Article 48 states that a legal person seeking to rely on this provision must be formed in accordance with the law of a Member State and have its registered office, central administration or principal place of business within the Community.[123] As the ECJ has noted, the registered office 'serves as the connecting factor with the legal system of a particular State, like nationality in the case of natural persons'.[124] Thus, on the face of it, companies from third countries may not rely on Article 48. Given the nature of companies, however, it is possible for subsidiaries of legal persons to be established within the EC, allowing a transnational corporation to enjoy indirectly the benefits of Community freedoms. Furthermore, it is suggested that the analogy between registered office and nationality as the connecting element between the natural or legal person and the legal system of a Member State is somewhat misleading. Nationality usually carries with it some element of identity or loyalty and is usually not an easy matter to change. By contrast, it is comparatively easy for a company to establish subsidiaries in different countries[125] and it is questionable how much identity or loyalty is attached to that link.[126] If the ECJ is concerned with regulation and enforcement, however, although the link through a registered office may have some relevance for these

---

121 See Cases C-51/96 and 191/97 *Christelle Deliège, supra* n. 7 discussed above.

122 Case C-70/95 *Sodemare SA, Anni Azzurri Holding SpA, Anni Azzurri Rezzato Srl* v. *Regiona Lombardia, supra* n. 29.

123 See also the General Programme for the Removal of Restrictions on the Freedom to Provide Services (O.J. English Special Edition (2nd Series) IX, p. 3).

124 Case 270/83 *Commission* v. *France* [1986] ECR 273 at p. 304.

125 Though note Article 43 cannot be interpreted as conferring 'on companies incorporated under the law of a Member State a right to transfer their central management and control their central administration to another Member State while retaining their status as companies incorporated under the legislation of the first Member State': Case 81/87 *R.* v. *H. M. Treasury et al., ex parte Daily Mail and General Trust PLC* [1988] ECR 5483 at paragraph 24.

126 To a certain extent the ECJ has recognised there is a difference between natural and legal persons. In Case 81/87 *R.* v. *H. M. Treasury et al., ex parte Daily Mail and General Trust PLC, ibid.*, the ECJ noted that there could not be a precise parallel between companies and individuals: 'Companies are the creatures of law and, in the present state of Community law, creatures of national law.' paragraph 19.

purposes, for the regulation of individuals the test of residence appears more relevant.

IV Conclusions

The definition of services adopted by the ECJ has been broad. Such an approach is understandable from the perspective of Community law, given the threat to its uniformity and effectiveness inherent in a narrower interpretation. Nonetheless, some aspects of the jurisprudence appear problematic, notably as regards the boundary between the economic and the non-economic. Non-economic actors and services might properly be seen as more appropriately the preserve of the Member State. Furthermore, the impact of the services jurisprudence on the provision of public services highlights not just the tension between the Member States and the Community, each seeking to assert their own competence, but also the tension between different policy objectives within the Community legal order. This latter point again raises the question of which values should be dominant in the European Community and whether amendments to the Treaty have a noticeable influence on the interpretation of the Treaty freedoms.

Chapter 10

Outline of the Freedom to Provide Services

Article 49 contains a prohibition on discrimination regarding the provision of services by a person in one Member State who is established in another. Although this seems a simple proposition, there are a number of different aspects to the right conferred by Article 49. These reflect not only the fact that the right can involve the movement of a person, whether it be the service provider or the recipient, from one Member State to another, but also the different types of service that may be provided. This chapter outlines the bundle of rights which make up the right to provide (or receive) services, including the scope of the right when the services themselves move (telecommunications or insurance services, for example) and the persons against whom the rights may be enforced. This chapter also contains a brief overview of the secondary legislation relating to the mutual recognition of qualifications, as the legislation and jurisprudence of the ECJ in this are intertwined. Any difficulties arising from the scope of the right and the ECJ's interpretation of it will be considered in more detail in the next chapter.

I Whose Actions are Caught?

As with the provisions relating to goods, a preliminary question is whether Article 49 imposes obligations on private parties as well as Member States (and public bodies). Article 49 is not specifically addressed to the Member States. Instead, it is phrased in terms of a general prohibition on discrimination. Given that the signatories of the Treaty are the Member States, it is clear that Article 49 catches their actions. In this respect, Article 49 has similarities to Articles 28 and 29. A sharp contrast between the two sets of provisions lies in the ECJ's approach to the actions of private parties. Whereas for goods the horizontal effect of Articles 28 and 29 is, at best, contested,[1] the ECJ accepted relatively early on in its

---

1 Discussed in Chapter 3.

jurisprudence that Article 49 might have some form of horizontal effect, although its precise scope was not always clear.

In *Walrave and Koch*,[2] the ECJ applied the principle prohibiting discrimination set out in two of the Treaty articles which concern the free movement of people: Articles 39 and 49 (the then Articles 48 and 59 respectively). In imposing this obligation on non-state actors, the ECJ emphasised the foundational and mandatory nature of the prohibition on discrimination.[3] The ECJ also referred to the need to avoid private parties neutralizing the removal of governmentally imposed barriers to the free movement of people; and to the need to ensure uniformity of protection throughout the Community. The ECJ seemed thus to have two main concerns: the centrality of the prohibition on discrimination to the common market project; and the need to ensure uniformity of Community law. Although *Walrave* opened up the possibility that Article 49 could attach to the actions of private parties, certain points remained the subject of debate. In particular, would all actions of private parties be caught or just some of their actions? Further, how and where would any boundaries be drawn? If we consider effectiveness and uniformity of Community law as the central elements of the Court's reasoning, a broad view of Article 49's field of application follows. By contrast, the judgment in *Walrave*, based as it was on references to the 'mandatory' nature of rules, suggested that there would be limits to the obligations imposed by Article 49 on private parties. Clearly we could argue about the meaning of 'mandatory' for these purposes. Further, would horizontal direct effect occur only in cases of direct and overt discrimination, as appeared to be the case in the field of sex discrimination?[4] Finally, was the ruling in *Walrave* limited to circumstances in which there was a collective agreement, such as that in issue in *Walrave*?

It seems that the question of whether Article 49 should be seen as having a general form of horizontal effect has now been answered. *Angonese*[5] concerned the decision of a bank not to employ Angonese because he had not passed the requisite language exams. Angonese had tendered proof of his language skills, but these alternative qualifications were not accepted. The ECJ held that the fact that the bank was a private party was irrelevant in determining whether there had been a finding of a violation of the Treaty. As it had earlier emphasised in *Walrave*,[6] what was important was the need to ensure that the dismantling of state imposed barriers would not be undermined through the re-imposition of other

2 Case 36/74 *Walrave* v. *Union Cycliste Internationale* [1974] ECR 1405.
3 See also Case 13/76 *Dona* v. *Mantero* [1976] ECR 1333.
4 Case 43/75 *Defrenne* v. *Sabena* (No. 2) [1976] ECR 455.
5 Case C-281/98 *Angonese* v. *Cassa di Rispamio di Bolzano SpA* [2000] ECR I-4139.
6 Case 36/74 *Walrave, supra* n. 2.

barriers resulting from private action. This approach suggests that the Court remained concerned with ensuring the effectiveness of Community law (or the rights of individuals), rather than looking for certain formal criteria, such as the existence of collective agreements. Furthermore, the ECJ accepted that the rules in issue constituted indirect discrimination, thereby refuting the suggestion that horizontal direct effect would be limited to cases of direct discrimination. Although *Angonese* concerned workers, Articles 39, 43 and 49 seem to have been interpreted in this context in parallel, as they have been in other cases.[7] *Angonese* can therefore be seen as relevant for identifying the scope of private parties' obligations under Community law in relation to services as well as for workers. On this basis, Article 49 has general horizontal effect.

On one level, given the consistent thread in the ECJ's case law regarding the need to ensure the effectiveness of Community law,[8] the horizontal nature of Article 49 is not surprising. Looked at against the backdrop of Articles 28 and 29, and the concerns expressed in relation to those articles, however, one might question why a different approach has been taken in relation to people than was adopted for goods. It is true that there are some structural differences between the goods provisions and those relating to services. Moreover, in some instances the similarities between the freedom to provide services and the free movement of people might cause issues to arise in relation to services that do not occur when goods are in issue. Not the least of these differences between goods and services is the fact individuals have rights whereas goods do not. Do these differences justify the difference between the goods and services? Although a broad interpretation of Article 49 will provide greater protection for individuals' rights, there is a concern as to whether all private parties will be aware of their obligations under Community law, especially where those obligations have been interpreted broadly and national law permits, or even requires, the challenged behaviour. Simply put, would imposing obligations on individuals always be fair or practicable?

II Scope of Article 49 – Subject Matter

The main thrust of the right concerns the provision of services. Originally, it seemed the main difficulties would affect the service providers themselves. Provision was made in the Treaty to ensure that EC nationals

---

7 Case C-415/93 *Union Royale Belge des Sociétés de Football Association ASBL* v. *Jean-Marc Bosman* [1995] ECR I-4921.

8 See the justification for the introduction of direct effect and supremacy of Community law: e.g. Case 6/64 *Costa* v. *ENEL* [1964] ECR 585.

seeking to exercise their freedom to provide services were able to do so effectively. Thus, the Treaty provided for the drawing up of a General Programme for the abolition of the restrictions on the freedom to provide services within the Community. The programme was drawn up during the early years of the Community, in 1961.[9] It parallels the equivalent programme in respect of the right to freedom of establishment. The need for harmonizing legislation was perceived as central to ensuring the free cross-border provision of services from an early stage in the Community's development. The purpose of the General Programme was therefore to identify the areas in which Community secondary legislation was required to facilitate the freedom to provide services through the elimination of discrimination in various fields. These included the recognition of diplomas and certificates and other evidence of formal qualifications, or in respect of the need for prior authorisation or the 'issuance of a document such as a foreign merchant's card or a foreign professional's card'.[10] Many of the directives issued related to establishment as well as the freedom to provide services. The resulting framework is discussed briefly in Section V below. Harmonization in general is discussed further in Chapter 13.

Notwithstanding the fact that the drafters had recognised the need for secondary legislation, the ECJ ruled that the right set out in Article 49 had direct effect,[11] thus reducing the necessity for harmonizing legislation, although not eliminating it entirely.[12] In the ECJ's view, the proposed directives would not grant new rights, they would merely clarify rights already granted directly by the EC Treaty itself.[13] The impact of the secondary legislation was thus to facilitate the exercise of those rights by making the exact scope of the rights and the mechanisms for their exercise clearer.[14] Given the difficulties encountered in agreeing harmonized sector specific rules prior to the Single European Act, the ECJ's approach to the direct effect of the Treaty article was essential in allowing individuals access to their Community law rights and also in ensuring the effectiveness of Community law itself. Even nowadays, when there is a more extensive legislative framework, an understanding of the ECJ's approach to Article 49 is needed. Not only will this be necessary in filling in lacunae in the protection offered by the secondary legislation, but that legislation must in

9 OJ [1974] Spec. Ed. 2nd Series IX.

10 General Programme, *ibid.*, p. 4.

11 Case 33/74 *Van Binsbergen* v. *Bedrijfsvereniging Metaalnijverheid* [1974] ECR 1307.

12 Contrast the Commission's view: Commission Communication, SEC (74) final.

13 See for example the ECJ's comments in Case 48/75 *Royer* [1976] ECR 497.

14 Case 2/74 *Reyners* v. *Belgium* [1974] ECR 631 at 652, albeit in relation to the right of establishment.

any event be understood within the scope of the relevant Treaty provisions.[15]

The scope of the prohibition in Article 49 has been interpreted widely, covering the structure, nature and location of service providers and their functions and manner in which those functions are carried out. As a general proposition, Article 49 covers those rules that relate to the exercise of economic activity that do not fall within the scope of employment relationship or constitute the exercise of the right of establishment. It does not appear to matter whether the rule applies in respect of a person moving or to the provision of cross-border services. This is the case whether or not the case involves the right to provide services or the right to receive them.[16] Note that the Treaty does not give a migrant an absolute right to practise as a professional but instead permits them to do so on the same conditions as those which apply to the nationals of the host Member State. As a consequence some restrictions may be acceptable.[17] In intention then, the Treaty is not wholly deregulatory, though the difficulties with this point are discussed in greater detail in Chapter 11.

Obviously some rules have the potential to affect workers, establishment and services. The question in such a situation is one of context: that is, which Treaty provision applies rather than is this the type of rule that falls within the scope of Community law? The relationship between these three freedoms is discussed in Chapter 9. Examples of such national rules are those relating to qualifications, noted above. Similarly, situations where the Member State does not recognise the qualifications or training of another Member State may be contrary to the Treaty, as may a failure to recognise the level or quality of supervision carried out by the home Member State authorities.[18] Higher levels of qualification cannot be required and where a Member State requires evidence of good character, provision must be made for accepting appropriate proof from other Member States. Migrants seeking to exercise their Community law rights have the right to join professional or trade organisations under the same conditions as the nationals of the host Member State. Other requirements, such as that of registering with a governing body in the host State could

---

15 Case C-158/96 *Kohll* [1998] ECR I-1931.

16 Case 186/87 *Ian William Cowan* v. *Trésor public* [1989] ECR 195.

17 Article 50, third paragraph.

18 Case C-340/89 *Vlassapoulou* v. *Ministrium für Justiz, Bundes- und Europaangelegenheiten Baden-Württemberg* [1991] ECR I-2354; Case C-104/91 *Aguirre Borrell and others* v. *Colegio Oficial de Agentes dela Propriedad Immobilieria* [1992] ECR I-3003; Case 205/84 *Commission* v. *Germany* (Insurance Services) [1986] ECR 3755, paragraph 47; Case C-76/90 *Manfred Säger* v. *Dennemeyer & Co. Ltd* [1991] ECR I-4221, paragraph 14.

constitute a restriction;[19] and certainly a prohibition on certain categories of persons so registering based on nationality or because they were already registered (established) in another Member State would violate Article 49.[20] Residence requirements, such as those found in the insurance services cases,[21] in general are unlikely to be compatible with the Treaty.[22] Rules of territorial exclusivity for the temporary provision of certain services equally would contravene Article 49.[23]

Even rules that do not prohibit the cross-border provision of services but subject them to extra requirements, could be caught. For example, rules making the exercise of the right more costly through the imposition of taxes or through the requirements that deposits or surety bonds must be paid in the host Member State will be viewed as contrary to Article 49. Administrative requirements, such as prior authorisations, would equally be likely to fall foul of that provision;[24] in *Vander Elst*[25] the requirement that undertakings established in another Member State were obliged to comply with French work permit requirements in respect of third country nationals who were legally working for the undertaking in another Member State prior to their being able to provide services in France was held to constitute a restriction contrary to Article 49. The unacceptability of the national rule was in this case compounded by the fee also payable and by the heavy administrative fine for non-compliance.[26] Similarly, rules in Luxembourg, which required a company temporarily in that State to pay into the Luxembourgoise social security fund when the company was liable to pay similar contributions in its state of establishment for the same period and when the workers were not entitled to any consequent benefits in Luxembourg, also fell within the scope of Article 49.[27]

Article 49 is, however, wider than rules relating strictly to the actual exercise of a professional activity itself. Thus the right covers the right to canvass, to advertise and to approach potential clients and a finalised

---

19 Case 5/83 *Rienks* [1983] ECR 4233.

20 Case 96/85 *Commission* v. *France* (Registration of Doctors) [1986] ECR 1475.

21 E.g. Case 252/83 *Commission* v. *Denmark* (Insurance) [1986] ECR 3713.

22 Case 33/74 *Van Binsbergen, supra* n. 11; Case 39/75 *Coenen* [1975] ECR 1547, paragraphs 6-8.

23 Case C-294/89 *Commission* v. *France* (Lawyers' Services) [1991] ECR I-3591.

24 See e.g. Case C-158/96 *Kohll, supra* n. 15, Case C-76/90 *Manfred Säger* v. *Dennemeyer & Co. Ltd, supra* n. 18.

25 Case C-43/93 *Vander Elst* [1994] ECR I-3803.

26 Case C-43/93 *Vander Elst, ibid.*, at paragraph 12. The position of posted workers has given rise to significant amounts of jurisprudence. The Community has now legislated on this issue.

27 Case 62 and 63/81 *Seco* [1982] ECR 223, paragraph 15.

contract in relation to the service to be provided[28] (or received)[29] is not necessary. Beyond this, Article 49 extends to matters that may be ancillary to the performance of professional activity but which are still necessary for its exercise. Examples are the right to enter into certain types of transaction – for example leases of land or buildings; the right to tender bids or to participate as a contractor or subcontractor in public contracts;[30] the right to borrow and to have access to various forms of credit;[31] and the right to benefit from aids granted by the State. Equally, provisions which required insurers to be established in the host Member State as a precondition to the obtaining of a tax break by the persons insured by that company were found to be contrary to Article 49.[32] This prohibition includes rules which grant benefits as a result of residence,[33] as well as rules which are not formulated as a residence requirement but have the same effect as such requirements.[34]

As is the case for Article 43, the ECJ has interpreted Article 49 more broadly still, so as to encompass within the prohibition of discrimination not only rules which relate specifically to the exercise of non-waged economic activity, but also rules which relate to general facilities which are of assistance to the migrant in seeking to exercise his rights. The most crucial of these is perhaps the right to move itself, together with the right to reside in the host Member State. Secondary legislation elaborates rights to leave one Member States and to enter another.[35] Article 1(1) requires Member States to abolish restrictions on the entry and residence, not only for those who wish to provide services but also, and in express terms, for

---

28 Case C-384/93 *Alpine Investments BV* v. *Minister van Financiën* [1995] ECR I-1141.

29 Case 186/87 *Ian William Cowan* v. *Trésor public*, *supra* n. 16. See Chapter 9.

30 See now Directive 93/96 co-ordinating procedures for the award of public supply contracts OJ [1993] L199/1 and Council Directive 93/37 concerning the co-ordination of procedures for the award of public works contracts, OJ [1993] L199/54.

31 The relationship between the right to provide services and the free movement of capital is discussed in Chapter 9.

32 Case C-300/90 *Commission* v. *Belgium* (Insurance Services) [1992] ECR I-305, paragraph 22. See similarly, Case C-204/90 *Bachmann* [1992] ECR I-249, paragraph 31. See also Case C-294/97 *Eurowings Luftwekehrs AG* v. *Dortmund-Unna* [1999] ECR I-7447.

33 See e.g. Case C-390/96 *Lease Plan* [1998] ECR I-2553 at paragraph 39 concerning rules determining the date from which interest will run following the service of notice to pay; Case C-484/93 *Svensson and Gustavsson* v. *Ministre du Logement et de l'Urbanisme* [1995] ECR I-3955 where the grant of an interest rate subsidy was dependent on obtaining the loan from a company established in the same Member State.

34 Case C-17/92 *Distibudiores Cinematogràphicos* [1993] ECR I-2239, paragraph 16.

35 Directive 73/148 OJ [1973] L172/14.

those who wish to move to receive services.[36] Family members, as defined in the Directive, are granted similar rights. Articles 2 and 3 specify that all persons who fall within the scope of the Directive have the right to leave their national territory and to be issued with a passport or identity card. Correspondingly, they also have the right to enter another Member State on production of valid identity papers. Those providing or receiving a service have the right to remain in the host Member State for the period during which the service is provided; where this right of residence exceeds three months the host Member State should issue a 'right of abode' to the migrant as proof of residence.[37] Similar provisions relate also to family members and are co-terminous with the rights of the service provider or recipient. More broadly, Article 49 has also been held to cover the right to equal access to housing[38] (rather than just business premises) and also to the right to equal access to acquire housing. Although rules such as the Italian preferential loan system would be more likely to affect those seeking to establish themselves, the ECJ has held that,

> '...it cannot be held *a priori* out of the question that a person, whilst retaining his principal place of business in one Member State, may be led to pursue his occupational activities in another Member State for such an extended period that he needs to have permanent housing there and that he may satisfy the conditions of a non-discriminatory nature for access to social housing.'[39]

The extent of the scope of Article 49, especially in the context of social benefits, is slightly unclear. Although the examples given above clearly relate closely to the exercise of a profession, the same cannot be true of *Cowan*.[40] This case concerned a British national on holiday in France, coming within the scope of the EC Treaty by virtue of the fact that he was travelling to receive services, in this case, those of the tourist industry. After being mugged, he sought compensation from the French state. In agreeing that in this context he should not be discriminated against on grounds of nationality, the ECJ argued:

> 'when Community law guarantees a natural person the freedom to go to another Member State, the protection of that person from harm in the Member State in question, on the same basis as that of nationals and persons residing there, is a corollary of that freedom of movement. It follows that the

36 See also Joined Cases 286/82 and 26/83 *Luisi and Carbone* v. *Ministero del Tesoro* [1984] ECR 377.

37 Article 4(2) Directive 73/148, *supra* n. 35.

38 Case 63/86 *Commission* v. *Italy* [1988] ECR 29.

39 Case 63/86 *Commission* v. *Italy, ibid.*, paragraph 19.

40 Case 186/87 *Cowan* v. *Trésor public, supra* n. 16.

> prohibition of discrimination is applicable to recipients of services within the meaning of the Treaty as regards protection against the risk of assault and the right to obtain financial compensation provided for by national law when that risk materialises.'[41]

Although one might accept that the security of the person is necessary to encourage people to exercise free movement rights, it is hardly very closely connected with that right. Arguably *Cowan* is an isolated example.[42] Nonetheless, the issue of the scope of social rights that migrant EC nationals may expect has become complicated by the fact that individuals seem now to have the right to travel to receive services, including some of those provided as a service as a matter of public policy (e.g. health care).[43] The introduction of European citizenship suggesting that in some instances individuals might be able to claim benefits by reference to the citizenship provisions rather than the traditional free movement right itself may compound this difficulty.[44]

III Scope of the Non-discrimination Principle: A Question of Market Access

Most of the above rules were characterised by the ECJ as discriminatory. One issue that needed addressing was whether Article 49 would be limited to discriminatory rules or whether the ECJ should extend the scope of this provision to 'indistinctly applicable' rules, or rules that hindered market access, as it did for goods. The starting point for tracing this development can be found in *Van Binsbergen*,[45] a case which concerned a Dutch national, qualified as a lawyer in the Netherlands, who practised Dutch law in the Netherlands. He then moved to Belgium but sought to continue his practice before the Dutch courts, a practice which he ran from home. The Dutch authorities sought to prevent him from doing so because he was no longer established in the Netherlands and, according to Dutch law, only

41 Case 186/87 *Cowan* v. *Trésor public*, *ibid.*, paragraph 17.

42 See also e.g. Case C-20/92 *Hubbard* v. *Hamburger* [1993] ECR I-3777 regarding a requirement that non-nationals must deposit security for costs and consider Case C-60/00 *Mary Carpenter* v. *Secretary of State for the Home Department* [2002] ECR I-6279, regarding family members' residence rights, discussed further in the next chapter.

43 The breadth of individuals' rights and the nature of the internal situation are discussed further in Chapter 9.

44 For relationship between the services provisions and citizenship see Case C-274/96 *Bickel* v. *Franz* [1998] ECR I-7637.

45 Case 33/74 *Van Binsbergen* v. *Bedrijfsvereniging Metaalnijverheid*, *supra* n. 11.

those who were established in the Netherlands could act as legal representatives before the Dutch courts. Van Binsbergen sought to rely on Article 49; that is, his freedom to provide services from Belgium to the Netherlands. The ECJ held that Articles 49 and 50 take effect against discrimination based on the grounds of a person's nationality or on 'the fact that he resides in a Member State other than that in which the service is to be provided.'[46] As the ECJ made clear in subsequent judgments, such a requirement would have,

> 'the result of depriving Article 59 [now 49] of all its effectiveness, a provision whose very purpose is to abolish restrictions on the freedom to provide services of persons who are not established in the State to which the service is to be provided.'[47]

The effect of the rules at issue in *Van Binsbergen*[48] was to preclude absolutely the cross-border provision of legal services. What would be the position of other rules that did not preclude the provision of such services and which applied both to those resident in the host Member State and to those established elsewhere? The question arose in relation to a requirement that employment agencies be licensed by the host Member State irrespective of whether the agency in question was licensed in its home Member State and therefore already subject to regulatory supervision there.[49] In this case the ECJ seemed to suggest that the application of the rules of the host Member State to a service provider not established in the home Member State might be discriminatory when it did not take account of home regulation. The host Member State in such an instance would be failing to treat different circumstances differently and, in effect, such service providers would be subject to a double level of regulation.

---

46 Case 33/74 *Van Binsbergen* v. *Bedrijfsvereniging Metaalnijverheid*, *supra* n. 11, paragraph 10. See also Joined Cases 110 and 111/78 *Ministère public and Chambre syndicale des agents artistiques et impresarii de Belgique* v. *Van Wesemael* [1979] ECR 35, paragraph 27 and Cases 62 and 63/81 *Seco*, *supra* n. 27, paragraph 8.

47 Case 205/84 *Insurance Services*, *supra* n. 18, paragraph 52. This approach has been repeated in many cases – see for a more recent example Case C-222/95 *Société Civile Immobilière Paroldi* v. *Banque H. Albert de Bary et Die* [1997] ECR I-3899, paragraph 31. A similar approach in respect of rules which negate the very essence of the right has been taken in respect of establishment too – see Case C-212/97 *Centros Ltd* v. *Erhvervs-og Selskabsstyrelsen* [1999] ECR I-1459 discussed in Chapter 9.

48 Case 33/74 *Van Binsbergen*, *supra* n. 11.

49 See Joined Cases 110-111/78 *van Wesemael*, *supra* n. 46, paragraph 30, and Case 279/80 *Webb* [1981] ECR 3305, paragraph 16.

The approach taken in the employment agency cases[50] was developed further in the German insurance company cases.[51] German rules required, amongst other provisions, that insurance companies established and regulated in other Member States must still obtain a German authorisation for their activities in Germany. The ECJ again stated that national rules could not be applied blanket fashion to a service provider established in another Member State. Nonetheless the ECJ accepted that host Member State rules could be used to protect certain public interests. In the event that such a public interest was not protected by the regulation of the home Member State then the host Member State rules could be justified. The insurance cases provided the basis for a four-stage test that the Court still uses to determine whether Article 49 has been violated in the case of a *prima facie* breach:

1) the national rules in issue apply to those established in the Member State as well as to those who are established in another Member State (in the terminology of the case law relating to goods, they are 'indistinctly applicable');
2) the rules protect the public interest;
3) they are proportionate in that they achieve the end desired in no more intrusive manner than necessary; and
4) account is taken of home Member State regulation.

If all four criteria are satisfied, no violation of Article 49 will have occurred, although the national rule may operate to put the non-national service provider (or recipient) under an additional burden.[52]

There are a number of points to be noted at this stage. Rules that duplicate home State regulation are contrary to Article 49. A rule that is not duplicated in the home Member State may be acceptable under the terms of Article 49, but this will not necessarily be the case, even if the national rule does not impose a double burden. It is important to note that only those rules that protect the public interest may be saved by reference to this approach.[53]

Although the debate has been framed in terms of discrimination so far, it would seem that the jurisprudence of the ECJ is not concerned, or at

---

50 Joined Cases 110-111/78 *van Wesemael*, *supra* n. 46 and Case 279/80 *Webb*, *ibid*.

51 Case 205/84 *Insurance Services*, *supra* n. 18.

52 This is similar to the argument relating to goods as to whether the *Cassis de Dijon* (Case C-120/78) 'mandatory requirements' constitute derogation from Article 28 or operate instead to determine its scope. This point is discussed further in Chapter 7.

53 Case C-154/89 *Commission* v. *France* (Tour Guides) [1991] ECR I-4221; Case C-198/89 *Commission* v. *Greece* [1991] ECR I-727, paragraphs 16 and 18. The scope of the public interest justification will be discussed in Chapter 12.

least not solely concerned, with discrimination.[54] This point is less clear than it might be as the ECJ has not always made it entirely clear what the term, 'discrimination' actually means.[55] The approach in the *German Insurance* cases[56] and subsequent rulings indicates a move away from a discrimination based approach: Article 49 does not require that cross-border service providers or recipients are subject to an extra burden. It is here that we see parallels developing with the approach taken in *Cassis de Dijon*[57] in relation to goods, based on mutual recognition and a rule of reason.[58] The underlying assumption in the insurance cases and in subsequent judgments is that what is permissible in one Member State should be acceptable throughout the Community. Similarly, in the case of rules that are expressed to apply equally to those established in the host Member State and those established in another Member State – in goods terms, indistinctly applicable measures, proportionate rules that protect 'mandatory requirements' may be permitted.

These suggested parallels became much clearer with the ECJ's ruling in *Säger* v. *Dennemeyer.*[59] Säger was a specialist in patent renewal services who claimed that the provision of such services by Dennemeyer, a company incorporated in England and Wales, was contrary to German rules that required the providers of such services to have obtained certain qualifications. The provision of patent renewal services was not subject to regulation in the United Kingdom. The German court referred the question of the rule's compatibility with Article 49 to the ECJ. The ECJ in answering this question chose not to focus on the issue of discrimination or the negating of the essence of the rights, as it had done in previous judgments. Instead, it adopted an approach very similar to that which it had taken in *Cassis*[60] as regards the free movement of goods. Crucially, it held that:

> '... Article 59 [now 49] of the Treaty requires not only the elimination of all discrimination against a person providing services on the ground of his

---

54 On discrimination see e.g. Case 52/79 *Procureur du Roi* v. *Debauve* [1980] ECR 833, paragraph 21, Case C-279/80 *Webb, supra* n. 49, paragraph 21, Cases 62 and 63/81 *Seco, supra* n. 27, Case C-381/93 *Commission* v. *France* (Maritime Services) [1994] ECR I-5145 and Case C-158/96 *Kohll, supra* n. 15.

55 The issue of discrimination is discussed further in Chapter 11. See also Chapter 5 regarding goods.

56 Case 205/84 *Insurance Services, supra* n. 18.

57 Case 120/78 *Rewe* v. *Bundesmonopolverwaltung fur Branntwein* (Cassis de Dijon) [1979] ECR 649.

58 See Chapters 4 and 5 for a further discussion of the case in relation to goods.

59 Case C-76/90 *Manfred Säger, supra* n. 18.

60 Case 120/78 *Cassis de Dijon, supra* n. 57.

nationality but also the abolition of any restriction, even if it applies without distinction to national providers of services and to those of other Member States, when it is liable to prohibit or otherwise impede the activities of a provider of services established in another Member State where he lawfully provides similar services.'[61]

As with goods, equal burden or trade neutral rules may be caught by Article 49 just as much as those that impose an additional burden on the cross-border service provider, whether the rule is phrased in neutral terms or not.

What the ECJ introduced with *Säger* v. *Dennemeyer* was a broad, effects-based test, albeit a test that seems not to be quite as broad as that introduced in relation to goods by *Dassonville*.[62] Whereas the test in *Dassonville* emphasised that any effect on inter-state trade to trigger the application of Community law and, in particular, Article 28 could be indirect or even potential, the test in *Säger* seems to require a slightly more concrete impediment to the provisions of services. Whether the distinction between the approach for goods and that taken in respect of services is purely semantic is another question. The level of hindrance required and the question of whether the change to an indistinctly applicable test was necessary or desirable is an issue discussed further in Chapter 11.[63] It is, however, an approach that now seems well established and in general use, whether the situation relates to services themselves moving, to service providers moving and, despite the precise phraseology used by the ECJ in *Säger* v. *Dennemeyer*, to those moving to receive services. The ECJ adopted the same approach in relation to lotteries,[64] to cold calling in respect of financial services[65] and, apparently, also in relation to the right to receive health care.[66] Whether the services jurisprudence has adopted another aspect of the goods case law, the distinction between 'product requirements to be met' and 'selling arrangements'[67] has been the subject of some debate. This point is discussed further in the next chapter, although it would generally seem that the distinction does not arise in relation to services. [68]

---

61 Case C-76/90 *Manfred Säger*, *supra* n. 18, paragraph 12; contrast the holding in Case 52/79 *Procureur du Roi* v. *Debauve*, *supra* n. 54, paragraph 16.

62 Case 8/74 *Procureur du Roi* v. *Dassonville et al.* [1974] ECR 837.

63 See also Chapter 5 in relation to goods.

64 Case C-275/92 *Schindler* [1994] ECR I-1039.

65 Case C-384/93 *Alpine Investments BV*, *supra* n. 28.

66 Case C-158/96 *Kohll*, *supra* n. 15.

67 Joined Cases C-267 and 268/91 *Keck and Mithouard* [1993] ECR I-6097.

68 Case C-384/93 *Alpine Investments*, *supra* n. 28; Case C-17/00 *Françoise de Coster* v. *Collège des Bourgmestres et Echevins de Watermael-Boitsfort* [2001] ECR I-9445.

The restrictions in these cases were on the whole rules imposed by the receiving state. Article 49 may also apply to those imposed by the Member State of establishment – in effect these may be seen as a form of restriction on export.[69] In principle, Article 49 could apply irrespective of whether the rule is directly or indirectly discriminatory (or indistinctly applicable). In *Alpine Investments*[70] the Dutch government sought to prevent companies cold calling customers, even when those potential customers were not resident in the Netherlands, relying on a mandatory requirement to justify the rule. In *de Agostini*,[71] the ECJ viewed the Swedish restriction on advertising aimed at children as limiting the freedom of advertisers based in Sweden to approach broadcasters established elsewhere but who were broadcasting programming back to Sweden. A similar approach was adopted in *Gourmet*[72] regarding the ability of advertisers to sell advertising space in respect of advertisements for alcoholic beverages in the light of Swedish rules limiting where such advertisements could be displayed.

IV The Cross-border Element

A consistent element in the ECJ's case law in respect of all of the four freedoms is that there must be a cross-border element to bring the case within the scope of EC law. In other words, EC law does not apply to purely internal situations. This is implied by the wording of Article 49 itself and has been re-iterated by the ECJ in many judgments.[73] This does not mean that the issue is reduced to the situation where an individual physically moves from one Member State to another to provide the service, although such a situation would clearly be caught within the Treaty rules. In the *Tourist Guides* cases, the ECJ held,

> 'the provisions of Article 59 [now 49] must apply in all cases where a person providing services offers those services in a Member State other than that in

69 See e.g. Case C-18/93 *Corsica Ferries Italia* [1994] ECR I-1783.

70 Case C-384/93 *Alpine Investments BV, supra* n. 28.

71 Joined Cases C-34-36/95 *Konsumentombudsmannen* v. *de Agostini* and *TV Shop i Sverige* [1997] ECR I-3843, paragraph 50.

72 Case C-405/98 *Konsumentombudsmannen* v. *Gourmet International Products AB* [2001] ECR I-1795.

73 Case 52/79 *Procureur du Roi* v. *Debauve, supra* n. 54, paragraph 9; Case C-64 and 65/96 *Land Nordrhein-Westfalen* v. *Uecker* and *Jacquet* v. *Land Nordrhein-Westfalen* [1997] ECR I-3171, paragraph 16; Case 134/95 *USSL No 47 di Biella* v. *INAIL* [1997] ECR I-195, paragraph 19; Case C-332/90 *Steen* v. *Deutsche Bundespost* [1992] ECR I-341, paragraph 9.

which he is established, wherever the recipients of those services are established.'[74]

This is the case whether or not the right is being asserted against the host or the recipient Member State.[75] As noted in Chapter 9, the ECJ expanded this to include the right to receive services. Thus, the relevant cross-border element may also be found when the recipient of the services moves from one Member State to another.[76] A cross-border element is also found in situations where the services themselves cross borders, such as in cross-border television broadcasting[77] and in investment services.[78] Recipients of such services may rely on Article 49 as against their own Member State.[79] Whether there is a cross-border element depends on the facts in each case, an issue that, *prima facie*, is for the national court to decide.[80] Sometimes, however, the ECJ has suggested that there is an EC element when the link has been somewhat tenuous, an issue discussed further in the next chapter.

V Recognition of Qualifications – Harmonization

As noted earlier, one of the key difficulties for anyone seeking to move or to provide services across borders concerns the professional qualifications required for the practice of a particular profession or occupation by the different Member States because there are significant differences between the educational systems of the different states. Although a detailed analysis of the relevant secondary legislation falls outside the scope of this book, a brief overview will be provided, against which the Article 49 case law may be assessed. Where the directives apply, in principle reference should be made to them rather than to the Treaty freedoms, although the directives must be understood in the light of the Treaty provisions and relevant jurisprudence. In practice, then, the early ECJ rulings on Article 49 may

---

74 Case C-198/89 *Commission* v. *Greece*, *supra* n. 53, paragraph 9. See also Case C-154/89 *Commission* v. *France* (Tour Guides), *supra* n. 53, paragraph 9.

75 Case C-18/93 *Corsica Ferries Italia*, *supra* n. 69, paragraph 30.

76 Joined Cases 286/82 and 26/83 *Luisi and Carbone* v. *Ministero del Tesoro*, *supra* n. 36, paragraph 10.

77 Case C-56/96 *VT4* [1997] ECR I-3143 at paragraph 17; Case C-14/96 *Denuit* [1997] ECR I-2785 at paragraph 23.

78 Case C-384/93 *Alpine Investments*, *supra* n. 28, at paragraph 21.

79 Case C-294/97 *Eurowings Luftverkehrs*, *supra* n. 32, Case C-17/00 *de Coster*, *supra* n. 68.

80 Case 52/79 *Procureur du Roi* v. *Debauve*, *supra* n. 54, paragraph 9.

still be relevant, especially as there may still be gaps in the rules provided by the harmonizing legislation.[81]

The initial approach to the harmonization of standards was sector-specific, regulating in some detail the training for particular professions. Although certain sectors are still regulated in this way – for example lawyers, doctors, dentists, pharmacists, midwives and architects – the institutions subsequently developed a different approach; that of a general system for the recognition of qualifications. Whereas the directives regulating particular professions tend to lay down minimum standards in respect of the relevant profession and guarantee automatic recognition of the professional title throughout the Community, the general system does not do so. Instead it seeks to provide a system for establishing the equivalence of qualifications. This approach means that less detailed regulation at Community level is required and avoids the necessity of most, or all, Member States having to amend their rules governing specific professions.

There are two general directives: one relates to the recognition of higher education diplomas awarded after at least three years' study,[82] the second supplements the first extending the same principles beyond three year degrees.[83] The mutual recognition system under the Higher Education Diploma Directive applies to regulated professions, that is, where the pursuit of an activity is regulated in at least one Member State, either directly or indirectly, by reference to a diploma.[84] To fall within the terms of the Directive, the diploma must be a higher education certificate awarded following the completion of a course of at least three years' duration and that the certificate shows that the holder has the professional qualification required for the pursuit of the profession in the Member State in which the certificate was awarded.[85] Article 3 contains the basic principle: that where a profession is subject to the holding of a diploma, the regulatory authority may not determine that a migrant has inadequate qualifications where either the migrant has a diploma from another Member State entitling him to pursue the activity in question in that Member State; or where the Member State of origin does not regulate the profession in question, but the migrant has pursued the activity full time for at least two years in the previous ten. Article 4 attempts to deal with discrepancies in the training systems between Member States by

---

81 See for example, Case C-340/89 *Vlassapoulou*, *supra* n. 18.

82 Council Directive 89/48 [1989] OJ L 19/16.

83 Council Directive 92/51 [1992] OJ L 209/25.

84 'Diploma' is defined in Article 1(a) of Directive 89/48, *supra* n. 82.

85 The Directive does not cover diplomas conferred in third countries. A Council Recommendation on such diplomas recommends that Member States should recognise such qualifications, [1989] OJ L 19/24.

allowing the host Member State to require the applicants to satisfy 'compensation measures', such as providing proof of professional experience; completing an adaptation period (the extent of which is limited by the Directive); or taking an aptitude test. Article 7 then outlines the circumstances in which professional titles may be used. A similar approach based on mutual recognition is adopted in the supporting directive on post secondary education training and professional experience.

The general system is more flexible than the sectoral approach; the sectoral approach is slow and difficult to amend and there is therefore a risk that the guarantees contained in the sectoral directives may become outdated, especially given the difficulties Member States have had in coming to agreement in respect of some activities. Further, a similarity of approach can be detected between the Court's approach towards the regulation of services in general and that adopted in the mutual recognition system which forms the basis of the Higher Education Diploma. The general system is, however, not without its flaws, notably the uncertainty as to when the compensation measures will be required. Although in practice recognition has often been granted by the host Member State requiring the application of compensation measures, the position will not be clear to the migrant in advance. Further the fact that the system requires a case-by-case assessment of applications results in an administrative burden for Member States' regulatory bodies and increases the risk of delays in the requests being processed.[86] Additionally, a case-by-case approach can lead to an inequality of approach in practice and, potentially, there is also a risk of abuse. In any event, a number of Member States have not implemented the directives fully.

The Commission has recently launched a consultation process on improving mutual recognition. Fourteen sector specific directives have already been updated as part of the Simplified Legislation for the Internal Market (SLIM) initiative. The SLIM initiative is aimed at making Community legislation clearer and more accessible. The amending directive simplifies existing sector specific directives by consolidating the various requirements that had been scattered through the texts of the directives. Requirements for the professional and relevant regulatory bodies are now organised by Member States. Member States may notify the Commission directly of any changes in the relevant national system. It is hoped that the new system will be able to react more swiftly where there is need for change. Additionally, the Directive will require Member States to take rapid decisions on requests for recognition. In doing so, Member States will now be required to take into account experience gained in other Member States. Further, Member States will be required to take into

86 The Commission has noted, for example, that Greece has not dealt with applications regarding the profession of optician.

account, though not necessarily themselves recognise, the recognition of non-community qualifications by any Member State. The Commission hopes to simplify the general system also, although the process of consultation is not at the time of writing complete and there are therefore no specific proposals available. It is unlikely that any legislative development could render the ECJ's jurisprudence in this area superfluous.

VI Conclusions

In general, it seems that similar concerns underlie the services case law as can be found in the goods jurisprudence. One of the main questions is the proper scope of Article 49 and consequently the areas of policy that remain within the competence of the Member States. As a consequence, a particular concern is whether Article 49 should be concerned only with discrimination or with access to the market. The difficulties surrounding this question will be considered further in the next chapter. It should be noted, however, that the problems in this area might be exacerbated by the fact that Article 49 covers not just the provision of services, but also deals with the movement of people. As such, the jurisprudence will have to take into account the fact that individuals are not just factors of production or consumers, but are human beings and therefore also have a social side. Furthermore, this human aspect of service providers and recipients (as well as workers and those seeking to establish themselves) has been re-emphasised by the introduction of European citizenship[87] and the need to treat all citizens of Europe equally.[88] The difficulty here is that in many areas, social concerns link into areas of policy that have been jealousy guarded by the Member States, notably social security and the provision of public services. Should special rules apply in these areas, or should they be treated simply as internal market questions?

---

87 Article 18 EC *et seq.*

88 C-85/96 *María Martínez Sala* v. *Freistaat Bayern* [1998] ECR I-2691; Case C-274/96 *Criminal proceedings against Horst Otto Bickel and Ulrich Franz, supra* n. 44. See also Communication on Directive 64/221, discussed further in Chapter 12.

Chapter 11

Difficulties arising from the Article 49 Jurisprudence

I Introduction

The determination of the proper scope of the freedom to provide services is important, as measures falling within Article 49 EC, even if subsequently found to be acceptable by virtue of the rule of reason or of the Treaty provisions derogating from that freedom, will be assessed within the Community legal order by reference to values established by that order.[1] Member States' freedom to regulate in many fields is consequently circumscribed. Questions regarding the nature of an internal situation falling outside the scope of Community competence and that of the test to be applied to determine the application of Article 49 are clearly central to any discussion about the scope of the freedom to provide services. The issues are complicated by the many different ways in which the freedom to provide services may arise.[2] It can involve the movement of people or the movement of the service itself; the provision or the receipt of services; and include the provision of services as 'imports' as well as 'exports'.[3] As well as considering the test for the application of Article 49, in this context, we might question the degree to which the services case law deviates from that relating to goods and, if it does, why? Against such a backdrop, it is hardly surprising that the boundaries of Article 49 seem, on occasions, to be a little uncertain. This chapter seeks to identify the more problematic areas in the ECJ's services jurisprudence, particularly those areas in which questions have arisen and remain unresolved.

II Scope of Article 49 – Discrimination and Access to the Market

Article 49 is clearly phrased in a comparative manner, comparing the treatment of those established in a given Member State with those who

---

1 See further Chapter 12.

2 See further Chapter 9.

3 Case C-384/93 *Alpine Investments BV* v. *Minister van Financiën* [1995] ECR I-1141.

were not. The case law outlined in Chapter 10 has, however, expanded the range of measures potentially falling within Article 49 to include not only directly discriminatory measures, but also those that have an indirectly discriminatory effect and, arguably, even some measures which apply equally. Since *Säger*,[4] which brought the services jurisprudence broadly into line with the *Cassis de Dijon*[5] approach to goods, measures that in 'goods' terminology would be called indistinctly applicable, now fall within Article 49. We are then faced with a similar question to that arising in respect of Article 28: how do we determine what should be caught by the Treaty and what should not? The EC does not have a general competence to regulate all trade; an impact on inter-state trade must be shown.[6] So, what sort of level of impact is required and when does an inter-state element arise? What seems to be two elements can be broken down further, even if the ECJ does not expressly adopt such an analysis. The internal situation can be seen as describing the position when none of the service provider, the service recipient or the service itself cross a border. Equally, an internal situation could be seen as arising when the effect of the rule is too remote from the cross-border provision of services. Linked to this issue is another question, that of the type or scope of rights granted by Article 49. Remoteness is a different consideration from the level of hindrance required before a measure is caught by Article 49, although sometimes the issues might be seen as alternative responses to the question of whether Article 49 applies in a given case.[7] This section considers the first of these interpretations of an internal situation before considering the level of hindrance necessary to trigger Article 49. Remoteness is discussed briefly in Section IV.

As with other freedoms, Article 49 does not apply to purely internal situations. Given the variety of ways in which the freedom can manifest itself, however, the circumstances in which no cross-border element would occur is limited, especially were the ECJ to take a similar approach to that adopted in relation to goods: that of adopting an objective or abstract test. Following *Guimont*,[8] internal situations, as far as Article 28 is concerned, are limited to circumstances in which the rule the subject of complaint could never affect imports. The position regarding services is not, however,

4 Case C-76/90 *Manfred Säger* v. *Dennemeyer & Co Ltd* [1991] ECR I-4421.

5 Case 120/78 *Rewe* v. *Bundesmonopolverwaltung für Branntwein (Cassis de Dijon)* [1979] ECR 649.

6 Case C-97/98 *Jägerskiöld* v. *Gustafsson* [1999] ECR I-7319.

7 This can be seen in relation to the early Article 28 jurisprudence dealing with the free movement of goods discussed in Chapter 5.

8 Case C-448/98 *Criminal Proceedings against Jean-Pierre Guimont* [2000] ECR I-10663 and also Joined Cases C-321-4/94 *Jacques Pistre* [1997] ECR I-2343, discussed in Chapter 5.

as clear-cut. *Jägerskiöld*[9] concerned a dispute between two Finnish nationals' fishing rights in Finland. The relevant rules may also have had an effect on tourists travelling from abroad to fish. The ECJ found there to be an internal situation; it did not, however, address the issue of the hypothetical tourist industry.[10] Similarly in *RI.SAN*,[11] which concerned an Italian rule, the ECJ noted that economic operators from other Member States could be affected by the rule as well as Italians. Nonetheless, the Court held that this was an internal situation because *RI.SAN* 'which challenges the legality of the choice made by the municipality, has its seat in Italy and does not operate on the Italian market in reliance on freedom of establishment or freedom to provide services'.[12] As it did in *Jägerskiöld*, the ECJ thus judged whether there was an internal situation on the facts of the case, and not by reference to an objective test.

Deliège[13] is more problematic. The case is open to a narrow and a broad interpretation. In *Deliège*, the ECJ found there to be no internal situation. Although Deliège, an athlete, was challenging the national rules of her profession, the ECJ found a transfrontier element as Deliège had, after all, competed abroad and would do so again. On the one hand this reasoning suggests that an actual cross-border element will be required, however slight. On this assessment, *Deliège* is in line with cases such as *Jägerskiöld*[14] and *RI.SAN*,[15] in which the Court looked at the facts of the case in issue to determine if there was an out of state element. *Deliège*, however, also suggests that if even just once in an individual's career there is occasion to exercise free movement rights, then that individual's entire career could come within the protection of EC law. Such an interpretation raises questions about the longevity of migrant or cross-border status. These issues are discussed further below in Part IV of this chapter.

In contrast to these cases that take a comparatively broad view of the internal situation, *SETTG*[16] shows the ECJ taking an expansive approach to the definition of cross-border elements. It seems to adopt an interpretation similar to that which it took in relation to goods. *SETTG* concerned a Greek rule that affected only those tour guides with a particular Greek qualification that, according to EC law, the Greek Government could not require cross-border service providers to have. In

---

9 Case C-97/98 *Jägerskiöld* v. *Gustafsson, supra* n. 6.

10 This case could arguably be seen as a form of remoteness case too.

11 Case C-108/98 *RI.SAN Srl* v. *Comune di Ischia* [1999] ECR 1-5219.

12 Case C-108/98 *RI.SAN, ibid.*, paragraph 21.

13 Joined Cases C-51/96 and C-191/97 *Christelle Deliège* v. *Ligue Francophone de Judo et Disciplines Associées ASBL et al.* [2000] ECR I-2549.

14 Case C-97/98 *Jägerskiöld* v. *Gustafsson, supra* n. 6.

15 Case C-108/98 *RI.SAN, supra* n. 11.

16 Case C-398/95 *SETTG* v. *Ypourgos Ergosias* [1997] ECR 1-3091.

practice, it would be unlikely (albeit not impossible) that tour guides based in other Member States would obtain the Greek licence. Certainly the existence of the group of persons that rule would affect was hypothetical. The ECJ held that,

> '[t]he mere fact that tourist guides from another Member State do not need such a licence when they accompany a group of tourists to Greece does not mean that they cannot have an interest in acquiring the said diploma ...' [17]

The Court concluded that 'such rules may affect the right of self employed tourist guides from another Member State freely to provide services ...'.[18] The approach in *SETTG* indicates that the ECJ will look at whether the rule could ever have a transfrontier effect.

Since *SETTG*[19] predates *Jägerskiöld*[20] and *Deliège*,[21] we might dismiss *SETTG* as an aberration. The approach in *SETTG* finds some support in other case law, however. In the more recent case of *de Coster*,[22] a Belgian rule concerning the imposition of a tax on the installation of satellite dishes was the subject of a challenge. De Coster was resident in Belgium. Although the ECJ has repeatedly held that a service provider can rely on Article 49 as against its home State, there must still be some transfrontier element.[23] Here, de Coster was challenging under Article 49 a rule relating not to the service itself, but affecting the supply of goods. The national rule did therefore not directly relate to services. Nonetheless, the ECJ equated the tax with a direct charge on a service and assumed that Article 49 applied because it was more likely to affect non-Belgian broadcasters than domestic broadcasters. Although this may be the case, the reasoning of the Court does not refer specifically to any concrete examples; certainly the Court did not discuss the recipient's access to transfrontier television services. The reasoning in this case therefore re-emphasises the more abstract view of whether or not a transfrontier element arises. Here, broadcasters established in other Member States could have been affected by the national rule and the ECJ did not seem particularly concerned with whether there actually was such a broadcaster so affected. These abstract cases also show that there are links between the

---

17 Case C-398/95 *SETTG, ibid.*, paragraph 12.

18 Case C-398/95 *SETTG, ibid.*, paragraph 13.

19 Case C-398/95 *SETTG, ibid.*

20 Case C-97/98 *Jägerskiöld* v. *Gustafsson, supra* n. 6.

21 Joined Cases C-51/96 and C-191/97 *Deliège, supra* n. 13.

22 Case C-17/00 *Françoise de Coster* v. *Collège des Bourgmestres et Echevins de Watermael-Boitsfort* [2001] ECR I-9445.

23 Case C-294/97 *Eurowings Luftverkehr* [1999] ECR I-7447.

finding of a cross-border element and the finding of a restriction discussed further below. In this there are similarities to the goods case law.[24]

Sodermare,[25] in which Article 49 was found not to apply, illustrates a slightly different problem. The case concerned a Luxembourg company which, through its Italian subsidiaries, sought to provide care homes for the elderly in Italy. In doing so, the company had clearly exercised its freedom of establishment, but was it also exercising its right to provide services? The ECJ pointed out that, as the company was established in Italy and providing services in Italy, there was no transfrontier element to the provision of services. What, however, if those at the care home included non-Italians? When recipients move to receive services, both recipient and service provider may, in principle, rely on Article 49. The ECJ, however, took the view that the service recipients in such a situation would have exercised their right of establishment and Article 49 would not apply.[26] This reasoning would seem to lead to anomalies as far as the service provider is concerned. Whereas a recipient moving to another Member State falls within the scope of EC law irrespective of whether Article 43 or 49 is concerned, for the provider of the service the situation is different. Such a service provider, which has not moved itself, apparently only falls within the scope of EC law if the persons to whom it is providing the service have exercised their rights under Article 49, rather than Article 43. A person established within a Member State suing another in that Member State constitutes an internal situation. The approach in *Sodermare* therefore also re-emphasises the concrete assessment of the internal situation question.

As regards the question of the nature of the hindrance, on a superficial level there is a clear answer. In *Säger*,[27] the ECJ set down a test for the application of Article 49: that provision applies 'when it is liable to prohibit or otherwise impede'[28] the provision of services. This potentially is a very broad test, so one might question what it means in practice. Even before *Säger*, the scope of Article 49 had been wide. Based on discrimination against the cross-border provision of services, it covered both direct and indirect forms of discrimination. Clearly, rules that require service providers to be established in the Member State in which the service is to be provided, or which submit non-established service providers to special conditions,[29] would prevent or put at a disadvantage

24 See Chapter 5.

25 Case C-70/95 *Sodermare* v. *Regione Lombardia* [1997] ECR I-3395.

26 Case C-70/95 *Sodermare*, *ibid.*, paragraph 38.

27 Case C-76/90 *Säger*, *supra* n. 4.

28 Case C-76/90 *Säger*, *supra* n. 4, paragraph 12.

29 See e.g. Case 427/85 *Commission* v. *Germany* (Lawyers Services) [1988] ECR 1123 concerning obligations imposed on non-resident lawyers that were not imposed on

those providing cross-border services. This sort of rule would be objectionable, not because it would constitute indirect discrimination on grounds of nationality, but because it would impose restrictions directly on the cross-border provision of services. Nationality restrictions, apart from constituting a violation of Article 12 EC, are likely to be indirectly discriminatory in the context of cross-border service provision because those who would not satisfy such a criterion are more likely to be established in another Member State.[30] It seems, however, as though the prohibition in Article 49 has in any event been equated with a prohibition on discrimination on grounds of nationality.[31] This approach reflects the requirement in Article 54 that, as long as restrictions have not been abolished, such restrictions should be applied without distinction on grounds of nationality or residence.

Furthermore, rules which duplicate home country regulation can also be seen as discriminatory, even if phrased in neutral terms, where they subject the service provider to additional level of regulation which is unnecessary. *Seco* concerned the question of whether employer's contributions were due in respect of workers in the host Member State, when payments had been made in respect of those workers in the home Member State.[32] In that case, the ECJ remarked that legislation requiring the employer to pay again in the host Member State,

> 'proves in economic terms to be more onerous for employers established in another Member State, who in fact have to bear a heavier burden than those established within the territory.'[33]

---

resident lawyers; Case 96/85 *Commission* v. *France* (Registration of Doctors) [1986] ECR 1475, paragraph 16 – restriction on non-established doctors providing medical services to more than one patient within a two-day period.

30 Case 33/74 *Van Binsbergen* [1974] ECR 1299, paragraph 25, and the 'insurance cases': Case 252/83 *Commission* v. *Denmark* [1986] ECR 3713, paragraph 16; Case 205/84 *Commission* v. *Germany* [1986] ECR 3755, paragraph 25; and Case 206/84 *Commission* v. *Ireland* [1986] ECR 3817, paragraph 16. This point was re-emphasised more recently by the Advocate-General in Case C-283/99 *Commission* v. *Italy* (Security Guards) [2001] ECR I-436, Opinion, paragraph 20.

31 See e.g. Case C-288/89 *Stichting Collective Antennevoorziening Gouda* v. *Commissariat voor de Media* [1991] ECR I 4007, paragraph 10; Case C-76/90 *Säger*, *supra* n. 4, which in the landmark test for a restriction emphasises the centrality of a prohibition on nationality which has been picked up in numerous judgments: e.g. Case C-264/99 *Commission* v. *Italy* (Haulage Operators) [2000] ECR I-4417. See also the reasoning in Case C-79/01 *Payroll Data Services (Italy) Srl e.a.* [2002] ECR I-8923, paragraph 15.

32 Case 62 and 63/81 *Seco* [1982] ECR 223.

33 *Ibid.*, paragraph 9.

In other words, we are seeing 'dual burden' rules that occur through there being different regulatory systems in the various Member States.[34] It is not the rule itself that causes the difficulty, but the fact that another Member State, which has some jurisdictional claim, operates a different system and neither takes the other into account. The problem arises from dual regulation and not necessarily from the content of the rule. Nonetheless, such rules would fall within Article 49 on a discrimination-based analysis.

Interestingly, the line of reasoning established in cases such as *Seco*[35] appears to fly in the face of the express wording of Article 49. This suggests cross-border service providers should operate on the same terms as those established in the host Member State; that is, national regulations should apply. The ECJ has repeatedly held, however, that there is a fundamental difference between the person seeking to establish him or herself and the person intermittently providing services.[36] To treat them the same would, in fact, be to discriminate against the person providing services.[37] The case law of the ECJ and the approach of the institutions reflected a distinction between services and establishment, this distinction based on the 'home country' principle. By contrast, those establishing themselves would be expected to fit in to the host country's scheme of regulation in a way that would be impossible for those only temporarily providing services.[38]

The *TV10* decision[39] could be analysed within this framework. TV10 was broadcasting continuously into the Netherlands from another Member State, Luxembourg. Looking at the distinction noted above, as the service was neither intermittent nor temporary, TV10 could not claim that it (or the services) should not be subject to the full Dutch regime. The ECJ viewed the company as established in the host Member State, despite its lack of any physical presence in the host Member State. Certainly, if one focusses on the continuity of the link, this judgment has much to commend it.

---

34 See e.g. Case 110 and 111/78 *Ministère Public* v. *Van Wesemael* [1979] ECR 35, especially paragraphs 29 and 39; Case 279/80 *Webb* [1981] ECR 3305, especially paragraph 21.

35 Cases 62 and 63/81 *Seco*, *supra* n. 32.

36 In this there are reflection of the approach taken by the Commission in its Explanatory Memorandum to the General Programme for the Abolition of Restrictions on Freedom to Provide Services: COM 960) final OJ Sp. Ed, Second Series, IX, 3, pp. 22-23.

37 Case 427/85 *Commission* v. *Germany* (Lawyers' Services), *supra* n. 29, paragraph 42.

38 See also view of Advocate-General in Case C-108/98 *RI.SAN*, *supra* n. 11, when he argued that the provision of waste manage services could not be provided under Article 49 because of the continuity and regularity of contact required to carry out the contracts.

39 Case 23/93 *TV10 SA* v. *Commissariaat voor de Media* [1994] ECR I-4795.

Nonetheless, does it make sense to describe a service as establishment?[40] The Court could have split the services case law into two categories: one relating to the movement of persons in which the provision or receipt of services would be temporary; and one concerning the cross-border movement of the service itself, which could be provided continuously or frequently. Unfortunately, the reasoning of *TV10* itself would not support such an analysis. One could argue that the ECJ missed an opportunity to provide a more nuanced view of the scope of Article 49, reflecting the different circumstances in which the freedom to provide services can arise, preferring instead a unitary view of Article 49.

The boundary between services and establishment on which *TV10* is based is discussed further in Chapter 9. Nonetheless, it has long been suggested that some rules are, by their nature, less likely to affect services than establishment, or vice versa.[41] Thus, a requirement to register as an artisan or an architect would be compatible with Article 43, provided that qualifications and experience obtained in other Member States would be recognised, whereas such a requirement on its own would appear to constitute a restriction within Article 49.[42] Interestingly, the Advocate-General in the recent *Canal Satellite Digital*[43] case suggested that where registration was declarative and involved no particular cost or administrative effort, it would not of itself be a restriction. The ECJ in its judgment did not take up this point, seeing the obligation as a restriction and, in doing so, following a consistent line of cases concerning the requirement to register.

As noted above, *Säger*[44] marks a significant shift in the approach of the ECJ. It moves away from a concern about discrimination between those based in one Member State and another, and instead focusses on the existence of a restriction. This may seem insignificant given the breadth of circumstances in which a discrimination-based test could operate, but in

---

40 See further Chapter 9.

41 Marenco, G., 'The Notion of Restriction on the Freedom of Establishment and the Provision of Services in the Case-law of the Court' (1991) *YEL* 11, at p. 132, suggested that a rule in Case 168/85 *Commission* v. *Italy* [1986] ECR 2945 reserving the right to bid for allocation of pharmacies would affect the right of establishment rather than the freedom to provide services; more recently Tison, M., 'What is "General Good" in EU Financial Services Law?' (1997) 24(2) *LIEI* 1 – 46, pp. 6-7 that there is a distinction between institutional and functional rules in this context. Of course, some rules – such as a nationality requirement – would seem to affect both the freedom to provide services and the right of establishment: see e.g. Case C-283/99 *Commission* v. *Italy* (Security Guards) [2001] ECR 436.

42 Case C-58/98 *Corsten* [2000] ECR I-7919, paragraph 45.

43 Case C-390/99 *Canal Satellite Digital SL* [2002] ECR I-607, Opinion at paragraph 42.

44 Case C-76/90 *Säger*, *supra* n. 4.

some instances, however, the distinction would be crucial. Under a discrimination-based test, a Member State could ban entirely the provision of a service: it disadvantages both domestic and overseas service providers equally. A discrimination-based test would, however, catch national rules that prohibited the provision of certain services from another Member State or even those that reserved the provision of services to a national monopoly. In both instances some element of the domestic market would have gained an advantage at the expense of non-established service providers, even if some national providers were so disadvantaged also. A restriction-based test would catch both types of measure, arguably limiting the scope of Member States' freedom to determine what is acceptable within their own territory.[45] Of course, a Member State could seek to justify such a restriction, but even the very fact that a Member State is put in the position of justifying its policy is illustrative of a limited competence. Member States' competence is further limited as any such policy would have to fall within a head of derogation (as defined by the ECJ) and be subject to a proportionality test.[46]

The change from discrimination-based test to one centred on the existence of a restriction is linked to another shift. Rather than focussing on the individual rights, there is an emphasis on the service itself. Although the ECJ always highlighted the need to ensure that cross-border services are not precluded,[47] there has increasingly been a greater interest in the actual provision of services. In the earlier jurisprudence, a discriminatory effect was required. Now, any impediment to the provision of the service, even if it applies equally, apparently can trigger the application of Article 49. In taking this approach, the ECJ has prioritised the movement of services over Member States' freedom to regulate. As has been suggested elsewhere,[48] this trend is exemplified by the ECJ's references in more recent case law to the free *movement* of services rather than to the free provision of services.[49] This change has had two linked consequences. Firstly, there can be a broader notion of what might constitute a restriction, which need not be so tightly linked to an actual impact on the cross-border

---

45 See Case C-275/92 *Schindler* [1994] ECR I-1039 regarding the absolute ban of large lotteries and Case C-67/98 *Zenatti* [1999] ECR I-289 which reserved the organisation of gaming to two organisations: both sets of rules were deemed to be restrictions.

46 See further Chapter 12.

47 See cases where the ECJ referred to residence requirements as the very negation of the right: e.g. Case 33/74 *Van Binsbergen*, *supra* n. 30.

48 Hatzopoulos, V., 'Recent Developments of the Case Law of the ECJ in the Field of Services' (2000) 37(1) *CMLRev* 43-82, at p. 60.

49 See e.g. Case C-158/96 *Kohll* [1998] ECR I-1931.

provision of services.[50] The impact identified may be more abstract and hypothetical, with, as already noted, consequent difficulty in identifying the internal situation. Further, no *de minimis* argument will be accepted. For example, in so far as *SETTG*[51] should not be seen as constituting an internal situation, the group affected by the rules in that case would be small. Nonetheless, Article 49 would apply.

These points bring us back to the question of what constitutes a restriction. Despite the fact that the *Säger*[52] test does not appear as broad as the *Dassonville*[53] test, the abstract way in which the ECJ has interpreted its case law has ensured a wide application for Article 49. The test in *Säger* could even be interpreted subjectively, meaning that the scope of Article 49 would be virtually limitless, in particular where individuals are involved, as it would be their opinion of deterrence which would define Article 49. The wording of the *Säger* test, in any event, does not seem to require a particularly high level of deterrence, being in some cases no more than a measure 'liable to dissuade' the cross-border provision of services[54] or a measure that renders the provision of such services 'less attractive'. Thus, as noted, the mere requirement of registration will trigger the application of Article 49. In the *Italian Architects' Qualifications* case, the ECJ argued that the Italian rule whereby non-Italian qualified architects wishing to obtain recognition of their qualification are required to submit their original diploma or a certified copy,

> 'gives rise to additional obstacles for all architects applying for recognition of their qualifications, having regard to the risk of the original diploma being lost or of possible delay on the part of the Member State of origin in awarding that diploma and the additional steps and costs resulting from the procedures for certifying true copies of original diplomas.'[55]

---

50 Contrast the views of Barnard, C., 'Fitting the Remaining Pieces into the Goods and Persons Jigsaw?' (2001) 26 *ELRev* 35–59, p. 42 who suggests that the ECJ has been concerned to find an impact on cross-border trade 'in all the cases concerning non-discriminatory measures imposing restrictions on free movement of persons', citing Case C-275/92 *Schindler, supra* n. 45, which concerned a ban on lottery tickets, in support of her proposition as regards services.

51 Case C-398/95 *SETTG, supra* n. 16.

52 Case C-76/90 *Säger, supra* n. 4.

53 Case 8/74 *Procureur du Roi* v. *Dassonville et al.* [1974] ECR 837, see further Chapters 4 and 5.

54 Case C-118/96 *Safir* v. *Skattemyndigheten i Dalarnas Lan* [1998] ECR I-1919, paragraph 26.

55 Case C-298/99 *Commission* v. *Italy* (Architects' Qualifications) [2002] ECR I-3129, paragraph 37.

Submission of documents to regulatory bodies can be seen as an unavoidable part of the qualification process, as those bodies need to ensure conditions for qualification have been satisfied. This example therefore suggests that Article 49 would be easily triggered.

Furthermore, in some cases the ECJ has described the freedom to provide services as precluding 'the application of any national legislation which has the effect of making the provision of services between Member States more difficult than the provision of services purely within one Member State'.[56] The Court here is not suggesting that there needs to be any disadvantage for a service provider in being established in another Member State, but rather that the cross-border services themselves must be protected.[57] Originally, the cases that adopted this approach concerned the transport industries in which an essential facet of the service was movement. The same test has since been applied in other contexts.[58] Clearly these cases emphasise the importance of the single market and have links to the ECJ's original starting point regarding rules that negate the freedom to provide services.[59] It could be argued that, although the ECJ's ruling makes sense in the transport sector, they overlook the point that other contexts providing services to more than one recipient or destination may more effort than operating in a more limited manner. In this sense, we might suggest that the ECJ close to overlooking restrictions and obligations inherent in trading itself.

In some instances the ECJ seems to go beyond a test that compares the provision of the services in one Member State with another (or with more than one Member State). In the recent *Trade Fairs* case, the ECJ noted that time limits on the holding of trade fairs 'were liable to render the exercise of the freedom to provide services more difficult',[60] though it did not specify more difficult than what. It may be that this is short form for the test used in the transport cases. There is, however, still some risk that the ECJ may be seen as hypothesizing an abstract level of (European) regulation against which the national legislation is being compared. Such approach would have profound repercussions on Member States' freedom to regulate. Whether or not this is the case, this element of the ECJ's ruling

---

56 Case C-70/99 *Commission* v. *Portugal* (Air Travel) [2001] ECR I-2845, re-iterating the approach taken in Case C-381/93 *Commission* v. *France* (Marine Transport Services) [1994] ECRI-5145 and Case C-18/93 *Corsica Ferries* [1994] ECR I-1783 and Case 205/84 *Commission* v. *Germany* (Insurance Services) [1986] ECR 3755.

57 Marenco, G., *supra* n. 41, at p. 142 noted that this approach does not reflect the wording of the Treaty, which is based on discrimination against persons established in another Member State than that in which the service is provided.

58 See e.g. Case C-157/99 *Smits-Peerbooms* [2001] ECR I-5473.

59 Case 33/74 *Van Binsbergen, supra* n. 30.

60 Case C-439/99 *Commission* v. *Italy* (Trade Fairs) [2002] ECR I-305.

is essentially deregulatory; it is not concerned with discrimination or dual restrictions. Instead it is aimed at challenging national rules which might have the effect of partitioning off their territory in terms of the provision of particular services by discouraging non-established providers from entering that Member State's market. For the ECJ, it is irrelevant that companies established in Italy are likewise subject to these inconvenient rules. It is in this example that we can see the ECJ imposing free trade imperatives on a Member State's choices and thereby, again, limiting a Member State's competence in this regard.

Given the ease with which the Article 49 test may be satisfied, the emphasis in the case law often focusses on the justification for the restriction. Indeed, some cases blur the distinction between discussing the existence of a restriction with the justification for that restriction.[61] In part this is understandable, given the structure of the Treaty and the approach taken to such restrictions. Measures that do not discriminate on the face of the measures may be justified by reference to matters of overriding public interest. In such an instance, there would have been no violation of Article 49, rather than there having been a violation which could then have been saved by reference to a particular Treaty derogation. For such measures, therefore, the justification forms part of the finding of a violation or the absence of such a finding. In this we see a distinction between justification and defence[62] found in Article 28 and other areas of law, such as sex discrimination. Problematically, the ECJ has in some cases assumed the existence of a restriction and gone on to assess whether the national measure is justified by reference to Community law principles.[63] We might suggest that this is just an example of a very low threshold for the application of Article 49, which is balanced by the introduction of overriding public interest requirements. Nonetheless, the approach is questionable in terms of competence, as it is only if a restriction to cross-border trade exists that Community law principles should intervene in a Member State's freedom to regulate trade. Failing that, a Member State should be free to regulate in as restrictive and un-trade friendly a manner as it chooses.

---

61 This tendency has been noted in the literature: see e.g. Marenco, G., *supra* n. 41; Biondi, A., 'In and Out of the Internal Market: Recent Developments on the Principle of Free Movement' (1999/00) 19 *YEL* 461–491. See also cases discussed above.

62 This is the phraseology used by Ellis, E., 'Gender Discrimination Law in the European Community' in Dine, J., and Watt, B., *Discrimination Law* (Longmans, London: 1996).

63 Recent examples include Case C-390/99 *Canal Satellite Digital*, *supra* n. 43; Case C-298/99 *Commission* v. *Italy* (Architects' Qualifications), regarding proof of qualification, *supra* n. 55, see also Chapter 12.

The concern about the blurring of the two elements may well have been exacerbated by the move to a restriction-based test. *Webb*[64] and the earlier cases took into account home country regulation. In the absence of such home country regulation, a host country regulation that was proportionate would not create a dual burden situation. Looking at the reasons for the regulation would thus have made sense to identify if discrimination existed thus triggering the application of Article 49. For a restriction-based test, these issues are however irrelevant and therefore should be no reason for the ECJ to blend the two issues.

It is questionable what the obligation to take into account home State regulation means in any event. Does it mean, as the Advocate-General suggested in *Zenatti*,[65] that the Member State is entitled to take into account whether the home Member State regulates for services abroad? This issue has not been raised elsewhere but it seems to indicate a dichotomy between rules regulating access to the market and behaviour on that market. Whereas conditions for access are satisfied once, for example, by the acquisition of a qualification, the exercise of the profession is limited by continuing obligations. Market behaviour, additionally, may differ across different markets. In temporal and, importantly, geographic terms there may be different factors justifying regulation in the home and the host State. Furthermore, a home regulator may expend less energies on overseas operators for a variety of practical and resource related reasons.[66] Member States, notwithstanding the suggestion of the Advocate-General, have to assume that the home Member State is adequately regulating the service in question.[67] These difficulties are compounded by the impact of Article 49 on the ability of the host State to regulate non-established service providers. Cases such as *Canal Satellite Digital*[68] illustrate the difficulty for Member States in ensuring that cross-border service providers comply with regulation, even that in their home state as measures to enable review, such as the requirement to register or to prove qualification[69] are likely to be 'restrictions' within Article 49. Cross-border service provision brings with it practical difficulties in the enforcement of standards, no matter which State is responsible for regulation, and the effect of the ECJ's case law is likely to exacerbate these

64 Case 279/80 *Webb* [1981] ECR 3305.

65 Case C-67/98 *Zenatti, supra* n. 45, Opinion at paragraph 28, citing Case 110/78 *Van Wesemael, supra* n. 34, paragraph 30.

66 See the problems the ITC faces in supervising compliance with UK broadcasting regulation when the channels are broadcast through Europe.

67 Case C-11/95 *Commission* v. *Belgium* (Satellite Television) [1996] ECR I-4115.

68 Case C-390/99 *Canal Satellite Digital, supra* n. 43.

69 Case C-298/99 *Architects' Qualifications, supra* n. 55.

problems. In this sense, the ECJ's approach can again be seen as deregulatory, despite the express terms of the Treaty.

Where then, should the boundary of Article 49 lie? The ECJ resolved this problem with regard to Article 28 by introducing the distinction between selling arrangements and product requirements in the case of *Keck*.[70] Whether a similar distinction applies in the field of services is currently unclear, but the ECJ has interpreted the material scope of Article 49 widely. It could be that the jurisprudence has reached the equivalent state reached by the Article 28 case law in the early 1990s. Arguably it should therefore be limited in the same way. This issue arose in *Alpine Investments*,[71] which concerned a prohibition on cold calling, and in which a number of governments argued that Article 49 should not apply because the rule in question related to a selling arrangement. The ECJ disagreed: Article 49 applied, although the national rule could be justified.

Although it was clear that *Alpine Investments* took a different approach from *Keck* regarding selling arrangements, it was not clear why. Consequently the precise consequences of the ruling were unclear. There was some discussion as to whether *Alpine Investments* meant that the selling arrangements distinction would apply in some circumstances but not on the facts of that particular case; or whether selling arrangements would never apply to services.[72] On one line of reasoning, the ECJ was even seen as retreating from its position in *Keck*. Given, however, that in the field of goods the ECJ went on to repeat the *Keck* formula in many cases, *Alpine Investments* cannot be put forward to suggest that the ECJ has abandoned *Keck* completely. *Alpine Investments* may suggest, however, that *Keck* is not appropriate to services.[73] Services are, after all, different in nature from goods and, as a result, their selling and distribution arrangements may also differ. In particular, the notion of product characteristics may be difficult to maintain in the context of services. It is, nonetheless, not hard to envisage 'selling arrangements' regarding services: those who provide services do advertise and may be restricted as

---

70 Joined Cases C-267 and 268/91 *Keck and Mithouard* [1993] ECR I-6097 discussed in Chapters 4 and 5.

71 Case C-384/93 *Alpine Investments*, *supra* n. 3.

72 Friedbacher 'Motive unmasked: The ECJ, the Free Movement of Goods and the Search for Legitimacy' (1996) *ELJ* 226 suggests the former view: Weatherill, S., 'After *Keck*: Some Thoughts on how to Clarify the Clarification' (1996) 33 *CMLRev* 885 the latter: Hatzopoulos' note on the case (1995) 32 *CMLRev* 1427-1445 suggests three possible interpretations.

73 It should be noted that one way of limiting the impact of Article 49 is to view the matter as falling within Article 43, as happened in Case C-23/93 in *TV10*, *supra* n. 39. This point does not tend to be discussed in this context, however, and the anti-avoidance principle has been limited: see Chapter 9.

to where and when those services are provided. The question then should not be whether we can make a distinction between selling arrangements and requirements to be met, but rather whether selling arrangements (or rules equating to selling arrangements in the context of services) should fall within Article 49. It has been suggested that for professions there is a distinction between rules which govern the access to the activity, which are fundamental, and those which deal with its exercise – for example, where and when they may be provided, and that this would constitute the service related equivalent of the *Keck* distinction.[74] Although such an approach has been accepted in some national courts in other contexts, the ECJ seems to have gone out of its way to disregard such distinctions.[75]

Since *Alpine Investments*,[76] the message from the Court seems to be mixed. It has been suggested[77] that *de Agostini*[78] is authority for the proposition that the *Keck*[79] distinction does not apply to services. *De Agostini* concerned Swedish rules on television advertising that the ECJ considered to be selling arrangements in respect of the goods advertised. As regards the cross-border provisions of services, however, the ECJ considered the rules to fall within Article 49.[80] To suggest that this means that selling arrangements do not apply in the services context overlooks the fact that the Swedish rules had a different relationship to the provision of services than they did to the provision of goods. The advertising was the service itself, not the promotional material for another service.[81] The rules in issue thus precluded the provision of the service of advertising itself and therefore the 'selling arrangements' point would not have been relevant.

More recently, in *Canal Satellite Digital*,[82] which concerned both the provision of digital transmission services and digital decoders, the Spanish

---

74 See literature cited by Tison, M., *supra*, n. 41.

75 The discussion of Case C-439/99 the *Trade Fairs* case, *supra* n. 60, could have been discussed in this context, but was not.

76 Case C-384/93 *Alpine Investments*, *supra* n. 3.

77 Kaldellis, E., I., 'Freedom of establishment versus freedom to provide services: an evaluation of case law developments in the area of indistinctly applicable rules.' (2001), 28(1) L.I.E.I. 23-55, p. 30 Hatzopulos, V., 'Recent Developments of the Case Law of the ECJ in the Field of Services', *supra* n. 48, pp. 68–69 suggests that 'the view that *Keck* has in principle been transposed to services ... is considerably weakened'.

78 Joined Cases C-34-36/95 *Konsumentombudsmannen* v. *de Agostini* and *TV Shop i Sverige* [1997] ECR I-3843.

79 Joined Cases C-267 and 268/91 *Keck*, *supra* n. 70.

80 Joined Cases C-34-36/95 *de Agostini*, *supra* n. 78, paragraphs 50-52.

81 The position of teleshopping is slightly less clear. If it is seen as just another sales mechanism, then presumably the goods jurisprudence and Articles 28-30 would apply. See further Chapter 2.

82 Case C-390/99 *Canal Satellite Digital*, *supra* n. 43.

Government put forward the argument that, as regards the decoders, the requirement on suppliers to register as such, was a selling arrangement and therefore outside Article 28. The Advocate-General dismissed the argument, but equally only discussed the argument in relation to goods, suggesting that it was only relevant in relation to goods. The ECJ was much less clear. After stating that the registration requirement constituted a restriction contrary to Articles 28 and 49, it continued that,

> 'the need in certain cases to adapt the products in question to the rules in force in the Member State in which they are marketed prevents the abovementioned requirements from being treated as selling arrangements …'[83]

On the one hand, the reference to products would seem to imply that the ECJ was referring to Article 28 the free movement of goods. One the other hand, the digital decoders were essential for the provision of the television services, and so the argument cited applies just as much to the freedom to provide services as the free movement of goods. Moreover, the quoted statement from the ECJ occurs immediately after a discussion of both Article 28 and 49, suggesting that the points made in that section of the judgment apply to both freedoms. The confusion in this area is exacerbated by the Commission Communication on Satellite Dishes, which seems to imply that the *Keck* ruling applies to both goods and services.[84] By contrast, in a case involving the imposition of taxes on satellite dishes, which could be seen as a rule affecting the point of distribution of satellite television, the issue of whether this rule constituted a selling arrangement was not even raised.[85] There therefore remains considerable confusion on this issue. One point is clear: to date there has been no case in the context of services in which the *Keck* distinction has been successfully argued.

III Exports

Alpine Investments[86] raises other questions, notably whether the distinction found in the case law on goods between exports and import is also to be found in services. It is generally accepted that the test for the existence of MEQRs is stricter in relation to the export of goods under Article 29 than

83 Case C-390/99 *Canal Satellite Digital*, *ibid.*, paragraphs 29-30.

84 Commission Communication on Satellite Dishes, July 2001.

85 Case C-17/00 *de Coster, supra* n. 22. The cumulative effect of the Belgian rules on retransmission of satellite broadcast meant the tax was more likely to affect broadcasts from other Member States and it would therefore not have satisfied the 'apply equally in law and in fact' requirement.

86 Case C-384/93 *Alpine Investments*, *supra* n. 3.

imports under Article 28. The leading case in respect of exports is *Groenveld*.[87] It requires a two-stage test: as well as a distortion to trade, some form of advantage to the domestic market must be shown. *Groenveld* is a discrimination-based test, rather than a restriction-based test. In the earlier services case law on exports, it seemed as though the ECJ had adopted the *Groenveld* test, thereby preserving the distinction in approach to imports and exports that arises in relation to goods.[88] Indeed, the ECJ seemed to take this approach in *Peralta*,[89] a judgment handed down only a couple of months before the judgment in *Alpine Investments*. Nonetheless, *Alpine Investments* shows the Court taking a different approach. Without specifically addressing the point of whether the rule in issue concerned an export restriction, the ECJ introduced in *Alpine Investments* the same restriction-based test for the application of Article 49 as it had done in *Säger*,[90] a case which concerned imports. The lack of clarity in this area was compounded by the *French Maritime* case,[91] handed down shortly after *Alpine Investments*. The *French Maritime* case also concerned an export restriction on services. Despite the reasoning in *Alpine Investments*, the ECJ reverted to its earlier position in *Peralta* and based its judgment in the *French Maritime Case* on *Groenveld*.[92] In the space of a number of months therefore, the Court without explanation adopted an approach that, like the goods case law, distinguished between imports and exports, abandoned that distinction and then re-instated it.

The jurisprudence in this area remains unsettled. It is far from clear whether the ECJ has interpreted Article 49 in this context in line with its jurisprudence relating to the export of goods or with its rulings on the 'import' of services. It is suggested that the latter is more convincing: the ECJ has interpreted cases on the receipt of services in the same way as those on their provision, strengthening an argument for a general unified approach for services based on a restriction-based test. The ECJ also stated in the *French Maritime* case[93] that rules such as those in issue in that case, make the provision of services more difficult than in one Member State. This approach, which it has taken in subsequent cases, blurs the boundary between the *Groenveld* approach based on discrimination through advantage to the domestic market and the more usual services approach based on the notion of restriction. Furthermore, the interpretation of the *Groenveld* text in the context of Article 29 itself is no longer so clearly

---

87 Case 15/79 *Groenveld* v. *Produktschap voor Vee en Vlees* [1979] ECR 3409.

88 See Chapter 6.

89 Case C-379/92 *Peralta* [1994] ECR I-3453.

90 Case C-76/90 *Säger*, *supra* n. 4.

91 Case C-381/93 *Commission* v. *France*, *supra* n. 56.

92 Case C-381/93 *French Maritime Case*, *ibid.*, paragraph 21.

93 Case C-381/93 *Commission* v. *France*, *ibid.*

based on discrimination, although the ECJ has yet to take the step suggested by a number of commentators and move the Article 29 case law into line with the approach adopted with respect to the other freedoms.

IV Individuals and Ancillary Rights

The previous discussion has focussed to a significant extent on the case law where personal freedoms have not specifically been in issue. The rights of individuals to move to provide and to receive services do raise problems that might not occur when rules relating to the provision of services themselves are in issue. One particular question that arises when the movement of people is involved is the level or type of ancillary rights to which migrants will be entitled, especially when they are migrating for very short periods or to receive services. Although workers have been expressly granted social rights, reflecting the fact that their main residence will be in the host Member State and that they should be encouraged to integrate into the host country, the assumption relating to services initially seemed to be that social rights would be dealt with by the home Member State, rather than as a matter of EC law. Is this, or should this be the case, especially in the light of European citizenship? These issues have attracted some judicial attention.

Perhaps the leading case in this area is *Cowan*.[94] Cowan was mugged whilst on holiday and claimed that he, as a migrant within the terms of Article 49, was entitled to payment from a fund set up by the French government to compensate the victims of such crimes. The French government, however, argued that the fund was to benefit only French nationals; the fund, according to the government, was based on national solidarity which presupposed a closer bond with the state than that exhibited by a tourist. Further, the rules limiting the scope of payments from the fund did not impose any restriction on free movement.[95] The ECJ agreed with Cowan, however, holding that,

> '[w]hen Community law guarantees a natural person the freedom to go to another Member State the protection of that person from harm in the Member State in question, on the same basis as that of nationals and persons residing there, is a corollary of that freedom of movement.'[96]

The fact that the fund was financed by the French state was irrelevant.

---

94 Case 186/87 *Ian William Cowan* v. *Trésor public* [1989] ECR 195.
95 Arguments summarised Case 186/87 *Cowan, ibid.*, paragraph 16.
96 Case 186/87 *Cowan, ibid.*, paragraph 17.

Cowan[97] suggests a number of points. Firstly, recipients of services will be treated on the same basis as those providing services. Further, a very broad notion is given to the rights to which individuals are entitled and that the level of disincentive need not be high nor need it be focussed particularly closely to the free movement right itself. Equally, the provision in *Cowan* discriminated directly on the grounds of nationality and thus contravened one of the fundamental Treaty principles. Once within the scope of the Treaty by virtue of the freedom to provide – or receive – services, Article 12, the general prohibition on grounds of nationality, can come into play. Nonetheless, from the terms of the ECJ's judgment, it seems that the scope of protection is in some way connected with the freedom of movement. The question then is, what is 'a corollary of that freedom of movement'?

The more recent case of *Bickel and Franz*[98] concerned similar issues. In this case, two tourists were arrested during their stay in Italy. They sought to rely on an Italian rule, which provided that residents of a particular province could use the German language in their dealings with the authorities. Bickel and Franz were not, however, permitted to use German at their trials, as they were not members of the community the rule was intended to protect. This rule was not directly discriminatory on grounds of nationality, although it would work to the detriment of non-nationals the most and could therefore be seen as indirectly discriminatory. The trial of Bickel and Franz, and particularly the operation of this rule, would not seem particularly close to the freedom to provide services. It does not relate specifically to the tourist industries, instead regulating relations in Italian society generally. Nonetheless, the ECJ once again relied on the right to receive services to bring Bickel and Franz within the scope of Community law and then referred to the non-discrimination principle, stating that,

> '[national] legislative provision may not discriminate against persons to whom Community law gives the right to equal treatment or restrict the fundamental freedoms guaranteed by Community law.'[99]

Although *Bickel and Franz* re-affirms *Cowan*,[100] it has not clarified the required degree of connection between the national rule and the movement of persons before a hindrance to the exercise of the relevant free movement

---

97 Case 186/87 *Cowan, ibid.*

98 Case C-274/96 *Criminal Proceedings against Horst Otto Bickel and Ulrich Franz* [1998] ECR I-7637.

99 Case C-274/96 *Bickel and Franz, ibid.*, at paragraph 17.

100 Case 186/87 *Cowan, supra* n. 94.

rights is created.[101] In one sense, this point is of less significance as an individual may rely on Article 12 when within the scope of the Treaty and even, as was suggested by *Bickel and Franz*, on the provisions relating to European citizenship.[102] One thing is clear: being able to bring yourself within Article 49 will have a huge impact on a government's ability to restrict benefits to those who migrate even temporarily. This might cause concerns in respect of those travelling to receive services, such as medical services.[103]

The impact of Article 49 can be seen in another context in *Carpenter*.[104] In this case Mr and Mrs Carpenter both resided in the UK. He was a British national, she was a third country national. She was originally given leave to enter the UK for six months under British immigration laws, but overstayed that leave. She only subsequently married Carpenter. The Home Office sought to deport her. The Carpenters challenged that order on the basis that she had the right to remain under Community law. Community law gives migrants the right to take their families with them when they exercise their free movement rights, and this includes individuals moving temporarily to provide services. The Carpenters did not, however, seek to exercise a right to go to another Member State. Instead, they were seeking to rely on Article 49 as against the UK government. They claimed they fell under Community law because Mr Carpenter provided services to other Member States. Clearly, there is a cross-border element here but was it enough to trigger Article 49 and, if so, would Mrs Carpenter's connection sufficiently close to be protected by Article 49? It is interesting to note that the referring court divided the question into two aspects: firstly has an EC service provider the right to rely on Community law to provide a non-national spouse with a right to residence; secondly, is the position affected by the non-national's spouse's indirect contribution, for example looking after children, to the provision of services?

The Commission suggested to the ECJ that this situation constituted an 'internal situation', to be compared with cases such as *Morson and Jhanjan*,[105] in which Belgian nationals, who had never exercised any of their free movement rights, sought unsuccessfully to rely on Community

---

101 Although the ECJ has not made this point, there seems to be some move towards the approach taken with regard to workers in Case 207/78 *Even* [1979] ECR 2019, in which the key factor is residence on host territory. The difficulty with this analysis is that service recipients need not reside in the host Member State.

102 Article 18 *et seq.*

103 See Chapter 9.

104 Case C-60/00 *Mary Carpenter* v. *Secretary of State for the Home Department* [2002] ECR I-6279.

105 Joined Cases 35 and 36/82 *Morson and Jhanjan* [1982] ECR 3723.

law to gain entry to Belgium for their third country national relatives. The ECJ took a different approach. It pointed out that it had previously held that under Article 49 a service provider could rely on Article 49 as against the home Member State provided that the services were provided to others in another Member State.[106] Here, a significant proportion of Mr Carpenter's business was in providing services to those in other Member States.[107] The ECJ then reasoned that:

> '... the separation of Mr and Mrs Carpenter would be detrimental to their family life and, therefore, to the conditions under which Mr Carpenter exercises a fundamental freedom. That freedom could not be fully effective if Mr Carpenter were to be deterred from exercising it by obstacles raised in his country of origin to the entry and residence of his spouse.'[108]

In doing so, it seemed either to conflate the two elements of the question referred by the national court, or to ignore the second element.[109] Certainly, the ECJ did not base its judgment on the contribution Mrs Carpenter made to Mr Carpenter's business activities. Instead, the ECJ seems to have viewed Mrs Carpenter's residence as part of the general bundle of rights to which Mr Carpenter was entitled under Community law. The ECJ then went on to discuss the impact of the right to family life contained in Article 8 ECHR but, interestingly, only with regard to an assessment of whether a restriction on the Article 49 rights could be viewed as acceptable. As noted elsewhere, the ECJ can only rely on Community fundamental freedoms once it has found the situation already to within the scope of Community law.[110] The ECJ concluded that the UK immigration rules constituted an infringement of Article 49 that was not proportionate to the aim pursued.

Carpenter[111] is a development in determining the scope or potential impact of Article 49. The national rules in this case had a much more indirect effect on the provision of the service, affecting the general

---

106 Case C-384/93 *Alpine Investments, supra* n. 4.

107 Case C-60/00 *Carpenter, supra* n. 104, paragraph 37.

108 Case C-60/00 *Carpenter, ibid.*, paragraph 39.

109 The question referred by the national court questioned whether Council Directive 73/148/EEC on the abolition of restriction on movement and residence within the Community for nationals of Member States with regard to establishment and the provision of services, which provide service providers and recipients the right to take their families with them when they go to another Member State, also covered this situation. The ECJ held it did not.

110 Case C-260/89 *ERT* [1991] ECR I-2925, paragraph 43 and Case C-368/95 *Familiapress* [1997] ECR I-3689. See also discussion in Chapter 7 relating to goods.

111 Case C-60/00 *Carpenter, supra* n. 104.

environment in which the service provider found himself. The ECJ seemed to base its reasoning on the fact that the Community has accepted that families should be allowed to stay together, especially where the separation could be of a long duration. One may suggest different motivations for the acceptance of this point. The ECJ might have been concerned about the migrant in a social context. Alternatively potential migrants would undoubtedly be dissuaded from exercising their rights if their families could not accompany them, particularly in the case of workers or establishment when a more permanent link with the host Member State is envisaged. There is consequently a link between the exercise of the free movement rights and the right for migrants to have their family members accompany them. The situation in *Carpenter* does not fit this profile. There are two differences. Firstly, in *Carpenter* it is not the exercise of Community rights that would operate to separate the family, as the family does not have the right under the rules in Member State of origin to be together in the first place. Secondly, given the fact that Carpenter was based in the UK with only short trips abroad, the dissuasion argument does not apply. Perhaps recognising the difference from the 'normal' migration pattern, the argument was put forward that the family rights were operating to facilitate the actual exercise of the freedom to provide services. The Advocate-General suggested that this element of the Carpenters' argument was irrelevant.[112] As noted above, the ECJ did not address the issue, but by referring to the importance of family rights implicitly seems to have rejected it. This leaves us with a broad definition of family rights, making the determination of when Article 49 applies more significant.

Although the second limb of the Carpenters' argument might have operated to limit the breadth of this right, it is unsurprising that the ECJ did not look into the issue. There are philosophical problems with valuing individuals' family lives through the prism of what that person contributes to someone else's working life. Further, such an approach would raise the question of the extent to which Member States are under an obligation to facilitate individuals' rights of free movement. Drawing the line between restrictions that have too remote an effect on inter-state trade and those that affected an indirect contribution would be difficult. With the possible exception of *Peralta,*[113] there has not been a consistent line of jurisprudence which views some rules as being too remote from trade to fall within Article 49. This position is by contrast to that operating in respect of other freedoms.[114] This may, of course, be because the cases

112 The Advocate-General placed greater emphasis on the right to family life.

113 Case C-379/92 *Peralta, supra* n. 89. Note that neither the discussion of the Advocate-General nor the ruling of the Court refer to the issue using the phraseology that the impact of the rule upon the provision of services was too indirect or remote.

114 See Chapter 5 and in respect of workers, Case C-190/98 *Graf* [2000] ECR I-493.

have not arisen before the ECJ. Given the impact of citizenship and human rights on the services jurisprudence, it would seem likely that the ECJ would accept such an argument only in cases in which individuals were not personally involved.

We have seen that service providers may rely on Article 49 as against their country of origin. This may arise when the service provider is disadvantaged in seeking to export a service. The ECJ has also held that migrants may rely on Community law rights on their return to their Member State of origin.[115] If individuals lost out on their return under national law, a disincentive to their exercising Community law rights in the first instance would arise. This ruling might operate to turn what *prima facie* appears to be an internal situation into one involving Community law when someone who has been a migrant is involved.[116] The problems in this area arise because it is not clear how long an individual's rights as a migrant would last and whether the duration of this period would be affected by the length of the stay in the host Member State or by the types of right relied upon. The ECJ has given no definitive answer to these questions, although it is clear from some earlier case law that the rights accrued, or at least some of them, do not expire immediately on return. *Carpenter*[117] also illustrates this point: although Mr Carpenter provided cross-border services, his entire business was not cross-border. It would, however, make no sense to suggest his family life rights should switch on and off depending on when and whether he was dealing with a client based in another Member State. Similarly, what would happen when Mr Carpenter retired? This line of reasoning would seem to become less compelling were we to consider restrictions which, rather than applying to his social environment, applied more directly to the provision of the service itself: such restrictions have in general little impact when services are not provided.[118]

Clearly there is some potential for abuse arising from the longevity of ancillary rights, which becomes more important when we consider the breadth of circumstances to which Article 49 may apply. Article 49 does not just apply when an individual repeatedly provides cross-border

---

[115] See e.g. Case C-370/90 *Singh* [1992] ECR I-4265.

[116] Watson, P., 'Free Movement of Workers: A One Way Ticket?' (1993) 22 ILJ 68. This argument is not necessarily limited to natural persons but could apply to companies.

[117] Case C-60/00 *Carpenter*, *supra* n. 104, see also discussion in Joined Cases C-51/96 and C-191/97 *Deliège*, *supra* n. 13. Similar issues have arisen in Case C-109/01 *Akrich*, Opinion of 27 February 2003.

[118] There are possible exceptions to this statement, for example rules which prohibit the provision of a service with the territory of a Member State, where Article 49 is used to try to argue that the Member State should not stop the cross-border provision of services.

services; Article 49 applies also on receipt of services, even when the transaction is not long-lived. It would seem that an EC national, who went on holiday within the EC and met someone at the holiday destination and married that person even after the migrant returned to the Member State of origin, would be entitled under EC law to return with the spouse to the Member State of origin, that is unless the rights of service recipients are more constrained than the rights of those who provide services. From *Cowan*[119] and *Bickel and Franz*,[120] and given the impact of European citizenship, we cannot be certain that such a difference would justify a lower level of protection. Potentially, the jurisprudence limits the scope of Member States to regulate in areas that typically are considered to be central to Member State competence, such as immigration and criminal law and procedure. It may be that the ECJ will come under some pressure to clarify the limits of Article 49 and, in particular, the relationship between service recipients and the longevity of ancillary rights.

V Discrimination

As with goods, there is some confusion concerning the use of discrimination within the Article 49 jurisprudence. We see similar problems arising in relation to the use of the term 'discrimination' as occur in the case law on Article 28. To avoid duplicating the discussion in Chapter 5, this chapter will not deal with the issues in depth but will merely summarise the difficulties in this area by reference to examples arising in the services jurisprudence. Discrimination was used to identify the scope of Article 49.[121] It is also used to determine whether a measure may be justified by reference to the heads of derogation identified in the Treaty, or whether such national measures may also be justified by reference to overriding reasons. The difficulty is that discrimination appears to have different meanings in these two contexts; discrimination in the context of the application of Article 49 being a broader notion than the concept used to determine whether a national rule might be justified by reasons of overriding public interest. The precise limit of discrimination in this latter context is not clear. Inconsistencies can be found in the jurisprudence, as a recent case, *de Coster*,[122] illustrates. The rules in question imposed a tax on the installation of satellite dishes. Insofar as these rules had an impact on the cross-border provision of services it was likely also to affect domestic satellite broadcasters, although there was a

---

119 Case 186/87 *Cowan*, *supra* n. 94.

120 Case C-274/96 *Bickel and Franz*, *supra* n. 99.

121 See discussion above and Marenco, G., *supra* n. 41.

122 Case C-17/00 *de Coster*, *supra* n. 22.

potential for cable retransmission of domestic services that was not available to non-established broadcasters. The Advocate-General suggested that this was a discriminatory measure, whereas the ECJ viewed the matter as indirectly discriminatory.

There is another level of confusion arising in this context. Some commentators suggest that only restrictions which are not indirectly discriminatory may be justified by reference to overriding reasons of public interest.[123] Yet, the ECJ has in a number of cases found that those rules which operate to the detriment of nationals of other Member States can be justified by non-Treaty grounds of derogation, although it may not have addressed the point of whether the relevant national measure was discriminatory or not.[124] It is submitted that indirect discrimination should be capable of justification by reference to overriding reasons of public interest. Otherwise the combined effect of the broad interpretation of indirect discrimination and the limited grounds of justification would have a significantly limiting effect on the Member States' powers to regulate and, arguably, destabilize the balance of powers. Certainly such an approach would be in line with that taken in sex discrimination cases, where indirectly discriminatory measures may be justified by 'objective justifications', as well as that taken in relation to free movement of goods.[125]

Member States' power to freedom to regulate is particularly important when we consider the provision of public services. Public services are often provided by state monopolies. A state monopoly will certainly fall within Article 49,[126] but should the rules establishing state monopolies be viewed as discriminatory so as to affect the scope of justification? Despite the fact that such measures will given an advantage to one operator, usually domestic, all other service providers will be equally disadvantaged. In *ERT*,[127] the ECJ discussed the national rules by reference matters of overriding public interest, indicating that these rules were not directly discriminatory. Although state monopolies are worthy of a book in their own right, just two points will be made here. Firstly, an approach which

---

123 Wathelet, M., 'The Influence of Free Movement of Persons, Services and Capital on National Direct Taxation: Trends in the Case Law of the Court of Justice' (2001) 20 *YEL* 1-33, p. 11.

124 Case C-204/90 *Hanns-Martin Bachmann* v. *Belgium* [1992] ECR I-249; Case C-120/95 *Nicholas Decker* v. *Caisse de Maladie des Employés Privés* [1998] ECR I-1831.

125 See further Chapter 5.

126 Contrast the position regarding goods where there is a separate provision, Article 31 EC. Nonetheless state monopolies have been held to fall within Article 29. See further Chapter 6.

127 Case C-260/89 *ERT*, *supra* n. 110.

sees such rules as indirectly discriminatory and which thereby permits state rules to be assessed in the light of wider societal objectives is in line with a wider view of concerns protected by the Community. Matters of overriding public interest are broader than those set down in the express Treaty derogation, as interpreted by the ECJ.[128] The second point relates to the definition of discrimination where state monopolies are concerned. Cases such as *ERT* suggest that that state monopoly rules are not considered directly discriminatory. Even within the confines of the services jurisprudence the rules by which such an assessment is made are not clear,[129] but the case law under Article 29 confuses this picture. One might argue that any difference in approach is based on the distinction between goods and services, or exports and imports. The difficulty with this argument is that some service monopolies act to impose a restriction on the export of goods and the two sets of provisions could potentially affect one set of national rules.[130] For example, for environmental reasons, waste may be required to be processed locally. Such rules, in the context of Article 29 have been viewed as discriminatory. This would indicate a difference between the two provisions, for which there is no obvious reason.

VI Conclusions

The services jurisprudences has developed to bring it broadly into line with the Article 28 case law, in that the trigger for the application of Article 49 is the existence of a restriction rather than a test based on discrimination. If we assume that the aim of the provision is the removal of barriers and the creation of an internal rather than the prohibition of discrimination, such a move is necessary. Significantly not only does such an assumption

---

128 State monopolies can also be caught by the competition rules, which provide specific exception in Article 86(2) for the providers of services of general economic interest. Furthermore the new Article 16 EC accepts that Member States should be free to provide public services as they each deem appropriate; though, it should be noted that Article 16 is expressed to operate without prejudice to other Community policies, notably the competition provision. The impact of this provision is discussed by Ross, M., 'Article 16 E.C. and services of general interest: from derogation to obligation?' (2000) *ELRev*. 22.

129 Although not concerning a state monopoly, there is, for example, dissent between the Advocate-General and the ECJ Case C-17/00 *de Coster, supra* n. 22, as to whether rules that adversely affect some but not all domestic providers as well as non-established providers should be viewed as discriminatory.

130 See Chapter 2 and Chapter 9 on which set of rules should apply in a given set of circumstances.

contradict the express wording of Article 49, but it also has implications for the division of competence between the Community and the Member States. Community competence has been expanded with the result that a greater number of national measures will be subject to review by the Community legal order of its values.

Moving from a discrimination-based test has also introduced questions as to where the boundary of Article 49 lies. Discrimination has an inherent boundary that is not present when a broad restriction-based test is used. A restriction, seen as a disincentive, could include many national rules not immediately connected with inter-state trade. Within this category of 'unintentional' restrictions, how should one distinguish between those that fall within Community competence and those that fall outside it? One suggestion is that a distinction analogous to that introduced into Article 28 by *Keck* should be, or has been, incorporated into Article 49 jurisprudence. This would mean that the development of the jurisprudence in the relation to the two freedoms would develop further similarities. There is, however, little clarity in the case law currently. Accepting this as justification for such a change could overlook crucial differences between goods and services. As a general comment, however, the ECJ needs to be wary of case law which overextends Article 49, whereby cases with little integrationist merit are brought challenging national rules that are remote from inter-state trade, such as planning or social provision.

There is a tendency to think of the Article 49 case law as unified; that Article 49 constitutes one freedom. Article 49, however, covers a variety of circumstances. The Court seems to have taken the same approach, irrespective of whether the provider of the service or its recipient is seeking to rely on Article 49, although there are inconsistencies in the jurisprudence relating to the export of services. Of course, one might argue that any distinction is based on the nature of exports and that we should expect to see greater parallels between Article 29 and Article 49 in this context, rather than to see a unified approach to all aspects of Article 49. The issue of a unified approach brings us to another fault line in the services jurisprudence. This lies between the services as economic transactions and services as a personal freedom. Although the ECJ has adopted a restriction-based approach in both contexts, there is a difference in terms of the types of rule that will fall within the scope of Article 49. These differences arise from the fact that the social context of individuals must be taken account, factors which do not arise in the field of banking or telecommunications, for example. Moreover, it is in the aspect of the services case law that European citizenship comes into play. Although this is illustrative of broader concerns being taken into account, the consequence of the ECJ's approach is that, again, Member States' competence is limited.

Chapter 12

Derogation from the Right to Provide Services

I Introduction

Article 55 EC provides that the derogation principles contained in Article 46 in respect of the free movement of workers apply also in respect of services. Thus measures which *prima facie* fall foul of Article 49 may be justified on grounds of public policy, public security or public health. In addition to the Treaty provision itself, which applies to both legal and natural persons, Article 55 has been implemented in respect of natural persons by Directive 64/221,[1] which is directly effective.[2] As with Articles 28 and 29 regarding goods, the treaty-based justifications have been supplemented by grounds of overriding public interest where the relevant national rule is indistinctly applicable, or non-discriminatory. The provisions derogating from the treaty freedoms are important for identifying the extent to which Member States remain free to prioritise other policy areas over the creation of the single market. This chapter will first discuss the scope of Directive 64/221 and then consider the extent of Article 55 and the other public interest grounds of justification in the light of competing interests recognised by the Treaty.

As a general point, and in common with all treaty provisions derogating from the four freedoms, these articles have been interpreted narrowly[3] and are subject to a proportionality test.[4] Furthermore, no derogation from the free movement principle can be justified by reference to an economic policy,[5] nor can it be used as a precondition to the acquisition of entry and residence rights. In addition to these provisions, which apply regarding entry to the host Member State, each Member State may limit access to its public service to its own nationals. In all instances when a Member State seeks to rely on Article 55 or a reason of overriding

---

1 OJ Sp. Ed 1964, No. 850/64, p. 117.

2 Case 41/74 *van Duyn* v. *Home Office* [1974] ECR 1337.

3 Case 352/85 *Bond van Adverteerders* v. *Netherlands* [1988] ECR 2085.

4 Case 353/89 *Commission* v. *Netherlands* (Mediawet) [1991] ECR I-4069 at p. 4094.

5 *Ibid.*, at p. 4093.

public interest, these must be read in the light of human rights obligations as understood by the ECJ.

II Directive 64/221

Directive 64/221 implements not just the derogation from the freedom to provide services but also the corresponding provisions relating to the free movement of workers and the right of establishment. It provides for 'special measures concerning the movement and residence of foreign nationals which are justified on the grounds of public policy, public security and public health'. The Directive can be divided into two sections: the first part elaborates the substantive scope of public policy, public security and public health; the second part guarantees to migrants certain procedural rights. The Directive covers not only the migrant who is economically active but also any family members of such a migrant, whatever their status and whether or not they are third country nationals. The Directive provides rights for those who move to provide services and those who move to receive services; it seeks to identify the circumstances in which measures taken by the Member States limiting individuals' freedom of movement may be justified. The Directive is limited in that it applies only to rights of entry to the host Member State; it does not deal with discrimination as regards access to the market, nor does it deal with the rights of legal persons or the situation in which services themselves move. Such issues would be dealt with either directly under Article 55 or as a reason of overriding public interest, discussed further below. The main focus of the jurisprudence to date, however, has been on the scope of public policy, public health and public security within the scope of the Directive.

a) Substantive Rights

The scope of 'public policy' is somewhat unclear, as is the notion of 'public security'. Certainly there is no definition of the terms within the Treaty or Directive 64/221, although the Directive sets out some limitations on the use of both these concepts. Article 2(2) states that public policy and public security do not include measures taken to service economic ends and in this we see parallels to the approach adopted in respect of the derogation from the free movement of goods. Presumably the same difficulties in determining the boundary between economic concerns and other policy objections, which arise in the goods jurisprudence,[6] occur here also. Further, according to Article 3(2) previous criminal convictions

6 See Chapter 7.

in themselves do not constitute grounds for taking measures against an individual. Neither public policy nor public security may justify general administrative measures in excess of the production of a valid identity card or passport and expiry of an identity card or passport will not justify expulsion. As can be seen in *Royer*,[7] an individual's right of residence does not depend on the possession of a residence permit; a residence permit merely provides proof of the right. The right itself, however, is derived from the Treaty and administrative systems set up by Community secondary legislation should not frustrate the primary Treaty goals.

None of this provides an exhaustive definition of public policy or, indeed, public security. It thus falls to the ECJ to fill in the gaps. The leading case on public policy is generally regarded as being *Bouchereau*.[8] In that case the ECJ held that the existence of a criminal conviction could 'only be taken into account in so far as the circumstances which gave rise to that conviction are evidence of personal conduct constituting a present threat to the requirements of public policy'.[9] Thus, past conduct does not necessarily constitute a present threat, although the ECJ recognised that it may indicate a propensity to a certain type of behaviour. The ECJ then went on to lay down the classic test for public policy, that there is a genuine and sufficiently serious threat to the requirements of public policy affecting one of the fundamental interests of society.[10] Although the 'fundamental interests of society' are an equally vague concept and one that it seems Member States are in principle to determine, the ECJ through the introduction of the term 'fundamental' has limited the potential scope of the public policy derogation and re-emphasised that a derogation from a Treaty freedom may not be used as a disguised restriction on free movement.

Although there will always be a distinction between the Member State's freedom of action vis-à-vis its own nationals and those of another Member State, in that a state may not deport its own nationals, it seems one way of verifying the genuine nature of the claimed serious threat is to verify the state's approach to the behaviour objected to in respect of its own nationals. Thus parallels in approach can be seen between public policy in respect of services and Article 30 in relation to goods (discussed in Chapter 7). The level of repressive measures permitted to the Member State by this test is open to question. One example where the issue was raised is the early case of *van Duyn*.[11] Although the case concerned the scope of derogation from workers' rights of free movement, the ECJ's

---

7 Case 48/75 *Procureur du Roi* v. *Royer* [1976] ECR 497.

8 Case 30/77 *R.* v. *Bouchereau* [1977] ECR 1999.

9 *Ibid.*, at pp. 2012–13.

10 *Ibid.*, at p. 2014.

11 Case 41/74 *van Duyn* v. *Home Office, supra* n. 2.

interpretation of the Directive would seem to have a more general relevance. Van Duyn was a Dutch national who sought to enter the UK to work for the Church of Scientology. The UK took no measures of any description against the Church of Scientology in the UK, although the Church itself was clearly the subject of official disapproval. The British authorities refused van Duyn entry on public policy grounds and van Duyn challenged this decision. The ECJ accepted the public policy justification in this case.[12]

Since then, however, a tightening of the ECJ's assessment of Member State 'repressive measures' can be seen and it is arguable that the ECJ's approach in *van Duyn* is merely a product of its time, taking place against the backdrop of the British referendum on EC membership. Thus in the later case of *Adoui and Cornaille*,[13] the ECJ did not accept that Belgium could justify taking measures against Adoui and Cornaille on the grounds that they were suspected of being prostitutes, as no similar repressive measures were taken in respect of Belgian prostitutes. In *Adoui and Cornaille*, the ECJ held that Member States must show that repressive measures or other genuine and effective measures were taken to combat the offending conduct in respect of their own nationals. Although the Member States need not criminalise the behaviour in question, the burden of proof lies on the relevant Member State to show appropriate measures apply in all cases.

An important point to note is that in any case, the threat to the public policy concern must arise exclusively from the personal conduct of the individual against whom the Member State seeks to take measures (Article 3(1) of the Directive). As noted earlier, the Directive states that a previous criminal record would not suffice in this context. Even if an individual commits a criminal act, that individual cannot necessarily be deported and certainly cannot be deported if the aim of that deportation is to discourage other immigrants from the same sort of behaviour.[14] More recently, in *Donatella Calfa*,[15] a case concerning an individual's right to travel to receive tourist services, a Greek rule, which provided for automatic deportation of non-nationals who had been convicted of certain offences, was found to be inconsistent with the requirements of the Directive. The ECJ in this case held that, in the light of European citizenship (introduced by TEU), Calfa's expulsion could be based only on conduct other than the commission of the offence. This would seem significantly to restrict the freedom of authorities to deport individuals.

---

12 In this case there was no discussion of whether the UK's freedom of action in refusing van Duyn entry should be limited in the light of van Duyn's freedom of religion.

13 Cases 115 and 116/81 *Adoui and Cornaille* v. *Belgium* [1982] ECR 1665.

14 Case 67/74 *Bonsignore* v. *Oberstadtdirektor* [1975] ECR 297.

15 Case C-348/96 *Donatella Calfa* [1999] ECR I-11.

Article 4 of the Directive deals with public health. The freedom of Member States to take action in this context is limited; they can rely only on those diseases set out in the Annex to the Directive which relate to highly infectious or contagious diseases such as tuberculosis; drug addiction or profound mental disturbance. In particular, the Commission issued a Communication that states that the free movement of persons with HIV/AIDS must be safeguarded.[16] The grounds in the Annex can be divided into two categories. In the first category fall highly infectious diseases, where the risk is contagion arising from the mere presence of the infected individual, a point the ECJ seemed to accept in *Gül*.[17] The right of the Member States to limit the free movement of individuals in this context can be seen as a form of quarantine. By contrast, neither drug addiction nor profound mental disturbance, which fall into the second category, are contagious in this way.

It is evident that the concerns that might underpin this second category are different from that of a direct and specific risk of a disease spreading rapidly. Two particular possible concerns spring to mind. The first is that Member States are seeking to protect their populations from the actions of drug addicts (for example, theft to fund an addiction or attacks on doctors to obtain drugs) or those of persons who are mentally disturbed (unprovoked attacks on passers-by). The problem with this analysis is that it does not take into account the fact that not all drug addicts and persons suffering from profound mental disturbance are potentially dangerous in this way. Further, the concerns addressed might better be described as public order or public security issues – in relation to which it must be the personal conduct of the individual concerned that is the basis for refusal of entry rather than membership of a particular group. Additionally, if the actions of persons who are ill are to be taken into account in determining whether they constitute a risk to the public health, surely the actions of those who carry infections falling outside the current list should also be taken into account? This would clearly result in a potentially wide and, as far as individual rights are concerned, intrusive exception to the free movement rights. The argument does, however, serve to illustrate what seems to be the somewhat arbitrary inclusion of the second category of persons within the scope of Article 4 and the Annex to the Directive.

The second possibility is that Member States are implicitly concerned about the potential costs arising from the need to care for or rehabilitate such persons, who might have a right to enter a Member State to receive treatment without in anyway being economically active or self-supporting.[18] Of course, the ECJ tends to reject arguments based on

---

16 COM (1999) 372.

17 Case 131/85 *Gül* v. *Regierungspräsident Düsseldorf* [1986] ECR 1573.

18 See further Chapters 8 and 11.

economic grounds, although it should also be noted that it has accepted justifications relating to the viability of social security systems.[19] Whatever the rationale, it would seem that public health as an exception to free movement may cover more circumstances than might be necessary. Nonetheless, as noted earlier in relation to the Directive in general, Article 4 of the Directive may not be used to access the services market; the grounds set out in the Directive may be used in the context of access to Member State territory. Thus, the regulation of the medical profession does not fall within the scope of this provision,[20] although such concerns might be relevant as far as the public health derogation in Article 55 itself is concerned. The scope of the public health exception under Article 55 is discussed further below.

Diseases or disabilities that occur after a first residence permit, according to Article 4(2) of the Directive, 'shall not justify refusal to renew the residence permit or expulsion from the territory'. Whether this would protect an individual who is making repeat trips to a Member State is another question. Further, given the expansion of the scope of the right to receive medical services, there may be a clash between such an individual's right to obtain those services where the individual has a disease listed in the Annex and the Member State's interest. Presumably, even when medical authorities had agreed to treat the individual, the Member State would still be able to take action to protect public health.

b) Procedural Rights

The Directive also provides procedural rights, of which only an overview follows.[21] The Member State must take a decision regarding first entry within six months of the date of the application and during that time the applicant it permitted to stay within the host Member State. Individuals, were their application to be refused, should be given certain minimum periods of time in which to leave the country. In all such cases, the individual is to be informed of the grounds for the reason to expel 'unless this is contrary to the interests of the security of the State involved'.[22] The

---

19 Case C-204/90 *Bachmann* v. *Belgium* [1992] ECR I-249. See also Case C-368/98 *Abdon Vanbraekel and Other* v. *Alliance nationale des mutualités chrétiennes (ANMC)* [2001] ECR I-5363 and Case C-157/99 *Geraets-Smits* v. *Stichting Ziekenfonds VGZ* and *Peerbooms* v. *Stichting CZ Groep Zorgverzekeringen* [2001] ECR I-5473.

20 Case 131/85 *Gül, supra* n. 17 at p. 1589.

21 For more detailed criticism of the Directive's procedural guarantees see e.g. O'Keeffe, D., 'Practical Difficulties in the Application of Art. 48 of the EEC Treaty' (1982) *CMLRev* 35; and notes on *Gallagher*, cited below, by O'Leary, S., (1996) 33 *CMLRev* 777 and White, R., (1996) 21 *ELRev* 241.

22 Article 6 of the Directive.

reasons should be sufficiently precise and comprehensive to allow the applicant to take effective steps to prepare an appeal.[23] Article 8 provides that all public law remedies should be open to such applicants in challenging an unfavourable decision, although the ECJ in *Shingara*[24] accepted that there were inherent differences between the situation of a national and non-national which could be reflected in terms of the procedures available to the applicant. Article 9 provides a safety net reflecting the minimum requirements of natural justice. Thus, where there is no right of appeal under national law to a court of law or where any such review is limited to the legal validity of the decision, the applicant has the right not to be deported until an opinion has been obtained from a 'competent authority of the host country' on the matter. The authority must not be the same body that made the original decision to expel[25] and the opinion on the desirability of deportation must be made within reasonable temporal proximity of the time that order will be executed.

III Scope of Treaty Provisions beyond Directive 64/221

As noted, the Directive does not cover all situations; there is still need for the underlying Treaty derogation. It might be assumed that the Treaty articles would cover both access to the Member States' territory and access to the market itself: the Treaty freedoms are, after all, expressed in terms of right of access to the market; access to the Member State is ancillary to that right. In the *Security Guards* case, the ECJ, citing *Gül*,[26] held that,

> '[t]he right of Member States to restrict freedom of movement for persons on grounds of public policy, public security or public health is not intended to exclude economic sectors such as the private security sector from the application of that principle, from the point of view of access to employment, but to allow Member States to refuse access to their territory or residence there to persons whose access or residence would in itself constitute a danger for public policy, public security or public health.'[27]

---

23 Case 36/75 *Rutili* v. *Ministre de l'Intérior* [1975] ECR 1219.

24 Cases C-65 and 111/95 *R.* v. *Secretary of State for the Home Department, ex parte Shingara* [1997] ECR I-2163.

25 See Case 36/75 *Rutili* v. *Ministre de l'Intérior, supra* n. 22 but contrast Case C-175/94 *R.* v. *Secretary of State for the Home Department, ex parte Gallagher* [1995] ECR I-4253.

26 Case 131/85 *Gül supra* n. 17 at paragraph 17.

27 Case C-114/97 *Commission* v. *Spain* (Security Guards) [1998] ECR I-6717, at paragraph 42.

On the face of it, this looks as though the ECJ is, however, limiting Article 55 to access to the territory.[28] It is submitted that this is not necessarily the case: the concern the ECJ is expressing here is that whole sectors of the economy should not be removed from the scope of the EC Treaty. Arguably, should a derogation refer to a specific instance limiting access to a particular contract (i.e. the services market), the ECJ would be prepared to consider whether the derogation is justified. In *Centros*,[29] which admittedly concerned a legal person rather than a natural person, the ECJ was prepared to consider a derogation in relation to a rule which affected access to the market; similarly in *Kohll*,[30] which concerned the right of an individual to go to another Member State to receive medical treatment and to be reimbursed for that treatment in the home Member State, the ECJ considered a public health argument which was not primarily concerned with Kohll's access to the territory of the host Member State but with the operation of national health care systems. It may be that this distinction is of limited significance, as many of the more obvious circumstances when a derogation under public policy or public security might arise in relation to access to the market are likely to fall within the scope of the public service exception, considered below.

a) Public Policy

Public policy is potentially a wide concept. Arguably, since Article 30 enumerates in more detail various heads of derogation that are not all included in Article 55, the public policy derogation as regards services is wider than the public policy derogation in relation to goods, perhaps including those heads of derogation which Article 30 specifically mentions. It might be argued that the ECJ has implicitly taken this approach. It accepted issues of public morality as falling within the scope of public policy when considering prostitutes' rights. It also introduced industrial and commercial rights into Article 55 by analogy with Article 30 in the *Coditel* case.[31] The position is not, however, clear-cut: some elements of public morality relating to rules limiting gambling have been characterised as consumer protection issues which constitute interests of overriding public importance. Similarly the prevention of the exploitation of individuals' weakness for gambling and the maintenance of order in

---

28 See e.g. Wyatt and Dashwood *European Union Law* (4th edition) (Sweet and Maxwell, London, 2000) at p. 485.

29 Case C-212/97 *Centros Ltd* v. *Erhvervs-og Selskabsstyrelsen* [1999] ECR I-1459.

30 Case C-158/96 *Kohll* v. *Union des Caisses de Maladie* [1998] ECR I-1931.

31 Case 62/79 *Coditel SA* v. *Ciné Vog Films SA* [1980] ECR 878. See also Cases C-92 and 326/92 *Phil Collins* v. *Imtrat Handelsgesellschaft mbH* [1993] ECR I-5145.

society have been viewed as matters of overriding public interest.[32] It may be that an expansive approach to public policy here is unnecessary, given the juridical development of matters considered to be of overriding public interest (discussed in more detail below), rather than public policy. This difficulty, of course is, that such justifications will only apply to a more restrictive category of national rules: that is, they will apply only to those measures which are not on the face of it discriminatory. Discriminatory measures may be saved only by reference to the heads of derogation expressed in the Treaty itself.[33]

It seems as if the ECJ has adopted a parallel approach to the concept of public policy under the Treaty as in Directive 64/221: in *Commission* v. *Spain* (Security Guards),[34] the ECJ when considering the scope of public policy referred specifically to the test in *Bouchereau*.[35] Presumably the introduction of citizenship will have a similar impact on the interpretation of Articles 46 and 55 as on the Directive. One possible problem, however, is that they may be relied on by legal persons to whom citizenship would not attach, as well as natural persons. Other concerns relating to public policy have been identified by secondary legislation: for example, the protection of the telecommunications network from harm and the need to ensure that broadcasts do not include programming which might seriously impair the physical, mental or moral development of minors nor contain any incitement to hatred on grounds of race, sex, religion or nationality.[36] These issues are a matter to be determined by the individual Member State, but, as ever, secondary legislation is interpreted to comply with Treaty obligations and the scope of Member State freedom is thus circumscribed.

---

32 Case C-275/92 *Schindler* [1994] ECR I-1039 at paragraph 58; Case C-124/97 *Markku Juhani Läärä, Cotswold Microsystems Ltd, Oy Transatlantic Software Ltd* v. *Kihlakunnansyyttäjä (Jyväskylä), Suomen Valtio (Finnish State)* [1999] ECR I-6067 at paragraph 33.

33 Case C-353/89 *Commission* v. *Netherlands* (Mediawet), *supra* n. 4 at 4093-4. See further Chapters 10 and 11. Interestingly, the ECJ in Case C-124/97 *Läärä, supra* n. 32, did not consider whether the award of an exclusive licence constituted an indistinctly or distinctly applicable measure.

34 Case C-114/97 *Commission* v. *Spain, supra* n. 27, at paragraph 46.

35 Case 30/77 *R.* v. *Bouchereau, supra* n. 8.

36 Council Directive 89/552/EEC as amended, Article 22. It should be noted that the Television without Frontiers Directive (Directive 89/552/EEC, as amended) additionally prescribes the measures that the Member State should take in such an instance and there is therefore less likelihood of an issue arising as to its proportionality.

b) Public Security

There is little case law on this aspect, although the ambit of public security as regards goods and services might differ, as public security in the field of goods relates to the external as well as the internal sphere. As noted earlier, certain elements of public security have been subsumed into the discussion about the scope of public service. One further issue concerning the scope of public security arises following the amendments introduced by the Treaty of Amsterdam. The changes included the insertion into the EC Treaty of some policy areas previously dealt with by the Justice and Home Affairs (JHA) pillar of the EU and, effectively, the Schengen Convention system for removing border controls. The new section of the EC Treaty contains separate provisions for the free movement of peoples, including separate derogation provisions. These heads of derogation include national security. It is not yet clear how the separate elements of the EC Treaty will operate and inter-relate. Coherency seems to have suffered from the amendments introduced by ToA. A further complicating issue is that certain policies which may indirectly affect national security, such as decisions relating to police co-operation against terrorism, remain with the JHA.

c) Public Health

As we have seen, Directive 64/221 describes at least part of the content of the public health exception. Article 4 of the Directive relates to a Member State's reaction to a specific and, as regards contagion, direct risk that operates from the point of entry into the Member State.[37] Might public health extend beyond this negative conception to a view of public health that includes general and/or positive measures, such as public health education, ensuring health care standards or the provision of a health care system? In this context, changes to the concerns expressly protected by the Treaty might be significant.

As noted, *Gül*[38] is authority for the proposition that whole sectors cannot be excluded from the scope of the Treaty. A similar point arose in *Kohll*.[39] There the ECJ had to decide whether a Member State could rely on the public health exception in relation to rules restricting the right to obtain medical treatment abroad, which were based on a concern to ensure the quality of medical services. The ECJ started by referring to *Gül* and

---

37 Compare the position under Article 30: initially the public health exception there was characterised by reference to specific risks but has since developed to include more general or less direct threats. See Chapter 7.

38 Case 131/85 *Gül supra* n. 17.

39 Case C-158/96 *Kohll, supra* n. 30.

then went on to point out that the conditions for training for and pursuing the profession of doctor and dentist have been harmonized.[40] There was therefore no scope for the use of Article 46 or 55.[41] It is important to note that the ECJ did not expressly rule out the possibility that concern for medical standards might fall in the scope of public health; the ruling here was tied to the fact that the relevant professions had been harmonized. This point is re-emphasised by the more recent case of *MacQuen et al*.[42] In that case, which concerned restrictions on the type of eye examinations opticians could carry out, the ECJ held that in the absence of harmonization a Member State remained free to regulate, albeit whilst respecting the basic Treaty freedoms. It then held that:

> 'The choice of a Member State to reserve to a category of professionals holding specific qualifications, such as ophthalmologists, the right to carry out objective eyesight examinations ... may be regarded as an appropriate means by which to ensure attainment of a high level of health protection.'[43]

Although the ECJ applied the first part of the proportionality test in this case, it would seem that in principle the ECJ accepted that such concerns about quality of medical services may fall within Article 55.

Kohll also addressed the question of the provision of national health care. The financing of a health care system raises a number of possible grounds for derogation. As the ECJ has previously held, the risk of seriously undermining the financial balance of a social security system may constitute an overriding reason in the general interest.[44] The ECJ specifically held that the objective of maintaining a balanced medical and hospital service open to all, although intrinsically linked to the financing of the social security system, could fall within the public health derogation 'in so far as it contributes to the attainment of a high level of health protection'.[45] It is to be presumed that the ECJ did not mean to exclude the provision of a universal medical and hospital service which operated at a

---

40 See Council Directive 78/686/EEC OJ [1978] L 233/1; Council Directive 687/EEC OJ [1978] L 233/10; Council Directive 93/16/EEC OJ [1993] L 165/1. Other medical professions have also been the subject of sector specific Community regulation, although not all. See also Chapter 13.

41 It has been questioned whether this approach provides adequate protection given the difference in standards of quality assurance with the various Member States: see Roscam Abbing, H.D.C., 'Public Health Insurance and Freedom of Movement within the European Union' (1999) 6 *European Journal of Health Law* 1 at p. 4.

42 Case C-108/96 *Denis MacQuen et al* [2001] ECR I-837.

43 *Ibid.*, at paragraph 30.

44 Case C-158/96 *Kohll*, *supra* n. 30, at paragraph 41.

45 *Ibid.*, at paragraph 50.

basic level from the scope of Article 55. The distinction between the overriding interest argument (that is the need to finance the system) and the balanced service argument seems fine. Presumably, the latter concern relates to the provision and allocation of resources more generally, rather than the financing of such resources. This issue is more fully elaborated in *Smits-Peerbooms*,[46] discussed below. As a separate point, the ECJ also agreed in *Smits-Peerbooms* that Member States may place restrictions on the freedom to provide medical services 'insofar as the maintenance of a treatment facility is essential for the public health and even the survival of the population'.[47] This would seem to justify the same sorts of rules as already discussed, but for different reasons. Despite the finding of principle, when the ECJ considered the issue of necessity, the Luxembourg rules were found not to be necessary for the purpose.

Kohll was closely followed by two cases: *Vanbraekel*[48] and *Smits-Peerbooms*.[49] Both concerned national rules which sought to limit the freedom of individuals to travel to another Member State to receive treatment unavailable in the home Member State and the circumstances in which the costs of that treatment would be reimbursed by the home Member State's health care system. Unsurprisingly the applicants in these cases relied on *Kohll*. In *Vanbraekel*, the applicant was seeking reimbursement for her medical expenses at the rate allowed in her home Member State rather than at the rate allowed by the Member State which treated her. The problem was that the host Member State reimbursed at a lower rate (80% of costs) than that of the home Member State (100%). Not being fully reimbursed if you travel to receive treatment seems a clear disincentive to the exercise of individual free movement rights. The ECJ re-iterated the grounds which might justify a *prima facie* violation of Article 49 identified in *Kohll*, but held that none of these reasons justified the limitations on the right to receive services. In reaching this conclusion, the ECJ seemed to assume that the impact of one person circumventing Member State rules on treatment available[50] and seeking reimbursement at the higher rate would have little impact on a Member State's social security system, which is no doubt the case. It does, however, ignore the cumulative impact of more than one person seeking to claim in this way

46 Case C-157/99 *Smits-Peerbooms*, *supra* n. 19.

47 *Ibid.*, at paragraph 51. The reference to 'population' would seem to be to national groups, emphasising the Member States' responsibilities to their own citizens.

48 Case C-368/98 *Abdon Vanbraekel*, *supra* n. 19.

49 Case C-157/99 *Smits-Peerbooms*, *supra* n. 19.

50 The distinction in the goods case law between products caught by home insurance package, to which free movement principles apply, and those which are not so covered and to which the free movement principle does not apply. See Case 238/82 *Duphar* [1984] ECR 523. The principle seems unaffected by Case C-158/96 *Kohll supra* n. 30.

and the ECJ's reasoning is, arguably, incompatible with a Member State's need to control allocation of resources. Some unanswered questions remained: what is the position where the host Member State reimburses to a higher level than that of the home Member State; and what if the treatment is more expensive in the host Member State than in the home Member State? Until the ECJ rules otherwise, it would seem that the paying Member State would be able to impose some budgetary limitations.[51]

Smits-Peerbooms[52] similarly re-iterated the grounds for derogation identified in *Kohll*, so again the question here was whether the national measures were necessary and proportionate. In contrast to the ruling in *Vanbraekel*, the ECJ in this case actually identified in more detail the issues at stake for the Member States. The Court identified that planning – including the number of hospitals, their geographical distribution, the mode of their organisation and their equipment, and the types of medical services they offer – is necessary to meet the underlying policy concerns. The ECJ concluded that,

> 'if insured persons were at liberty, regardless of the circumstances, to use the services of hospitals with which their sickness fund had not contractual arrangements ..., all the planning which goes into the contractual system in an effort to guarantee a rationalised, stable, balanced and accessible supply of hospital services would be jeopardised at a stroke.'[53]

Again, however, any prior authorisation system must still be justified in relation to the issues of overriding interest and be proportionate.

The recent case law is also noteworthy as it allows us to make some assessment of the impact of Article 152, introduced by the TEU but amended by ToA. The change introduced by the ToA re-emphasises the obligation on the Community to ensure that a high health level of human health protection is obtained. Article 152(1) requires that 'a high level of human health protection shall be ensured in the definition and implementation of all Community policies and activities'[54] and tracks the

---

51 van der Mei, A.P., 'Cross-Border Access to Medical Care within the European Union' (1998) 5 *Maastricht Journal* 277 at p. 295.

52 Case C-157/99 *Smits-Peerboom, supra* n. 19.

53 Case C-157/99 *Smits-Peerboom, supra* n. 19, at paragraph 82.

54 The original text inserted by TEU read 'The Community shall contribute towards ensuring a high level of human health protection by encouraging co-operation between the Member States and, if necessary, lending support to their action.' The new version seems to make clear that health considerations are not to be ring fenced into specific policy actions but must be taken into consideration through the Community's actions.

terms of Article 3(1)(p) EC, which sets out the general Treaty objectives.[55] Furthermore, Article 152(5), inserted by ToA, states that 'Community action in the field of public health shall fully respect the responsibilities of the Member State for the organisation and delivery of health services and medical care.'[56] There are two questions which arise from this change: whether following ToA the scope of the public health exception has been enlarged and whether the introduction of the new provision indicates that the provision of national health care would fall into the exclusive competence of the Member State. This issue of the scope of public health has been considered in a number of post-Amsterdam cases, notably *MacQuen et al*,[57] *Van Braekel*[58] and *Smits-Peerbooms*.[59]

As regards the scope of public health, the ECJ seems to have taken the same approach both before and after the changes introduced by the ToA: *Vanbraekel*[60] and *Smits-Peerbooms*[61] follow the same approach as *Kohll*, although with differing degrees of sophistication in analysis. Interestingly, it appears as though the ECJ has blurred the distinction between the public health exception and the requirement for a high level of health protection. This can be seen in *Kohll*, *Vanbraekel*, *Smits-Peerboom* and *MacQuen et al*.[62] In *MacQuen,* the ECJ linked the level of protection permitted by the Treaty with the terms of Article 55; i.e. the standard public health exception that defines by reference to a specified risk. This could support the argument that the four freedoms and the derogation therefrom are now to be understood in the light of the obligation to provide for a high level of health protection.[63] Indeed, following *MacQuen* it would seem as if the

---

Consider also the changes introduced in relation to environmental and consumer protection and cultural policy. See Chapters 1 and 7.

55 For relationship between general Treaty objectives and the four freedoms see Chapter 1.

56 Note that this emphasises Member State competence to a much higher degree than Article 42 (ex-51), which provides the legal basis for Regulation 1408/71 on the application of Social Security Schemes to Employed Persons, to Self-employed persons and to Members of their Families moving within the Community. It aims at the co-ordination of such schemes, not at their harmonization. The interpretation of this provision has been affected by the concept of European Citizenship.

57 Case C-108/96 *Denis MacQuen et al*, *supra* n. 42.

58 Case C-368/98 *Abdon Vanbraekel*, *supra* n. 19.

59 Case C-157/99 *Smits-Peerbooms*, *supra* n. 19.

60 Case C-368/98 *Abdon Vanbraekel*, *supra* n. 19.

61 Case C-157/99 *Smits-Peerbooms*, *supra* n. 19.

62 Case C-108/96 *Denis MacQuen et al*, *supra* n. 42.

63 Similar arguments have been made regarding consumer protection and environmental protection, see Chapter 7. As regards environmental protection, consider the reasoning in Case C-379/98 *PreussenElektra AG* v. *Schleswag AG* [2001] ECR I-2099.

requirements of Article 152 (or Article 3(1)(p)) are the same as those of the public health exception. Worryingly, however, it does not seem as though Article 55 is to be read more broadly in the light of Article 152, as might have been anticipated in the light of the requirement to read EC policies so as to ensure a high level of protection. Rather, it seems as if the new level of protection required by Article 152 adds nothing to health protection, or at least provides no greater safeguards to public health from the side effects, via deregulation, of the creation of the internal market. Thus Article 152 seems to be being interpreted by reference to Articles 49-55, rather than Article 152 influencing the impact of the free movement of services rules.

Interestingly, in *MacQuen* the ECJ instructed the national court, in assessing the proportionality of the measure, to take into account changes in the profession and technological developments which themselves affect the level of risk to public health. Thus matters that may fall within the scope of the exception may change over time. Whether this means that risks to health will decrease in the light of new technology or may pose further or greater threats is not specifically addressed by the ECJ.[64]

Vanbraekel[65] and *Smits-Peerbooms*[66] concern the public provision of health care and its relationship with the freedom to receive services. Despite the recognition of Member States' competence in this area, the ECJ effectively held that the individuals in question were entitled to receive the treatment and to be reimbursed for the costs. As the change in UK government policy regarding the use of German health care facilities to treat NHS patients shows, this judgment will have a profound impact on the health systems of the Member States. The judgments reinforce the point, illustrated elsewhere, that the ECJ has prioritised various objectives within the Community legal order differently, with the creation of the internal market receiving a very high priority.[67] The inclusion of public sector provision in the internal market has affected the relationship between state and citizen, perhaps creating the base for a form of European public health provision. In this there are links, albeit implicit, between the effects of these rulings and European citizenship. Nonetheless, it is questionable whether the ECJ's jurisprudence 'fully respect[s] the responsibilities of the Member States' in terms of the organisation of their health care systems, as required by Article 152.

---

64 On the impact of science and technology, see the amendments to Article 95 (ex-100a), discussed further in Chapter 13.

65 Case C-368/98 *Vanbraekel*, *supra* n. 19.

66 Case C-157/99 *Smits-Peerboom*, *supra* n. 19.

67 See discussion of culture, below and Chapter 7 regarding the derogation from the free movement of goods.

IV Public Service

The scope of the public service exception has been the subject of much litigation, the Member States seeking a relatively broad interpretation; the Commission and the ECJ adopting a narrower approach. Article 45 states that the provisions regarding establishment are inapplicable 'so far as any given Member State is concerned, to activities which are connected, even occasionally, with the exercise of official authority.' This provision, as with the other derogations, has been extended by Article 55 to apply to services. It is very unlikely that a Member State would seek to rely on this provision in relation to the right to receive services.

There are two basic issues to resolve regarding Article 45: what sort of responsibilities fall within the public service exception; and whether, in assessing if a given situation falls within the scope of the public service exception, a functional or institutional approach should be taken. In resolving these questions, the basic issue of identification of public service is for the Member States, subject, as always, to the ultimate confines of Community requirements. The ECJ has taken a strict approach to this issue. Despite the difference in wording between Article 39(4) and 45, the ECJ has adopted a parallel approach between the two provisions.

In *Reyners* v. *Belgium*[68] the Belgium Government sought to argue that the profession of advocate was excluded from the provisions on establishment as it involved the exercise of official authority. The ECJ held that the crucial test for the application of the public service derogation was that there be a 'direct and specific connection'[69] with the exercise of official authority. This test has since been re-iterated many times.[70] In *Reyners*, the ECJ identified the tasks that advocates typically carried out, such as legal consultation, co-operating with the courts and defending parties before the courts, but held that these could not be considered as being connected with the exercise of official authority as '[t]he exercise of these activities leaves the discretion of judicial authority and the free exercise of judicial power intact'.[71]

Although the reasoning in *Reyners* makes it clear that the ECJ will take a functional approach to determining whether the public service exception applies,[72] it does not provide further guidance on the nature of the direct and specific connection required. In a subsequent case, relating to the free

68 Case 2/74 *Reyners* v. *Belgium* [1974] ECR 631.

69 *Ibid.,* at paragraph 45.

70 See e.g. Case C-42/92 *Thijssen* [1993] ECR I-4047, paragraph 8; Case C-114/97 *Commission* v. *Spain* (Security Guards), *supra* n. 27, at paragraph 35.

71 Case 2/74 *Reyners* v. *Belgium, supra* n. 68 at paragraph 53.

72 The functional criteria were specifically applied in Case 152/73 *Commission* v. *France* [1974] ECR 153.

movement of workers, the ECJ held that the public service exception could only be applied to those safeguarding the interests of the State and did not apply automatically to all civil servants.[73] It further identified the basis on which the public service exception operated: that of the special loyalty presumed on the part of a citizen towards the state of which he is a national, a point that has been re-iterated on a number of times.[74] One might question the impact of European citizenship on this point; the issue has not yet been addressed by the ECJ. Thus the criteria for identifying the exercise of official authority remain twofold:

1) an objective element requiring the direct or indirect participation in the exercise of powers conferred by public law; and
2) a subjective element relating to the intention of the post – that it must be intended to safeguard the interests of the state. It is this second element that ties in to the notion of loyalty.

This test is cumulative rather than in the alternative. Thus, although the functioning of the state railway system is no doubt important and in times of crisis could be crucial to the well being of the state,[75] neither criteria are satisfied. By contrast, where judicial powers are exercised as part of the service carried out it seems that the necessary link will be shown; this is the implication from *Reyners* and a further case involving traffic experts.[76] There, the role of the expert did not fall within the scope of the public service exception where his reports were not binding on the national court as, again, the exercise of judicial power was left intact.[77]

It seems where there is some element of coercion over fellow citizens, the holders of such power may well have the necessary link with the State, though – equally – such powers must go beyond those of the average person on the street. The ECJ has been sceptical about the existence of such 'extra' powers, as can be seen in the *Spanish Security Guards* case.[78] There, private security guards were held not to fall within the scope of the exception, as they were not vested with the powers of constraint although they carried guns, carried out surveillance and were empowered to arrest

73 Case 149/79 *Commission* v. *Belgium* [1980] ECR 3881.

74 See e.g. Case C-4/91 *Bleis* v. *Ministère de l'Education Nationale* [1991] ECR I-5627.

75 Compare reasoning in Case 72/83 *Campus Oil* v. *Minister for Industry and Energy* [1984] ECR 2727 discussed in Chapter 7.

76 Case C-306/89 *Commission* v. *Greece* [1991] ECR I-5863.

77 *Ibid.*, at paragraph 7. See also Case C-42/92 *Thijssen*, *supra* n. 70 regarding the 'auxiliary and preparatory functions' of a Commissioner for a body which exercised official authority regarding the relevant decisions – again there was no direct and specific connection.

78 Case C-114/97 *Commission* v. *Spain* (Security Guards), *supra* n. 27.

those committing offences. According to the ECJ, '[m]erely making a contribution to the maintenance of public security, which any individual may be called on to do, does not constitute exercise of official authority.'[79]

In the subsequent *Italian Security Guards* case[80] the ECJ was seemingly still more restrictive in its views. In the Italian case, the security guards had the authority to arrest those committing a serious criminal offence. In this, the Italian rules were similar to the Spanish. Italian security guards were, additionally, empowered to arrest people committing a minor offence. The Commission accepted that when security guards arrest a person during the course of a minor offence, 'for which police officers are empowered, but not obliged' to arrest the perpetrator, they are, exercising a function which is normally reserved to the police'.[81] The ECJ concluded, however, that the Italian Government could not rely on the public service exception, stating that the security guards' powers did not go beyond the powers of private citizens. In taking this approach, the ECJ did not fully address the arguments put forward by the Italian government suggesting that a distinction must be drawn between guards who act solely within the context of a private-law contract and the guards and firms in issue here, who were subject to control by the public authorities. They had to swear an oath undertaking to pursue only the public interest. Furthermore, their reports could have a probative effect in court hearings. In this aspect, the ECJ's reasoning seems insufficient. The concern, as the Commission had noted, was to ensure that an entire sector was not excluded from the scope of the Treaty by reference to elements ancillary to the guards' work. Although it may be thought that the ECJ underplayed the role of security guard by equating their role to one that any private individual might undertake, it is clear that the security guards' function did not require particular loyalty to the state arising from the bond of nationality. The problem from the Community perspective is not that the Member States seek to regulate security guards, although any such national regulation would have to be compatible with Article 49, but that they sought to do so by reference to an express nationality criterion.

Given the propensity of the Member States to seek to rely on the public service provisions with regard to a wide number of public servants, the Commission issued a Communication on the subject of the scope of the public service exception.[82] It suggested that only in rare exceptions would the derogation be available and identified activities which it considered to be 'sufficiently remote from the specific activities of the public sphere'. According to the view of the Commission, which seems in line with the

79 *Ibid.*

80 Case C-283/99 *Commission* v. *Italy* (Security Guards) [2001] ECR1-436.

81 *Ibid.*, at paragraph 15.

82 Commission Communication OJ [1988] C72/2.

ECJ's jurisprudence, the following are unlikely to benefit from the public service derogation:

1) public health care services;
2) teaching in State educational establishments;
3) research for non-military purposes in public establishments; and
4) public bodies responsible for administering commercial services.

Despite the fact that the Commission issued this Communication more than a decade ago, there still are recent cases, as the *Italian Security Guard* case illustrates, on this point. The basic principles on which the cases will be decided do not seem to have changed.

V Requirements of Overriding Public Interest

Säger v. *Dennemeyer*[83] confirmed that measures which are not discriminatory but which still on the face of it trigger Article 49 can nonetheless be justified on grounds of public interest. In this holding, the ECJ effectively introduced a rule of reason into the services case law and a degree of parallelism between the jurisprudence of the goods and services sector. As is the case with mandatory requirements, it seems that the category of possible justifications is not closed: the ECJ has held consumer protection[84] and advertising, fairness of commercial transactions,[85] professional conduct,[86] public morality,[87] environmental protection[88] and cultural policy objectives all to constitute such justifications.[89] The ECJ has also found intellectual property rights to justify rules that *prima facie*

83 Case C-76/90 *Manfred Säger* v. *Dennemeyer & Co. Ltd* [1991] ECR I-4221.

84 Case C-384/93 *Alpine Investments BV* v. *Minister van Financiën* [1995] ECR I-1141; Case 252/83 *Commission* v. *Denmark* (Insurance) [1986] ECR 3713. See Chapter 7.

85 Case C-384/93 *Alpine Investments BV, supra* n. 84; Joined Cases C-34-36/95 *Konsumentombudsmannen* v. *de Agostini* and *TV Shop i Sverige* [1997] ECR I-3843.

86 Case C-76/90 *Manfred Säger, supra* n. 83; Case 33/74 *Van Binsbergen* v. *Bedrijfsvereniging Metaalnijverheid* [1974] ECR 1307.

87 Case C-275/92 *Schindler, supra* n. 32; Case C-124/97 *Läärä, supra* n. 32.

88 Case C-37/92 *Criminal Proceedings against José Vanacker and André Lesage* [1993] ECR I-4947. The Advocate-General in this case commented that environmental protection was considered a mandatory requirement in relation to goods and 'the same must apply to the freedom to provide services' at paragraph 65. The ECJ did not pick this point up, dealing with the case as one concerning goods. On the scope of environmental protection see Chapter 7.

89 For a list of rule of reason exceptions see Case C-353/89 *Commission* v. *Netherlands* (Mediawet), *supra* n. 4.

are contrary to Article 49.[90] Given that the scope of consumer protection and commercial fairness as well as environmental protection have been discussed in Chapter 7, and there are similarities in the scope of those concepts as regards both goods and services, these matters will not be dealt with again here. Instead, in this section we will consider the notion of 'culture' as that is one mandatory requirement which has not been fully elucidated by the ECJ in relation to goods.[91]

As noted, the ECJ has in principle accepted the notion of culture as a matter of overriding public interest in the context of Article 49 EC. Such acceptance does, however, raise the question of what is meant by cultural policy; given the multitude of potential meanings for the notion of 'culture', it could mean virtually anything. One possibility is that the culture protected by overriding interests in relation to Article 49 is similar in scope to the values protected by Article 30, that is, to 'national treasures possessing artistic, historical or archaeological value'. In other words, does culture in this context protect only high culture? Certainly, in the *Tourist Guide* cases,[92] a notion of high culture was seemingly accepted. There the French Government argued that the general interest included a proper appreciation of places and things of historical interest and the widest possible dissemination of knowledge of the artistic and cultural heritage of the country.[93] Further, in *Commission* v. *Italy*, the ECJ held that 'the general interest ... in the conservation of the national historical and artistic heritage can constitute an overriding reason'.[94] It would seem from these cases that the notion of high culture is broadly construed, as the ECJ accepted that the justification extends not just to those who create or preserve such culture, but also to those who facilitate access to cultural facilities and disseminate information about them, even where that information is conveyed at a very basic level. Although the principle may well have been accepted, the ECJ has taken a stringent line on the type of measures that would be acceptable, applying the usual necessity and

90 Case 62/79 *Coditel SA* v. *Ciné Vog Films SA* [1980] ECR 878; Cases C-92 and 326/92 *Phil Collins* v. *Imtrat Handelsgesellschaft mbH* [1993] ECR I-5145; Case 195/87 *Ministère Public* v. *Tournier* [1989] ECR 2521. The scope of intellectual property rights is discussed in Chapter 8.

91 The ECJ has not expressly recognised cultural policy as a mandatory requirement, although it seems implicit in Cases 60 and 61/84 *Cinéthèque SA* v. *Fédération Nationale des Cinémas Françaises* [1985] ECR 2605.

92 Case C-154/89 *Commission* v. *France* (Tour Guides) [1991] ECR I-659; Case C-198/89 *Commission* v. *Greece* (Tour Guides) [1991] ECR I-727; Case C-180/89 *Commission* v. *Italy* (Tour Guides) [1991] ECR I-709.

93 Case C-154/89 *Commission* v. *France* (Tour Guides), *ibid.*, at paragraph 16.

94 Case C-180/89 *Commission* v. *Italy* (Tour Guides), *supra* n. 92 at paragraph 20.

proportionality tests. In the *Tourist Guide* cases, the national measures were held to be disproportionate.

The ECJ had the opportunity to consider cultural policy again in the *Mediawet* cases.[95] These two cases concerned Dutch legislation which established a monopoly corporation responsible for the broadcasting of advertisements on television in the Netherlands, profits from which were distributed amongst the Dutch media (including the press), so as to encourage the reflection of the views of the various cultural, philosophical and social sections of Dutch society. Clearly this is a much broader conception of 'culture' than seen in the *Tourist Guide* cases,[96] yet the ECJ accepted it as a potential overriding requirement. The ECJ did not, however, seem to have a particularly clear notion of the concept of culture to be protected. In accepting the Dutch government's proposition, the ECJ referred specifically to Article 10 ECHR, almost turning the issue into a question of freedom of expression and of equality of access, despite the specific reference to the 'cultural tasks' of the system – such as managing a sound library, keeping film archives and managing orchestras and choirs.[97] The ECJ did, however, accept that the maintenance of programme quality itself might be an object of cultural policy. Insofar as all these activities are included within 'culture' it seems that the ECJ does not accept that culture is linked to a particular state: broadcasters cannot be under an obligation to have 'all or some of their programmes produced by a Dutch undertaking'.[98]

One area in which the link between Member State and culture would be hard to dismiss is with regard to language. There has been little discussion of this point regarding services,[99] although the issue has arisen

---

95 Case C-288/89 *Stichting Collective Antennevoorziening Gouda* v. *Commissariat voor de media* [1991] ECR I-4007; Case C-353/89 *Commission* v. *Netherlands* (Mediawet), *supra* n. 4.

96 Case C-180/89 *Commission* v. *Italy* (Tour Guides), *supra* n. 89; Case C-154/89 *Commission* v. *France* (Tour Guides), *supra* n. 92; Case C-198/89 *Commission* v. *Greece* (Tour Guides), *supra* n. 92.

97 Case C-353/89 *Commission* v. *Netherlands* (Mediawet), *supra* n. 4, at paragraph 29.

98 Case C-353/89 *Commission* v. *Netherlands* (Mediawet), *ibid.*, at paragraph 31. Note, however, the European programme quotas are permissible under the Television without Frontiers Directive, *supra* n. 36 and, in many Member States, in practice this turns into a national requirement.

99 Language requirements did arise in relation to the Belgian rules relating to cable television. These arguments were dismissed mainly it seemed because the rules were characterised as discriminatory and could therefore be saved only by reference to the express Treaty derogation: the ECJ held that cultural policy did not fall within public policy. See Case C-211/91 *Commission* v. *Belgium* (Access to Cable Television) [1992] ECR I-6757.

in relation to workers and goods, albeit with different results. Given the various ways in which services can occur, the jurisprudence from both the workers and goods areas might also be relevant here. Language requirements for workers are considered an exception to the rules relating to non-discrimination – perhaps because in many, if not all, jobs the ability to communicate is vital. The ECJ went further in *Groener*, however.[100] The case concerned an Irish rule that required that teachers pass an oral test in Irish, even when they would be teaching in English. The ECJ noted that,

> 'although Irish is not spoken by the whole population, the policy followed by the Irish government for many years has been designed not only to maintain but also to promote the use of Irish as a means of expressing national identity and culture.'[101]

The ECJ here is emphasising that individual national identities can be protected within the Community, a point that the Advocate-General had made emphatically. Of course, any such measures must be proportionate,[102] so, for example, the Irish Government could not require that the relevant language tests be taken in Ireland.[103]

This judgment may be open to criticism on the grounds that it seems to contradict the clear wording of Article 3 of Regulation 1612/68. Further, although the ECJ applied a proportionality test, it did not consider whether the application of the language requirement satisfied the necessity or proportionality tests as it has done with other mandatory requirements and overriding interests (which, arguably it would have failed). The ECJ rather contented itself with looking to the level of language required and the operation of the test. It is debatable whether *Groener*[104] can be seen as authority for the proposition that Member States have exclusive competence as regards language requirements. *Groener* itself interprets secondary legislation rather than the terms of the Treaty and the terms of the judgment are very much limited to the facts; Irish was the constitutionally recognised first language. What would be the position, for example, as regards a regional language policy? In any event, the *Mediawet*

100 Case 378/87 *Groener* v. *Minister for Education* [1989] ECR 3987.

101 *Ibid.*, paragraph 18.

102 In this there is a difference of approach between the ECJ and the Advocate-General, who spoke of drawing the line between Member State competence and Community competence. See *ibid.*, Opinion at paragraph 16. The ECJ emphasised that a Member State cannot encroach upon a free movement right: see judgment at paragraph 19.

103 Contrast Case C-281/98 *Angonese* v. *Cassa di Rispamio di Bolzano SpA* [2000] ECR I-4139.

104 Case 378/87 *Groener, supra* n. 100.

cases,[105] that were decided shortly after *Groener*, indicate a more limited freedom being left to the Member States. Equally, the position seems somewhat different as far as language requirements in the context of goods are concerned. Rather than seeing the matter as one of culture, the ECJ has viewed such issues through the lens of consumer protection and has taken a limited view of the extent of language requirements on labelling.[106]

The TEU introduced a new article, Article 151 EC, which gave the EC cultural competence. In some ways, the provision is schizophrenic, referring just as much to the cultures of the Member States as to Community policy and Community culture. Article 151(1) obliges the Community to 'contribute to the flowering of cultures of the Member States, whilst respecting their national and regional diversity and at the same time bringing the common cultural heritage to the fore.' Specifically, Article 151(4) states that the Community, which includes its institutions, is to take 'cultural aspects into account under other provisions of this Treaty, in particular to respect and to promote the diversity of its cultures'. This would suggest an interpretation of mandatory requirements that took more account of the individual Member States' concerns about cultural autonomy. To date, Article 151 has been raised in one case in connection with the freedom to provide services, concerning the Television without Frontiers Directive and programming requirements. The Belgian government sought to rely on Article 151 to justify the Belgian regulatory requirements, but the ECJ dismissed the argument out of hand. To a certain extent this approach is understandable; it would be easy for a Member State to try to disguise protectionism as culture seen as the traditional way doing things in a given Member States. Given, however, that the Community has recognised the importance of the broadcast media in the creation of identity and backed this up with the imposition of quota requirements for European programming, there seems to be a double standard at work. It is questionable whether such a dismissive approach is necessary, especially given the strict application of necessity and proportionality tests even where overriding requirements are recognised.

VI Proportionality

Proportionality is central to a national measure's acceptability under EC law even if that measure, in principle, falls within accepted grounds of derogation. The ECJ seems to have adopted a similar test in relation to justification derived from the express wording of the Treaty and reasons of overriding public importance. Essentially, the test is what one would

105 Case C-353/89 *Commission* v. *Netherlands* (Mediawet), *supra* n. 4.

106 See e.g. Case C-369/89 *Piageme* v. *BVBA Peeters* [1991] ECR I-2971 and Chapter 7.

expect from the case law relating to the other freedoms:[107] the measure achieves a public interest objective; is no more than necessary to achieve that objective and is proportional. From cases such as *Webb*,[108] it follows that Member States are required to take into account regulation in the home Member State. Two points arise. Firstly, it is not clear whether the requirement to take home State regulation into account goes to the proportionality of the measure or to a finding of a restriction in the first place.[109] Furthermore, it has been suggested that the ECJ has not always adopted the same approach to the assessment of proportionality.[110] In the *Mediawet*[111] case (prohibition on advertising) and *Vanbraeckel* (limitations on medical services),[112] the ECJ did not accept that the measures were proportionate, though in *Zenatti*[113] (prohibition on gambling) and *Läärä* (restriction on gambling)[114] it did. The reasoning in *Läärä* and *Zenatti* is not such that convinces the reader that the rules in question are any more proportionate than those in other cases. In both *Zenatti* and *Läärä* the ECJ reasons negatively, arguing that the mere fact that there are differences between Member States' regulatory systems does not mean that the higher levels of regulation are unacceptable. Whilst this is undoubtedly the case, it does not help us identify why these particular rules are proportionate when others are not. It would also seem clear that it is not the *nature* of the restriction that is relevant. Both *Mediawet* and *Vanbraekel,* and arguably *Zenatti*, could be seen as indistinctly applicable rules, whereas *Läärä* might be seen as discriminatory – although the Court did not address this issue in *Läärä*. It would therefore appear that different areas are treated more cautiously than others, with public morality related issues perhaps being deemed more sensitive than others.

VII Conclusions

There are marked themes running through this area of law. There is one set of distinctions between discriminatory rules and indistinctly applicable rules resulting in different grounds of justification for the two types of rule.

---

107 See regarding goods Chapter 7.

108 Case 279/80 *Webb* [1981] ECR 3305.

109 See Chapter 11.

110 Biondi, A., 'In and Out of the Internal Market: Recent Developments on the Principle of Free Movement', (1999/00) 19 *YEL* 461 at p. 463 and Tridimas, T., *The General Principles of EC Law* (OUP, Oxford, 1999) at p. 140.

111 Case 353/89 *Commission* v. *Netherlands, supra* n. 4.

112 Case C-368/98 *Abdon Vanbraekel, supra* n. 19.

113 Case C-67/98 *Zenatti* [1999] ECR I 7289.

114 Case C-124/97 *Läärä, supra* n. 32.

Whether this distinction carries a great deal of significance is less clear: the ECJ has adopted a unitary approach to their interpretation and in some instances has blurred the boundary between the two categories. There is also a distinction between the case law relating to the freedom to provide services as a personal freedom and services seen as an economic transaction akin to the provision of goods. In the former category specific rules apply. Further, in this context the scope of the derogation is tightly construed with less emphasis, or less need to rely, on proportionality. The introduction of European citizenship, in particular, has had a noticeable impact on the scope of any derogation available to Member States vis-à-vis European nationals. In this context an amendment to Part I of the EC Treaty has affected the understanding of the subsequent provisions. In the latter category, by contrast, the ECJ seems to have taken a wider view of the interests worthy of protection, especially as regards the existence of matters of overriding public interest, but used the proportionality test to great effect in controlling the number of national rules found to be justified under EC law. Overall, one can identify that although the ECJ may recognise matters deserving of protection in a wide range of areas, especially as regards the protection offered through interests of overriding importance, the value ascribed to them in practice is questionable. This is most obvious particularly by the areas in which Treaty amendment highlighted the need to ensure particular interests are safeguarded and, in some cases, given a high level of protection, as can be seen in the case of public health. Furthermore, even where interests are recognised, the application of necessity and proportionality tests also limits Member States' freedom, which also ensures that the creation of the internal market continues to be prioritised. The impact of amendments to the Treaty, reflecting wider values, other than the introduction of citizenship, have had a limited impact on the interpretation of the derogation from the freedom to provide services.

Chapter 13

Harmonization

The preceding chapters have dealt primarily with negative harmonization, contained in the jurisprudence of the ECJ under Articles 28, 29 and 49, which operates to strike down national legislation that is incompatible with the free movement of goods or the freedom to provide services. Negative harmonization has not been without it critics, however. Notably, there has been concern that the operation of the Treaty freedoms has led to a deregulatory impulse throughout the Community and to a lowering of standards in areas affected by the internal market.[1] The response to this problem at Community level is also not without disadvantages. As illustrated elsewhere,[2] the Treaty derogation provisions and mandatory requirements may in some instances justify certain national rules which result in barriers to trade through divergent regulatory practices. Harmonization measures are the solution to these problems, being seen either as an attempt to achieve uniformity across the Community in such areas, or as a response to a regulatory gap[3] caused by negative harmonization. On either characterisation, the appropriate response would be at Community level. On this view, a clear, simple picture of the division of competence emerges: where the internal market or common market requires regulation, Community legislation is enacted, which may then require implementing legislation within each of the domestic legal systems. Such an approach has the advantage of including legislative and political organs within the process of law-making and, as a result, Community secondary legislation also seems more legitimate than judicial activity.

Like many simple pictures, this view gives a distorted impression of reality. There are a number of problems in this area concerning the

1 McGee, A. and Weatherill, S., 'The Evolution of the Single Market – Harmonization or Liberalisation' (1990) 53 *MLR* 578 at p. 581 note that 'the *Cassis de Dijon* decision is fundamentally deregulatory' because of its emphasis on mutual recognition.

2 See Chapters 7, 8 and 12.

3 See the comments of Advocate-General Fennelly in Case C-376/98 *Germany* v. *European Parliament and Council of the European Union* (Tobacco Advertising Directive) [2000] ECR I-8419 at paragraph 65: 'In adopting legislative acts the Community stands in the place of the Member States and gives weight to national policy concerns which are not the subject of specific Community competence.'

complexity and types of legislative processes and the actors involved. There is also a lack of clarity as to the scope a harmonizing measure will, in a given case, have. As a result, the relationship between national law, the Treaty freedoms and derogations, and the harmonizing legislation is opaque. There are, consequently, tensions in this area, both horizontally and vertically. As regards the horizontal relationships, the different regulatory techniques reveal tensions between the regulatory and deregulatory forces, as well as within[4] and between policy objectives (notably the creation of the internal market and the social and environmental policies). The vertical aspect concerns the question of whether regulatory competence lies with the Member States or the Community. This chapter aims to provide an overview of the main Treaty bases used for legislation in the area of free movement of goods and services, as well as the different legislative techniques. It will then look at the relationship between the different levels of Community law (for example between the Treaty and directives and between different types of directives) and also between Community law and national law to try to identify if harmonization provides an effective mechanism whereby competing policies (in particular, the completion of the internal market and other societal objectives) can be reconciled and protected.

I Community Competence

Article 5 EC makes express the requirement that had always been understood: that the EC institutions can only take action, such as the enactment of legislation, within the scope of the EC's powers. Indeed, Article 253 EC states that all regulations, directives and decisions must identify the reasons for action. This involves not just an explanation of the purposes of the legislation but also the basis in the Treaty for the legislation. The determination of the constitutionality of Community action requires a two-stage enquiry. First is the proposed action within the scope of Community competence and secondly should the Community institutions act? The first question is about the attribution of powers; the second, the exercise of those powers.

As regards the first question, the tasks of the Community are set out in Article 2 with activities that the Community may undertake to fulfil those tasks enumerated in Articles 3 and 4. These provisions are broadly drawn but do not give the Community general power to act.[5] Although questions

---

4 Dehousse, R., 'Community Competences: Are there Limits to Growth?' in *Europe after Maastricht*, Dehousse, R., (ed.) (Munchen Law Books in Europe, 1994).

5 A point re-iterated recently by the Advocate-General in Case C-376/98 *Germany* v. *European Parliament and Council*, *supra* n. 3 at paragraph 60.

might well arise as to precisely which actions fall within their scope, there are a number of specific provisions that give the institutions express authority to act in particular fields.[6] These provisions generally outline the type of action to be taken and the procedure by which any community measure is to be enacted. For example, Article 47(1) EC provides authority for the enactment of directives for the mutual recognition of diplomas, certificates and other evidence of formal qualification. It further specifies that in agreeing the terms of such directives, the institutions are to use the co-decision procedure.[7] Harmonization of legislation relating to turnover taxation, by contrast, may only take place when the Council acts unanimously, after consulting the European Parliament.[8] The competence of the Community is clear in these fields, as are the mechanisms for action.

What is the position when the particular field is not mentioned? As before, the same two questions arise: is the action within the scope of Community action in principle, that is within Articles 2-4; and does the Community have power to act? The ECJ has developed a number of doctrines to determine the proper scope of Community action although, given the clear centrality of the four freedoms to the creation of the common market or internal market, the issue will not be developed here. The next question relates to the power to act; clearly it would not be practicable to identify all possible areas in which internal market considerations might arise. Instead the Treaty has always contained certain 'general' or 'catch all' provisions, such as Article 94 (ex-100) and Article 308 (ex-235). Since the Single European Act (SEA), Article 94 has been supplemented by Article 95 (ex-100a). Article 47(2) EC, which provides for measures to be taken with respect to services, addresses the same functional concern of safeguarding the internal market with regard to the freedom to provide services. Rather than being defined in terms of substance, as the sector-specific provisions are, these provisions are defined by reference to a function. Their potential ambit, in terms of substantive fields in which they may have an impact, is broad and thus questions regarding the interrelationship between substantively defined provisions and these functional (or horizontal) articles, as well as questions regarding their relative status, are likely to occur.

---

6 Article 51 EC clarifies how transport services and banking and insurance services are to be dealt with. The boundary between other provisions is dealt with further below.

7 Article 251 EC. This procedure requires the Council to act by qualified majority voting and effectively gives the European Parliament the power of veto over any proposed measures. Of course, no Community measure may be enacted without the consent of the Council.

8 Article 93 (ex-99) EC.

a) Specific Treaty Bases

Article 308 Article 308 provides that, should action be necessary to attain in the course of the operation of the common market one of the Community's objectives, but the Community has not been provided with the necessary powers, the Council may take the appropriate measures. Potentially, this provision is very broad, and as commentators[9] have noted, it has been used in a wide variety of situations: the protection of the environment; the promotion of sex equality; the creation of new institutions and the grant of food aid to non-associated countries.[10] This wide use reflects the breadth of the Community's objectives. Article 308 cannot, however, be used to extend the Community's powers, as the ECJ made clear in Opinion 2/94 on *Accession to the ECHR*.[11] Although some Treaty amendments giving express competence to the Community in a given field post-date the use of Article 308 in that field (for example the introduction of specific provisions in the environmental field or that of consumer protection in Articles 174 and 153 respectively), these amendments presumably constitute the clarification (and possibly extension) of the existing scope of the Treaty as illustrated by the prior use of Article 308.

Article 308 is also limited by the fact that it can only be used where the European Community has not been given the power to act. Given the existence of the general harmonizing provisions, Article 94 and 95 EC, as well as the extension of express provisions in some areas, it would seem difficult to find the requisite lack of powers within the fields of free movement of goods and services. Indeed, the use of Article 308 would seem to have become less prevalent; it seemingly goes against the spirit of the time with its increased emphasis towards action by the Member State in the doctrine of subsidiarity.[12]

Article 94 Article 94 provides that the Council, acting unanimously, may issue directives for the harmonization of national laws 'as directly affect the establishment or functioning of the common market'. The fact that Article 94 is phrased to include matters that affect the functioning of the common market widens the potential scope of this provision, despite the

---

9 See e.g. Weiler, J.H.H., 'Transformation of Europe' (1991) 100 *Yale Law Journal* 2403 at p. 2445-6.

10 In a draft report, the European Parliament noted that Article 308 had been utilised some 700 times: Draft Report on the Division of Powers between the European Union and the Member States (2001/2024 (INI)) at point F.

11 Opinion 2/94 *Accession to the ECHR* [1996] ECR I-1759.

12 See also the comments of the Bundesverfassungsgeright in *Brunner* v. *TEU* [1994] 1 CMLR 59 on this point.

reference to national rules which 'directly affect' the common market. It seems that the reference to the functioning of the common market has been interpreted to refer to rules that cause the market to function more effectively. Thus, Article 94 has been used to bring flanking policies within the scope of the common market, the argument being that differences in the national arena relating to, for example working practices, result in a distortion of competition and affect the ability of the companies to compete throughout Europe. The emphasis would seem to be on ensuring an equal playing field in a broad range of areas: for example, rules relating to the environment[13] and consumer protection[14] have been found to fall within Article 94.

Article 95 Article 95 is specifically tied in to the achievement of the objectives set out in Article 14: that is the creation of 'an area without internal frontiers in which the free movement of goods, persons, services and capital is ensured'. It provides that the institutions, using the co-decision procedure, may enact measures for the approximation of national laws 'which have as their object the establishment and functioning of the internal market'. Article 95(2) specifically excludes certain areas from Article 95: fiscal provisions; provisions relating to the free movement of persons; or provisions relating to the rights and interests of employed persons. These excluded areas were perceived as too politically sensitive to permit the use of qualified majority voting, which brings with it the possibility that a Member State might be out-voted. Article 47(2), however, provides a broad basis for action within the field of services and establishment and has been seen as the equivalent provision to Article 95 in respect of those fields.[15] Article 95(3) then obliges the Commission, when putting forward proposals in the fields of health, consumer protection and the protection of the environment, to take as its base a high level of protection, taking into account any development in scientific facts.[16] This

13 Council Directive 87/217/EEC of 19 March 1987 on the prevention and reduction of environmental pollution by asbestos OJ [1987] L 85/40.

14 E.g. Council Directive 85/374/EEC of 25 July 1985 on the approximation of the laws, regulations and administrative provisions of the Member States concerning liability for defective products OJ [1985] L 210/29 and Council Directive 87/102/EEC of 22 December 1986 for the approximation of the laws, regulations and administrative provisions of the Member States concerning consumer credit OJ [1987] L 42/48.

15 Case C-376/98 *Tobacco Advertising Case, supra* n. 3 at paragraph 87.

16 See comments of Advocate-General Jacobs in Case C-377/98 *Netherlands* v. *European Parliament and Council of the European Union* (Biotechnological Inventions) [2001] ECR I-7079 as to the scope of this provision.

requirement is reflected in the sector-specific provisions introduced in respect of each of the areas.[17]

Article 95 refers to 'measures' making it arguably more flexible than Article 94 in this regard, as it would seem to give the institutions the choice of which legislative instrument to use. Typically, however, the directive has been the instrument of choice. As the directive as a legal form specifies the end to be achieved leaving the Member State to choose the means best suited to its own domestic legal system, it appears more flexible and more in keeping in with the concerns underlying the introduction of subsidiarity. This preference finds its expression in the Fourth Declaration annexed to the SEA which states that when selecting the measure to be used in respect of proposals under Article 95, 'the Commission shall give precedence to the use of the instrument of a directive if harmonization involves the amendment of legislative provisions in one or more Member States.' This is not to say that the regulation or decision are never used,[18] but that the declaration operates as a disincentive to the use of a legal form other than the directive. In its recent Communication on Simplifying and Improving the Regulatory Environment,[19] the Commission re-emphasised the importance of the distinction between regulations and directives, commenting that regulations should only be used when absolute uniformity of application is required in the Member States.[20] For many areas, especially where minimum harmonization is used, regulations would seem simply inappropriate.

Article 95 is different in scope from Article 94; Article 95 refers to the internal market whereas Article 94 refers to the common market. Logically, the scope of the internal market should be narrower than that of the common market, the latter including for example external relations or, indeed, competition policy. There has been a tendency, however, to treat the two expressions as synonymous.[21] Indeed, the ECJ has blurred any distinction between the terms.[22] In some directives, the reasoning by which the institutions show that Article 95 is the appropriate Treaty base is linked

---

17 See Articles 152, 153 and 174 EC.

18 See e.g. proposal for a European Parliament and Council Regulation concerning sales promotions in the Internal Market (COM (2001) 546 final), OJ C 75 E/11, but note that sometimes even when the Commission has proposed using the form of a regulation the Council has enacted a directive.

19 COM (2001) 726.

20 *Ibid.*, at p. 8.

21 See Mortelmans, K., 'The Common Market, the Internal Market and the Single Market, What's in a Market?' (1998) 35 *CMLRev* 101 at pp. 107-108 for the distinction between common market, internal market and single market.

22 Case C-41/93 *Commission* v. *France* [1994] ECR I-2867.

very strongly to that used in respect of Article 94. The recitals to the GMO Directive illustrate this point:

> 'Whereas disparity between the rules which are in effect or in preparation in the Member States concerning the deliberate release into the environment of GMOs (genetically modified organisms) may create unequal conditions of competition or barriers to trade in products containing such organisms, thus affecting the functioning of the common market; whereas it is therefore necessary to approximate the laws of the Member States in this respect.
>
> Whereas measures for the approximation of the provisions of the Member States which have as their object the establishment and functioning of the internal market should, inasmuch as they concern health, safety, environmental and consumer protection, be based on a high level of protection throughout the Community.'[23]

The first of the two recitals quoted specifically refer to the functioning of the common market, although the Directive was based on Article 95 alone. It is only in the second recital that we see a reference to the internal market.

The ECJ has given an expansive interpretation to Article 95. In the *Titanium Dioxide* case,[24] it confirmed that Article 95, as the above recitals suggest, concerns the functioning as well as the establishment of the single market and that the distortion of competition is of concern here too, as it is in Article 94. Article 95 covers remedial action in respect of existing barriers and preventative action in respect of likely future barriers. This approach would seem to be based on Article 3 EC which lists as one of the tasks of the Community the 'approximation of law to the extent required for the functioning of the common market'. It would equally seem to eradicate virtually any difference in scope between Article 94 and 95,[25] save as regards the express exclusions contained in Article 95(2). Thus, despite the wording in Article 95(1), that this provision is subject to the other Treaty bases, at least as far as its relationship with Article 94 is concerned it has become the rule rather than the exception. The choice of Treaty base is discussed below.

Even though Article 95 is broad, it is not unlimited. The institutions in their law-making are, in general, constrained by the four freedoms. Further,

---

23 Council Directive 90/220/EEC of 23 April 1990 on the deliberate release into the environment of genetically modified organisms OJ [1990] L 117/15.

24 Case 300/89 *Commission* v. *Council* (Titanium Dioxide) [1991] ECR I-2867.

25 See Directive 90/220/EEC, *supra* n. 23. In the case of the measures to be taken against air pollution the original directive (Directive 70/220/EEC) was based on Article 100 (now Article 94) whereas the amending directive (Council Directive 88/436/EEC) was based on Article 100a (now Article 95): OJ [1988] L 214/1.

Article 95 is not a provision giving the EC power to regulate commerce generally at the Community level, as the ECJ has recently confirmed.[26] To rely on Article 95 there must be some connection with the functioning of the internal market and the eradication of barriers to trade and distortions in the competitive environment. The question is the extent to which Article 95 can be seen as concerned with regulatory matters alone rather than with market liberalisation. This issue was discussed in the *Tobacco Advertising* cases.[27]

The cases challenged the legality of a directive which was enacted on Article 95 and which sought to prohibit the advertising of tobacco products. Amongst other arguments, it was alleged that the Directive had been enacted on the wrong treaty base.[28] The institutions argued that there was a cross-border element in tobacco advertising, sponsorship and promotional gifts and that national laws dealt with these items differently. It was this potential divergence that justified action at Community level to remove conditions distorting competition. Although the ECJ accepted that in principle action could be taken even against future barriers to trade, it clarified that there must be a real risk of barriers or distortion of competition arising to justify such action. The mere existence of disparities between national laws is, on its own, insufficient to warrant Community action. In contrast to the position under Articles 28 and 49, where there is no *de minimis* requirement, an appreciable distortion of competition would be required to trigger the use of Article 95.[29] The ECJ, in putting forward this point, emphasised the need to ensure that the division of competence between Community and national level was respected. In this case, although there were some differences in national treatment, they were not of a nature to justify a general ban on tobacco advertising; indeed the ECJ noted that the Directive in no way facilitated the free trade in promotional materials.[30]

There are a couple of issues to be considered. Although the ECJ emphasised the liberalising aspect of Article 95, it was careful to ensure that this case was not read as precluding the Community from taking any regulatory action whatsoever. In particular, it emphasised that the rules in

26 Case C-376/98 *Tobacco Advertising Directive*, *supra* n. 3.

27 Case C-376/98 *Tobacco Advertising Directive*, *supra* n. 3.

28 There were two challenges: one was a direct challenge by the German Government; the other arose through the English courts via an Article 234 reference on validity – see Case C-74/99 *R.* v. *SoS for Health, ex parte Imperial Tobacco* [2000] ECR I-8599.

29 Case C-376/98 *Tobacco Advertising Directive*, *supra* n. 3, paragraph 84. Advocate-General Jacobs, in the Case C-377/98 *Biotechnological Inventions* case *supra* n. 16, suggested that the ECJ's approach to distortions in competition was more rigorous than that taken regarding barriers to trade.

30 Case C-376/98 *Tobacco Advertising Directive*, *supra* n. 3, paragraphs 96-105.

issue were different from those in the Television without Frontiers Directive,[31] prohibiting the advertising of tobacco products on television.[32] By providing a base level of rules in that sector, the Television without Frontiers Directive facilitated the free movement of television broadcasts. As regards the level of interference that would be required to justify action, the ECJ distinguished this case from, for example, the *Titanium Dioxide*[33] case. Although the Court accepted that there might be a variation in the competitive environment for the advertising agencies throughout the Community, the effects of those differences in the view of the ECJ were simply too indirect. In the *Titanium Dioxide* case, however, the impact was directly felt on production costs, thus constituting an appreciable distortion in competition. Although the ECJ's analysis may well make sense in the light of the case in issue and perhaps the division of competence generally, it is questionable whether all directives hitherto based on Article 95 would satisfy the appreciable distortion test introduced by the *Tobacco Advertising* case. It further throws into question certain proposed Community action, for example the recent proposal for action in the field of consumer protection.[34] The Commission paper suggesting the need for Community action did not even address the issue of treaty base.

Nonetheless, the approach in *Tobacco Advertising*[35] was re-affirmed by the ECJ in the *Biotechnological Inventions* case,[36] which again concerned the choice of legal base, this time concerning a directive which sought to ensure that biotechnological inventions could be patented. Applying the approach in *Tobacco Advertising*, the ECJ concluded that,

> 'by requiring the Member States to protect biotechnological inventions by means of their national patent law, the Directive in fact aims to prevent damage to the unity of the internal market which might result from the Member States' deciding unilaterally to grant or to refuse such protection.'[37]

---

31 Council Directive 89/552 of 3 October 1989 on the co-ordination of certain provisions laid down by law, regulation or administrative action in Member States concerning pursuit of television broadcasting activities [1989] OJ L 295/15.

32 Whether the Community had competence, pre-TEU, to enact this directive was the subject of some discussion during the legislative process. See further below.

33 Case C-300/89 *Titanium Dioxide*, *supra* n. 24.

34 Commission Green Paper on European Union Consumer Protection, 2 October 2001, COM (2001) 531 final, The Commission Communication on European Contract Law, 11 July 2001, COM (2001) 398 final, did not identify an appropriate treaty base for any proposed action either.

35 Case C-376/98 *Tobacco Advertising Directive*, *supra* n. 3.

36 Case C-377/98 *Biotechnological Inventions* case *supra* n. 16.

37 Case C-377/98 *Biotechnological Inventions* case *supra* n. 16, paragraph 18.

Presumably, the difference between the two cases lies in the immediacy of the respective measures' impact on the market. Nonetheless it could be argued that the tobacco advertising rules were concerned with the unity of the market just as much as the rules on biotechnological inventions. Further, the patent rules would not ensure free movement of biotechnological inventions because, although Member States would be required to grant patent protection, Member States were not precluded from prohibiting the sale or distribution of such products. Given that the ECJ seemed to regard the rules' effect on trade as being self-evident in this case, the boundary between it and the *Tobacco Advertising* cases is not entirely clear.

Nonetheless, the test in the *Tobacco Advertising* cases has been reaffirmed recently in *R.* v. *Secretary of State for Health, ex parte BAT et al.*[38] Following *ex parte BAT*, the test for the use of Article 95 can be divided into two parts. As far as existing barriers are concerned, the measure must genuinely have the object of improving conditions and actually contribute to the elimination of current barriers or distortions in competition. For future obstacles the existence of the obstacles must be likely and the measure must be designed to prevent them. The test was satisfied in this case, although it is questionable whether the facts in this case have a noticeably greater impact than those in *Tobacco Advertising*. One might suggest that the practice here and in *Biotechnological Inventions* is close to that in the pre-*Tobacco Advertising* case jurisprudence. The scope of Article 95 when there are other possible Treaty bases is discussed further below.

The *ex parte BAT* case raises another question, that of the scope of the Community to take action if it has already acted in a given field. Effectively the argument is that if the Community has harmonized a field, it cannot take further action to avoid market distortions because the original harmonizing measure should have achieved that goal. This argument is particularly clear where Member States have no room for discretion. This argument was raised when the Community attempted to revise its regime on tar yield in tobacco products. The Court rejected the argument, commenting that the rules in issue were likely to give rise to barriers and that there were still some differences between Member States' regimes, as in some instances only minimum requirements were provided at Community level and the existing regime did not cover every aspect of the subject in issue. It then concluded,

> 'even where a provision of Community law guarantees the removal of all obstacles to trade in the area that it harmonizes, that fact cannot make it

---

38 Case C-491/01 *R.* v. *Secretary of State for Health, ex parte British American Tobacco et al*, judgment 10 December 2002.

impossible for the Community legislature to adopt that provision in step with other considerations.'[39]

The Court then went on to refer to the obligations on the Community to provide a high level of protection in areas such as health, contained in Articles 152(1) and especially Article 95(3). The Court also then referred to other considerations, such as social attitudes to smoking.

The reasoning in this case sends conflicting messages. On the one hand, the ECJ seemed keen to emphasise that discrepancies actually existed between Member States' legal systems causing barriers to trade. It then effectively argued that the existence of such discrepancies would not matter: existing harmonization cannot preclude further harmonization. This is a broad statement. The ECJ's next comments, emphasising the provisions which require Community action to take a high level of protection in certain areas, could be seen as suggesting that it would be only in these areas that the Community could re-regulate on the basis of Article 95. The next stage in the Court's argument undermines this supposition, however, as the ECJ accepted that the Community can take into account other considerations, such as social attitudes, which are not mentioned in the Treaty at all. Although it is beyond dispute that the Community may re-regulate, the circumstances in which it may do so are, following *ex parte BAT*, still open to some discussion.

One other crucial difference between Article 94 and 95 is the 'opt-out' clause contained in Article 95(4) and (5). This provision was included, apparently, to compensate for the loss of individual Member States' veto consequent on the use of qualified majority in Council. It provides that, should a harmonization measure have been agreed and a Member State still 'deems it necessary on grounds of major needs referred to in Article 30, or relating to the protection of the environment or the working environment', that Member State may maintain national measures. Article 95(5), introduced by the ToA, provides for the possibility of Member States introducing new national measures where there is new scientific evidence to support such a proceeding. In both instances, a Member State must notify the Commission of the national provisions together with the grounds for maintaining the measures. The obligation is on the Member State to provide enough supporting evidence. The Commission then has six months in which to approve or reject the measures, and in the event of a failure to make a decision, the Member State action will be deemed to have been approved. Until the Commission decision is made, the Community measure continues in force in the relevant Member State and may even have direct

39 Case C-491/01 *ex p. BAT, ibid.*, at paragraph 78.

effect.[40] The Commission is also under an obligation to consider whether Community harmonization measures are required in the area in which the Member State is maintaining the national measures. Article 95(9) provides a judicial review procedure whereby Member States or the Commission can bring the matter before the ECJ if it considers another Member State is making improper use of Article 95(4) or 95(5).

There are difficulties with Articles 95(4) and (5). Any derogation under Articles 95(4) or (5) could be permanent; neither Article 95(4) nor Article 95(5) is phrased in terms of a temporary measure. More fundamentally, by allowing Member States to adopt different standards the Community would be undermining the internal market project. As Advocate-General Tesauro noted, Article 95(4) is an exception to the fundamental principles of the uniform application of Community law and the unity of the market.[41] At a philosophical level, it illustrates a disagreement over the basic level of Community standards. In this sense, it is arguably different from the minimum harmonization approach discussed below.[42]

Despite these concerns, Articles 95(4) and (5) have not been frequently invoked.[43] Although the provision is clearly exceptional from the viewpoint of the Community,[44] as illustrated by the stringent approach taken by the ECJ to its interpretation, why has the provision not been more used? One possibility is the way the provision is limited. Any attempt to rely on it must be 'necessary' and relate to the grounds identified in Articles 95(4) and 95(5). These grounds in Article 95(4) reflect the terms of Article 30 (ex-36) with two additions, the protection of the environment or the working environment. Article 95(5) is more stringently drafted than Article 95(4). The grounds referred to in Article 95(5) are much narrower than those in Article 95(4), as it excludes those concerns found in Article 30. Additionally, the Member State must point to new scientific evidence

---

40 Case C-319/97 *Kortus* [1999] ECR I-3143. This case was decided on the basis of the pre-ToA amendments to Article 95; the Commission was therefore under no time constraints to make its decision.

41 Case C-41/93 *Commission* v. *France*, *supra* n. 22, Opinion paragraph 4.

42 On this point, see the comments of Advocate-General Saggio in Case C-319/97 *Kortus*, *supra* n. 40 at paragraph 26 of the Opinion.

43 A recent exception is the Swedish approach to the maximum admissible content of cadmium in fertilisers; Commission Decision of 24 May 2002, OJ [2002] L 138/24. In this case, the Swedish Act of Accession laid down specific transitional provisions in respect of the Swedish regime regarding cadmium in fertilisers and the notified national laws sought to continue this regime, which the Commission, having analysed the scientific evidence, agreed.

44 Although following the introduction of the 'flexibility' provisions following the ToA, arguably it is less unusual now.

and a problem that is specific to that Member State. These conditions are cumulative. According to the Court, this is because new measures are more likely to jeopardise harmonization as such measures could not be taken into account in the harmonisation process.[45] In either case, it would seem that the possibility of relying on a mandatory requirement style argument would be unsuccessful: any derogation is strictly interpreted and it would seem from the wording that the drafters of the Treaty had already assessed which mandatory requirement style justifications would be accepted in this context. Further, the measures cannot constitute a means of arbitrary discrimination, a disguised restriction on trade or an obstacle to the functioning of the internal market.[46] In making this assessment, it would seem clear that the Member States' interests asserted under Article 95(4) and (5) are not paramount: they must be carefully weighed against the impact of such measures on the internal market.

A further disincentive is the review procedure in Article 95(6)-(9). The Member States are obliged to notify the Commission of any measures retained or taken and the reasons for such action. The Commission itself is obliged to consider whether the terms of Article 95 are satisfied. The ECJ has again sought to ensure that this process is not merely a formality. When the Commission makes a decision it must be fully reasoned, and this requirement is not satisfied where the Commission merely re-iterates the wording of the Treaty, though the obligation to provide full reasons presumably would not be relevant when the default procedure introduced by the ToA applied.

It has also been suggested that the high level health status of livestock was excluded from the scope of Article 95 and therefore of Article 95(4) and (5) on the grounds that it is an area in which Member States' sensitivities might have been engaged. Case law clarified that such matters should be dealt with under the provisions dealing with agriculture. Further, the fact that Article 95(3) refers to a high level of protection may have deflected some Member States from taken action in the areas where Article 95(3) applied.

Choice of Treaty Base Given that there are a variety of legislative procedures[47] on which Community acts may be based and that these procedures give the various institutions[48] different degrees of influence

---

45 Case C-512/99 *Germany* v. *Commission* (Mineral Wood), judgment 21 January 2003.

46 Case C-41/93 *Commission* v. *France, supra* n. 22.

47 In addition to the co-decision and consultation procedures noted, there is a further procedure, the co-operation procedure. Following the rationalisation of the Treaty by the ToA, there are now few occasions when the co-operation procedure will be used.

48 The influence of the member States themselves will be affected depending on the position of the Council. The relative power of the individual member states will also be

within the legislative process, the question of which Treaty base should be used in a given situation may thus be a significant question, especially where the legislative proposal is in any way contentious. A Member State that knows itself to be in the minority on an issue and wishes to object to proposed legislation, for example, would probably prefer to see that issue dealt with as a matter of unanimity rather than under the co-decision procedure where it could be out-voted. With the repeated extension of the use of co-decision following successive amendments to the Treaty this issue may arise less frequently as discrepancies between voting procedures under the various legislative procedures will be fewer.

Determination of the appropriate Treaty base is ultimately to be reviewed by the ECJ. It has laid down a number of general principles to determine the appropriate provisions. The choice of legal base should be made in the light of objective factors capable of being reviewed judicially. We see here, again, a concern to ensure that the division of competence is respected. Where a Community measure is concerned with two or more distinct issues, multiple bases may be used.[49] There are two limitations on the application of this proposition. Where one aim is clearly the primary purpose with other objectives being secondary or incidental, then the Treaty provision reflecting the measure's main purpose should be used.[50] The ECJ has indeed held that a dual base should be used only when the Community act in question is concerned indivisibly with the various aims: a two-fold purpose is not enough to justify using more than one Treaty base.[51] The distinction between these two positions will be based on the facts in each case and in some instances may arguably be fine. Arguably, the ECJ has sometimes taken an inconsistent approach as to whether the question to be asked is about a proposal's centre of gravity or not. In the *MLIS Programme* decision,[52] the ECJ again emphasised that for more than one Treaty base to be used, the crucial point was whether two indisociable policies were involved. Applying this principle, the ECJ held that a decision regarding the provision of translation mechanisms for lesser-used Community languages was purely to do with industrial policy rather than

---

affected depending on the voting procedure used within the Council, notably whether or not qualified majority voting is used or not.

49 Council Directive 87/217/EEC, supra n.13, was based on Article 100 (now 94) and 235 (now 308) in respect of the impact on the common market and the impact on the environment. See Case 165/87 *Commission* v. *Council* [1988] ECR 5545, paragraphs 6–13; Case 242/87 *Commission* v. *Council* [1989] ECR 1425, paragraphs 33-37.

50 For example, Case C-155/91 *Commission* v. *Council* (Waste Disposal) [1993] ECR I-939 at paragraphs 19-21; Case C-377/98 *Biotechnological Inventions*, *supra* n. 16 at paragraph 27.

51 Case 300/89 *Commission* v. *Council* (Titanium Dioxide), *supra* n. 24.

52 Case C-42/97 *European Parliament* v. *Council* [1999] ECR I-869.

involving any element of culture. The ECJ did not explain why, which is unfortunate, given the close association between language and culture and the protection of diversity of cultures. The ECJ has reaffirmed that use of dual Treaty base should only be used in exceptional circumstances.[53]

The other proviso to using two Treaty bases is that they cannot be procedurally incompatible. In the *Titanium Dioxide* case,[54] the ECJ held it was impossible for a measure to be based on two Treaty provisions one of which required the use of the co-operation procedure and the other of which provided for Council unanimity and simple consultation of the European Parliament. Again, in such an instance, the test the ECJ use is the identification of the measure's 'centre of gravity'.[55] Where a measure could properly be based on internal market provisions, the fact that the measure may have other purposes will not necessarily take the measure outside the scope of the internal market provisions, whether or not there is another Treaty base that may be relied upon.[56] It is only when the internal market aspect of the measure has merely incidental effects that the measure should be based on the other treaty base to the exclusion of Article 95.[57] Again, in this context, the ECJ will look to a measure's centre of gravity to determine whether the internal market aspect is incidental, but not to exclude Community competence on this point when the internal market aspect is more than incidental.

Even given these guidelines, the boundary between Treaty bases is not clear, and sometimes seems to mutate. For example, legislation on equal treatment had been enacted on both Articles 94 and 308.[58] There have similarly been tensions between the use of Articles 94 and 95, as some of

---

53 Case C-491/01 *ex parte BAT*, *supra* n. 38.

54 Case 300/89 *Commission* v. *Council* (Titanium Dioxide), *supra* n. 24.

55 See e.g. Case C-197/93 *European Parliament* v. *Council* [1994] ECR I-2857; Case C-164 and 165/97 *Parliament* v. *Council* (Forestry Protection) [1999] ECR I-1139 at paragraph 14.

56 See Case C-376/98 *Tobacco Advertising Directive*, *supra* n. 3; Case C-377/98 *Biotechnological Inventions*, *supra* n. 16 at paragraph 28; Case C-62/88 *Greece* v. *Council* [1990] ECR I-1527, paragraphs 18-20.

57 Case C-70/88 *Parliament* v. *Council* (Chernobyl) [1991] ECR I-2041; Case C-271/94 *Parliament* v. *Council* [1996] ECR I-1689, paragraphs 32–33.

58 See Directive 75/117 of 10 February 1975 on the approximation of the laws of the Member States relating to the application of the principle of equal pay for men and women OJ [1975] L 45/19; and Council Directive 76/207/EEC of 9 February 1976 on the implementation of the principle of equal treatment for men and women as regards access to employment, vocational training and promotion, and working conditions OJ [1976] L39/40.

the environmental cases illustrate.[59] It should be noted that the dispute regarding treaty base are not limited to questions as to whether Article 94 or 95 should be used, but involve other provisions as well. As the *Titanium Dioxide* case[60] illustrates, the dispute centred on whether the measure was properly based on provisions relating to the protection of the environment or on the internal market provisions ensuring the free movement of goods. Given the broad approach to Articles 94 and 95 this issue is often far from clear. Another area which has not been addressed is the relationship between Article 95 and Article 52. Although Article 95(2) excludes the use of Article 95 in relation to the free movement of persons, this prohibition does not apply in relation to the movement of services themselves. Thus, the recent directives dealing with the telecommunications market are based 'in particular on Article 95', rather than any other provision such as those relating to services.[61] No reason was given, which might suggest a presumption towards the use of Article 95 where possible.

Further, it could sometimes be argued that the ECJ has given an extended notion to the needs of the internal market so as to ensure that measures for which the existence of a Treaty base would not otherwise be clear, falls within the competence of the EC. A similar tendency can be seen in relation to services. The Television without Frontiers Directive was enacted on the basis of the need to ensure the free movement of services, although a number of Member States argued that the measure constituted a matter of cultural policy for which the Community (at that stage) had not competence.[62]

Another problem that arises is the relationship between Article 95 (and possibly also the relevant provision relating to services – Articles 47(2) and 52) and the express competence in flanking policy areas such as consumer protection, public health, and commercial and industrial policy. In many instances the provisions convey a mixed message: they state that the areas in question are to be taken account of in other policy areas, such as the internal market, but also provide that harmonization is precluded. Where does this leave the use of Article 95 in these policy fields? On one view, the exclusion of the possibility of harmonizing measures constitutes a form of repatriation of legal power to the Member States, or at least a clear delimitation of Community competence. This view could be

59 Case 300/89 *Commission* v. *Council* (Titanium Dioxide), *supra* n. 24; Case C-155/91 *Commission* v. *Council* (Waste), *supra* n. 50.

60 Case 300/89 *Commission* v. *Council* (Titanium Dioxide), *supra* n. 24.

61 See e.g. Directive 2002/21/EC on a Common Regulatory Framework, OJ [2002] L 108/33; Directive 2002/19/EC on Access and Interconnection, OJ [2002] L 108/7.

62 Wallace & Goldberg, 'The EEC Directive on Television Broadcasting' (1989) 9 *Yearbook of European Law* 175; Niedobitek, M. *The Cultural Dimension in EC Law* (Kluwer Law International, 1997).

supported by the fact that Article 95 is expressed to be subject to other Treaty provisions. Alternatively, the need to take these policy concerns into account means that harmonizing measures should properly not be limited to market-driven concerns,[63] especially as Article 95(3) obliges the Community to take a high level of protection as its base in at least some of these areas.

It would seem as though the ECJ has adopted the latter of the two approaches. In the *Tobacco Advertising* cases,[64] the applicant Government argued that, as the Directive's principal concern was public health, its appropriate Treaty base should have been the specific public health provision, Article 152 EC, with Community action being constrained by the terms of that provision. Notably, Article 152(4) precludes harmonization. According to the applicant, using Article 95 was therefore an attempt to subvert the proper division of competence. Although, importantly, the ECJ agreed that the width of Article 95 should not be abused to circumvent an express exclusion of harmonization, the Court noted equally that Article 152(4) did not mean that harmonizing measures were precluded from having an impact on public health.[65] To the contrary, Article 152(1) provides for the inter-relationship of the various policies. It seems that, where a measure can be seen from an internal market perspective, the Community will have power to act using Article 95. Given that, as noted above, the ECJ found the connection between the Tobacco Advertising Directive and Article 95 to be insufficient, one cannot help but wonder whether the ECJ took the same standard into account when assessing this point. Of course, holding that this matter rightly fell under Article 152 and thereby excluding the possibility of harmonizing measures would have opened the door to many more challenges to harmonizing legislation on the basis that the substance of those measures properly fell within other substantively defined provisions, such as: culture; protection of the environment; and consumer protection. The ECJ's decision could be seen as a decision protecting the Community's competence to act in these fields and re-asserting the primacy of the internal market goal.

b) Techniques of Legislation

Over the years, the Community has adopted different approaches to the level of detail and degree of freedom allowed to Member States in areas where Community harmonizing measures were enacted. Although there is

---

63 Case C-180/96 *UK* v. *Commission* [1998] ECR I-2265; Case C-269/97 *Commission* v. *Council* [2000] ECR I-2257.

64 Case C-376/98 *Tobacco Advertising Directive, supra* n. 3.

65 See also Case C-377/98 *Biotechnological Inventions, supra* n. 16, paragraph 28 and Case C-491/01 *ex parte BAT, supra* n. 38.

some variety in commentators' approaches to categorisation of the types of technique used,[66] certain broad categories can be identified. The two main approaches to regulation seem to consist of total or exhaustive regulation on the one hand and minimum harmonization on the other.[67]

In the early years of the Community, the Community regulated in great detail, harmonizing measures setting out the entire scheme of regulation. Member States could not deviate in any way from the standards set out in the Community measures, save where specific safeguards applied.[68] This is referred to as total or exhaustive harmonization, as the Member States' policy choices have been foreclosed; they are limited to implementing the choices made at Community level and cannot rely on heads of derogation set down in the Treaty to justify action at national level. This style of regulation has become less popular, partly because it was difficult to agree at Community level the required detail to harmonize sectors exhaustively. Further, this approach to regulation is insufficiently flexible to deal with changing circumstances as amendment remained difficult. Slot[69] suggested that since 1975, it has been used only in relation to harmonization of products standards[70] under Article 95.

With the introduction of the 1992 programme, minimum harmonization, already in use in some instances, was more generally adopted. Using this technique, certain minimum harmonized rules are provided at Community level, with Member States free to set higher national rules, subject always to the constraints imposed by the four freedoms themselves. Usually the fact that a directive is based on the minimum harmonization approach is express from the terms of the directive, as can be seen in the Television without Frontiers Directive.[71] The use of minimum harmonization can also be implied.[72] Minimum harmonization is typically used in areas such as consumer protection and protection of the environment and this approach has now been incorporated in the Treaty provisions dealing specifically with these areas.[73]

---

66 Contrast for example McGee and Weatherill, *supra* n. 1 and Slot, P.J., 'Harmonization' (1997) 21 *ELRev* 378.

67 There are arguably further residual categories, optional and partial harmonization see Slot, *supra* n. 66.

68 See e.g. Council Directive of November 23 1970 OJ [1970] L 270/1.

69 Slot, *supra* n. 66 at p. 383.

70 Note new approach to technical standards too; for example, the Toy Safety Directive, Directive 88/378.

71 Directive 89/552, as amended, *supra* n. 31.

72 Case C-11/92 *R.* v. *Secretary of State for Health, ex parte Gallaher* [1993] ECR I-3545.

73 See e.g. Articles 153 and 174.

Although the use of minimum harmonization, which allows for upward flexibility of standards, may make it easier for Member States to agree Community measures, it does raise questions about equality of standards and, in particular, whether higher national standards can apply to imported products which meet the Community minima. This issue is discussed further below. In any event, it would seem that the ECJ is not be prepared to accept the argument that national products would be put at a disadvantage where they are subject to higher standards than imports. The ECJ would not strike down such higher national requirements; reverse discrimination is permitted under the EC Treaty.[74]

In conjunction with the move to minimum harmonization, two other changes in legislative technique can be noted: the first related to mutual recognition, the second a 'new approach' to technical regulations. Mutual recognition can be traced back to the *Cassis de Dijon* judgment.[75] It expressed the principle that what is acceptable in one Member State should be acceptable in another. An increased reliance on mutual recognition limits the areas in which harmonizing measures are needed to those where public interest requirements are at stake. Where mandatory requirements or matters falling within Articles 30 or 46 and 55 arise, national rules would not be struck down, with the result that potential barriers to trade, arising out of the operation of different legal systems, remain. Even within harmonization measures, there is a tendency to use mutual recognition. Thus rather than set a Community standard, Member States would be required to recognise the standards of other Member States. An example of this approach can be seen in the Directive on Higher Education Diplomas.[76]

The Commission has suggested that mutual recognition is 'a pragmatic and powerful tool for economic integration'.[77] By avoiding detailed Community legislation, mutual recognition allows greater observance of local, regional and national traditions and thus also provides for a wider variety of products to come on to the market. In this, mutual recognition is arguably in line with the requirements of the doctrine of subsidiarity. The reliance on mutual recognition has, however, been criticised because of the downward effect on standards it might have. Member States might be under pressure from their domestic industries to remove higher national standards so as to level the playing field to those lower (and presumably less expensive) standards applicable to their foreign competitors, as reverse

---

74 Case C-11/92 *Gallaher*, *supra* n.72.

75 Case 120/78 *Rewe* v. *Bundesmonopolverwaltung fur Branntwein* (Cassis de Dijon) [1979] ECR 649.

76 Directive 89/48 OJ [1989] L 19/16.

77 Commission Communication on Mutual Recognition in the Context of the Follow-up to the Action Plan for the Single Market, p. 4.

discrimination is permitted. Regulatory competition is a common feature of federal systems and, on some analyses, can be seen to produce benefits through innovatory approaches to questions of level and approach to regulation.[78] Given the lack of empirical evidence in this sphere, to a certain extent this issue comes down to a personal perspective.

Linked to the idea of mutual recognition is the new approach to technical standards. Following the Commission's determination that technical harmonization did not bring satisfactory results,[79] it suggested that, given most questions were dealt with on the basis of Article 28 and *Cassis de Dijon*,[80] the key issues were to identify the standards on which a presumption of conformity could be based; and to establish the conditions under which the burden of proof could be reversed. Following a Council Resolution on the subject,[81] the new approach to harmonization was based on the identification of essential safety requirements. The task of drawing up relevant technical specifications to safeguard these interests was devolved to expert standards committees. There has been some criticism that this approach has led to the privatisation of standards, with industry interests having a higher profile than other concerns. Although the standards remain voluntary, products complying with them are deemed to comply with the essential requirements set down in the relevant directive. Linked to this system[82] is a notification system, whereby Member States have to notify any technical measures so that the Commission can verify compliance with the Treaty. Failure to notify means that the technical regulations may not be relied upon – not just as against public bodies but in proceedings between private parties. Although this is not the place for a detailed discussion of the difficulties arising from the use of the Technical Regulations Directive[83] and the case law resulting there from, it should be noted that the effective removal in the case of this Directive of the bar on the horizontal direct effect of directives could prove a powerful tool in enforcement of EC law.[84] Nonetheless, the Council has recently noted that

---

78 See e.g., Sun and Pelkmans 'Regulatory Competition and the Single Market' (1995) 53 *JCMS* 67; Easterbrook, F. H. 'The State of Madison's Vision of the State: A Public Choice Perspective' (1994) 107 *Harvard Law Review* 1328, at pp. 1344-5.

79 COM (1985), 19 December 1985.

80 Case 120/78 *Cassis de Dijon, supra* n. 75.

81 Council Resolution of 7 May 1985 [1985] OJ C 136/1.

82 Although the original directive was enacted two years prior to the adoption of the new system.

83 For an early review see Burrows, N., 'Harmonization of Technical Standards: Reculer Pour Mieux Sauter?' (1990) 53 *Modern Law Review* 597.

84 Case C-194/94 *CIA Security* v. *Signalson* [1996] ECR I-2201; Case C-13/96 *Bic Benelux* [1997] ECR I-1753; Case C-443/98 *Unilever Italia SpA* v. *Central Food SpA* [2000] ECR I-7535 but contrast C-222/97 *Lemmens* [1998] ECR I-3711.

individuals and companies remain insufficiently aware of their rights in this field generally.[85]

II Subsidiarity

The second question, that of whether the Community should act, essentially concerns the operation of the doctrine of subsidiarity. The doctrine supposes that areas within Community competence fall into two categories: those in which the Community has exclusive competence and those in which competence is shared. Exclusive Member State competence falls outside the scope of Article 5 and the doctrine of subsidiarity as the Community will have no competence at all in this area.[86] Within exclusive Community competence, only the Community may act, and may do so when it feels such action is appropriate. There is, however, no provision by which the necessity of such action can be measured. Within fields where competence is shared, the question is twofold: should the Community or Member States act (or both, in conjunction); and what sort of action is appropriate.

The preliminary question is, of course, whether the field in question falls with the exclusive or concurrent competence of the Community. One of the principle problems with the doctrine of subsidiarity is that it presupposes that the distinction between areas of exclusive Community competence and shared competence is clear.[87] This is not the case, as the Treaty contains no list of exclusive Community competence. It has therefore fallen to the ECJ to determine the boundary between exclusive and concurrent competence. Equally typically, there is no definition of exclusive competence in the Treaty, which therefore also falls to the ECJ to determine. There has been significant academic debate on this issue,[88] but nowhere is there a clear, definitive statement as to the boundaries between the two.

---

85 Council Resolution of 28 October 1999 on Mutual Recognition, OJ [2000] C 141/5.

86 See Chapters 7, 8 and 12 for the relationship between the derogation provisions and the amount of exclusive competence allowed to Member States.

87 This issue is one which has been suggested needs to be resolved at the next IGC: one suggestion is that a list of exclusive Community powers should be identified, akin to the provisions in the German and Spanish constitutions; see Draft Report on the Division of Powers, *supra* n. 10 and Article 11 and 12 of the draft Constitutional Treaty.

88 See e.g., Emiliou, N., 'Subsidiarity: an Effective Barrier Against Enterprises of Ambition' (1992) 29 *CMLRev* 383; Swaine, E.T., 'Subsidiarity and Self Interest, Federalism at the European Court of Justice' (2000) 41 *Harvard International* L.J. 1 and literature listed below.

The approach to exclusive Community competence would seem to have clear links to a doctrine of pre-emption,[89] although the precise scope of pre-emption itself varies depending on the definition attributed to it.[90] Pre-emption is a doctrine seen in federal theory which, understood at a basic level, provides that action by one level of government, usually the federal level (or, here, Community), precludes action by the other (here, the Member States). Thus where the Community has pre-empted the field, the Community has exclusive competence. Of course, there are various interpretations of the doctrine of pre-emption, variously seeing it as narrower or broader, which reflect the positions taken regarding the determination of exclusive competence.

At its narrowest, Member States would be precluded from action inconsistent with existing Community legislation, a view of pre-emption which adds very little to the doctrine of supremacy of Community law – although at a theoretical level the two doctrines operate differently.[91] Pre-emption operates to preclude Member State action, whereas supremacy provides a rule to deal with a conflict between Member State and Community laws; this latter approach implies that both levels of government have been active in a given field. There are difficulties with this view of pre-emption, as we will see below. More broadly, pre-emption can be seen as describing fields in which Member States cannot act at all, irrespective of Community action. It would seem that there is a logical link between the strength of the doctrine of pre-emption adopted and the scope of the fields pre-empted. The stronger the version of pre-emption accepted, the narrower the policy fields that will be deemed to fall within the scope of pre-emption. The main issue then to be determined is the theoretical model to be used to determine the scope of exclusive competence.

During the earlier years of the EC, the ECJ seemed to take an expansive approach to the determination of Community exclusive competence.[92] For example, in *ERTA*, it held that '[t]he existence of

89 See e.g. Weiler, J.H.H., 'The Community System: the Dual Character of Supranationalism' (1981) 1 *YEL* 277.

90 Goucha Soares, A., 'Pre-emption, Conflicts of Powers and Subsidiarity' (1998) 23 *ELRev* 132, at p.133 for three modalities of pre-emption; Cross, E.J., 'Pre-emption of Member State Law in the European Economic Community: a Framework for Analysis' (1992) 29 *CMLRev* 447 and contrast the earlier position in Waelbroeck, M., 'The Emergent Doctrine of Community Pre-emption – Consent and Re-delegation' in Sandalow, T., and Stein, E., (eds) *Courts and Free Markets – Perspectives from the United States and Europe* Vol. II, (Clarendon Press, 1982).

91 Waelbroeck, *ibid.* and his distinction between the federal conceptual version and the pragmatic version of pre-emption.

92 Case 22/70 *Commission* v. *Council* (ERTA) [1971] ECR 263; Opinion 1/75 *Common Commercial Policy* [1975] ECR 1355.

Community powers excludes the possibility of concurrent powers on the part of the Member States'.[93] Further, in *Commission* v. *UK*,[94] the ECJ held that the expiry of the date by which the Community should have adopted measures in respect of the Community fisheries policy meant that Member States' competence was excluded even though the Community had not been able to agree a policy at that time. This would seem to suggest that the ECJ was adopting a broad approach to the notion of pre-emption. Since then, the ECJ seems to have been less keen to expand Community exclusive competence. In *Prantl*,[95] the ECJ commented that,

> 'once rules on the common organisation of the market may be regarded as forming a complete system, the Member States no longer have competence in that field unless Community law expressly provides otherwise.'

It should be noted that the reasoning in this case is based on the question of competence, not supremacy of EC law. The ECJ asserted the Member States' lack of power to act, rather than dealing with the consequence of a conflict between EC and national law. Nonetheless, it can be seen as a weaker form of pre-emption than that taken in *ERTA*, as the exclusion of Member State competence is linked to the existence of a complete systems of rules, though not necessarily Community action.

By the time of the introduction of the doctrine of subsidiarity by the TEU, the position regarding exclusive competence had still not been clarified. In *CERAFEL*,[96] for example, the ECJ seemed to envisage three possibilities: that Member States could not apply national rules within the scope of a common market – as long as the regulation of the latter exhaustively regulated the relevant area; or if the national rules would directly oppose the provisions of the Community system; or when the rules would constitute an obstacle to the functioning of the common system. Such a view seems to be a weak version of pre-emption, as it requires Community action to pre-empt the field. Markedly different views have been taken by commentators on the linked issue of exclusive competence. Toth,[97] for example, reasoning from the *ERTA* judgment,[98] took the view that the Community had exclusive competence in all areas where the Community had power to act and that, consequently, in reality there was no such thing as concurrent competence. By contrast, Steiner suggested that

93 Case 22/70 *ERTA*, *ibid.*, at p. 276.

94 Case 801/79 *Commission* v. *UK* (Fisheries Policy) [1981] ECR 1045.

95 Case 16/83 *Prantl* [1984] ECR 1299.

96 Case 215/85 *CERAFEL* v. *Le Campion* [1986] ECR 3513.

97 Toth, A.G., 'A Legal Analysis of Subsidiarity' in *Legal Issues of the Maastricht Treaty* O'Keeffe and Twomey (eds) (Wiley Chancery, 1994).

98 Case 22/70 *ERTA*, *supra* n. 92.

'the only areas in which the Community has exclusive competence are those in which it has already legislated'.[99] This latter position would indicate a narrow view of pre-emption.

What then of the internal market? Unlike the flanking policies, it has been suggested that the internal market is central to the Community's objectives and should therefore be seen as exclusive Community competence.[100] In more recent cases, certain Advocates-General have argued that the Community has exclusive competence in fields touched by Article 95, as only the Community has the ability to harmonize, although the ECJ has not adopted this reasoning.[101] To a large extent the answer to the question of whether the Community has exclusive competence within the internal market (especially action based on Article 95) depends on how we view exclusive competence and how we define the internal market. To date, these questions do not seem to have been addressed explicitly.

It is this author's contention that the better starting point for a determination of the nature of exclusive competence might be the earlier case law and a strong notion of pre-emption, though without making any comment about the fields in which exclusive competence might be found. Exclusive competence in this strict sense occurs irrespective of Community action.[102] There is a distinction between exclusive competence as seen in the *Fisheries Policy* case, where the Treaty was presumed to have set up a system which did not allow any Member State regulatory activity[103] and the situation where in principle Member States might have acted, but have since been excluded because of exhaustive Community regulation. In this latter situation there seems to be a danger of confusing the ideas of exclusive competence and total harmonization. The danger in accepting total harmonization as showing exclusive competence is that you remove the relevant measures from the subsidiarity test by virtue of the form of the measure itself, which is surely illogical. On this view, Community acts can be used to extend Community exclusive competence. A more coherent view is that 'exclusive' in this context is being used descriptively with

---

99 Steiner, J., 'Subsidiarity under the Maastricht Treaty' in *Legal Issues of the Maastricht Treaty*, *supra* n. 97.

100 This was the Commission's early view: Communication to the Council and Parliament outlining its proposals for the application of the subsidiarity principle, Bull EC 10-1992 at 116. See also Toth, *supra* n. 97.

101 Case C-376/98 *Tobacco Advertising Directive Case*, *supra* n. 3, Opinion at paragraph 142 and Case C-377/98 *Biotechnological Inventions*, *supra* n. 16 at paragraph 81. See also the somewhat self-contradictory view expressed in the Praesidium's Note outlining a Description of the Current System for the Delimitation of Competence between the European Union and the Member States (Conv 17/02) at point I(A)(a).

102 See Case 801/79 *Commission* v. *UK*, *supra* n. 94.

103 See also Case 159/73 *Hannoverische Zucker* [1974] ECR 129 at paragraph 4.

regard to the scope and nature of the Community act, rather than prescriptively in terms of defining what must happen as regards freedom to act within a particular policy area.

Further, what of other types of Community act, such as directives which give Member States a choice of ways to implement the directive or minimum harmonization directives which specifically permit Member States to maintain in force higher national standards? On one level the actions of Member States have been excluded: once a harmonization measure has been agreed, Member States must operate within that framework. Nonetheless, as far as minimum harmonization directives are concerned, Member States do retain some freedom to make policy choices (rather than executive and administrative decisions to implement Community policy), and so recourse to national law, within the boundaries permitted by general Treaty provisions, remains possible. Arguably, this situation cannot constitute either pre-emption or exclusive competence. The relationship between Community and national law would seem to vary depending on the terms of measure in question, which is surely inconsistent with a division of powers made at a constitutional level. Even within the scope of shared competence, Member State power is considerably constrained, although not pre-empted, by the operation of the doctrine of supremacy.[104]

If we cannot look to Community action to determine this question, then we need to assess by other factors the boundary of exclusive competence. If a strong notion of pre-emption is accepted, the areas in which it is found should be narrowly limited. There are a number of factors which weigh in favour of such an approach. Despite the ECJ's early rulings, the presumption must be that, in the absence of power being conferred on the Community, legislative freedom remains with the Member States. Further, if Member State competence were to be excluded even without Community action, there would be a risk of regulatory gaps.

Without seeking to identify all areas of exclusive Community competence, it is possible to deal with the issue of internal market. It should be noted that Article 95 does not constitute a general Community competence to regulate trade and may therefore be contrasted with some of the fields in which the ECJ has held there to be exclusive competence, such as agriculture or in relation to the common commercial policy.[105] The provisions in the Treaty that relate to the internal market are based on the assumption that Member States retain general economic competence (though this has been limited over the years with the various Treaty amendments), with the Community provisions operating to ensure that

---

104 Dehousse, R., 'Community Competences: Are there Limits to Growth?' *supra* n. 4.

105 *Supra* n. 92 and n. 94.

there is not an excessive burden on inter-state trade.[106] This presumption remains, even though the scope given to the free movement provisions has been interpreted very widely.

Both the recent *Tobacco Advertising*[107] and *Biotechnological Inventions*[108] cases questioned whether the enactment of certain directives, based on Article 95, was contrary to the doctrine of subsidiarity. In both cases, the Advocates-General suggested that harmonization under Article 95 constituted the exercise of exclusive Community competence. Both pointed out that, if harmonization proves to be necessary, only the Community can take harmonizing measures because of the territorial limitations on Member States. This argument on its own is unconvincing: there is a difference between being empowered to act in a given policy field and being able to take effective action in that area. Furthermore, it would effectively turn the determination of competence in the internal market field into a question of the substantive scope of Article 95.

The Advocate-General in *Tobacco Advertising* went further, however: he suggested that the need to complete the internal market constituted a separate policy area, just as separate substantive areas of policy do. In the light of the indeterminate scope of Article 95 arising from its functional nature, this argument seems very hard to accept, especially given the inter-relationship expressed elsewhere in the Treaty between internal market objectives and substantive policy areas. Furthermore, these are areas in which Member State involvement is envisaged. In the subsequent *Biotechnological Inventions* case, also concerning Article 95, the ECJ seemingly rejected this approach. It held:

> 'The objective pursued by the Directive ... could not be achieved by action taken by the Member States alone. As the scope of that protection has immediate effects on trade, and, accordingly, on intra-Community trade, it is clear that, given the scale and effects of the proposed action, the objective in question could be better achieved by the Community.'[109]

By applying the test in Article 5 EC when there is shared competence, the ECJ has implicitly rejected the notion of exclusive competence where Article 95 EC applies.

---

106 Waelbroeck, *supra* n. 90, p. 500.

107 Case C-376/98 *Tobacco Advertising Directive*, *supra* n. 3.

108 Case C-377/98 *Biotechnological Inventions*, *supra* n. 16.

109 Case C-377/98 *Biotechnological Inventions*, *supra* n. 16, paragraph 32.

Given that internal market measures are unlikely to be seen as falling within the exclusive competence of the EC,[110] the question of the application of subsidiarity arises. The doctrine of subsidiarity arguably reflects the tension in the expansion of Community competence in the TEU, both as regards actual policy areas and in terms of decision-making process, with the dilution of the powers of the Council. In fact the doctrine of subsidiarity can be seen as having roots in the changes introduced by the SEA: what was then Article 100r(4) limited Community action in the environmental field to where the objectives of environmental policy could 'be attained better at Community level than at the level of the individual Member States'. This approach countered a wide interpretation of the functional federalism of the Community's need to ensure the common market. The extent to which it is successful in this regard is debatable and probably depends more on the political will of the institutions than of the wording of the provision itself.

Once we have identified where the boundary of concurrent competence lies, the question becomes one of determining which level of government should act. As noted earlier, the doctrine of subsidiarity expressed in the second paragraph of Article 5 is not about the determination of competence between the Community and the Member States but about regulating the use of the powers attributed to the Community. There is a three-stage test for action at the Community level:

1) 'only and in so far as the objectives of the proposed action cannot be sufficiently achieved by the Member States'; and
2) 'can therefore by reason of the scale and effects of the proposed action be better achieved by the Community';
3) with any action by the Community not going 'beyond what is necessary to achieve the objectives of this Treaty'.

The first two elements have been linked together and have been described by the Commission as a test of comparative efficiency to assess the need for Community action. The third element, which only comes into play when it has been established that Community action is necessary,[111] is a requirement of proportionality. It thus limits how the Community's powers are exercised.

---

110 A point seemingly accepted by the European Parliament: it suggested that some areas within the internal market might fall within Community exclusive competence, however. See *supra* n. 10.

111 Commission Communication, *supra* n. 100. The cumulative nature of the test is not clear from the text of the provision.

The subsidiarity principle has been criticised for lack of clarity[112] and because of the danger that the requirement that the measure 'be better achieved by the Community' means that, given the inherently cross-border nature of much of the Community's activities, subsidiarity in practice will operate in favour of Community action. Despite the Commission's suggestion that this test is a test of 'added value' compared to what could have been achieved by action at the Member State level, the ECJ has recently accepted that harmonization can only take place at Community level.[113] This principle does not take us much further in assessing necessity of Community action, as the validity of that argument depends on an assessment of the need for harmonizing measures in the first place. There is, however, a danger that the application of the test of subsidiarity in Article 5 will become no more than the duplication of the assessment of whether Article 95 was properly used in the first instance.

It is debatable the extent to which introduction of Article 5 has had an impact on Community legislation. On one view its introduction embodied concerns, however ill-defined, felt at the political level. The Commission undertook to review whether all proposed legislation was necessary. The Commission abandoned a significant number of proposals and it now also undertakes pre-assessments of its draft proposals so as to determine whether or not to take action at Community level.[114] One might wonder how rigorous both processes have been. A decade later it is still stating that it 'intends to withdraw a hundred or so pending proposals dating from before 1999 and which are no longer of topical interest.'[115] The marked change in the Community's approach to regulation introduced at approximately the same time as the SEA, however, with the use of minimum harmonization and the 'new approach' to regulation signified a lighter regulatory touch generally allowing more flexibility for Member States within the framework laid down at Community level. This approach, although it predated the formal introduction of subsidiarity by the TEU, would seem in keeping with the principle. Nonetheless, it is not necessarily linked with subsidiarity and might be motivated more to ensure the efficiency of Community decision process than by any other consideration. Subsidiarity continues to be recognised as a problematic area, as the Convention on the Future of Europe shows. Whether amendments introduced following the next round of treaty revisions will improve

112 See difficulties relating to the detailed drafting of the provision identified in Steiner, *supra* n. 99 and Dehousse, *supra* n. 4.

113 Case C-377/98 *Biotechnological Inventions*, *supra* n. 16.

114 Commission Communication on Simplifying and Improving the Regulatory Environment, *supra* n. 19 at p. 7.

115 Commission Communication on Simplifying and Improving the Regulatory Environment, *supra* n. 19, p. 5.

matters seems, at best, highly uncertain: the current proposals seems to be aimed at monitoring implementation of subsidiarity than clarifying its scope.

III Relationship with National Law

From the above discussion, it can be seen that the level of flexibility and freedom of action allowed to Member States can vary between different types of legislation (with directives supposedly permitting more freedom than regulations) and even within types of legislation, depending on the approach taken to legislation. It is almost axiomatic that such variety will be reflected in the degree to which Member States may still rely on their own national provisions, via the operation of derogating provisions, in a given field. Where a measure harmonizes an area exhaustively, there is no scope for recourse to the Treaty derogations and, consequently, to Member State rules.[116] Where minimum harmonization applies, there is some scope left for Member State action, although questions as to its precise scope arise. Member States cannot rely on minimum harmonization to gain extra power contrary to the Treaty. Thus any national action would be circumscribed by Treaty principles, such as those contained in Articles 28-30 or 49 *et seq*. National measures permitted by Community legislation thus cannot constitute arbitrary discrimination, or be disproportionate barrier to trade, nor can they implement barriers for economic purposes.

It is arguable that where minimal harmonization has occurred, Member States may no longer rely on mandatory requirements to protect national provisions even where those provisions are indistinctly applicable. The basis for this argument is found in *Cassis de Dijon*.[117] The introduction of mandatory requirements in that judgment was prefaced by the proviso that the area should not have been harmonized. Given the importance of some of the areas which are not included in Article 30, such as protection of the environment, this would be a significant omission.[118] *Cassis de Dijon* was, however, handed down before the introduction of widespread minimum harmonization and it would therefore seem inappropriate to take an overly black letter approach to interpretation on this point. In some cases, moreover, it seems as if the Court has approved the reliance on mandatory requirements: in *Aher-Waggon*[119] Member States were permitted to set

---

116 See e.g. Case 190/87 *Oberkreisdirektor des Kreises Borken* v. *Handelsonderneming Moormann* [1988] ECR 4687; Case C-5/94 *R.* v. *Ministry of Agriculture, Fisheries and Food, ex parte Hedley Lomas (Ireland) Limited* [1996] ECR I-2552.

117 Case 120/78 *Cassis de Dijon, supra* n. 75.

118 See also Oliver, P. *Free Movement of Goods* (3rd edition), pp. 376-8.

119 Case C-389/96 *Aher-Waggon* [1998] ECR I-4473.

stricter rules provided they did not infringe the scope of action delineated by Article 28. Given the nature of the directive concerned noise pollution, it is hardly surprising that barriers to trade arising out of stricter rules could be justified on environmental grounds.[120] Whether this justifies recourse to mandatory requirements generally is another question: in *Aher Waggon* the directive itself was aimed at environmental concerns. Similarly, in the earlier *Red Grouse* case,[121] the ECJ noted that the discretion conferred by the directive in question had to be defined by reference to the 'principal objectives' of the directive. What this means is far from clear. It could be that the ECJ was concerned in this case, as the Advocate-General had been, to ensure that the Dutch Government was not trying to establish higher rules that would apply outside its own territory.

An argument suggesting the ECJ wishes to limit extraterritoriality of Member States' rules is supported by the approach of the ECJ in *Compassion in World Farming.*[122] There, the ECJ argued that UK rules imposed on the conditions of veal calves that were stricter than those required by the directive in question were not permissible despite the fact the relevant Community legislation was a minimum harmonization measure. The Court argued that, since there was no lawful veal crate system in the UK, effectively the rules were aimed at those calves for export. What was effectively a ban on exports to a Member State that complied with the terms of the directive was not only extra-territoriality, but 'would strike at the harmonization achieved by the directive'.[123] This limited the UK's permitted freedom to act, and apparently contradicted the terms of the directive. The reasoning has a certain logic, albeit one which prioritises free trade over other societal concerns. As the Advocate-General explained, any derogation from a fundamental freedom should be interpreted restrictively so as to prevent Member States from hindering trade on grounds not related to the national interest.[124] These judgments suggest that Member States are considered to have no interest in regulating goods, and possibly services, for export. This is a dubious assertion and one which is arguably inconsistent with the approach to exports under Articles 29 and 49.[125]

---

120 See also Case C-232/97 *Nederhoff* [1999] ECR I-6385.

121 Case C-169/89 *Gourmetterie Van den Burg* [1990] ECR I-2143.

122 Case C-1/96 *R.* v. *Minister of Agriculture, Fisheries and Food, ex parte Compassion in World Farming* [1998] ECR I-1251.

123 Case C-1/96 *Compassion in World Farming, ibid.*, paragraph 62.

124 See also Case C-5/94 *R.* v. *Ministry of Agriculture, Fisheries and Food, ex parte Hedley Lomas* [1996] ECR I- 2553, Opinion at paragraphs 22-38.

125 See e.g. Case C-5/79 *Groenveld* v. *Produktschapvoor Veeen Viees* [1979] ECR 3409 discussed in Chapter 6 and Case C-384/93 *Alpine Investments BV* v. *Minister van Financiën* [1995] ECR I-1141, discussed in Chapter 11.

These cases all concerned exports and problems relating to the potential extraterritoriality of national rules and might therefore be seen as not defining the relationship between national law and minimum harmonization generally. Another problem with minimum harmonization measures is whether a Member State may rely on permitted national measures at a higher standard than the Community minimum as against *imports* meeting the Community threshold. Where the directive contains a market access clause, the matter is clear: in such situations, Member States must permit products that comply with the Community standard. Whilst a product or service which fails to meet the Community minima cannot be lawfully marketed, the position regarding goods or services which meet neither the standards in the Member State of origin nor the host Member State is not clear. The ECJ has sought in some instances to limit the possibility of EC provisions being abused;[126] as regards the importing State, in some measures the wording of the market access provision is clear.

Where there is no market access clause within the directive, or implied into its terms, there is some discussion as to whether a Member State may rely on national provisions as against the imported products. On the one hand, Member States have been permitted to impose higher standards and the operation of normal Treaty rules will prevent abuse. On this reasoning, where there is no market access clause, Member States may impose higher national rules on imports.[127] Although this point was not expressly discussed in the *Tobacco Advertising* case,[128] the ECJ noted that there was no market access clause and that therefore the directive did not ensure free movement of goods. Implicitly, this supports the contention that, in the absence of such a clause, Member States may impose their own higher national standards on imports.[129] By contrast, other commentators have argued that the general presumption of mutual recognition means that, in the interests of creating the single market, higher standards may be relied on in relation to domestic products alone.

Even where there is exhaustive harmonization, the exclusion or limitation of Member States' competence applies only within the field of application of the Community act.[130] In *Campus Oil*,[131] for example, the

---

126 See further Chapter 9.

127 Slot, 'Harmonization', *supra* n. 66 takes this view.

128 Case C-276/98 *Tobacco Advertising Directive*, *supra* n. 3, paragraph 104.

129 Whether this suggestion on the part of the ECJ also implied that directives must include market access clauses, thus re-emphasising the de-regulatory nature of Article 95 is another question.

130 This is thus different from exclusive Community competence when an entire policy field is excluded.

131 Case 72/83 *Campus Oil* v. *Minister for Industry and Energy* [1984] ECR 2727.

ECJ commented that the Community legislation had not covered the field entirely and that there was therefore scope for reliance on Article 30 (ex-36) and national rules. It thus becomes necessary to determine the scope of the measures taken, and how any other relevant Community acts fit in. With increasing amounts of Community legislation, this latter point has become correspondingly more complex.

The case of television broadcasting illustrates some of the difficulties. The Television without Frontiers Directive[132] was enacted, in principle, to ensure the free flow of television broadcasts from Member State to Member State in a typically heavily regulated area, although the recitals also made brief mention of issues such as freedom of expression. The Directive placed primary regulatory responsibility on the individual Member States but then specified certain minimum content requirements. Member States were further under an obligation to ensure that broadcasts did not include material that offended against certain standards relating to the protection of minors and the eradication of incitement to hatred. Similar negative content rules applied to advertising, in addition to rules relating to quantity and timing of advertisements. The question arose as to what extent the Television without Frontiers Directive excludes other provisions dealing with advertising, whether at a Community or national level, when the advertising is broadcast?

This issue arose in *de Agostini*.[133] The case concerned Swedish rules relating to advertising aimed at children and regarding misleading advertising, neither of which issues were specifically dealt with under the Television without Frontiers Directive. There were two types of measure involved in this case: those prohibiting advertising aimed at children and those relating to misleading advertising. The Swedish authorities sought to argue that they retained the freedom to regulate the advertisements contained in the broadcasts on a number of grounds. In particular, they argued that the Television without Frontiers Directive did not regulate misleading advertising nor advertising aimed at children,[134] and therefore its provisions attributing regulatory jurisdiction[135] and ensuring access to the markets of recipient states were not determinative. In particular, they pointed to the Recitals, in particular Recital 17, which stated that the Directive,

---

132 Directive 89/552, *supra* n. 31.

133 Joined Cases C-34-36/95 *Konsumentombudsmannen* v. *de Agostini and TV Shop i Sverige* [1997] ECR I-3843.

134 The argument that the national rules regulated advertising whilst the Directive dealt with broadcasting was also put forward, but was unsuccessful.

135 The Swedish argument that all channels were Swedish channels was inconsistent with the approach the ECJ had taken to determining jurisdiction in earlier cases and therefore doomed to failure.

'is without prejudice to existing or future Community acts of harmonization, in particular to satisfy mandatory requirements concerning the protection of consumers and the fairness of commercial transactions and competition.'

As regards these concerns, there was additional Community legislation in existence, notably Directive 84/450/EEC[136] concerning misleading advertising; regarding children specifically, there were no relevant Community measures.

According to the Advocate-General, the central question was whether the issues the Swedes sought to regulate fell with the fields co-ordinated by the directive. The Advocate-General concluded that the Directive laid down minimum rules and standards regulating television advertising, including standards for the protection of minors.[137] As regards the misleading advertisements, he concluded that the 'infomercials' under discussion fell within the scope of the Television without Frontiers Directive and the fact that there was an earlier directive on misleading advertisements requiring certain Member State action could not change this. The Advocate-General specifically rejected a point accepted by the Commission; that is, the argument that because there is no express reference to misleading advertisements in the Directive, that field was not co-ordinated by the Directive. He argued that 'that proposition confuses two distinction issues, namely the fields co-ordinated by the directive and the specific matters regulated by it.'[138]

The ECJ took a different view. It held that the fields co-ordinated by the directive related to broadcasting as defined in Article 1a of the Directive[139] and therefore as regards other issues, such as advertising and sponsorship, the Directive provided only partial regulation. It therefore did 'not have the effect of excluding completely and automatically the application of rules other than those specifically concerning the broadcasting and distribution of programmes', leaving room for the operation of other Community measures and even national rules provided 'that they do not involve secondary control of televisions broadcasts'.[140] Although this might have the effect of undermining to some extent the transmitting state principle that had been established regarding the application of the Television without Frontiers Directive, any consequent disadvantage would be balanced by the need to ensure that the clear

---

136 Directive 84/450/EEC of 10 September 1984 relating to the approximation of laws, regulations and administrative provisions of the Member States concerning misleading advertising OJ [1984] L 250/17.

137 Joined Cases C-34-36/95 *de Agostini*, *supra* n. 133, Opinion paragraph 61.

138 Joined Cases C-34-36/95 *de Agostini*, *ibid.*, Opinion paragraph 80.

139 Joined Cases C-34-36/95 *de Agostini*, *ibid.*, at paragraphs 25-26.

140 Joined Cases C-34-36/95 *de Agostini*, *ibid.*, paragraphs 32-34.

intention of the Community legislature to harmonize the field of misleading advertising was safeguarded.[141]

Clearly this area is complex; that is a reflection partly of the fact that broadcasting is made up of a number of services (programme content, advertising, as well as distribution itself) and so lends itself to multiple regulation situations. Nonetheless, overlap between different types of European measure remains a possibility in many areas. It would seem that the Court's view, rather than that of the Advocate-General, is the better one. To have excluded all other possibilities of regulatory measure in an area which, by virtue of the use of minimum harmonization technique, encapsulated only a skeleton framework would have been excessively deregulatory and, as the Court itself pointed out, run contrary to the intent of the legislators. It is one thing to seek to exclude national legislation, quite another to prioritise one form of Community measure over another, especially where the wording does not authorise such an approach.[142]

Overlap of measures has occurred in other cases. In *Estée Lauder* v. *Lancaster*,[143] a number of advertising directives were in issue. There the Court sought to resolve the issues by interpreting the notion of a 'consumer' needing protection in the same manner for each of the directives and also in respect of the mandatory requirement of consumer protection. This has a certain logic to it. It should be noted, however, that the directives in issue were a total harmonization measure and a minimum harmonization measure respectively. Would it always be appropriate to interpret notions that delimit the scope of Member States' freedom to act in the same way? Different measures permit Member States' different degrees of freedom – thus minimum harmonization permits Member States to take action within a field delineated by the minimum level or regulation identified in the relevant directive and the outer scope of national action confined by the proportionality assessment in relation to mandatory requirements of the Treaty derogation provisions.[144] Total harmonization directives, by contrast, remove the possibility of Member State regulatory choice, and the level of regulation might be set within the boundaries of what might at an abstract level be permitted by the operation of

---

141 Joined Cases C-34-36/95 *de Agostini*, *ibid.*, paragraph 37.

142 See e.g. relationship between the two directives in Case C-232/97 *Nederhoff*, *supra* n. 120.

143 Case C-220/98 *Estee Lauder Cosmetics GmbH & Co OHG* v. *Lancaster Group GmbH* [2000] ECR I-117.

144 See AG Mischo who suggested that any Member State action irrespective of its impact on free movement must comply with the general principle of proportionality: Case C-2/97 *Borsana* [1998] ECR I-8597. The ECJ did not however take this approach. It would seem that proportionality comes into play only when triggered by an impact on free movement. See further Chapters 7 and 12.

proportionality on the field of Member State competence. On this basis, given the regulatory choices made at Community level as to how much freedom Member States should enjoy in a given area, should this be changed through the interpretation of Community measures' substantive provisions?[145]

The issue of how much scope remains for Member State action also arises in connection with the obligation on the Community in certain areas to take a high level of protection as its minimum level when harmonizing national laws. How much freedom does this leave Member States to take action at a higher level? This question has been addressed by the Court. Quite simply, taking a high level of protection as a base level is not the same as taking the highest possible level of protection; there would therefore still be room for Member States to take more stringent measures than those set out in the relevant directive.[146] The requirements of a high level of protection and the notion of minimum harmonization are, on this basis, not incompatible.

IV Conclusions

A number of themes can be discerned both as regards the relationships between the levels of government and even the institutions themselves; and regarding the shifting emphasis on different policy questions. The early years illustrate the emphasis on the creation of the common market, with Article 308 being used to describe flanking policy fields by reference to single market concerns. Although the use of total harmonization excluded independent Member State action from that field and left Member States very little choice in implementation, thus moving regulatory choices to the Community level, it should not be forgotten that both Article 308 and Article 94 require unanimity in Council, thus all the then Member States must, at least, have agreed to this process. Whilst a broad view of the needs of the (now) internal market remains, a greater degree of fluidity can be see regarding questions of competence and, as a consequence, the relative importance of different policy areas. For example, the increased use of minimum harmonization repatriated some competence,[147] albeit subject to

---

145 See, in a slightly different context the discussion of the interpretation of the Television without Frontiers Directive in Case C-6/98 *Arbeitsgemeinschaft Deutscher Rundfunkanstalten* (ARD) v. *PRO Sieben Media and others* [1999] ECR I-7599, Opinion paragraph 81.

146 Case C-284/95 *Safety Hi-Tech* v. *S&T* [1998] ECR I-1403 at paragraph 49.

147 Use of the co-decision procedure could also been seen as part of this process, as it allows the direct representatives of European Union citizens some say in the legislative process. Conversely, use of standard setting committees may to some extent have

the overall Treaty framework, and equally allowed Member States to make some room for other regulatory questions. Treaty amendments continue these trends. Inclusion of specific references to flanking policies has given these policies a higher profile and, in some instances, a higher status. It cannot be said then, that these issues are now viewed only from an internal market perspective. Nonetheless, internal market questions and flanking policies remain intertwined, so there is always the question of which takes priority in the case of conflict, and from which perspective these policies should be defined. Arguably, the ECJ continues to prioritise internal market concerns and Community competence. It seems likely that the precise inter-relationship between different policies and their consequent impact on Member States' and the Community's competence will remain contentious, at least for some little time, a point that has been recognised by the Convention considering the future of the EU.

privatised some elements of harmonization, with adverse consequences for accountability.

Chapter 14

Conclusions

In the Introduction, a number of issues were identified for further discussion. These included the question of whether the freedoms created a coherent system, particularly as regards the relationship between goods and services; the relationship between EC law and the laws of the Member States as defined by the freedoms; and the development of Community law in terms of the values it recognises.

As regards the first of these points, much has been written regarding the convergence of the case law between the four freedoms.[1] Certainly, between the free movement of goods and the freedom to provide services there are parallels in the ECJ's jurisprudence. This congruence manifests itself most clearly in the move from a discrimination-based test to one that focusses on the existence of a restriction, which can be seen in both Article 28 and 49 (though the position as regards exports is less clear). Similarly, both freedoms claim to operate within the economic sphere, the non-economic being the preserve of the Member States. This latter point is true also of Article 29. The definition of goods refers to commercial transactions and items which have a value.[2] For services, the key concept is that of remuneration.[3] In both instances, the terms have been interpreted widely, limiting the scope of the non-economic.

As regards the exceptions to the freedoms, again there are similarities, both structural and substantive. In structural terms we see that both freedoms have two forms of exceptions: the express provisions in the Treaty;[4] and the judge made exceptions: mandatory requirements and overriding interests. Article 29 is different here: only the Treaty derogation may be used. Despite the different terminology in some instances, similar elements make up the relevant tests for the application of the derogation,

1 Barnard, C., 'Fitting the remaining pieces into the goods and persons jigsaw?' (2001) 26(1) *ELRev* 35-59; Mortelmans, K., Towards Convergence in the application of the rules on free movement and on competition?' (2001) 38(3) *CMLRev* 613-649 who suggests that there is no systemic convergence between the application of the competition provisions and the free movement provisions.

2 See further Chapter 2.

3 See further Chapter 9.

4 Article 30 in relation to goods; Article 56 regarding services.

too. For both services and goods, not only must the national rule in question fall within one of the grounds of derogation, but that national rule must also satisfy the proportionality test as understood within the Community legal order. There are similarities in the grounds for derogation, and the ECJ sometimes refers to case law on the other freedoms when determining the scope and applicability of a justification in any given case. Perhaps the clearest example is *Bouchereau*,[5] a case concerning the public policy exception in relation to workers. This case now forms the test for public policy across the freedoms.

The freedoms are not, however, exactly the same. The differences arise from both the structure of the Treaty and the jurisprudence of the Court. Structurally, the provisions regarding the free movement of goods are spread over a number of articles, such as Article 25 regarding customs duties and Article 31 that deals with state monopolies of a commercial character. Even imports and exports are dealt with by separate provisions: Articles 28 and 29 respectively. For services, the comparable concerns are effectively all covered by Article 49. The original focus of the provisions is also different. Article 28 and 29 were drafted in terms of barriers: quotas and MEQRs, whereas Article 49 was conceived in terms of a comparison of treatment between those established in a Member State and those established outside it (but within the EC). The grounds of derogation also differ in some aspects: the grounds set out in Article 56 are narrower than those listed in Article 30, but the public policy exception for services finds no comparable provision in the section of the Treaty dealing with goods.

To some extent, such structural differences can be minimised, if thought desirable, through interpretation. There are, however, also differences in approach between the goods and services jurisprudence. The ECJ has sought to limit the application of Article 28 by the introduction of the distinction between product requirements and selling arrangements.[6] It is far from clear whether such a distinction has been introduced into the services case law.[7] It has been suggested that any such distinction arises from the intangible nature of services suggesting that a parallel approach in this context is not desirable. This argument is not entirely convincing, although the distribution chain for services is in general different from that of goods. As noted in Chapter 11, just because it may be difficult to define 'product requirements' in the light of delivery mechanisms for services, does not mean that it is impossible to distinguish between some product

---

5 Case 30/77 *R.* v. *Bouchereau* [1977] ECR 1999.

6 Joined Cases C-267 and 268/91 *Keck and Mithouard* [1993] ECR I-6097.

7 Case C-384/93 *Alpine Investments BV* v. *Minister van Financiën* [1995] ECR I- 1141; Joined Cases C-34-36/95 *Konsumentombudsmannen* v. *de Agostini* and *TV Shop i Sverige* [1997] ECR I-3843; Case C-390/99 *Canal Satellite Digital SL* [2002] ECR I-607, discussed Chapter 11.

requirements and some selling arrangements. For example, service providers advertise their services and at least some types of advertising would fall within the scope of selling arrangements. It may be, of course, that the boundary between product requirements and selling arrangements would fall in a different place for services than they do in respect of goods. It has been suggested that a more appropriate mechanism for determining which national measures would benefit from a rebuttable presumption that they are not contrary to Community law is the distinction between access to a profession and the terms on which the profession is exercised. The more fundamental of the two categories and the one most likely to have an impact on the cross-border provision of services is access to a profession. This approach is not wholly satisfactory either: not only does it find no support in the case law but it does not deal with all the circumstances in which services can arise. The real problem with the services jurisprudence is the breadth of such circumstances and that services can be seen in two ways: as an economic transaction or as a personal freedom, a fact which may make categorisation difficult for the services sphere. It also leads to distinctions between goods and services, for example circumstances, which simply would not occur in the goods context, such as family rights, may occur in the services case law.[8]

It may be, of course, that we should not expect a similarity of approach since the freedoms deal with objects that are fundamentally different. Although there is a clear distinction between, for example, goods and people, in some circumstances as identified in Chapters 2 and 9, that links, if not overlaps occur. On this basis, as Advocate-General Lenz suggested in *Bosman*,[9] the scope of rights should not vary arbitrarily merely because of a fluke of classification. Even accepting this point, to expect an exact duplication of the case law, given the substantive differences between the rights, is simply unrealistic. Instead, what we should be looking for is a unified general principle, which can be applied as circumstances demand in the various contexts. Arguably the case law, with its emphasis on the abolition of restrictions and the creation of the internal market through the facilitation of access, constitutes such a unified principle and that the central themes in the case law are as coherent as it is possible for them to be. Nonetheless, differences in approach between goods and services remain which are arguably more than an inherent, circumstance-based variation of a unified principle and may have significance for the outcome of a number of cases. In addition to the selling arrangements debate which remains problematic, another discrepancy which it is hard to explain as

8 See e.g. Case C-60/00 *Mary Carpenter* v. *Secretary of State for the Home Department* [2002] ECR I-6279, discussed Chapter 11.

9 Case C-451/93 *Union Belge des Sociétés de Football Association ASBL* v. *Jean-Marc Bosman* [1995] ECR1-4921.

inherent is the fact that, whilst Article 49 can be relied on as against private parties, Articles 28 and 29 cannot be so used, or at least not directly.[10] These differences make the determination of a situation as falling within goods or services significant. As has been illustrated, however, the ECJ's case law on this point is far from clear.[11]

Perhaps this last point has less significance than previously, or has been rather taken over by the ECJ's approach to the scope of application of the freedoms. The starting point for the relationship of the freedoms and their application was that they were mutually exclusive and that the services provision on the face of the Treaty should be used as a fall-back provision. More recent cases, such as *de Agostini*[12] and *Gourmet International Products*,[13] show both the goods rules and those relating to services being applied. Although it could be argued that each provision applies to a different factual context – in *Gourmet* the producer of the goods and the agency providing advertising for the goods – the same national rule is under challenge. In *Gourmet*, the rules challenged were those limiting the advertising of alcohol. In such situations, the services provision will, *de facto*, end up as the more significant. Even if a national rule constitutes a selling arrangement for goods, and on that analysis falls outside Community law, if it also affects services then it may well contravene Article 49; rendering the discussion under Article 28 effectively irrelevant. In passing, it should be noted that the cumulative approach to the application of the four freedoms is not limited to goods and services,[14] with the potential for a reversal of the Treaty provisions in that context also. The impact may not, in these other situations, have as noticeable consequences.

The Court's view of the scope of Articles 28-30 and Article 49 *et seq.* has consequences for the relationship of Community law with the various domestic legal orders on a number of levels. The Court's interpretation of the scope of the freedoms has been broad. This approach can be seen at all levels: in the definition of goods and services and in the test to determine when Articles 28, 29 or 49 apply. The approach taken to definition of services is amoral. Whilst this may be understandable in Community terms, it also means that issues are primarily dealt with in a trade-based environment, which is not always appropriate.[15] There are arguably other

---

10 See further Chapter 3.

11 See further Chapter 2.

12 Joined Cases C-34-36/95 *Konsumentombudsmannen* v. *de Agostini* and *TV Shop i Sverige*, *supra* n. 7.

13 Case C-405/98 *Konsumentombudsmannen* v. *Gourmet International Products AB* [2001] ECR 1-1795.

14 Case C-118/96 *Safir* v. *Skaltemyndigheten i Dalarnas Lan* [1998] ECR 1-1897.

15 See Chapters 2 and 9.

values that should have a higher status than a factor to be weighted against free trade. Surely human rights should be above the Community legal order, or have a higher value within that order, rather just than a factor to be taken into account by that system, especially in a system that now lays claim to the notion of citizenship and to respect fundamental rights?

Furthermore, in adopting an expansive view of these provisions' sphere of application, the Court has brought more national rules within the scope of EC law. This development means that such rules will be assessed by reference to Community standards, including the proportionality requirement. Given the essentially economic focus of the four freedoms, such an approach has repercussions for Member States' ability to prioritise non-trade concerns, such as those relating to social provision[16] or environmental protection, over those relating to free trade. This tendency can be seen in the approach to the provision of public health care, as well as in many cases involving the derogation from the Treaty freedoms and the operation of overriding matters of public interest. While the ECJ may be prepared to concede that there is a matter worthy of protection, it often concludes that the measures taken by the Member State are disproportionate. The consumer protection field is a clear example of this tendency.[17] The problem is exacerbated where the ECJ has judged measures by reference to their impact on trade.[18] The Community has been criticised for an approach that is essentially deregulatory and, on occasions, perhaps too deregulatory. Certainly, many issues are judged through the prism of trade concerns rather than being seen in their own right. This is particularly worrying given the width of the Community's competence.

Although harmonization might seem an answer to seem of these problems, it should be remembered that the EC's competence to legislate is limited; its main legislation making competence is linked to the creation and functioning of the common market or the internal market or to facilitate the four freedoms.[19] One might argue that such a limitation on approach is unimportant as an area of national regulation outside the creation or functioning of the common market should be unaffected by the four freedoms. The difficulty with this argument is that, should national legislation fall within the scope of Articles 28, 29 or 49, the protection of the relevant interests would be by derogation limited by the proportionality principles – the shortcomings of which were noted above – or by Community legislation. In general, such legislation, to fall within the scope of Community competence, has to be justified by reference to the common

16 See discussion in Chapters 9 and 11.

17 See Chapter 7 and literature cited therein.

18 This has happened in the environmental field: see Chapter 7.

19 See Chapter 13.

market, even though the national rule was not intended to regulate trade in the first place. Again, we see a trade-based emphasis in Community competence. The consequence of an enlarged view of the potential scope of negative harmonization seems to be a correspondingly broad view of positive harmonization to counter it. In any event, relying on the Community to legislate to compensate for the impact of negative harmonization re-emphasises the shift in competence that has occurred.

Quite apart from substantive issues, there are questions about the impact of the ECJ'S jurisprudence and Community secondary legislation on the domestic legal order. The electorates of all the Member States may want certain political choices put into effect, but the consequences of the four freedoms may be that a Member State is precluded from so doing. Although the governments of the Member States chose to sign the EC Treaty, is it correct that fifty years later those States are precluded from reviewing that decision, or rebalancing the Community? An answer to some of these concerns might be through changes to the Community legal order so as to give the Community power to protect the policy areas in which concerns arise, or to oblige the institutions to take a more nuanced approach to the application of the freedoms in the first place. We have indeed seen some such changes incorporated through Treaty amendment, indicating that there is political concern within the Member States about a broader range of issues, including culture and public health as well as consumer protection and protection of the environment. Similarly, the introduction of European citizenship indicates the development of a different type of Community.

The main problem with this proposition is whether the Community would give the same level of protection to these various concerns as would the Member States, assuming that they were agreed on that point. There are thus political difficulties even before judicial interpretation occurs. Furthermore, for these provisions to be effective in this regard, the Community, and particularly the ECJ, must take them into account when considering the scope of trade-based provisions. This, the ECJ seems, in general, unwilling to do. For example the protection of the environment enjoys a particularly high status,[20] although the jurisprudence in this area has not yet developed. Certainly, to the extent there are rulings considering the role of the environment, they are not consistent. Thus, in the lonely case of *PreussenElektra*,[21] the ECJ took into account the national measure's environmental purpose when determining whether there was a restriction for the purposes of Article 28.

---

20 Article 6 EC; Case C-379/98 *PreussenElektra AG* v. *Schteswag AG* [2001] ECR I-2099. See also draft Constitutional Treaty, Article III-4.

21 Case C-379/98 *PreussenElektra AG* v. *Schleswag AG ibid.*

So far this case has not been followed even in the environmental sphere and not all these areas enjoy the same level of protection as the protection of the environment does. The ECJ has also interpreted provisions relating to the free movement of persons in the light of European citizenship.[22] The use of citizenship has tended to support an extensive role for the free movement provisions, rather than curtailing them. Although this does not necessarily mean that European citizenship is not awarded a high status, the cases involving European citizenship are, as a result, difficult to see as examples of the ECJ balancing competing interests. In other areas, recent case law as regards both goods and services suggests that the Court continues to prioritise the four freedoms over other Treaty obligations, creating an unofficial hierarchy of norms. This can be seen particularly clearly in the field of services, where the co-ordination of social security was held to be subordinate to the freedom to provide services.[23] Similar concerns have arisen as regards goods and both lines of reasoning have had an impact on the interpretation of the new public health provision. It seems that the new, high level of public health is to be defined partly by the facility to provide cross-border medical services.

In general it would appear that, to the extent that these new provisions will have an effect at all, it is as to the scope of the derogation, thus leaving the trade-based focus of the Community untouched. This is somewhat worrying as the amendments to Articles 2 and 3 as well as the introduction of flanking policies referring to a high level of protection, suggest that some non-trade concerns should be taken into account in the determination of the scope of the internal market, if not given priority over it. There is a danger that, in not considering more fully these new provisions, that the ECJ is missing a political signal from some of the Member States themselves. Given the large and direct impact of Community law within Europe, such an approach could lead to a new crisis in legitimacy about the powers of the Union and the way those powers are interpreted. This is particularly problematic given that the Union is entering another phase of Treaty revision with the new version of the Treaty being put forward as a constitutional treaty and faces the tensions and difficulties of eastward expansion.

---

22 See e.g. Case C-348/96 *Donatella Calfa* [1999] ECR 1-11, discussed Chapter 12; and Case C-60/00 *Mary Carpenter*, *supra* n. 8. One might see the health care cases as an example of a European citizenship right; the draft Constitutional Treaty provides for the right to health care as an individual right of Article 11-35 following the terms of the Charter of Fundamental Rights (albeit not in the section entitled citizen's rights). The ECJ has made no reference to citizenship in its rulings.

23 Case C-158/96 *Kohll* v. *Union des Caisses de Maladie* [1998] ECR I-1931; Case C-368/98 *Vanbraekel* v. *ANNC* [2001] ECR I-5363. See Chapters 9 and 12.

Selected Bibliography

Books

Arnull, A., *The European Union and its Court of Justice* (Oxford: 1999)
Dehousse, R., (ed.), *Europe after Maastricht* (Munchen Law Books in Europe, Munich:1994)
Dine, J., and Watt, B., *Discrimination Law* (Longmans, London: 1996)
Eeckhout, P., *The European Internal Market and International Trade: A Legal Analysis* (Clarendon Press, Oxford: 1994)
Gormley, L.W., *Prohibiting Restrictions on Trade within the EEC* (Elsevier Science Publishers B.V., North Holland: 1985)
Hamilton, A., Madison, J., and Jay, J., *The Federalist* (William Benton, Chicago, London, Toronto, 1952)
Jans, J.H., *European Environmental Law* (2nd edition) (Kluwer, The Hague: 2000)
Krämer, L., *EC Environmental Law* (4th edition) (Sweet and Maxwell, London: 2000)
McGovern, E., *International Trade Regulation* (3rd edition) (Globefield Press, Exeter: 1995)
Niedobitek, M. *The Cultural Dimension in EC Law* (Kluwer Law International: 1997)
O'Keeffe, D. and Twomey, P.M., (eds), *Legal Issues of the Maastricht Treaty* (Wiley Chancery: 1994)
Oliver, P. *Free Movement of Goods in the European Community* (3rd edition) (Sweet and Maxwell, London: 1996)
Steyger, E., *National Traditions and European Community Law: Margarine and Marriage* (Dartmouth, Aldershot: 1997)
Trebilcock, M.J., and Howse, R., *The Regulation of International Trade* (2nd edition) (Routledge, New York: 1999)
Tridimas, T., *The General Principles of EC Law* (OUP, Oxford: 1999)
Weatherill, S., *EC Consumer Law and Policy* (Longmans, London: 1997)
Weatherill and Beaumont *EU Law* (3rd edition) (Penguin, London: 1999)
Wyatt and Dashwood, *European Union Law* (4th edition) (Sweet and Maxwell, London: 2000)

Articles and Contributions to Books

Alexander, W., 'Intellectual Property and the Free Movement of Goods – 1996 Case Law of the European Court of Justice' [1998] *International Review of Industrial Property and Copyright Law* 16

Barnard, C., 'Fitting the remaining pieces into the goods and persons jigsaw?' (2001) 26(1) *European Law Review* 35- 59

Biondi, A., 'In and Out of the Internal Market: Recent Developments on the principle of Free Movement' (1999/00) 19 *Yearbook of European Law* 461 – 491

Burrows, N., 'Harmonization of Technical Standards: Reculer Pour Mieux Sauter?' (1990) 53 *Modern Law Review* 597

Cross, E.J., 'Pre-emption of Member State Law in the European Economic Community: A Framework for Analysis' (1992) 29 *Common Market Law Review* 447

Daniele, L., 'Non-discriminatory Restrictions to the Free Movement of Persons' (1997) 22 *European Law Review* 191

Dougan, M., 'Minimum Harmonisation and the Internal Market' (2000) 37 *Common Market Law Review* 553

Easterbrook, F.H. 'The State of Madison's Vision of the State: A Public Choice Perspective' (1994) 107 *Harvard Law Review* 1328

Emiliou, N., 'Subsidiarity: An Effective Barrier Against Enterprises of Ambition' (1992) 29 *Common Market Law Review* 383

Friedbacher 'Motive unmasked: The ECJ, the Free Movement of Goods and the Search for Legitimacy' (1996) *European Law Journal* 226

Goucha Soares, A., 'Pre-emption, Conflicts of Powers and Subsidiarity' (1998) 23(2) *European Law Review* 132

Handoll, J., 'Article 48(4) EEC and Non-national Access to Public Employment' (1988) 13 *European Law Review* 223

Hatzopoulos, V., 'Recent Developments of the Case Law of the ECJ in the Field of Services' (2000) 37(1) *Common Market Law Review* 43-82

McGee, A. and Weatherill, S., 'The Evolution of the Single Market – Harmonisation or Liberalisation?' (1990) 53 *Modern Law Review* 578

March Hunnings, N., 'Case note on *Debauve* and *Coditel*' (1980) 17 *Common Market Law Review* 560

Marenco, G., 'The Notion of Restriction on the Freedom of Establishment and the Provision of Services in the Case-law of the Court' (1991) *Yearbook of European Law* 11

Mathews, C., 'Non-tariff Import Barriers and the Kennedy Round' (1964-5) 2 *Common Market Law Review* 403

Mei, A.P. van der 'Cross Border Access to Medical Care within the European Union – Some Reflection on the Judgments in *Decker* and *Kohll*' (1998) *Maastricht Journal of European and Comparative Law* 277

Mortelmans, K., 'Article 30 of the EEC Treaty and Legislation Relating to Market Circumstances: Time to Consider a New Definition?' (1991) 28 *Common Market Law Review* 115

Mortelmans, K., 'The Common Market, the Internal Market and the Single Market, What's in a Market?' (1998) 35(1) *Common Market Law Review* 101

Mortelmans, K., Towards Convergence in the Application of the Rules on Free movement and on Competition?' (2001) 38(3) *Common Market Law Review* 613-649

Quinn, M. and MacGowan., 'Could Art. 30 Impose Obligations on Individuals?' (1987) 12 *European Law Review* 163

Roscam Abbing, H.D.C., 'Public Health Insurance and Freedom of Movement within the European Union' (1999) 6 *European Journal of Health Law* 1

Slot, P.J., 'Harmonization' (1997) 21 *European Law Review* 378

Steiner, J., 'Drawing the Line: Uses and Abuses of Article 30 EEC' (1992) 29 *Common Market Law Review* 749

Swaine, E. T., 'Subsidiarity and Self Interest, Federalism at the European Court of Justice' (2000) 41 *Harvard International Law Journal* 1

Temmink, H., 'From Danish Bottles to Danish Bees: The Dynamics of Free Movement of Goods and Environmental Protection – a Case Law Analysis' (2000) 1 *Yearbook of European Environmental Law* 61

Tison, M., 'What is 'General Good' in EU Financial Services Law?' (1997) 24(2) *Legal Issues of European Integration* 1 – 46

Ubertazzi, L., 'Copyright and the Free Movement of Goods' [1985] *International Review of Industrial Property and Copyright Law* 46

van Calster, C., 'Court Criticises Restrictions on Free Movement of Waste' (1999) 24(2) *European Law Review* 170

Van Gerven, W., 'The Right of Establishment and Free Supply of Services within the Common Market' (1965-6) 3 *Common Market Law Review* 344

Waelbroek, M., 'The Emergent Doctrine of Community Pre-emption' in Sandalow, T., and Stein, E., (eds) *Courts and Free Markets* (Clarendon, Oxford: 1982)

Wallace, R. and Goldberg, D., 'The EEC Directive on Television Broadcasting' (1989) 9 *Yearbook of European Law* 175

Weatherill, S., 'After *Keck*: Some Thoughts on how to Clarify the Clarification' (1996) 33(5) *Common Market Law Review* 885

Weatherill, S., 'Recent Case Law concerning the Free Movement of Goods: Mapping the Frontiers of Market Deregulation' (1999) 36(1) *Common Market Law Review* 51

Weiler, J.H.H., 'The Community System: The Dual Character of Supranationalism' (1981) 1 *Yearbook of European Law* 277

Weiler, J.H.H., 'Transformation of Europe' [1991] 100 *Yale Law Journal* 2 403

White, E., 'In Search of Limits to Article 30 of the EEC Treaty' (1989) 26 *Common Market Law Review* 235

Wils, W. 'The Search for the Rule in Article 30 EEC: Much Ado About Nothing?' (1993) *European Law Review* 475

Index